TORITAN
Birds of a Feather

ACTER

KURO

Hot by crow standards, he speaks to Inusaki and mysteriously knows his name.

STORY

Inusaki is a private detective who spends more time doing odd jobs around his neighborhood than solving mysteries. He's been able to understand birds ever since he was little, an ability he's never liked. One day, a crow who somehow knows his name speaks to him, and Inusaki decides to name him Kuro. But for some odd reason, Inusaki can't seem to get Kuro off his mind. It gets so bad he even mistakes the voice of Mitsuru, his landlady's high school-aged son, for Kuro's. Over time, Inusaki realizes he's falling for the hot-for-a-crow Kuro and winds up brokenhearted (?). Mitsuru stops by to care for the depressed Inusaki, and, touched by his kindness, Inusaki starts falling for him instead. Then one day, out of the blue, Mitsuru kisses him!

NOZOMI INUSAKI

A 23-year-old private detective who does odd jobs around town and has the unenviable power to communicate with birds, making him more of a cat person. He somehow falls for a crow he's named Kuro. His crush gets so bad he confuses his landlady's son Mitsuru for the crow. After getting his heart broken and giving up on Kuro, he's cared for by Mitsuru, who out of the blue kisses him.

2

CHAR

&

ST

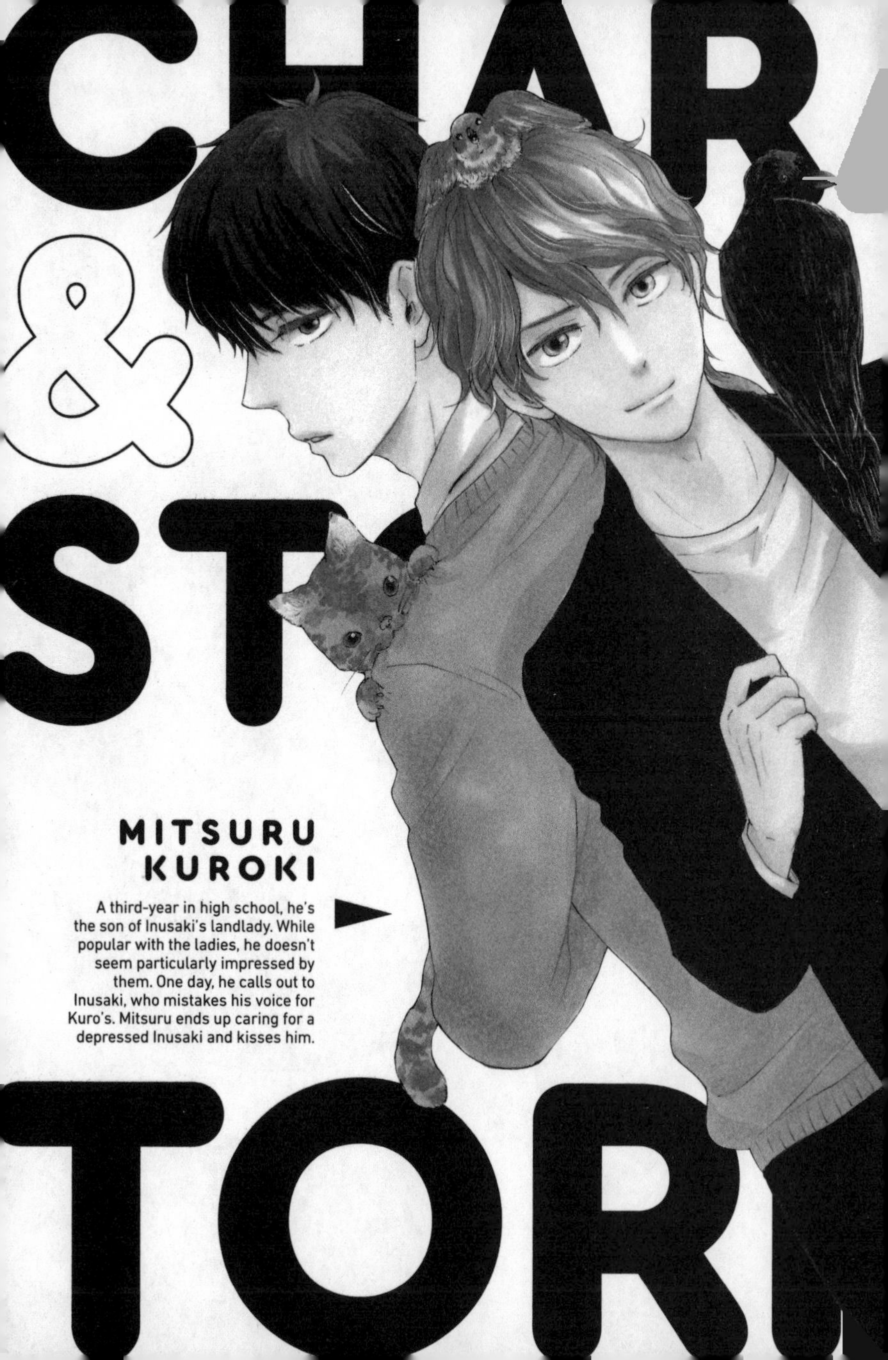

MITSURU KUROKI

A third-year in high school, he's the son of Inusaki's landlady. While popular with the ladies, he doesn't seem particularly impressed by them. One day, he calls out to Inusaki, who mistakes his voice for Kuro's. Mitsuru ends up caring for a depressed Inusaki and kisses him.

TORI

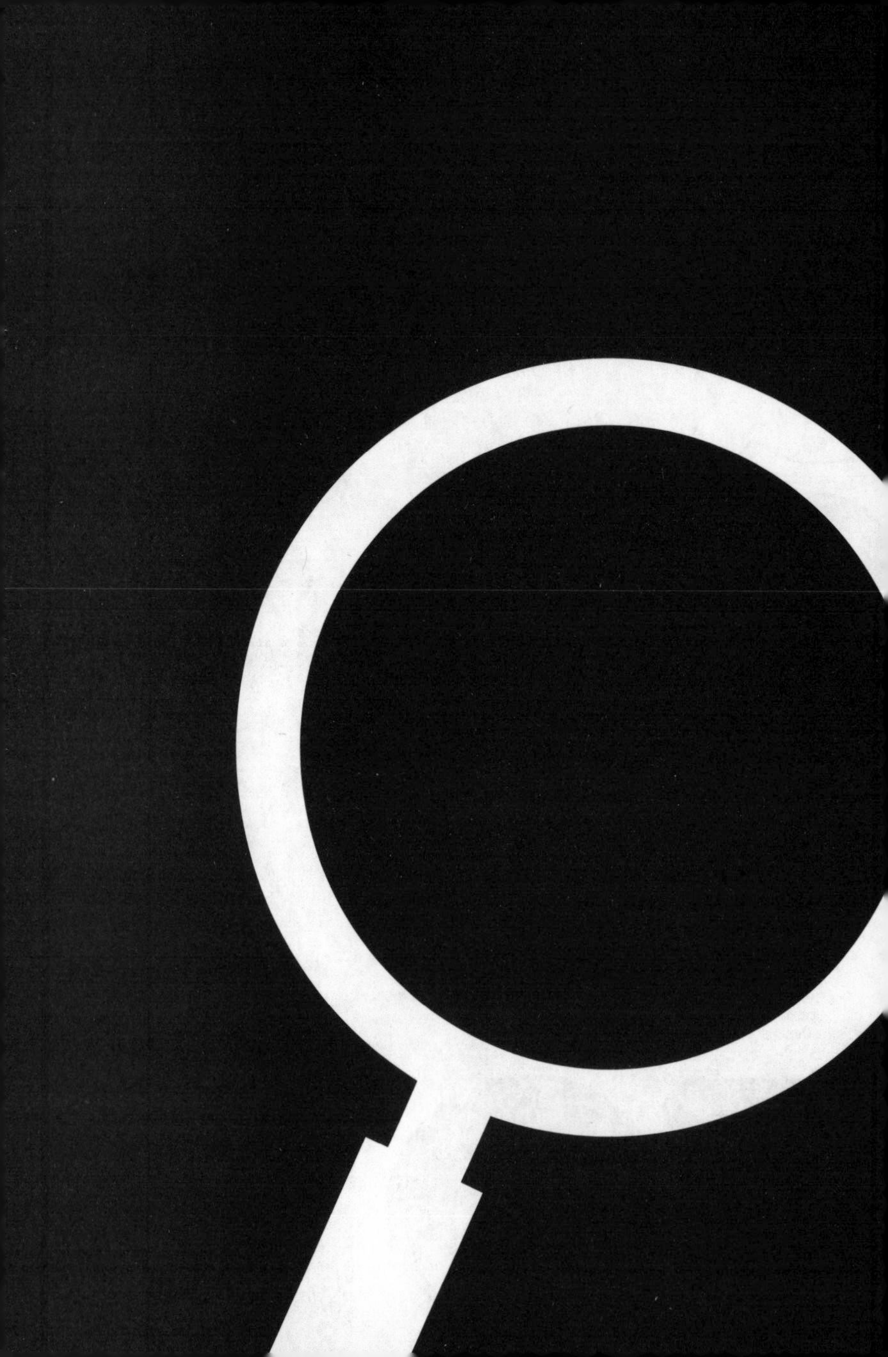

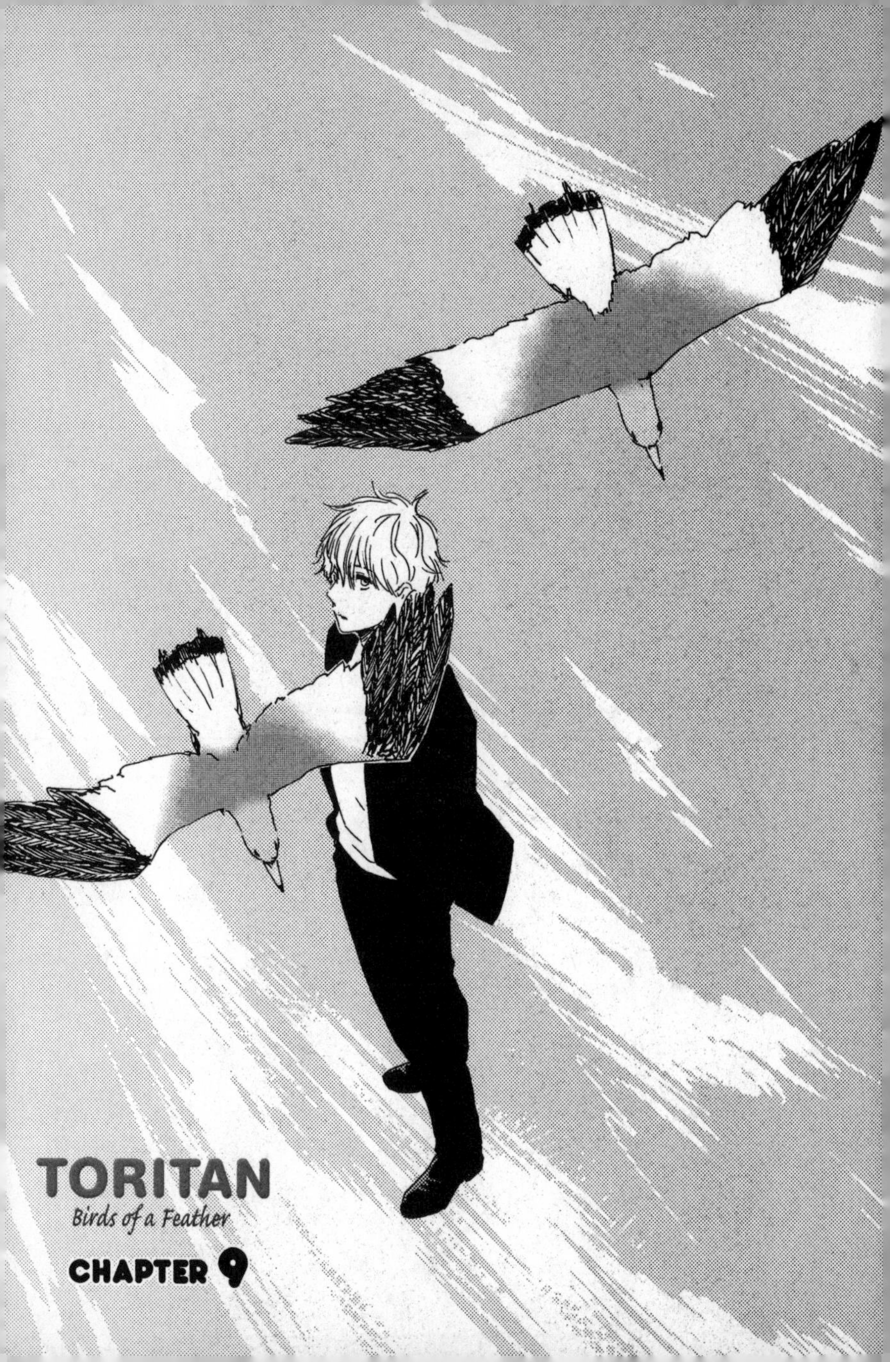
TORITAN
Birds of a Feather
CHAPTER 9

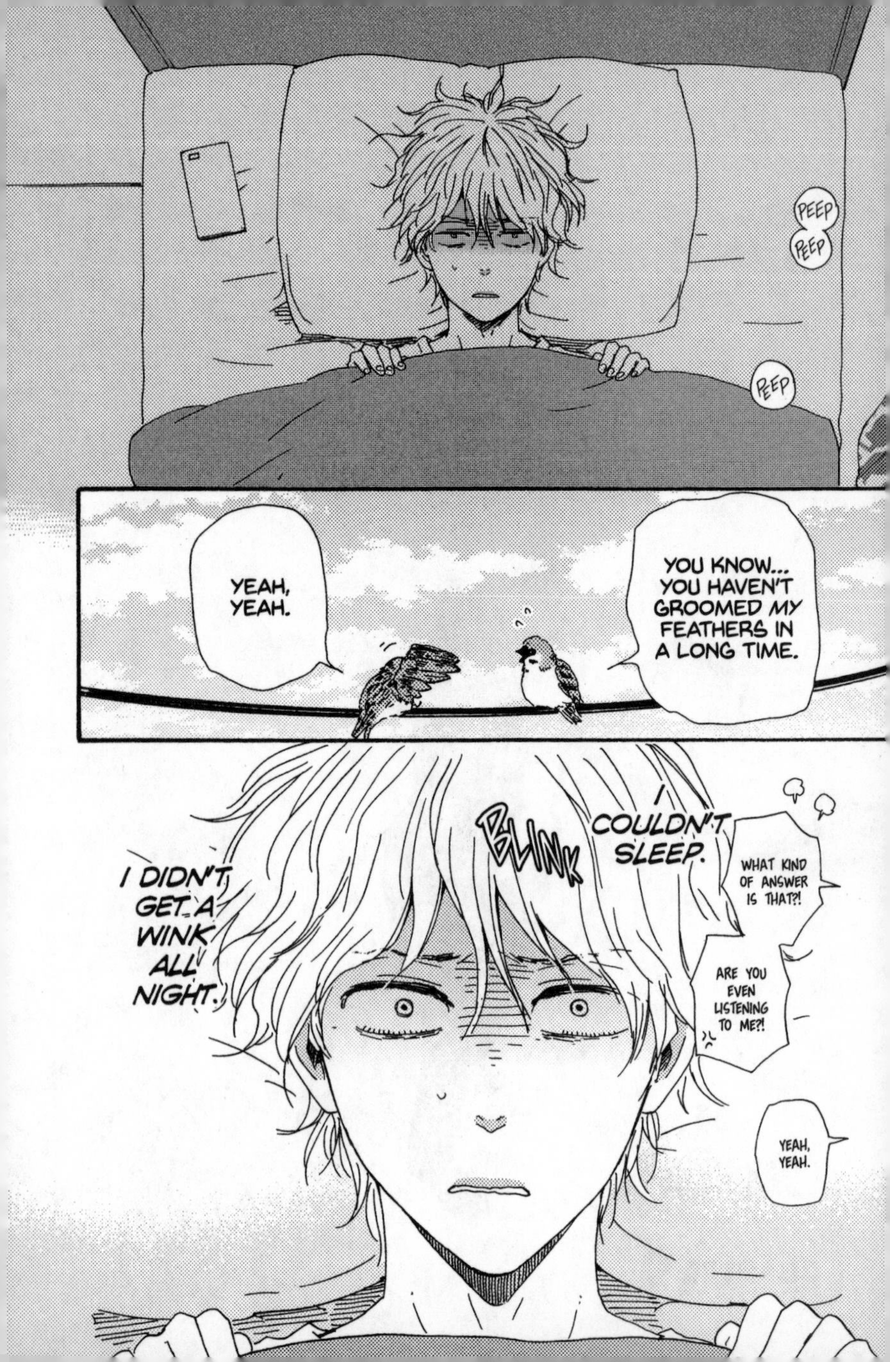
PEEP
PEEP
PEEP
YOU KNOW... YOU HAVEN'T GROOMED MY FEATHERS IN A LONG TIME.
YEAH, YEAH.
WHAT KIND OF ANSWER IS THAT?!
ARE YOU EVEN LISTENING TO ME?!
YEAH, YEAH.
I COULDN'T SLEEP.
BLINK
I DIDN'T GET A WINK ALL NIGHT.

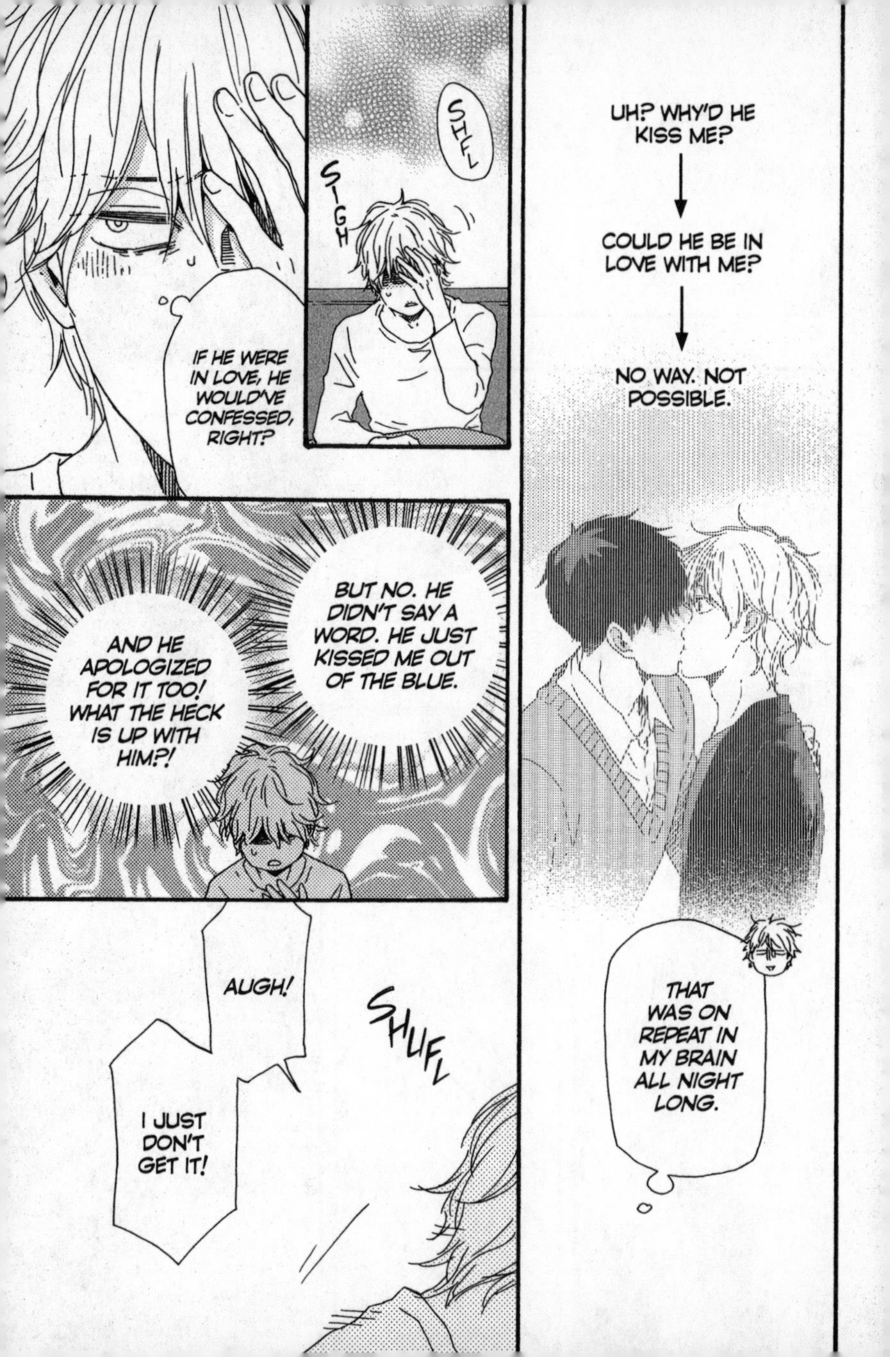

UH? WHY'D HE KISS ME?
COULD HE BE IN LOVE WITH ME?
NO WAY. NOT POSSIBLE.
THAT WAS ON REPEAT IN MY BRAIN ALL NIGHT LONG.
SHFL
SIGH
IF HE WERE IN LOVE, HE WOULD'VE CONFESSED, RIGHT?
BUT NO. HE DIDN'T SAY A WORD. HE JUST KISSED ME OUT OF THE BLUE.
AND HE APOLOGIZED FOR IT TOO! WHAT THE HECK IS UP WITH HIM?!
SHUFL
AUGH!
I JUST DON'T GET IT!

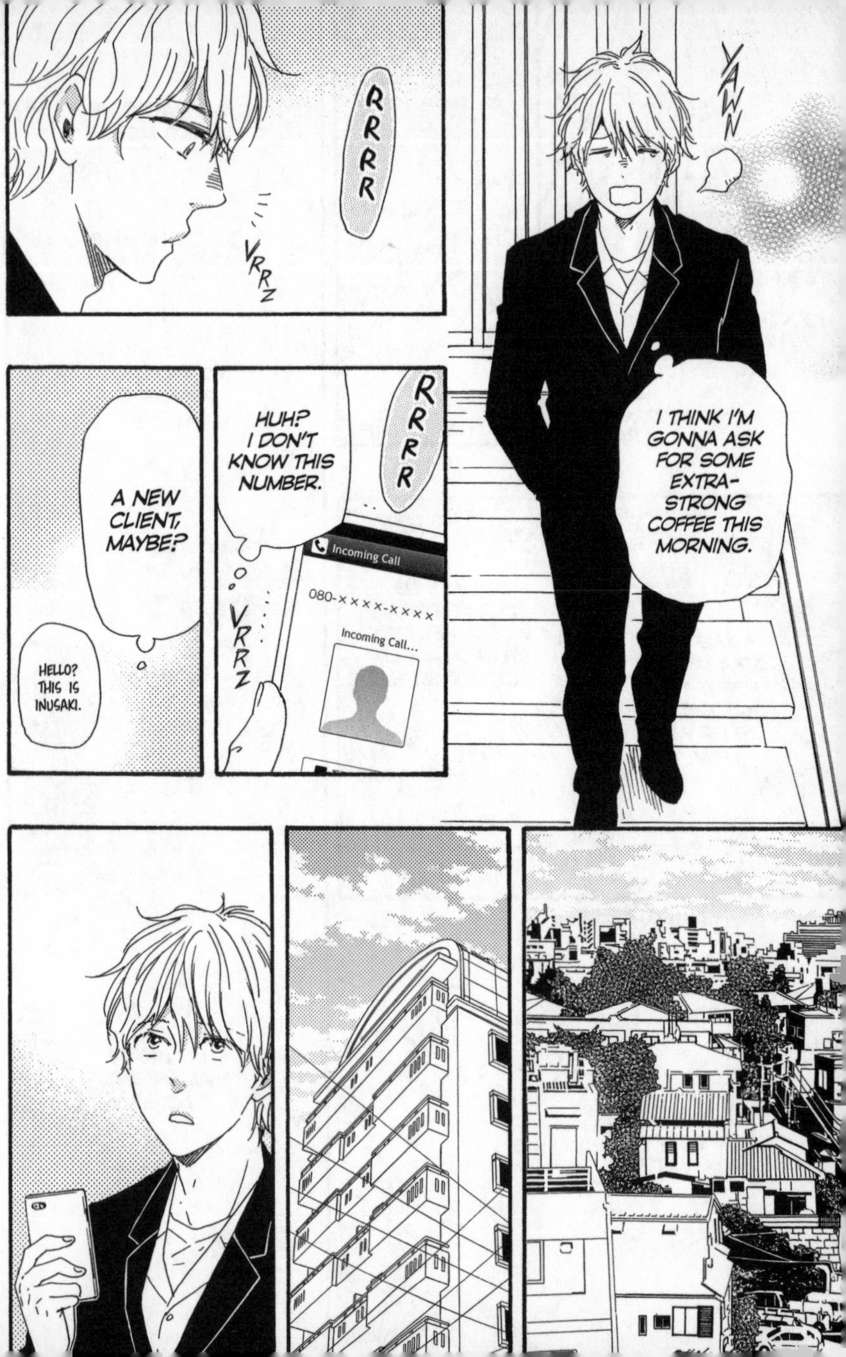
YAWN
I THINK I'M GONNA ASK FOR SOME EXTRA-STRONG COFFEE THIS MORNING.
RRRR
VRRZ
RRRR
HUH? I DON'T KNOW THIS NUMBER.
Incoming Call
080-××××-××××
Incoming Call...
VRRZ
A NEW CLIENT, MAYBE?
HELLO? THIS IS INUSAKI.

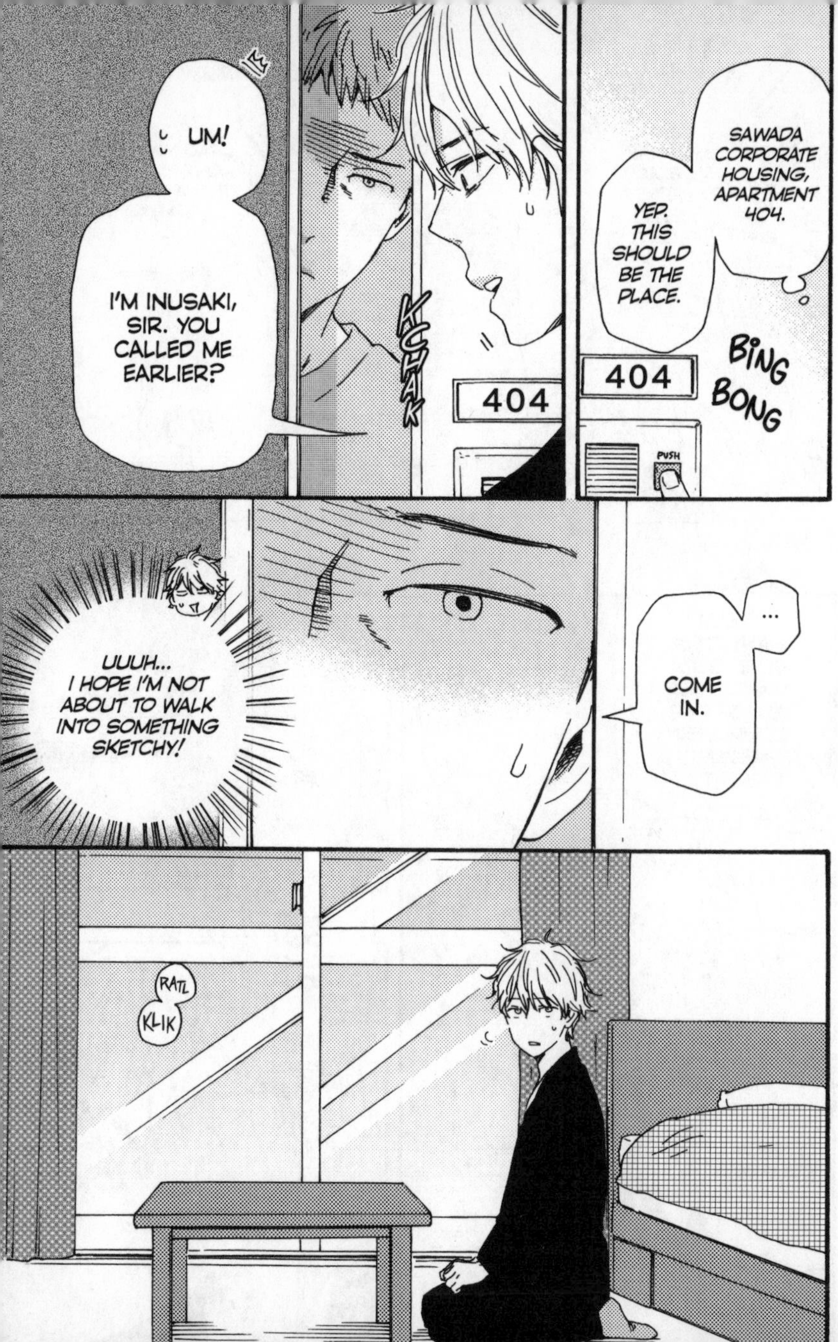
SAWADA CORPORATE HOUSING, APARTMENT 404.
YEP. THIS SHOULD BE THE PLACE.
404
PUSH
BING BONG
404
KCHAK
UM!
I'M INUSAKI, SIR. YOU CALLED ME EARLIER?
...
COME IN.
UUUH... I HOPE I'M NOT ABOUT TO WALK INTO SOMETHING SKETCHY!
RATL
KLIK

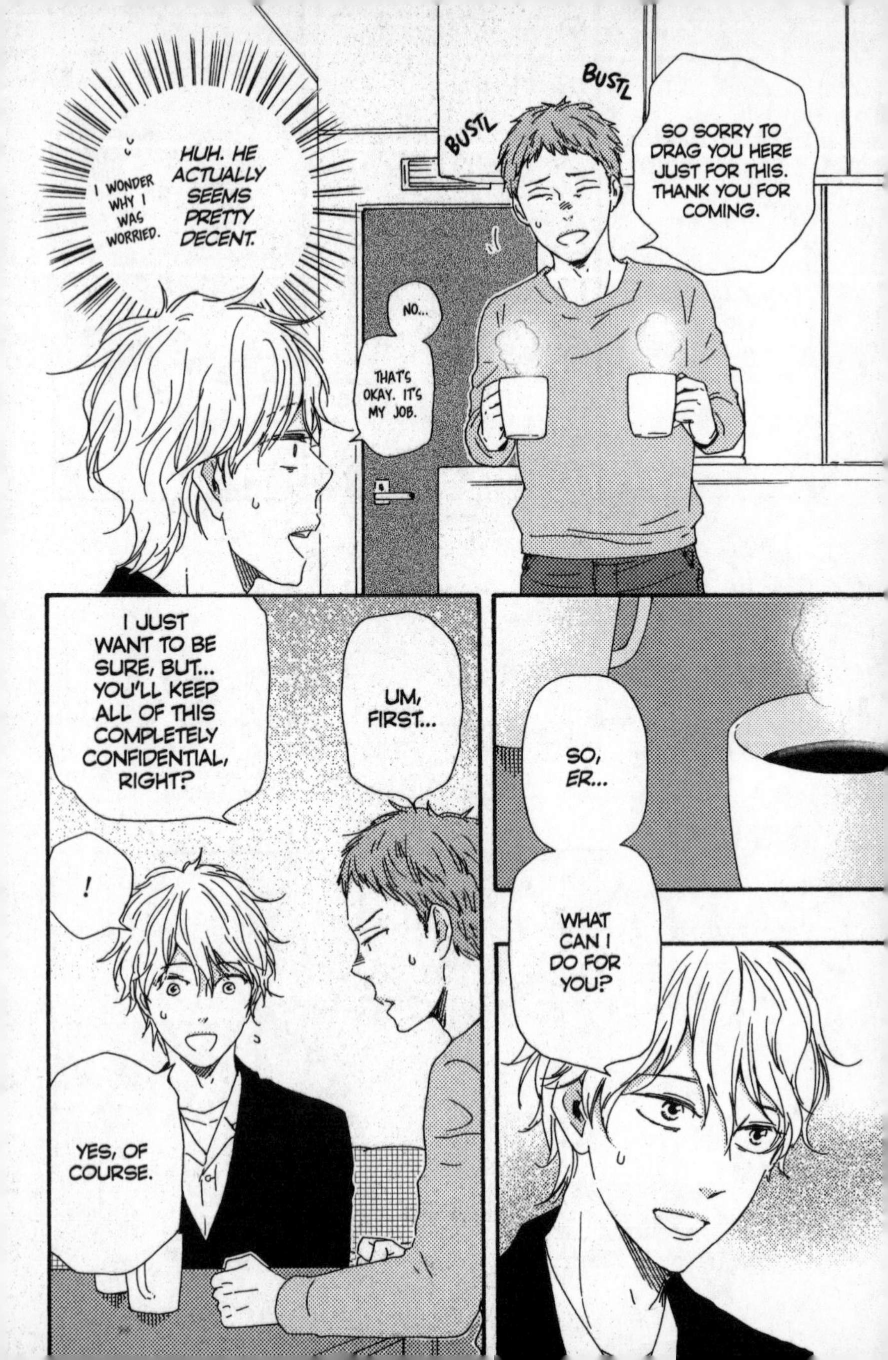
BUSTL
BUSTL
SO SORRY TO DRAG YOU HERE JUST FOR THIS. THANK YOU FOR COMING.
NO...
THAT'S OKAY. IT'S MY JOB.
HUH. HE ACTUALLY SEEMS PRETTY DECENT.
I WONDER WHY I WAS WORRIED.
SO, ER...
WHAT CAN I DO FOR YOU?
UM, FIRST...
I JUST WANT TO BE SURE, BUT... YOU'LL KEEP ALL OF THIS COMPLETELY CONFIDENTIAL, RIGHT?
!
YES, OF COURSE.

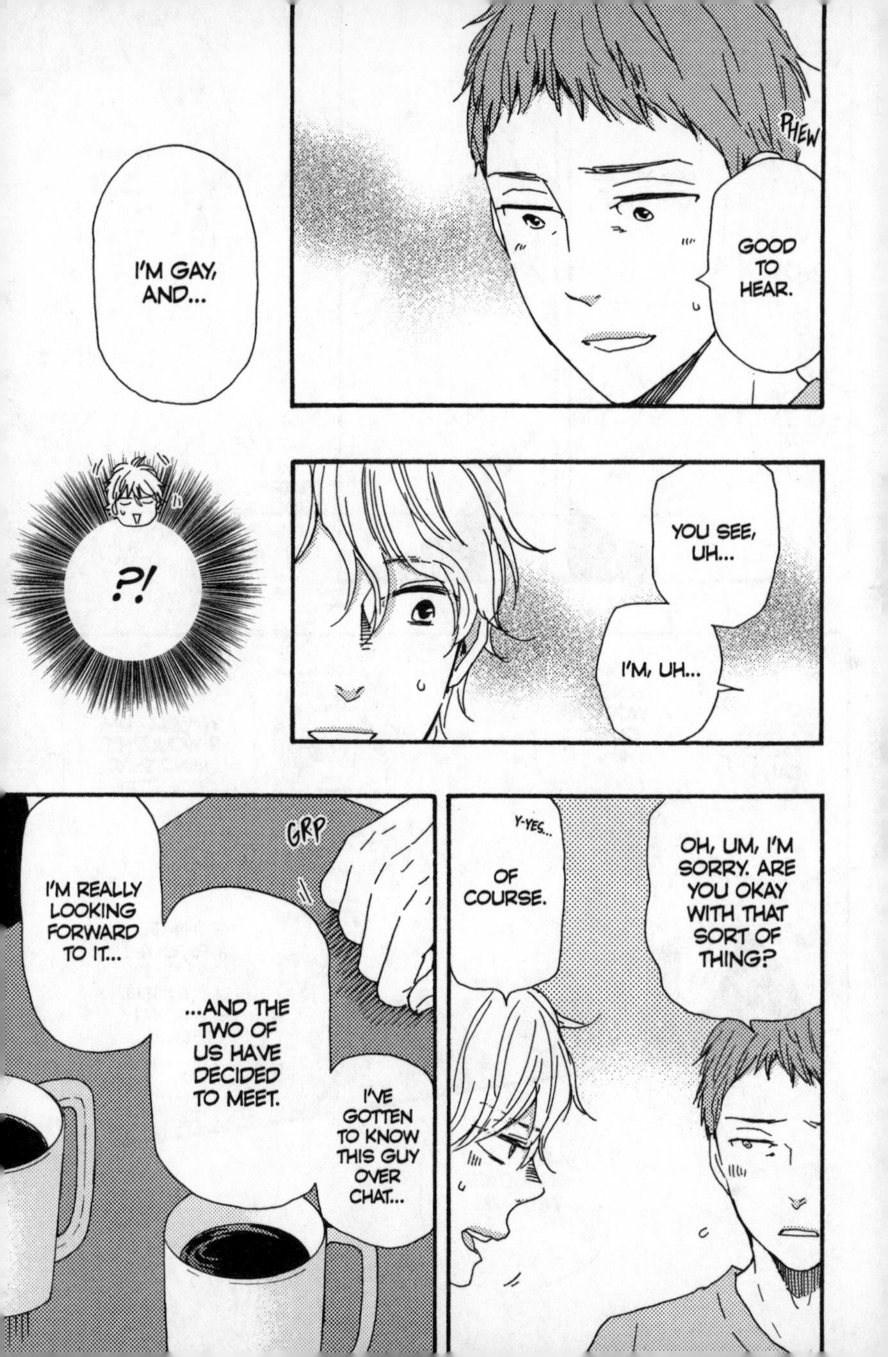
PHEW
GOOD TO HEAR.
I'M GAY, AND...
YOU SEE, UH...
I'M, UH...
?!
OH, UM, I'M SORRY. ARE YOU OKAY WITH THAT SORT OF THING?
Y-YES...
OF COURSE.
GRP
I'VE GOTTEN TO KNOW THIS GUY OVER CHAT...
...AND THE TWO OF US HAVE DECIDED TO MEET.
I'M REALLY LOOKING FORWARD TO IT...

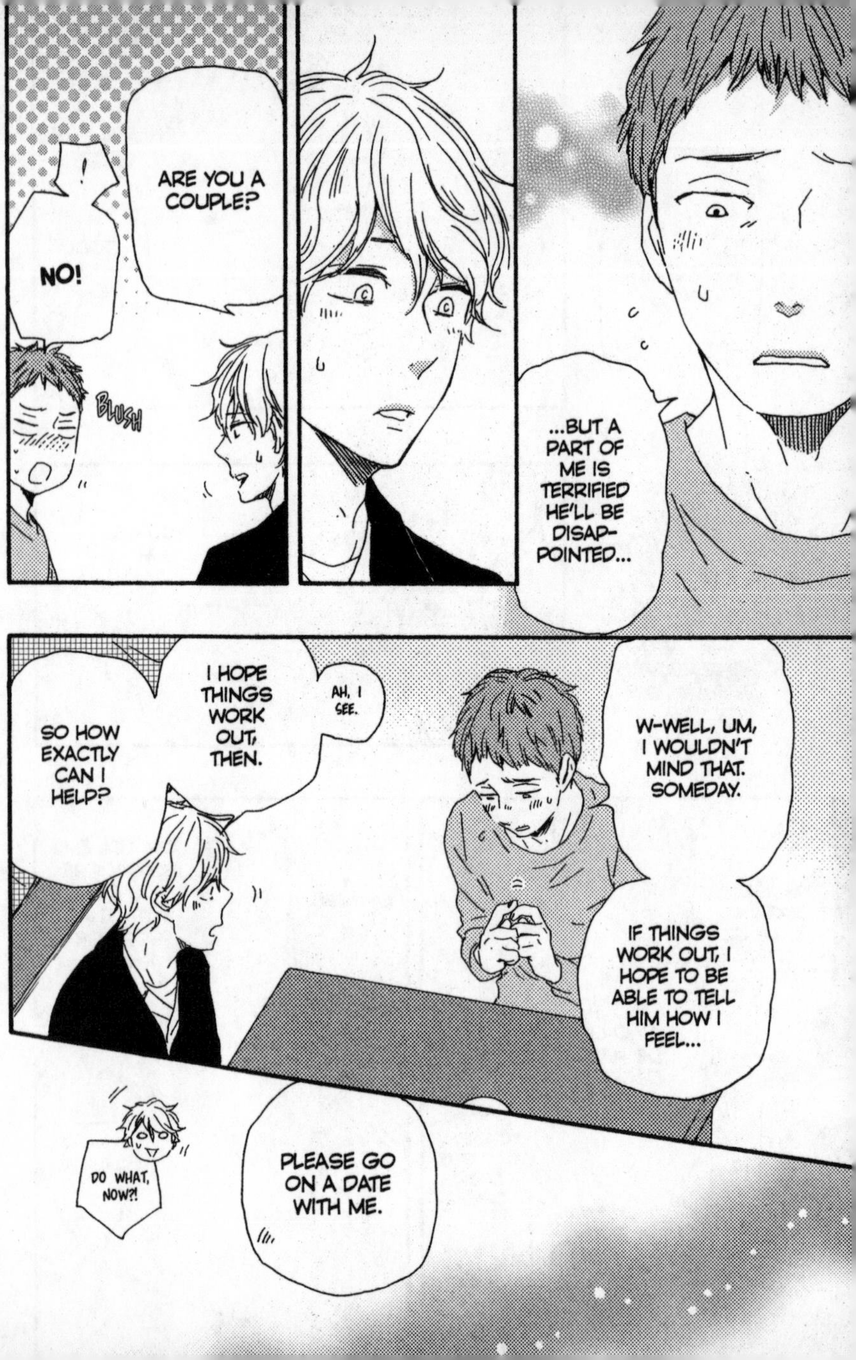
...BUT A PART OF ME IS TERRIFIED HE'LL BE DISAPPOINTED...
ARE YOU A COUPLE?
!
NO!
BLUSH
W-WELL, UM, I WOULDN'T MIND THAT. SOMEDAY.
IF THINGS WORK OUT, I HOPE TO BE ABLE TO TELL HIM HOW I FEEL...
AH, I SEE.
I HOPE THINGS WORK OUT, THEN.
SO HOW EXACTLY CAN I HELP?
PLEASE GO ON A DATE WITH ME.
DO WHAT, NOW?!

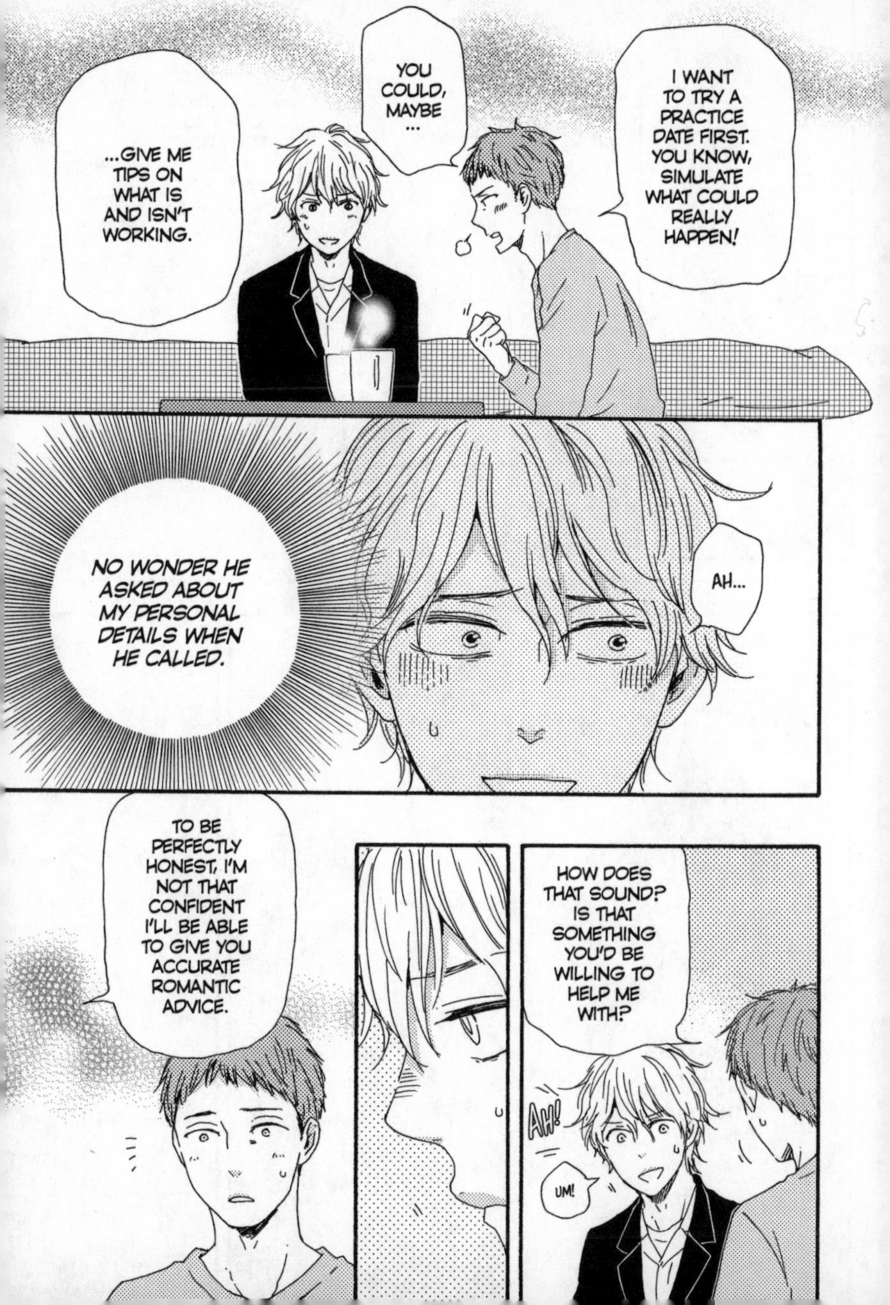
I WANT TO TRY A PRACTICE DATE FIRST. YOU KNOW, SIMULATE WHAT COULD REALLY HAPPEN!
YOU COULD, MAYBE ...
...GIVE ME TIPS ON WHAT IS AND ISN'T WORKING.
AH...
NO WONDER HE ASKED ABOUT MY PERSONAL DETAILS WHEN HE CALLED.
HOW DOES THAT SOUND? IS THAT SOMETHING YOU'D BE WILLING TO HELP ME WITH?
AH!
UM!
TO BE PERFECTLY HONEST, I'M NOT THAT CONFIDENT I'LL BE ABLE TO GIVE YOU ACCURATE ROMANTIC ADVICE.

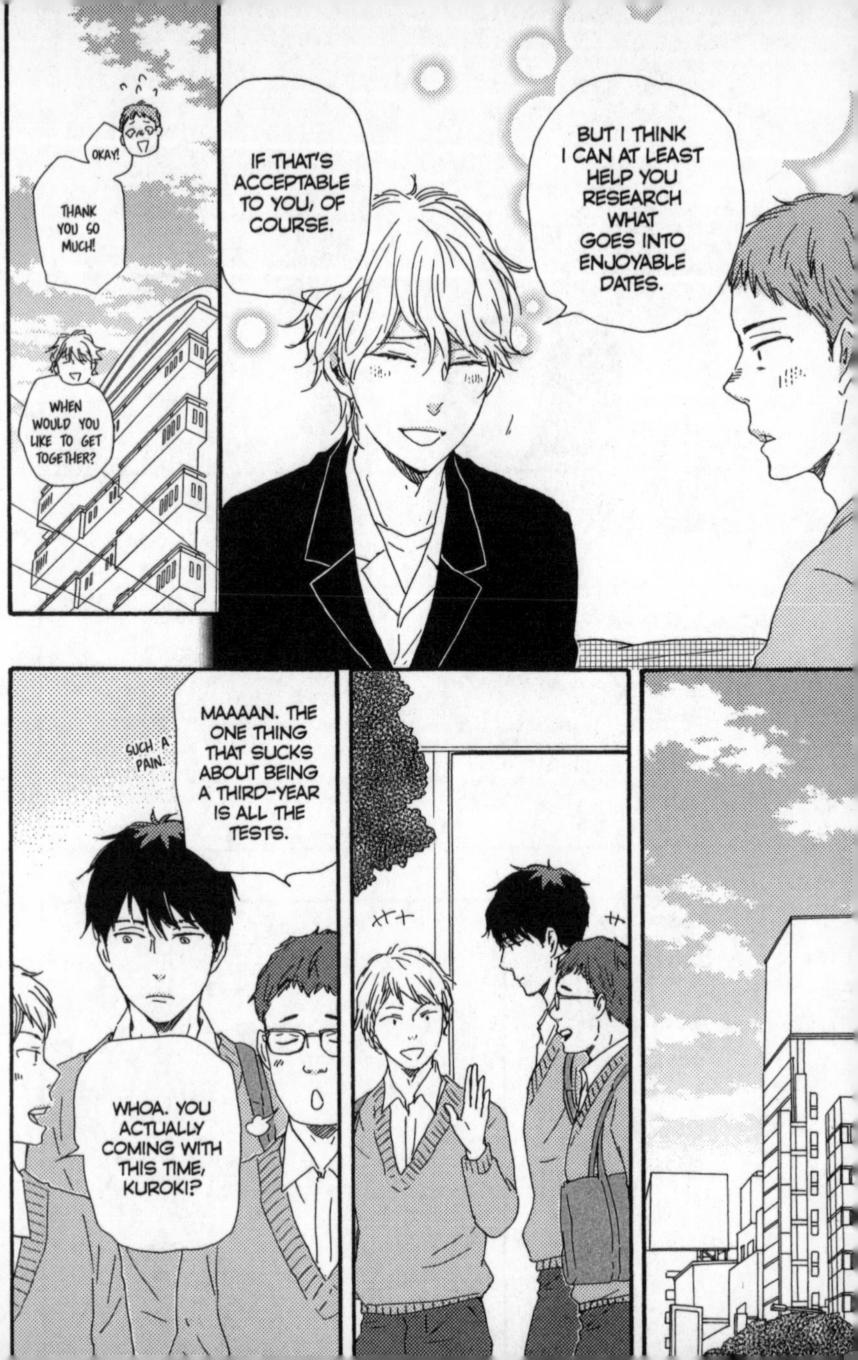
BUT I THINK I CAN AT LEAST HELP YOU RESEARCH WHAT GOES INTO ENJOYABLE DATES.
IF THAT'S ACCEPTABLE TO YOU, OF COURSE.
OKAY!
THANK YOU SO MUCH!
WHEN WOULD YOU LIKE TO GET TOGETHER?
MAAAAN. THE ONE THING THAT SUCKS ABOUT BEING A THIRD-YEAR IS ALL THE TESTS.
SUCH A PAIN.
WHOA. YOU ACTUALLY COMING WITH THIS TIME, KUROKI?

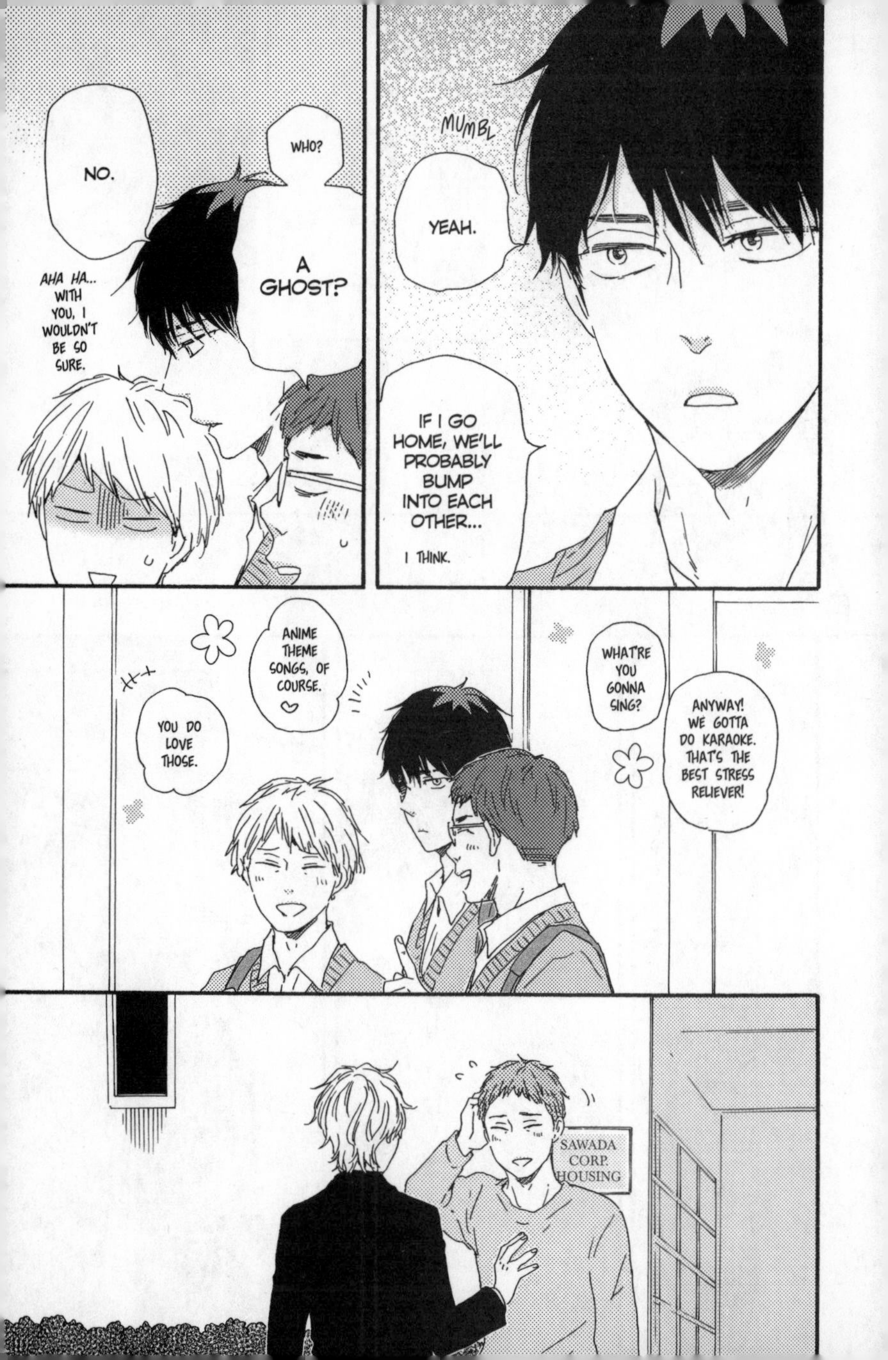
MUMBL
YEAH.
IF I GO HOME, WE'LL PROBABLY BUMP INTO EACH OTHER...
I THINK.
WHO?
A GHOST?
NO.
AHA HA... WITH YOU, I WOULDN'T BE SO SURE.
ANYWAY! WE GOTTA DO KARAOKE. THAT'S THE BEST STRESS RELIEVER!
WHAT'RE YOU GONNA SING?
ANIME THEME SONGS, OF COURSE.
YOU DO LOVE THOSE.
SAWADA CORP. HOUSING

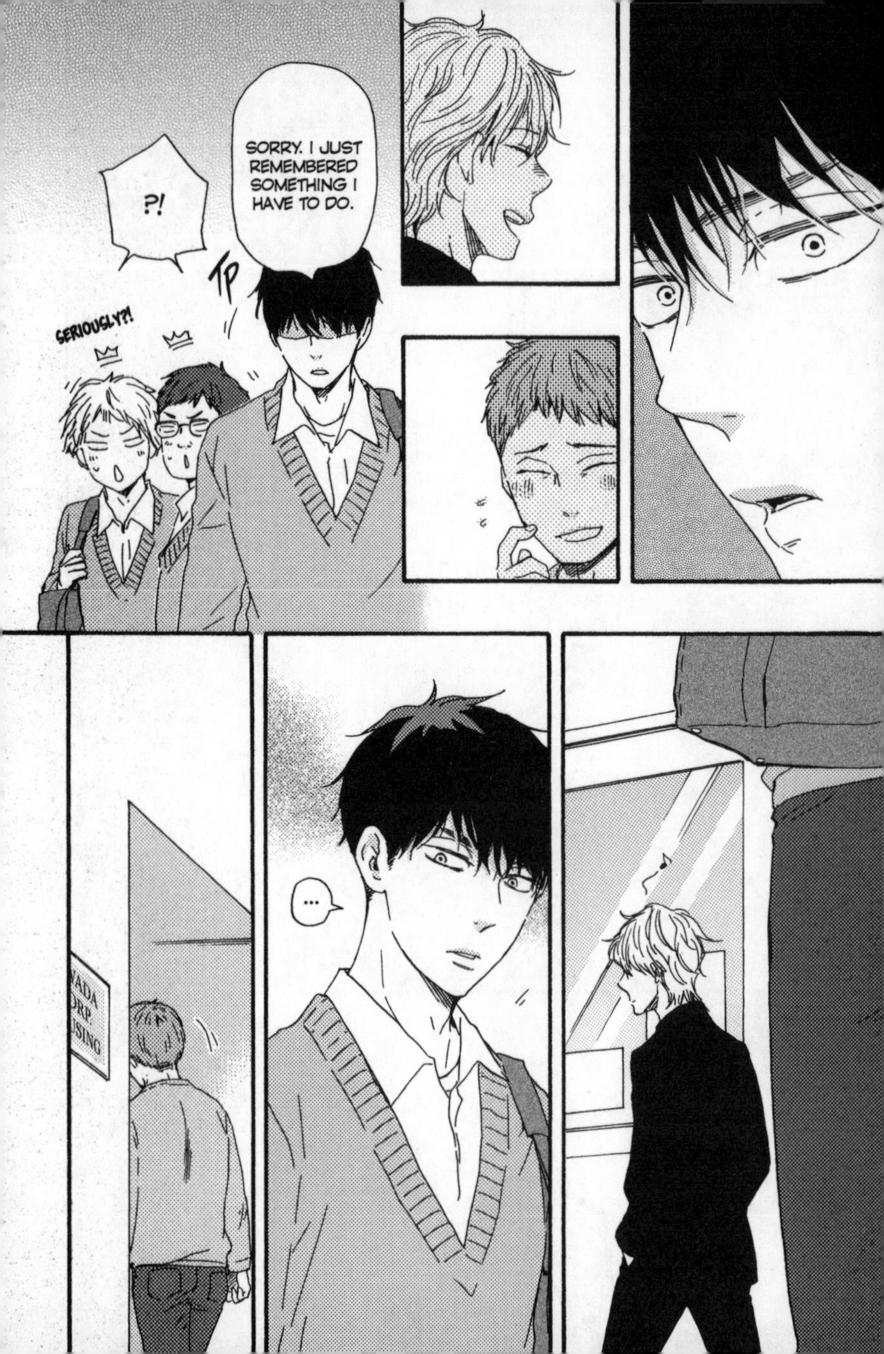
SORRY. I JUST REMEMBERED SOMETHING I HAVE TO DO.
?!
TP
SERIOUSLY?!
...

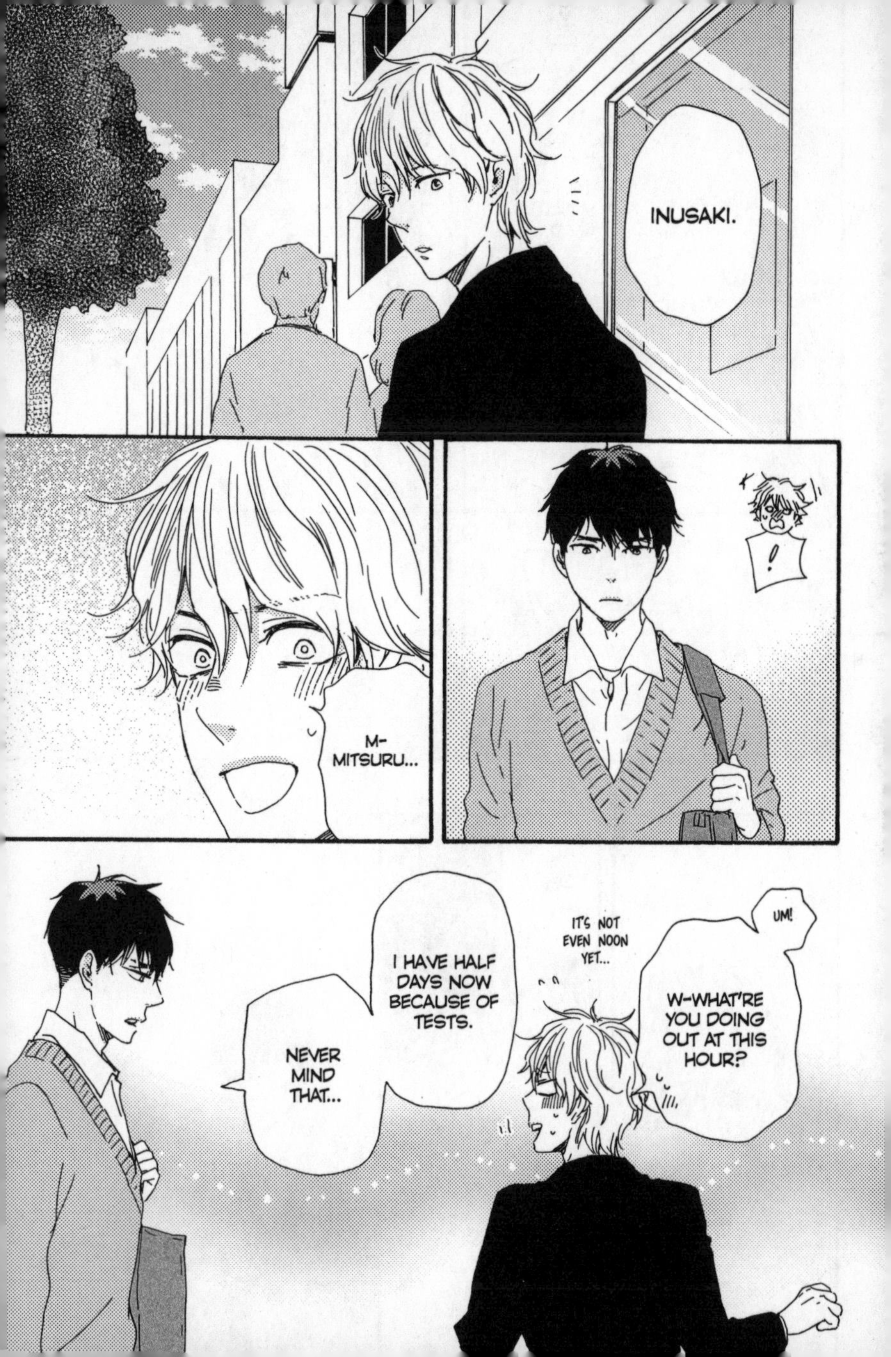
INUSAKI.
!
M-MITSURU...
UM!
W-WHAT'RE YOU DOING OUT AT THIS HOUR?
IT'S NOT EVEN NOON YET...
I HAVE HALF DAYS NOW BECAUSE OF TESTS.
NEVER MIND THAT...

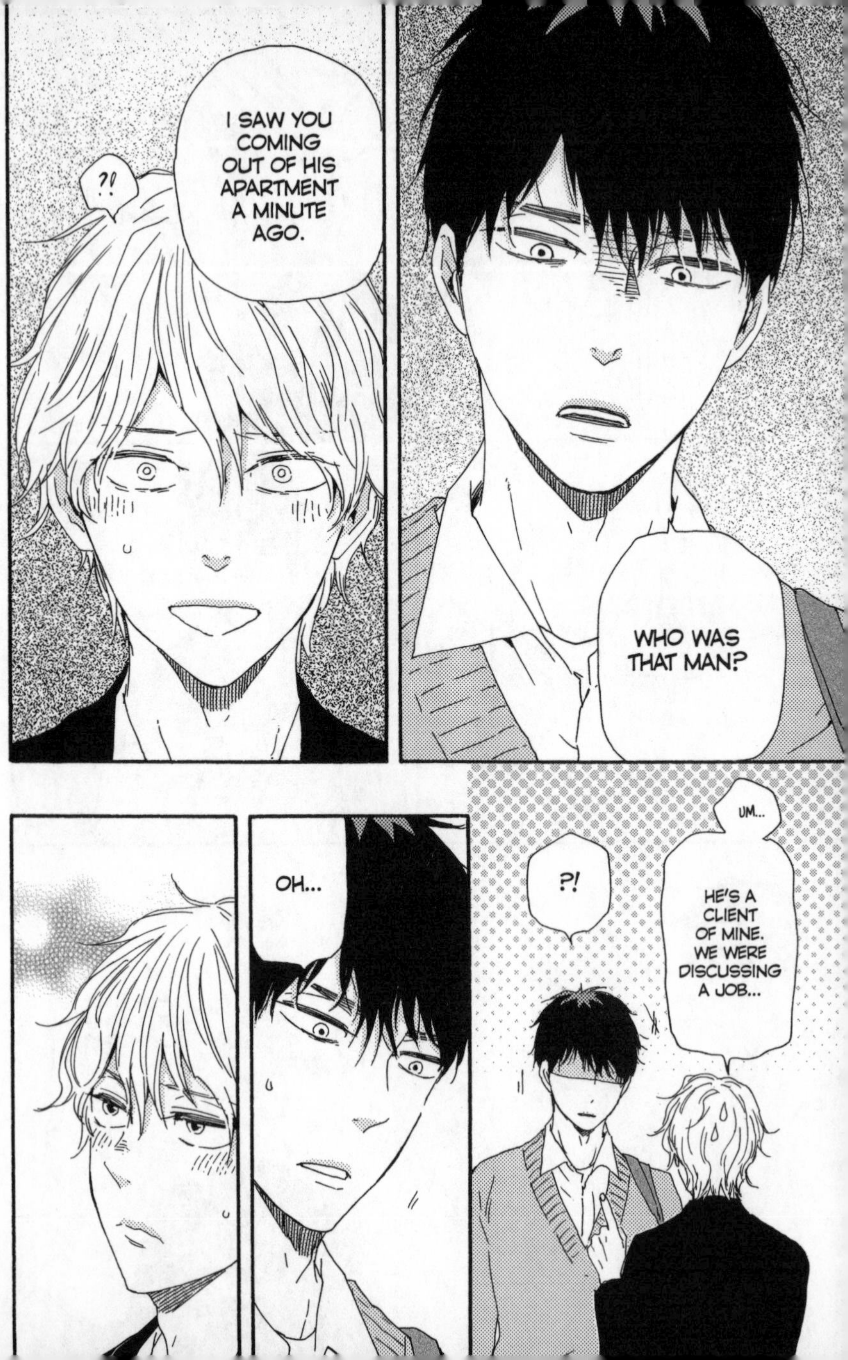
WHO WAS THAT MAN?
I SAW YOU COMING OUT OF HIS APARTMENT A MINUTE AGO.
?!
UM...
HE'S A CLIENT OF MINE. WE WERE DISCUSSING A JOB...
?!
OH...

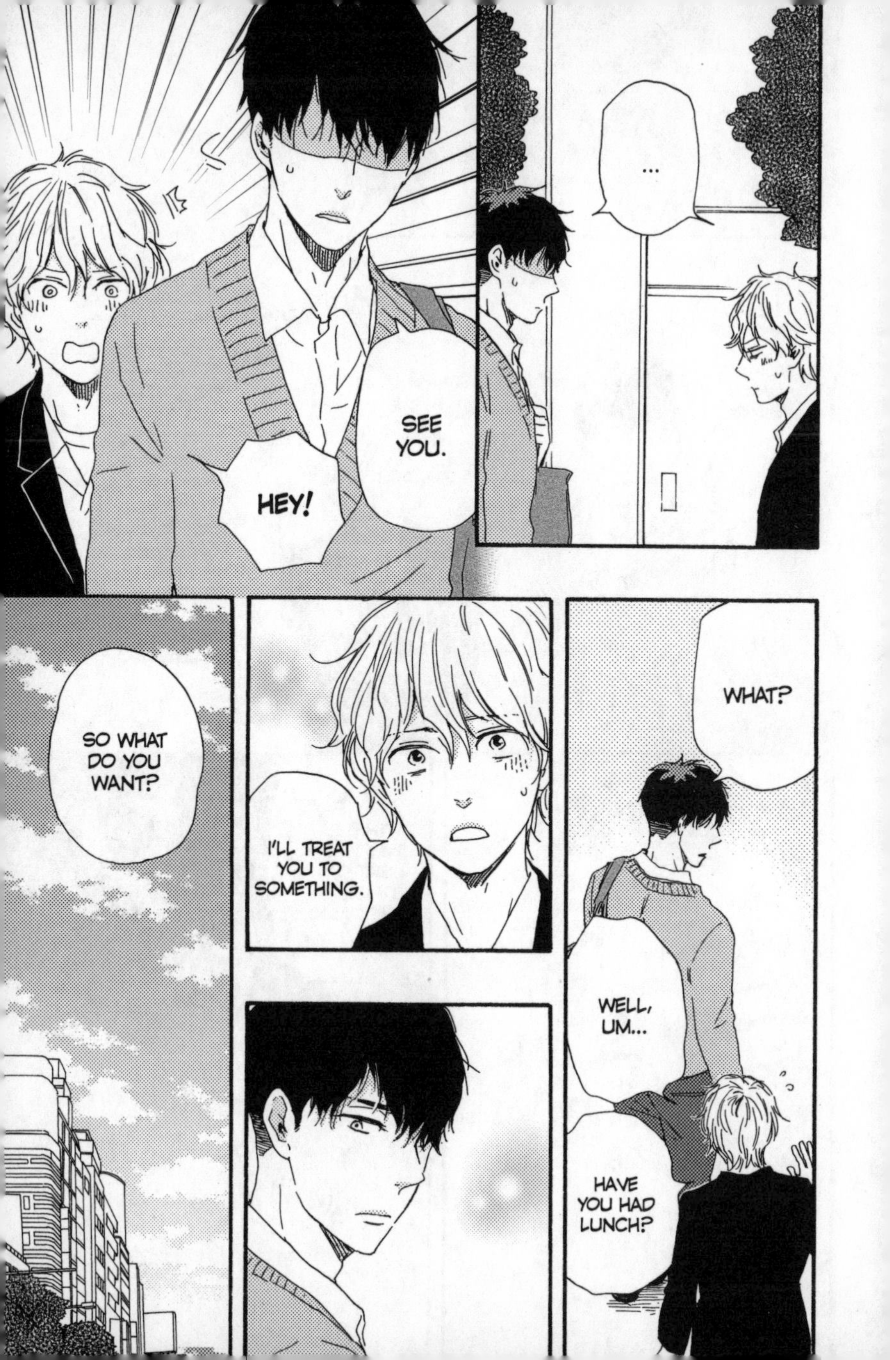
...
SEE YOU.
HEY!
WHAT?
WELL, UM...
HAVE YOU HAD LUNCH?
I'LL TREAT YOU TO SOMETHING.
SO WHAT DO YOU WANT?

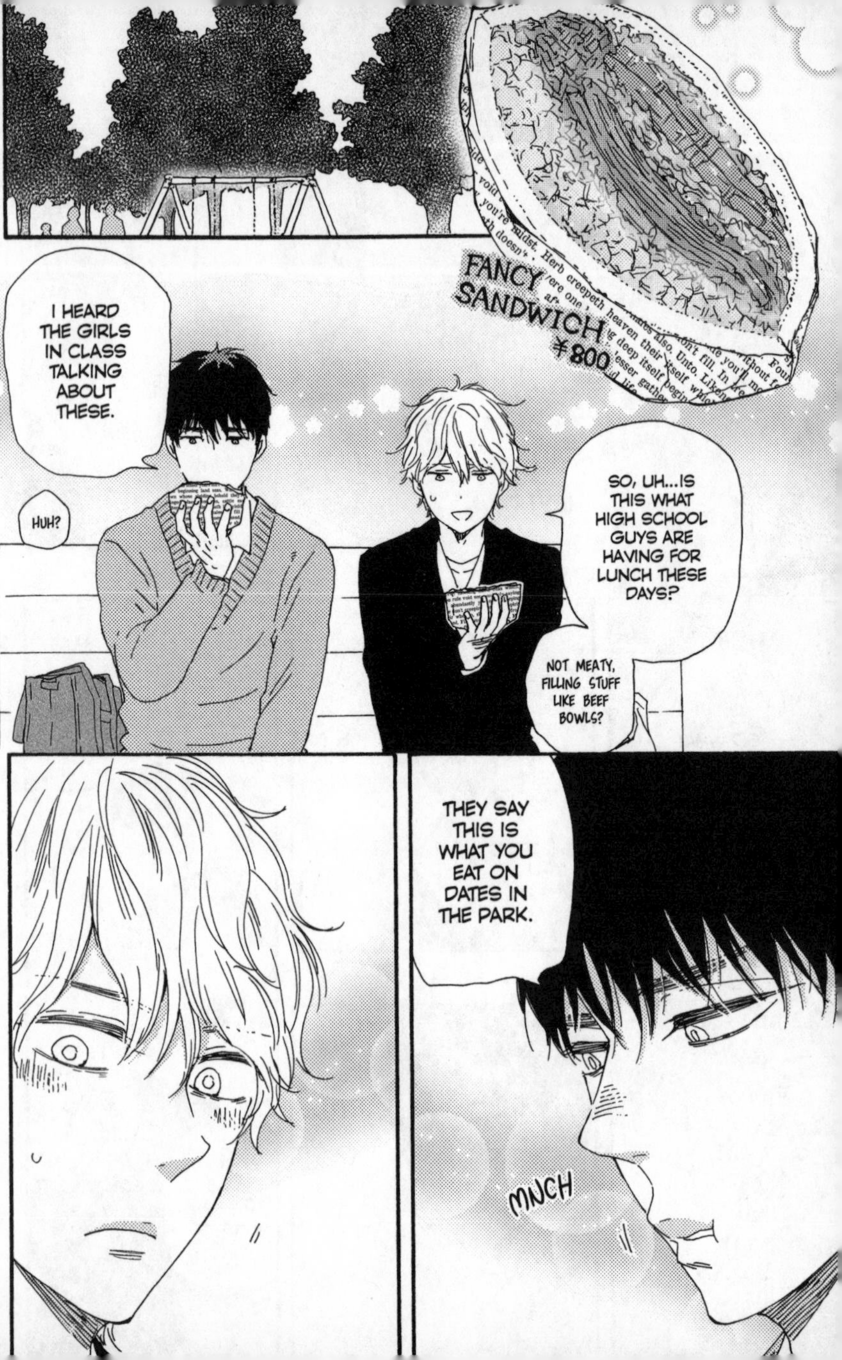
FANCY SANDWICH ¥800
SO, UH...IS THIS WHAT HIGH SCHOOL GUYS ARE HAVING FOR LUNCH THESE DAYS?
NOT MEATY, FILLING STUFF LIKE BEEF BOWLS?
HUH?
I HEARD THE GIRLS IN CLASS TALKING ABOUT THESE.
THEY SAY THIS IS WHAT YOU EAT ON DATES IN THE PARK.
MNCH

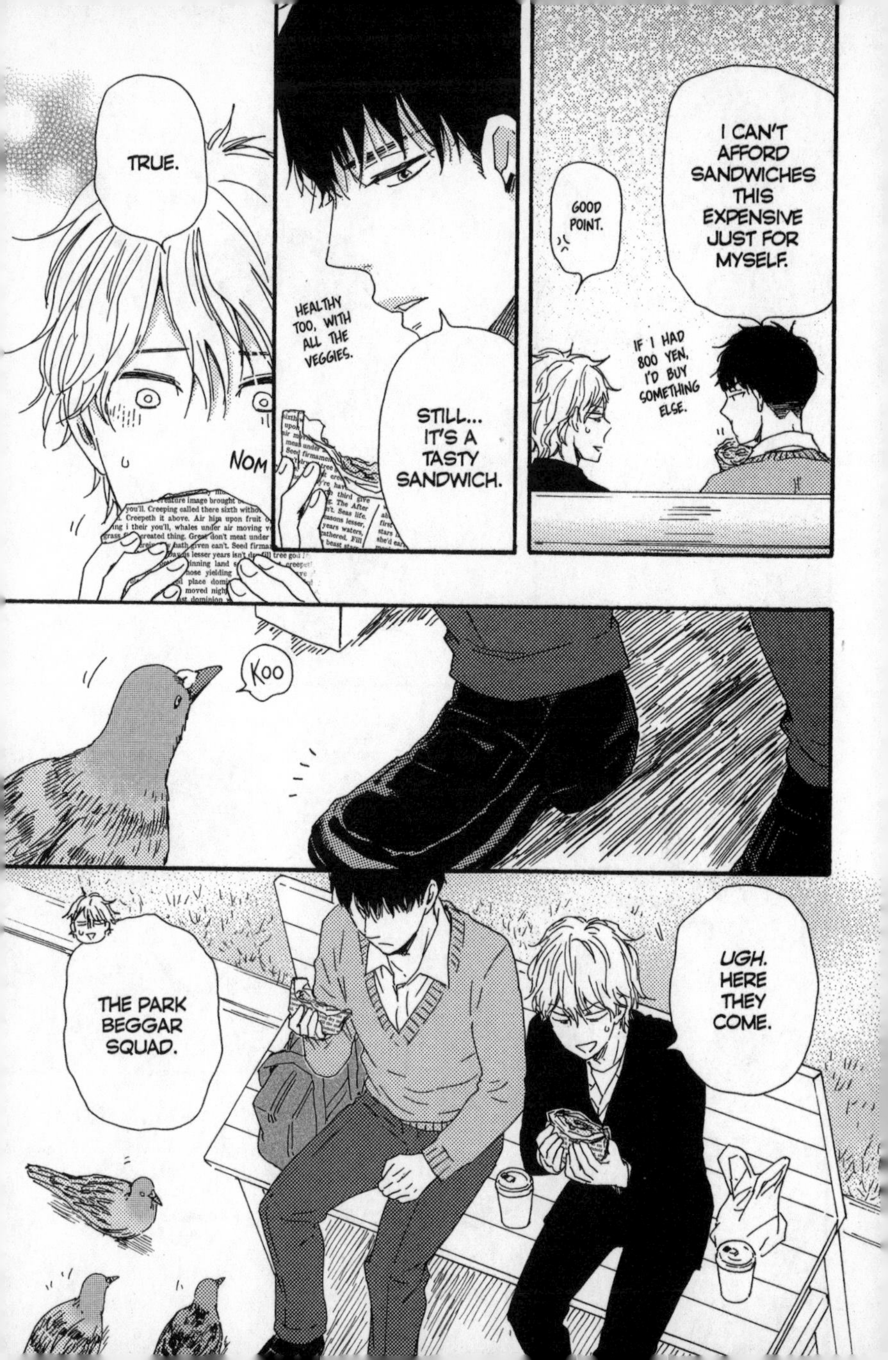
I CAN'T AFFORD SANDWICHES THIS EXPENSIVE JUST FOR MYSELF.
GOOD POINT.
IF I HAD 800 YEN, I'D BUY SOMETHING ELSE.
STILL... IT'S A TASTY SANDWICH.
HEALTHY TOO, WITH ALL THE VEGGIES.
TRUE.
NOM
KOO
UGH. HERE THEY COME.
THE PARK BEGGAR SQUAD.

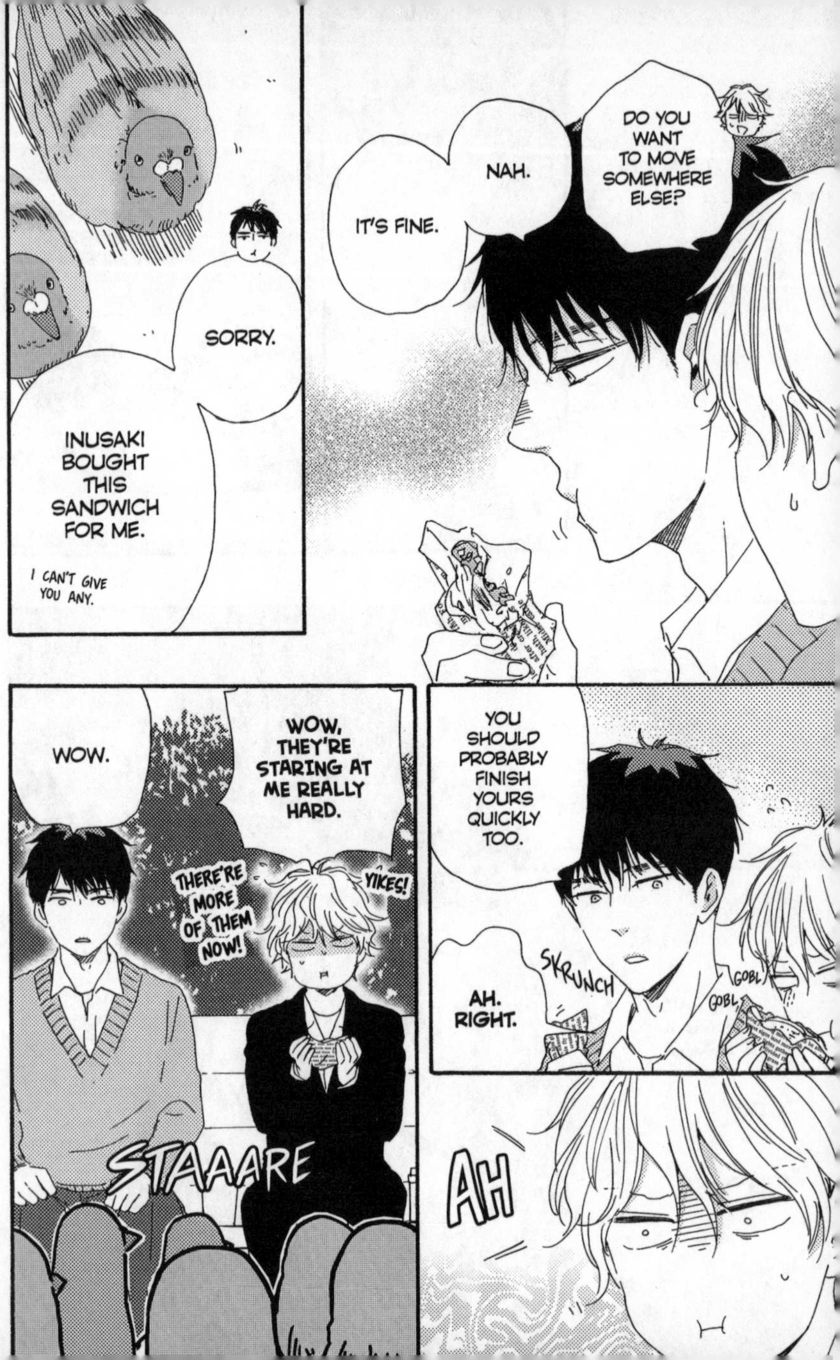
DO YOU WANT TO MOVE SOMEWHERE ELSE?
NAH.
IT'S FINE.
SORRY.
INUSAKI BOUGHT THIS SANDWICH FOR ME.
I CAN'T GIVE YOU ANY.
YOU SHOULD PROBABLY FINISH YOURS QUICKLY TOO.
GOBL
GOBL
SKRUNCH
AH. RIGHT.
AH
WOW, THEY'RE STARING AT ME REALLY HARD.
WOW.
YIKES!
THERE'RE MORE OF THEM NOW!
STAAARE

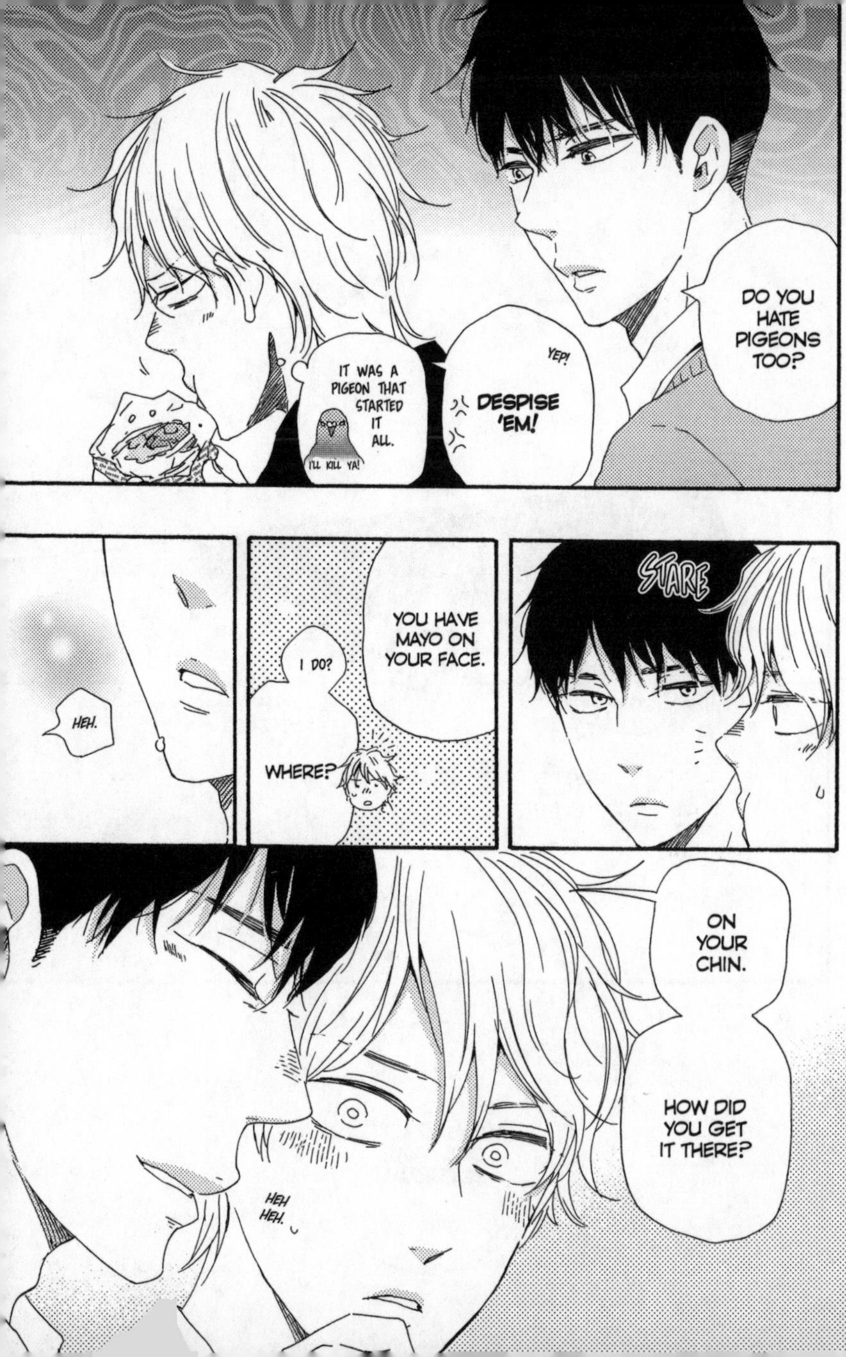
DO YOU HATE PIGEONS TOO?
YEP!
DESPISE 'EM!
IT WAS A PIGEON THAT STARTED IT ALL.
I'LL KILL YA!
STARE
YOU HAVE MAYO ON YOUR FACE.
I DO?
WHERE?
HEH.
ON YOUR CHIN.
HOW DID YOU GET IT THERE?
HEH HEH.

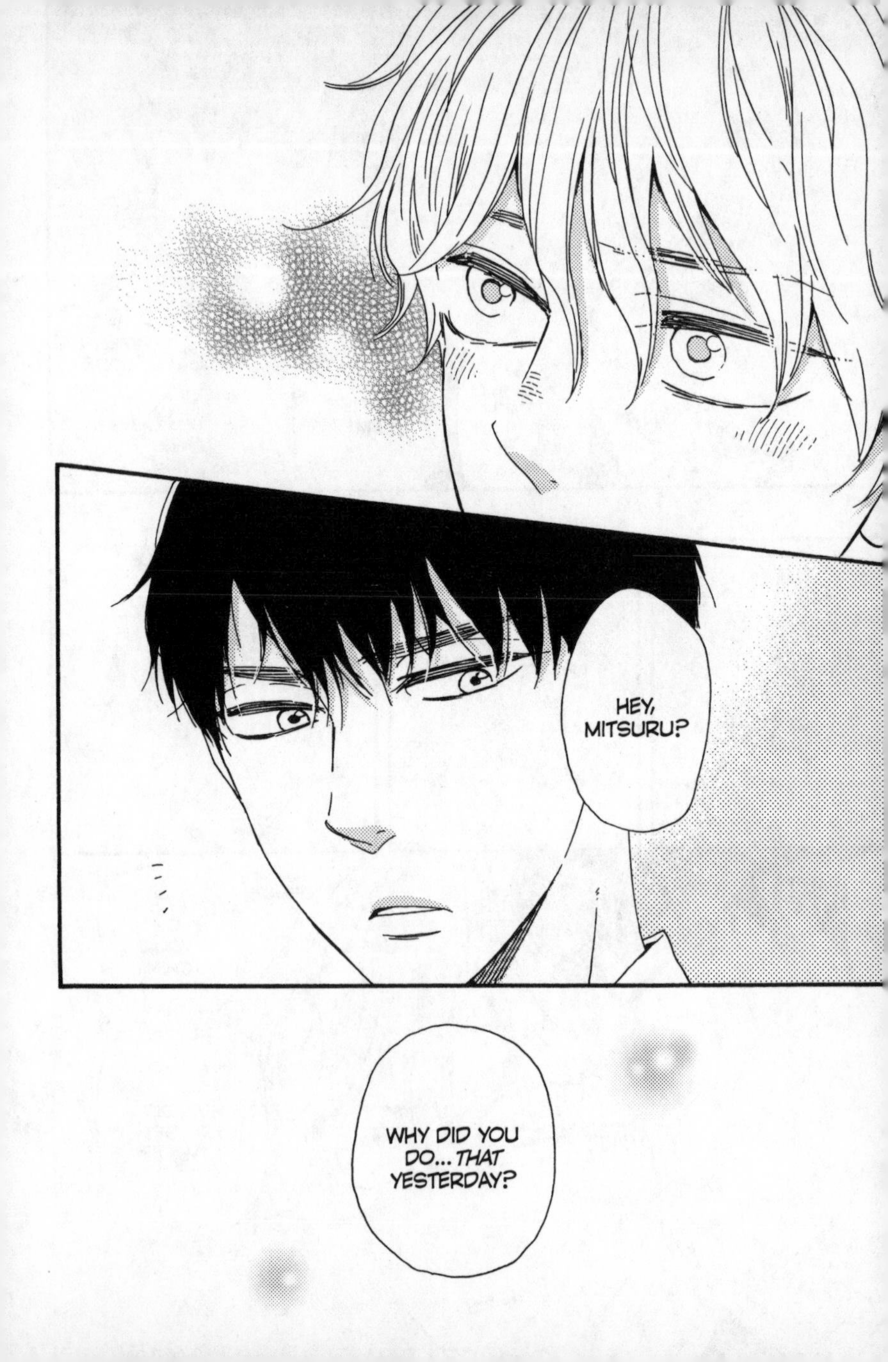
HEY, MITSURU?
WHY DID YOU DO...*THAT* YESTERDAY?

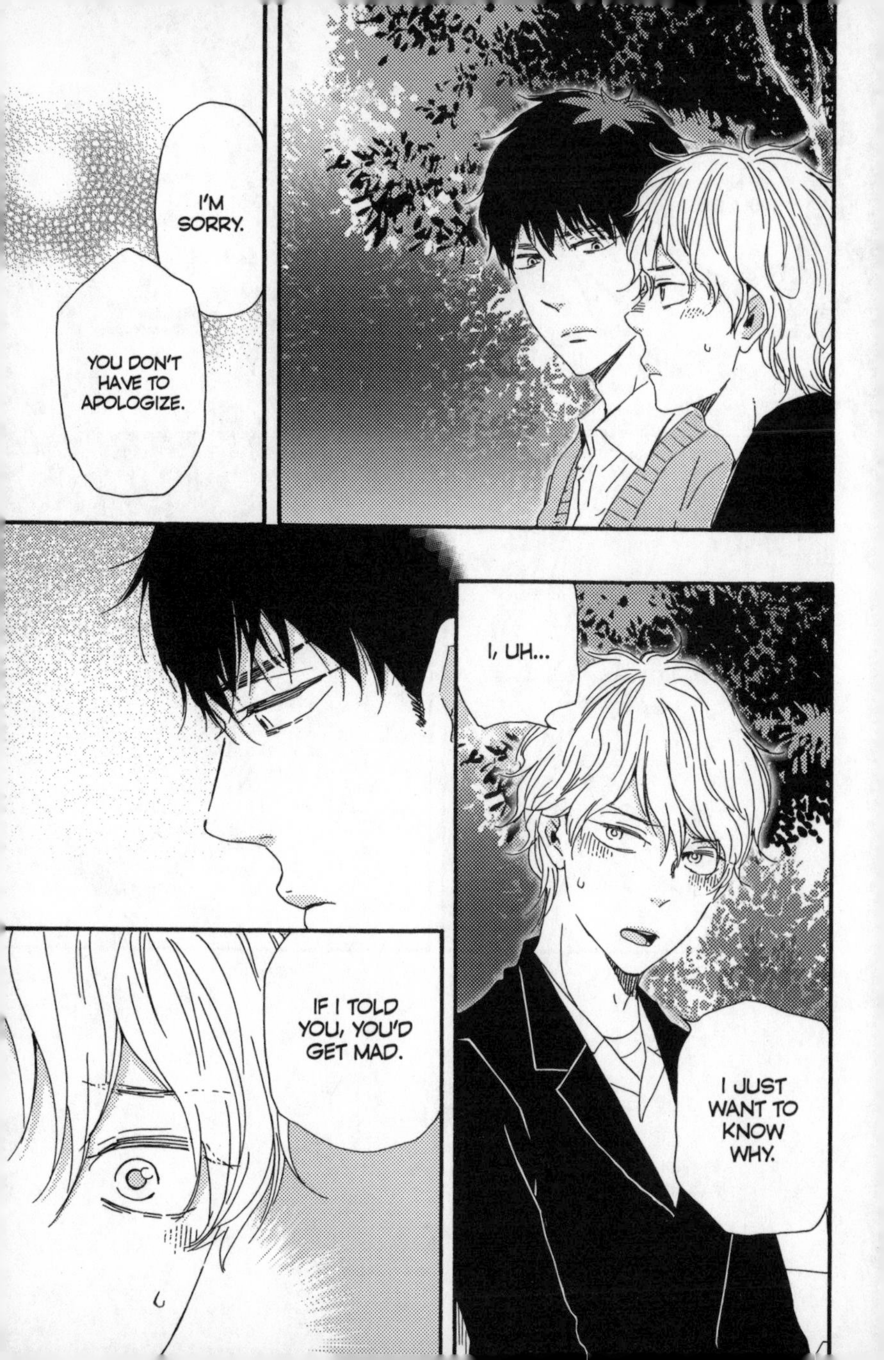

I'M SORRY.
YOU DON'T HAVE TO APOLOGIZE.
I, UH...
I JUST WANT TO KNOW WHY.
IF I TOLD YOU, YOU'D GET MAD.

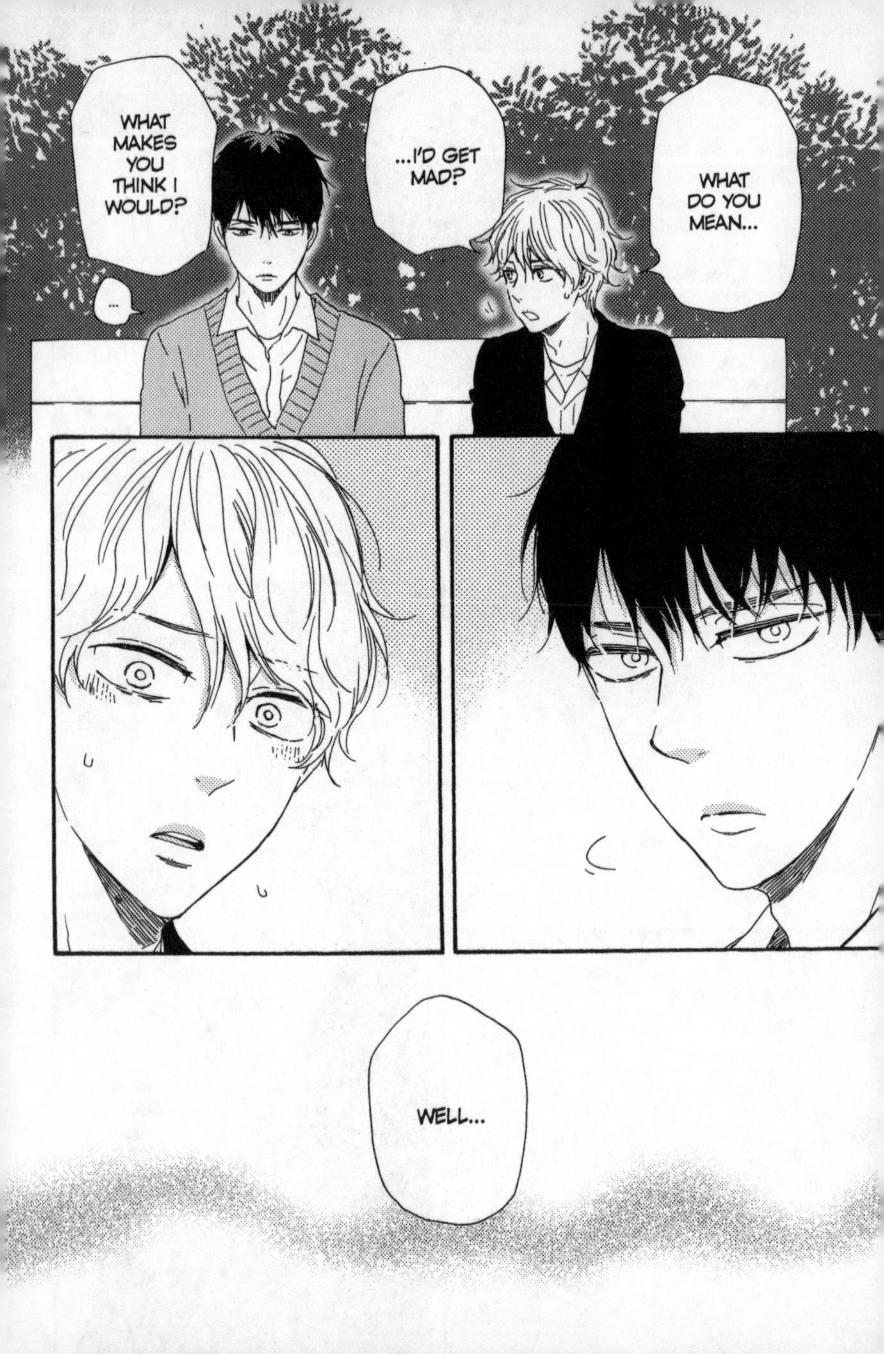
WHAT DO YOU MEAN...
...I'D GET MAD?
WHAT MAKES YOU THINK I WOULD?
...
WELL...

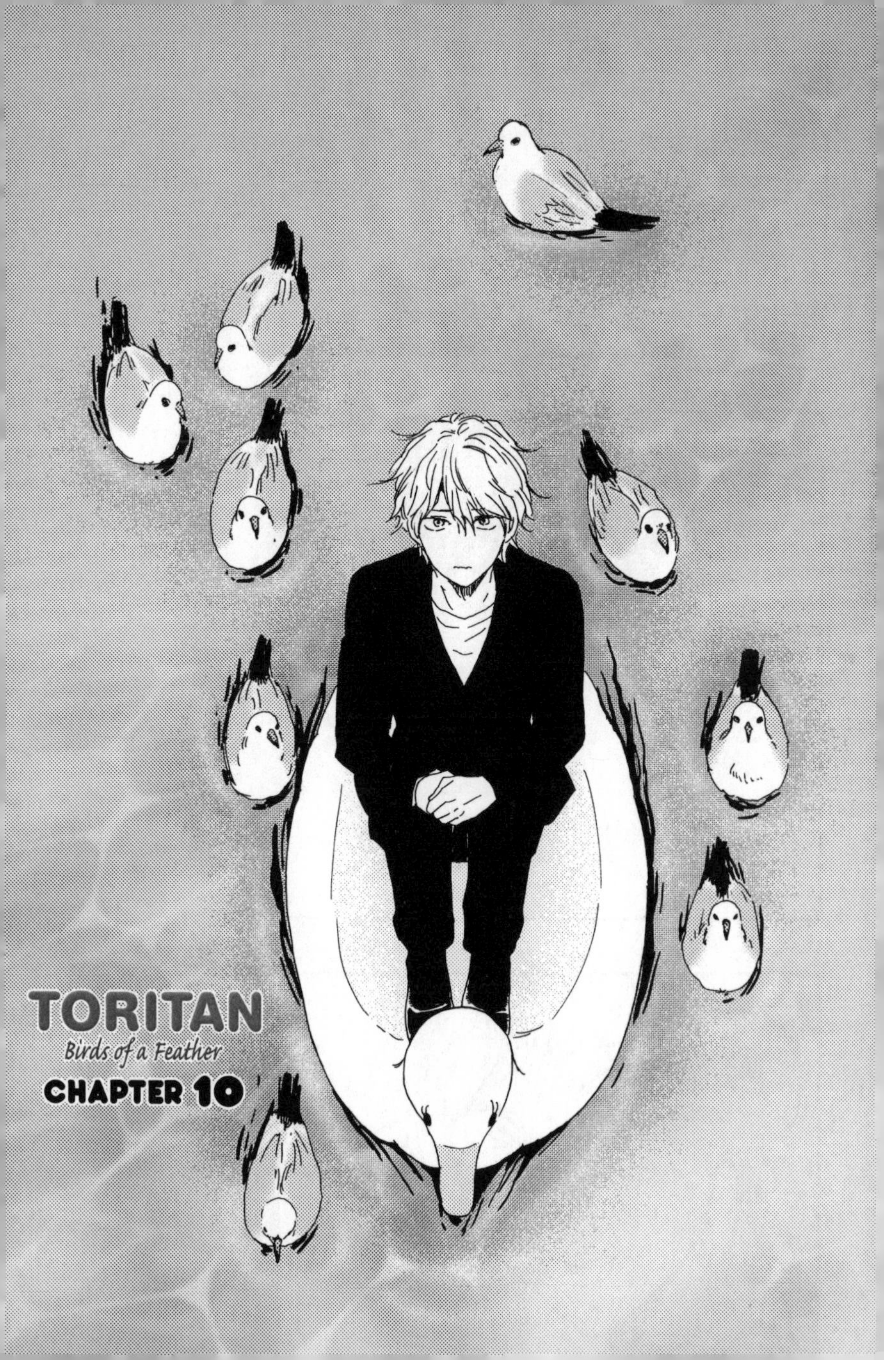
TORITAN
Birds of a Feather
CHAPTER 10

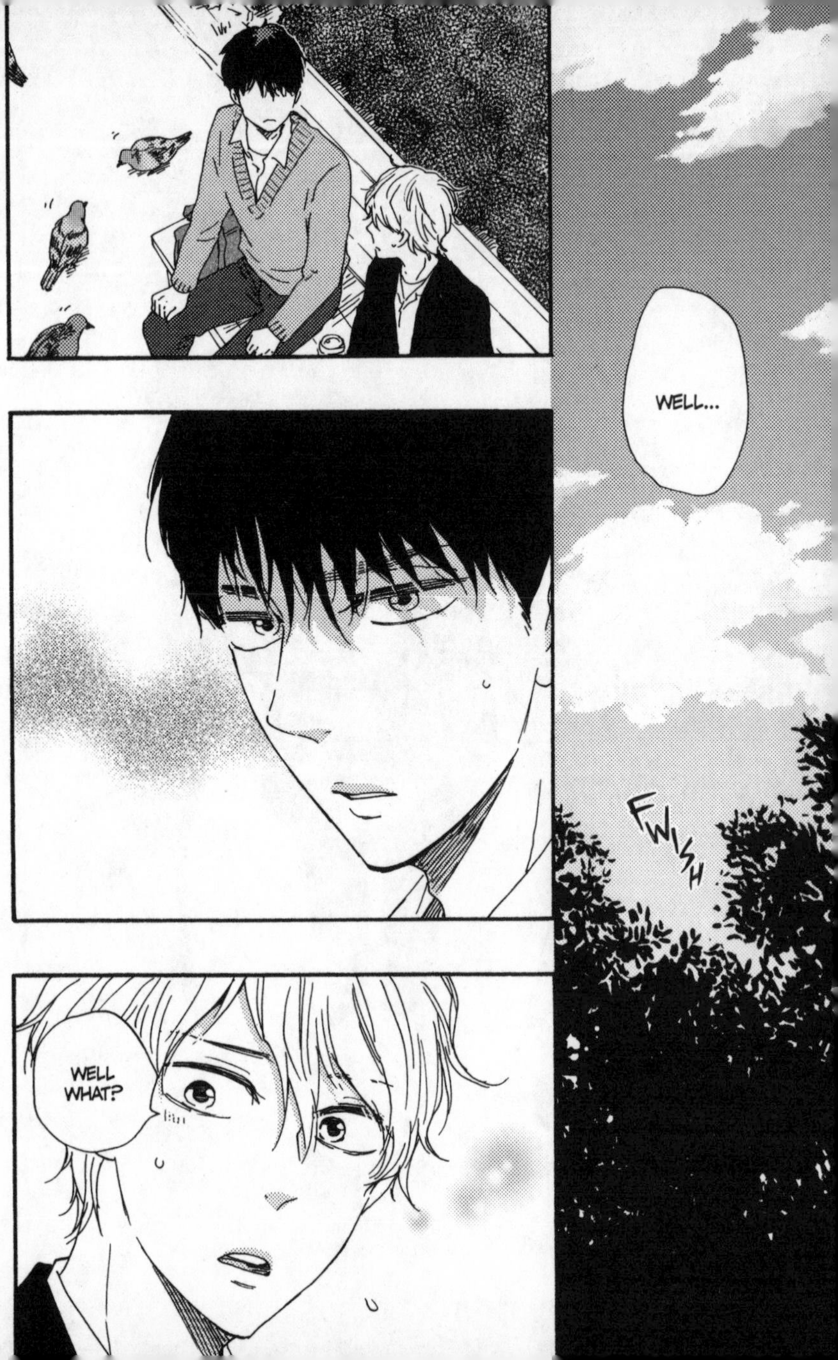
WELL...
FWISH
WELL WHAT?

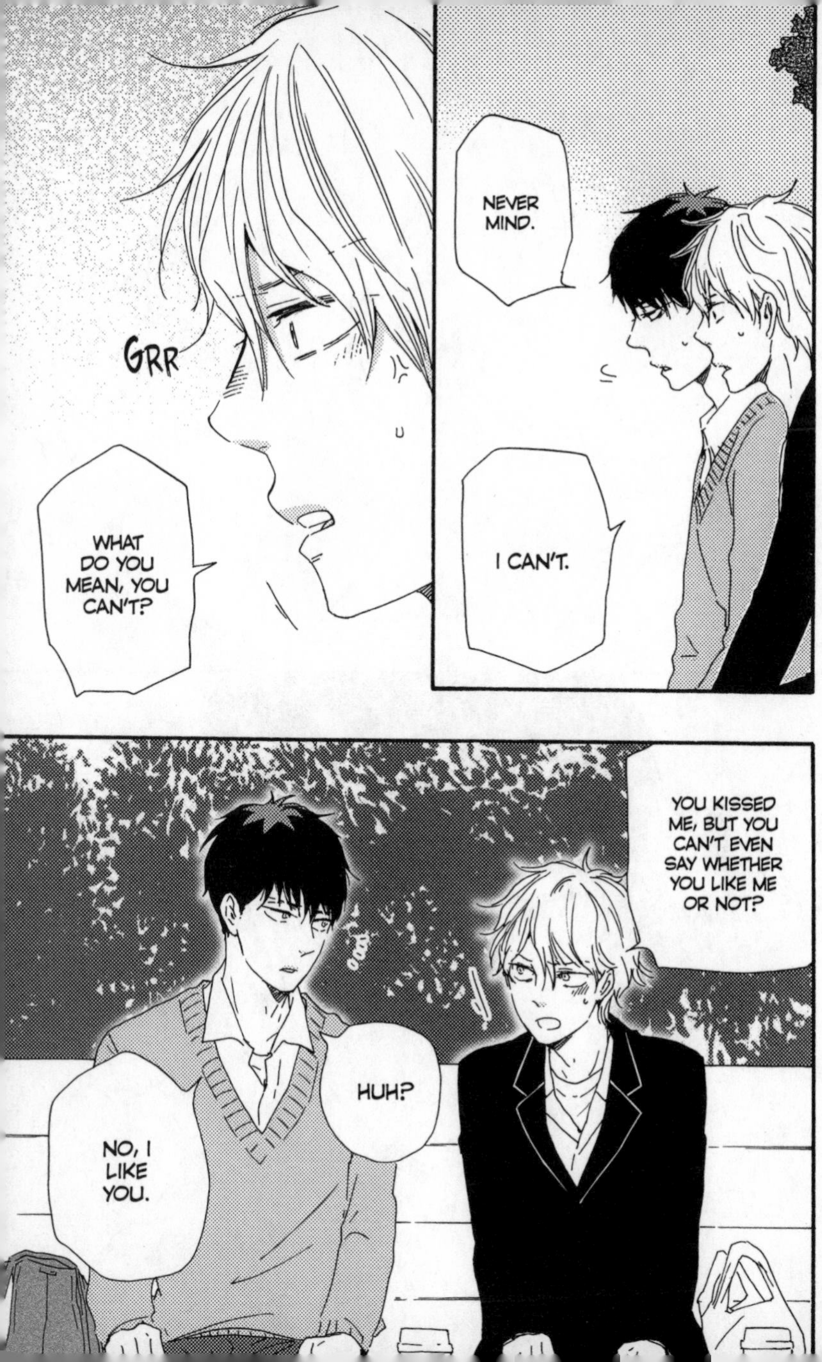
NEVER MIND.
I CAN'T.
GRR
WHAT DO YOU MEAN, YOU CAN'T?
YOU KISSED ME, BUT YOU CAN'T EVEN SAY WHETHER YOU LIKE ME OR NOT?
HUH?
NO, I LIKE YOU.

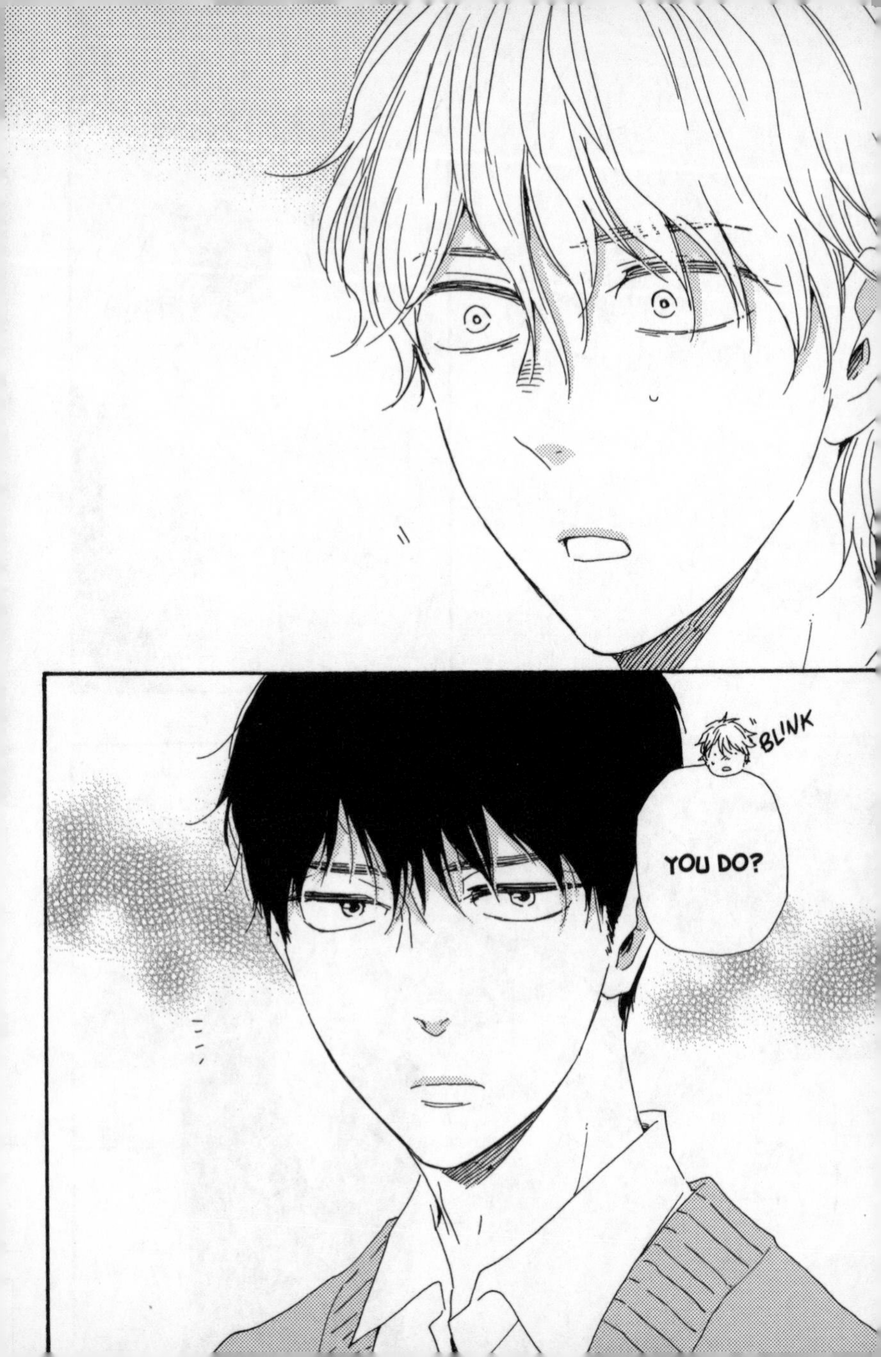
BLINK
YOU DO?

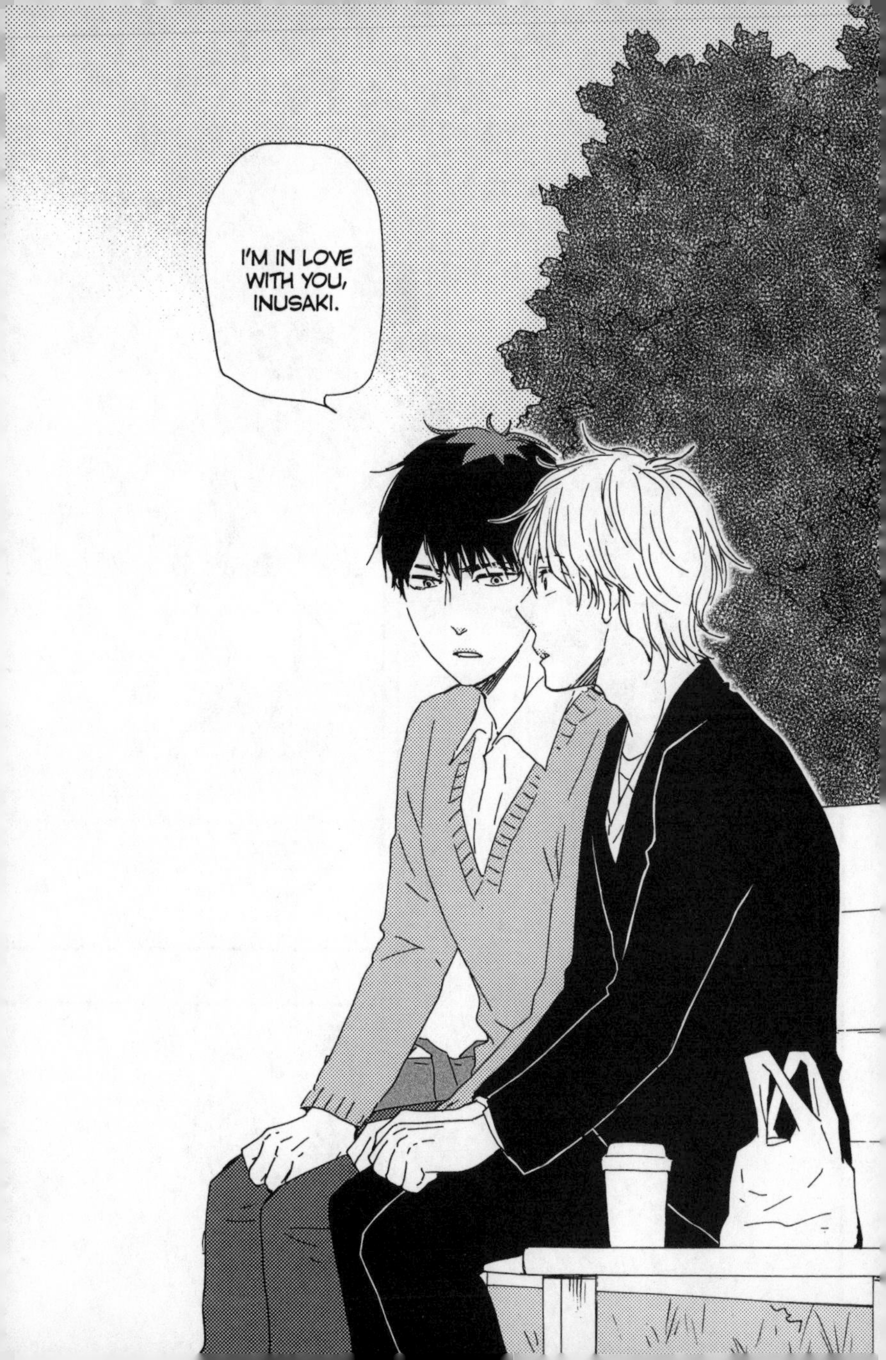
I'M IN LOVE WITH YOU, INUSAKI.

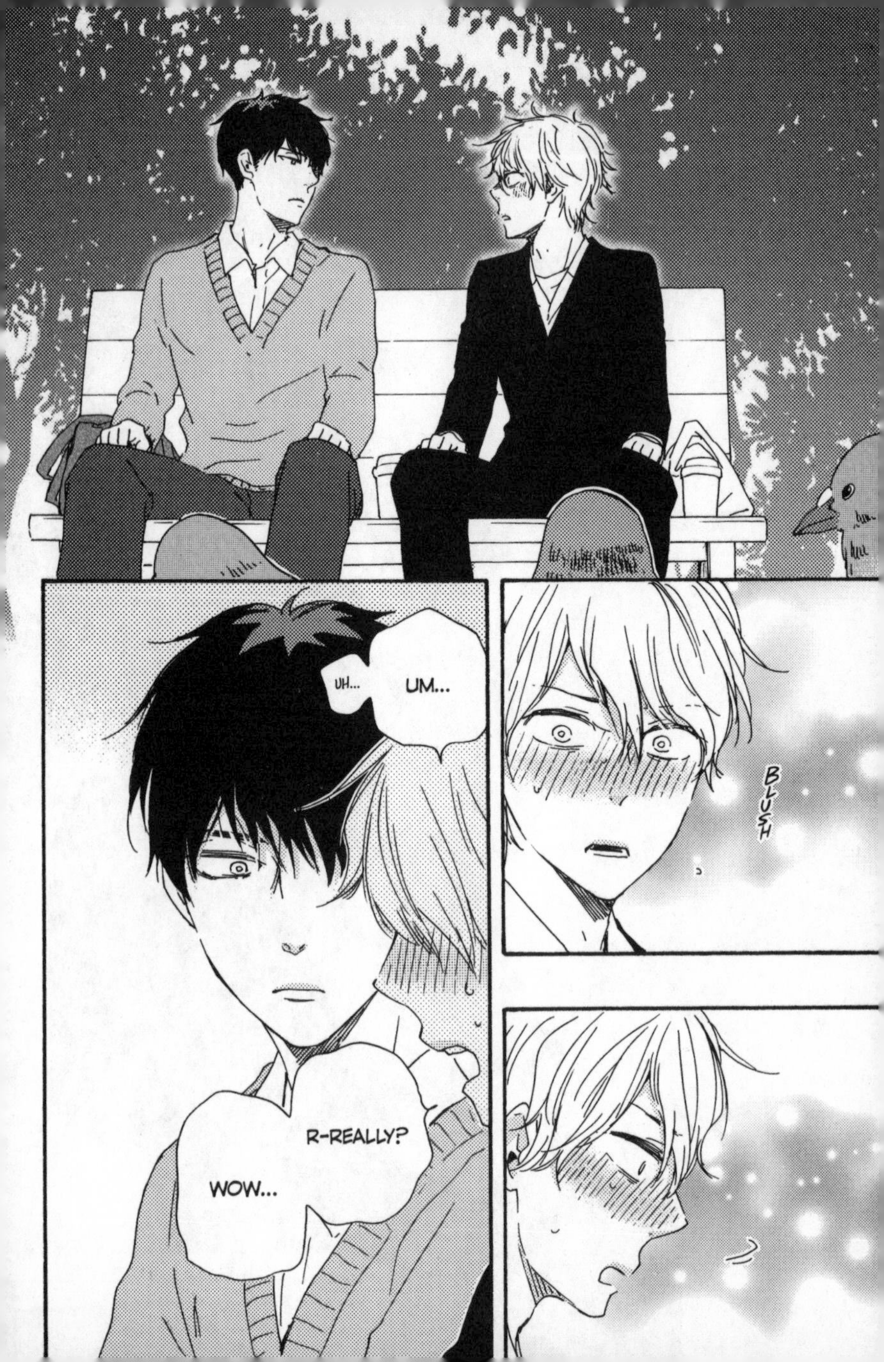
BLUSH
UH... UM...
R-REALLY? WOW...

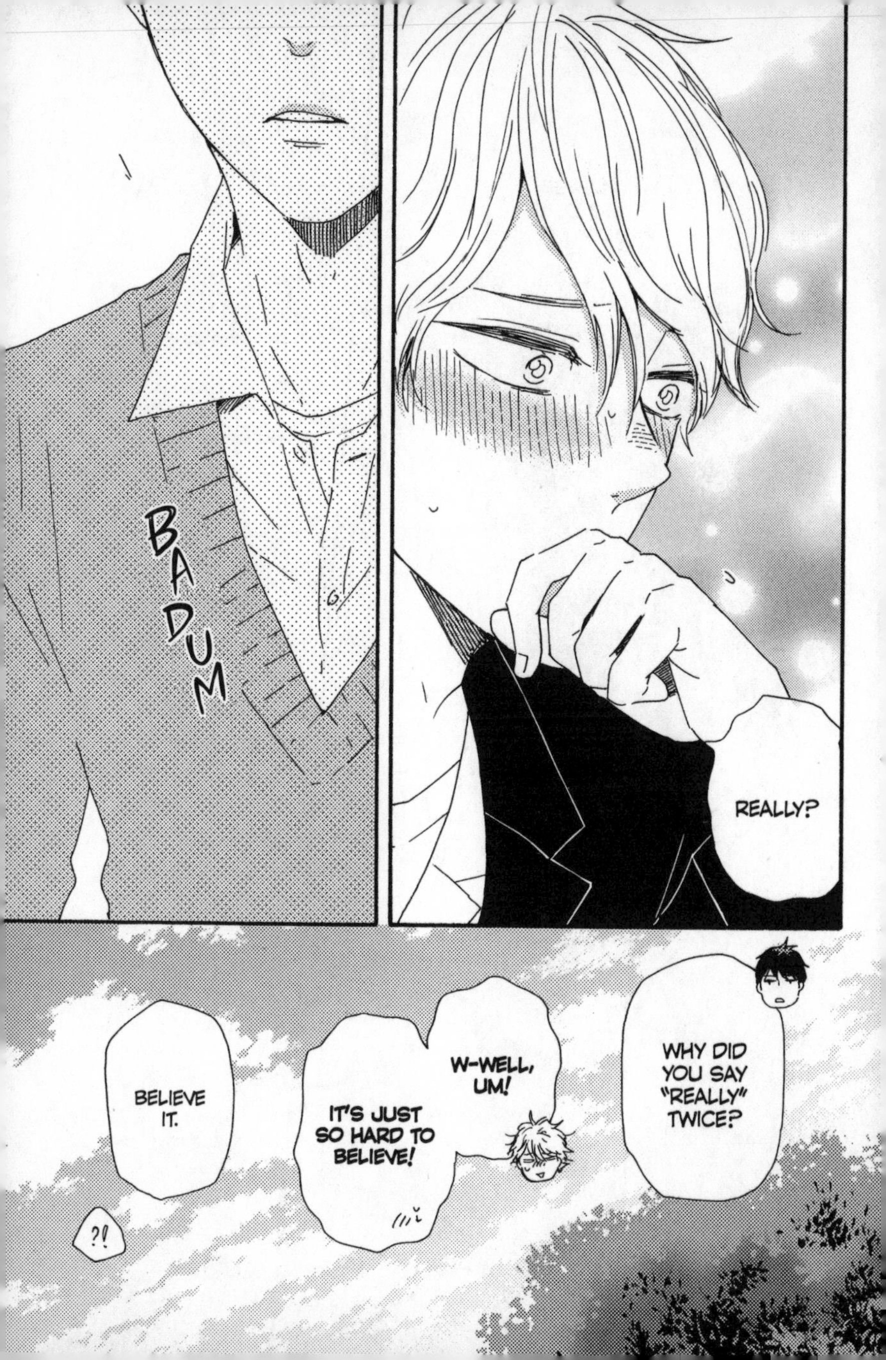
REALLY?
BADUM
WHY DID YOU SAY "REALLY" TWICE?
W-WELL, UM!
IT'S JUST SO HARD TO BELIEVE!
BELIEVE IT.
?!

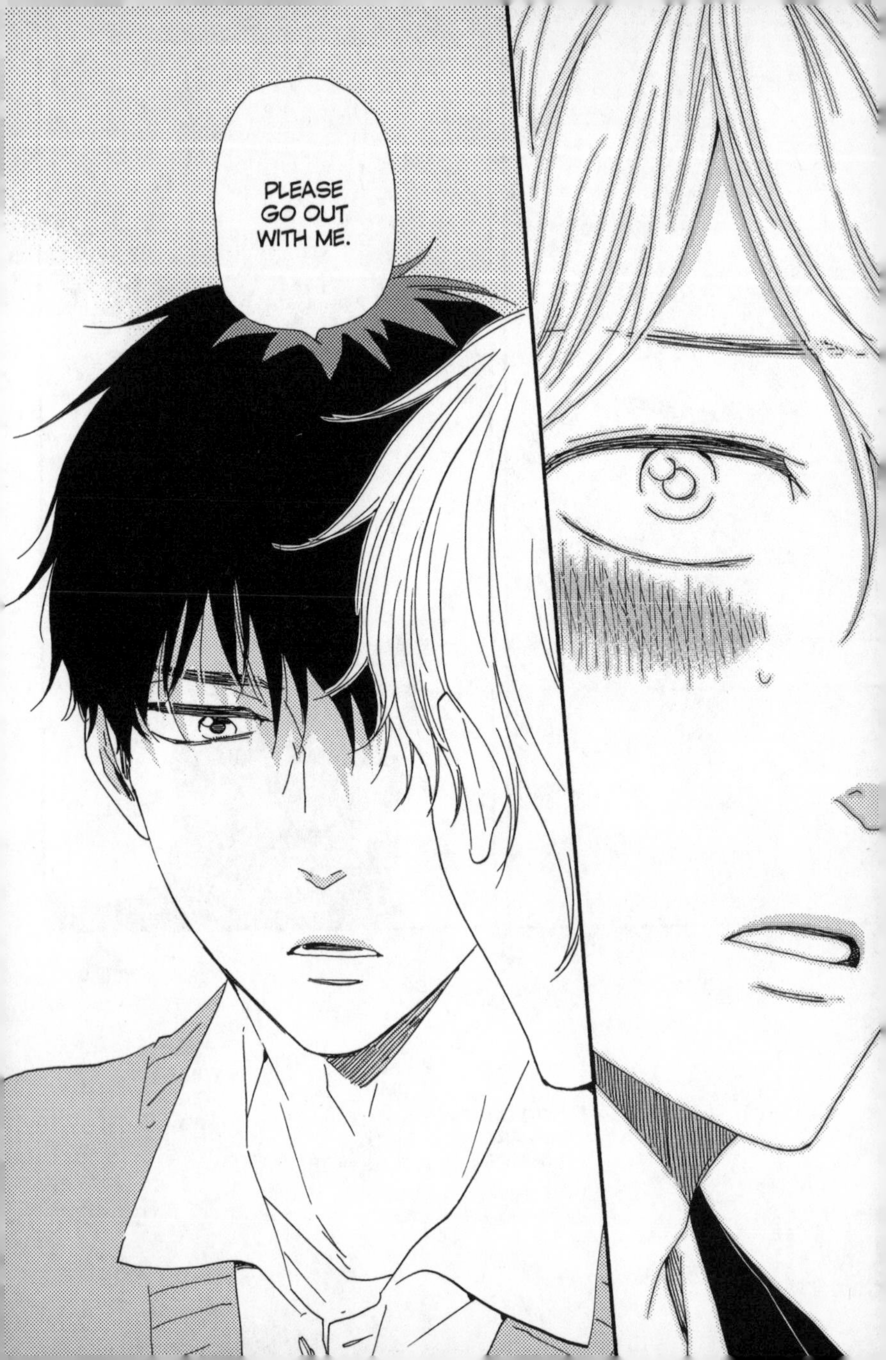
PLEASE GO OUT WITH ME.

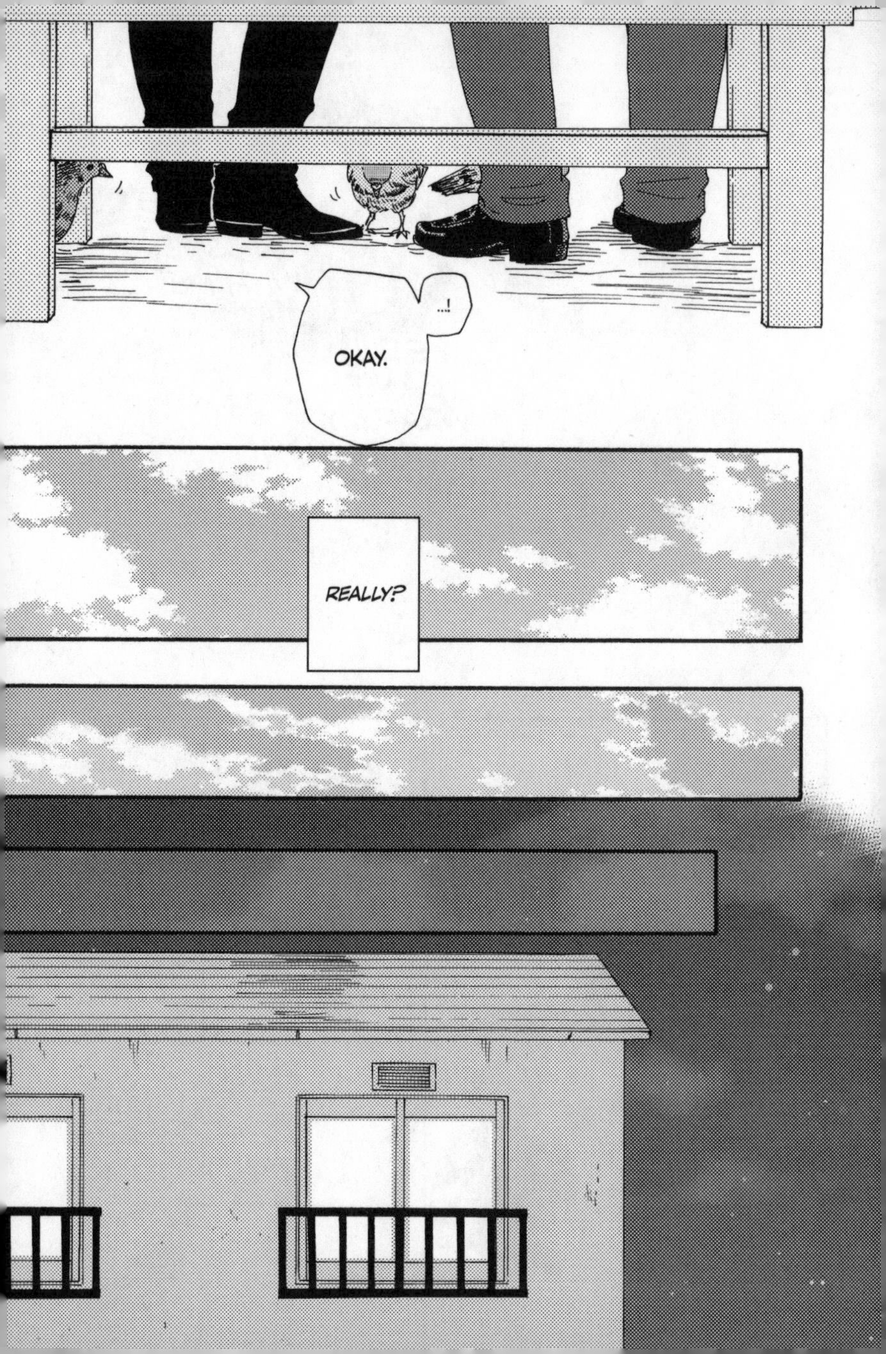
...!
OKAY.
...REALLY?

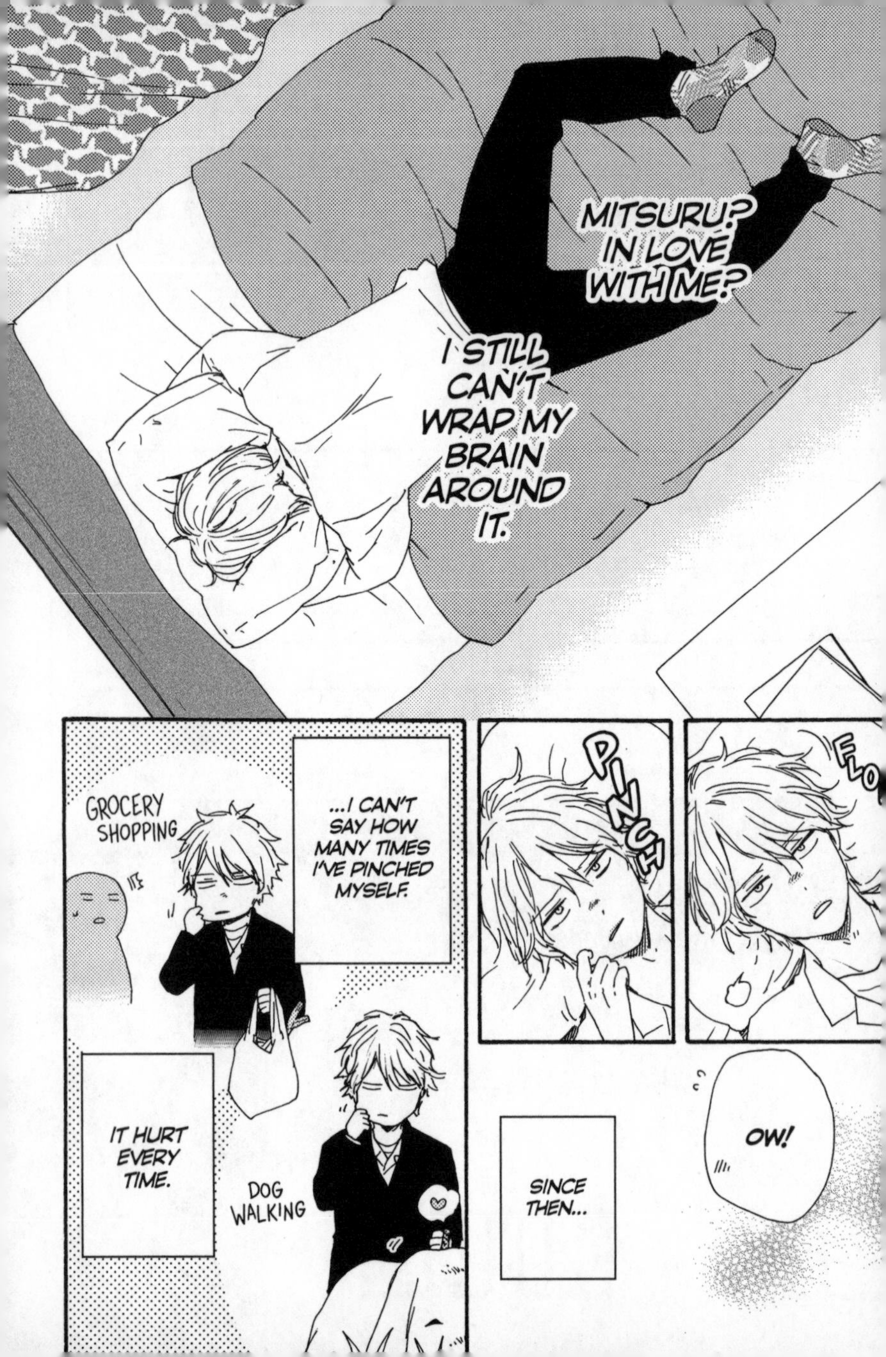
MITSURU? IN LOVE WITH ME?
I STILL CAN'T WRAP MY BRAIN AROUND IT.
FLO
PINCH
OW!
SINCE THEN...
...I CAN'T SAY HOW MANY TIMES I'VE PINCHED MYSELF.
GROCERY SHOPPING
IT HURT EVERY TIME.
DOG WALKING

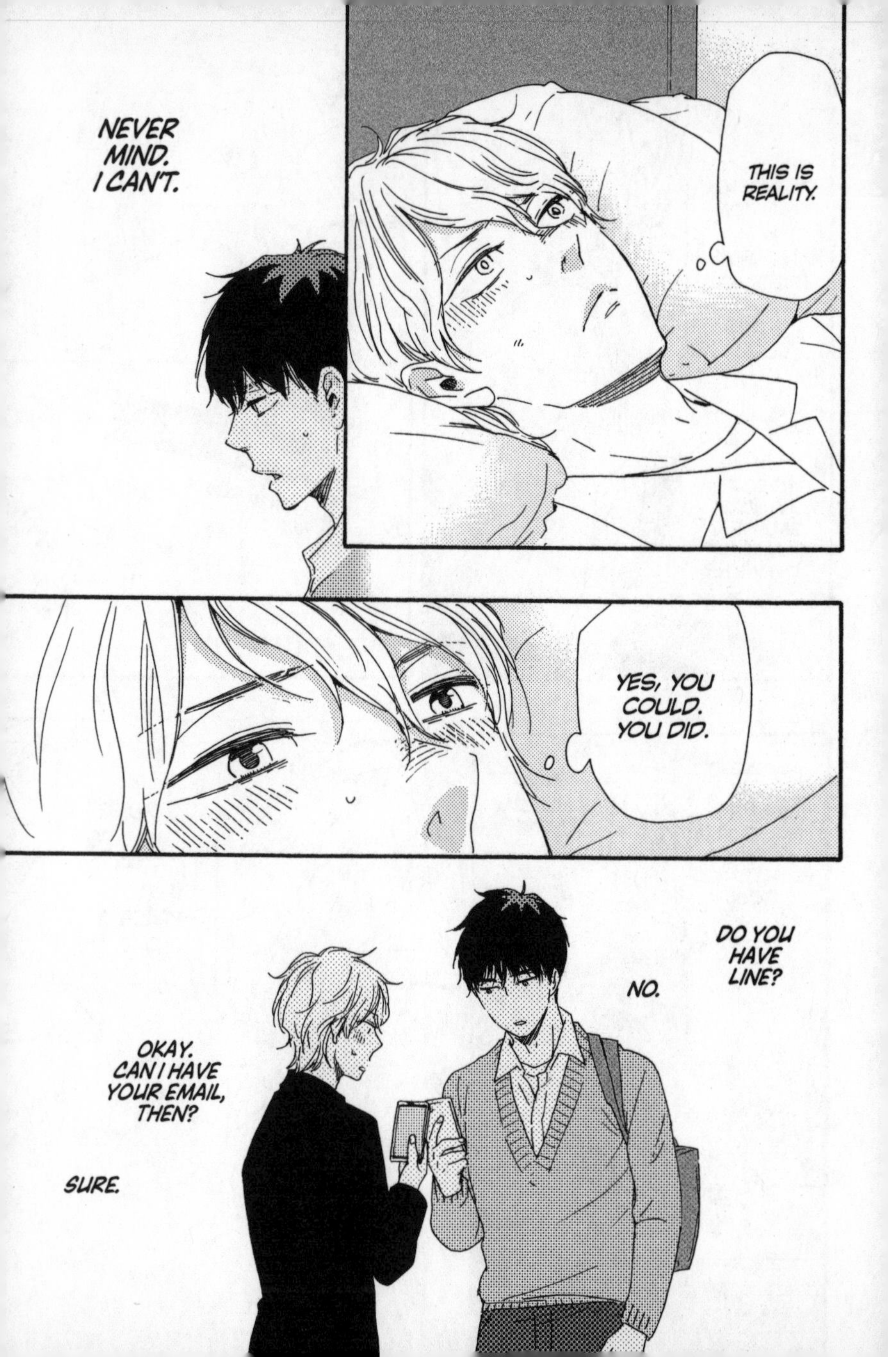
THIS IS REALITY.
NEVER MIND. I CAN'T.
YES, YOU COULD. YOU DID.
DO YOU HAVE LINE?
NO.
OKAY. CAN I HAVE YOUR EMAIL, THEN?
SURE.

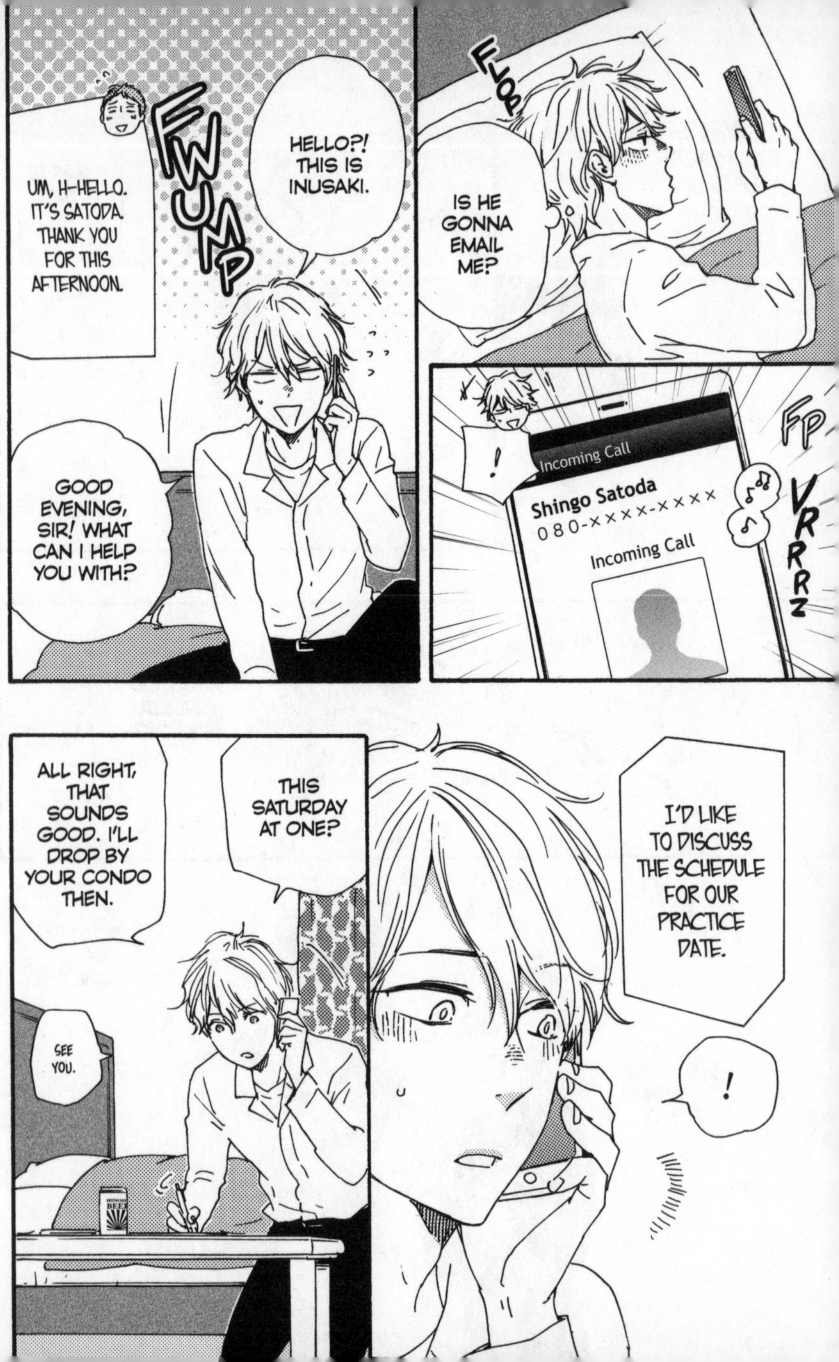

FLOP
IS HE GONNA EMAIL ME?
FP
VRRRZ
Incoming Call
Shingo Satoda
080-××××-××××
Incoming Call
!
FWUMP
HELLO?! THIS IS INUSAKI.
UM, H-HELLO. IT'S SATODA. THANK YOU FOR THIS AFTERNOON.
GOOD EVENING, SIR! WHAT CAN I HELP YOU WITH?
I'D LIKE TO DISCUSS THE SCHEDULE FOR OUR PRACTICE DATE.
!
THIS SATURDAY AT ONE?
ALL RIGHT, THAT SOUNDS GOOD. I'LL DROP BY YOUR CONDO THEN.
SEE YOU.

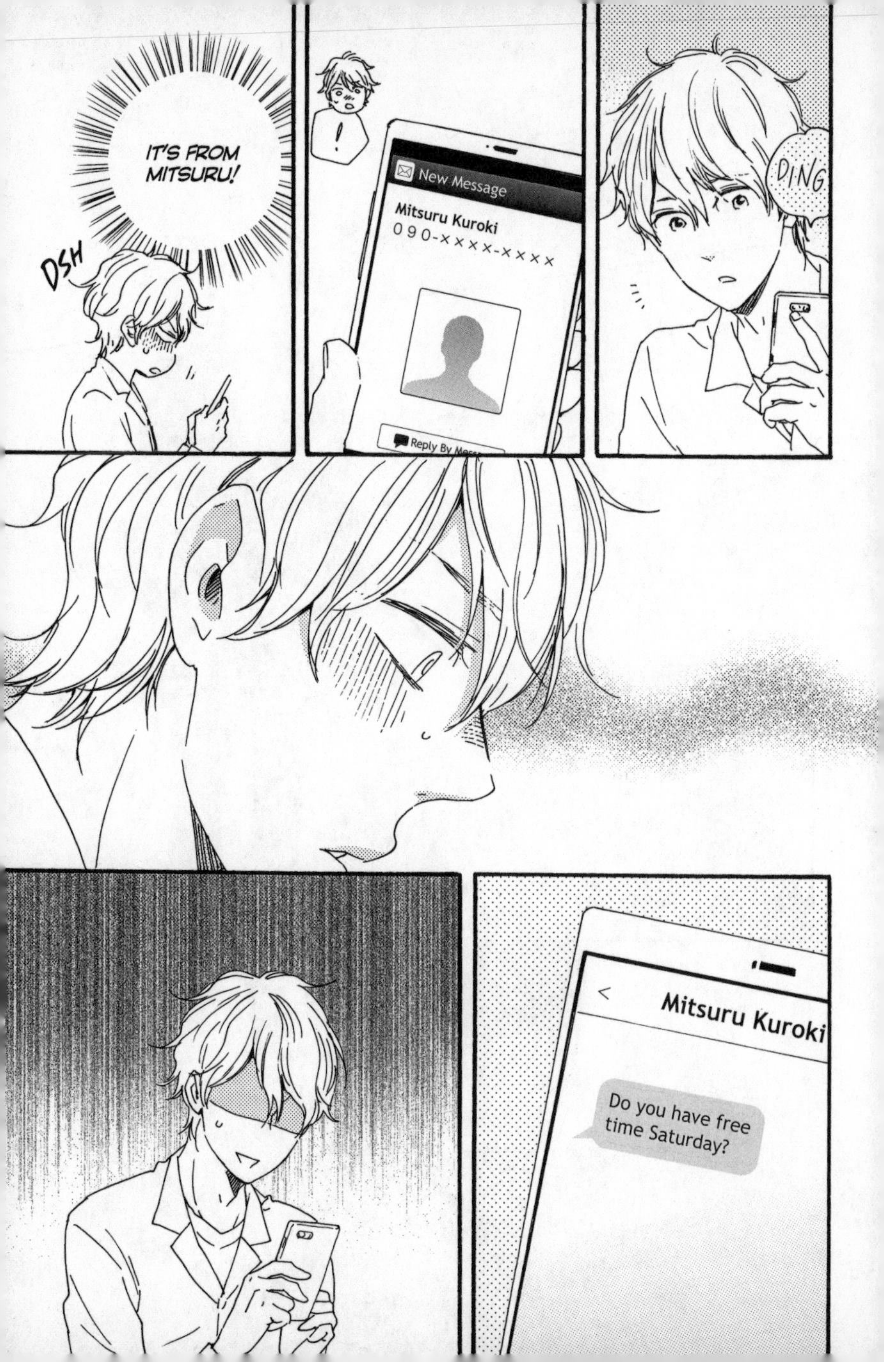
DING
!
New Message
Mitsuru Kuroki
090-××××-××××
Reply By Messa
IT'S FROM MITSURU!
DSH
<
Mitsuru Kuroki
Do you have free time Saturday?

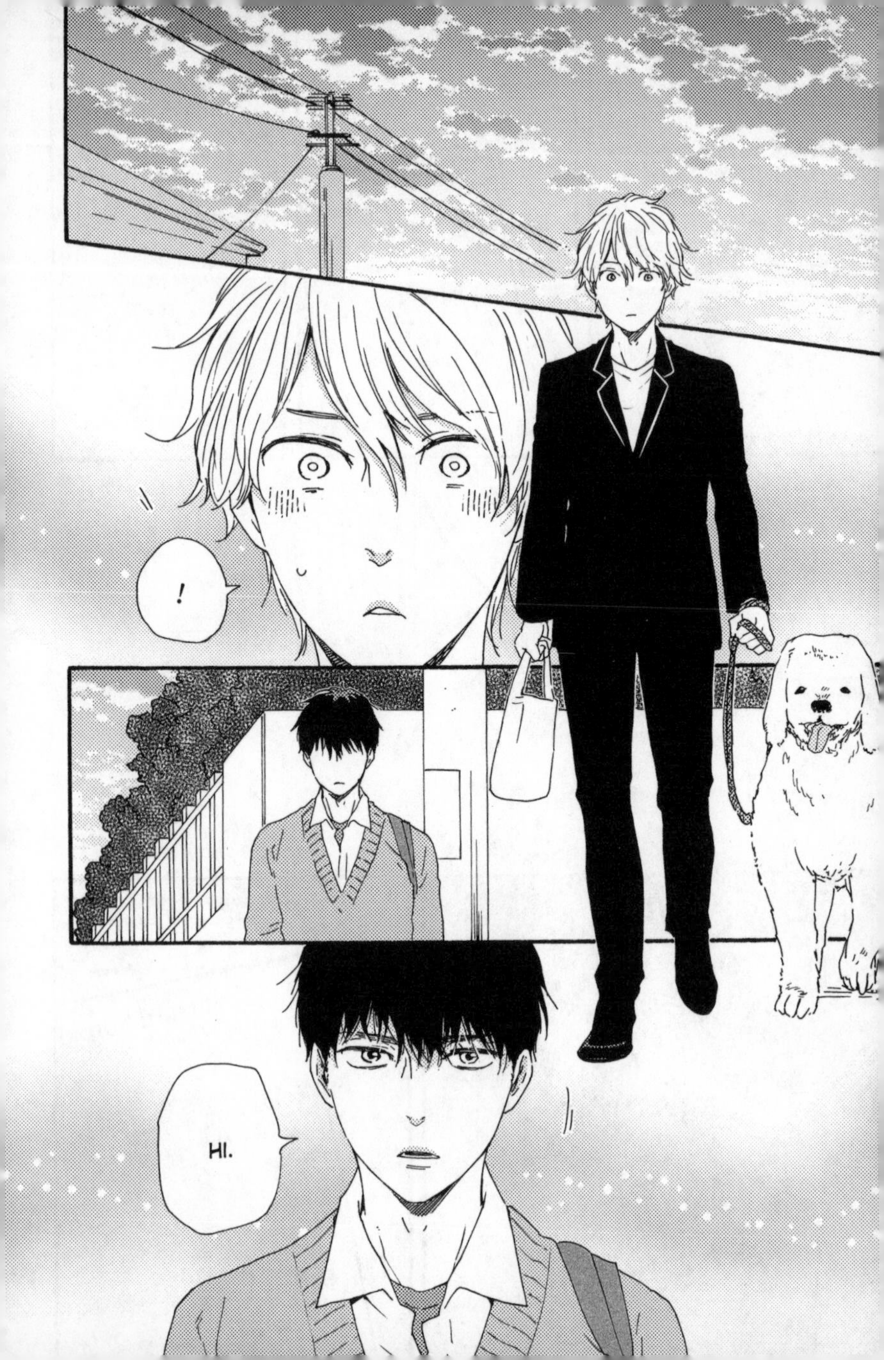
!
HI.

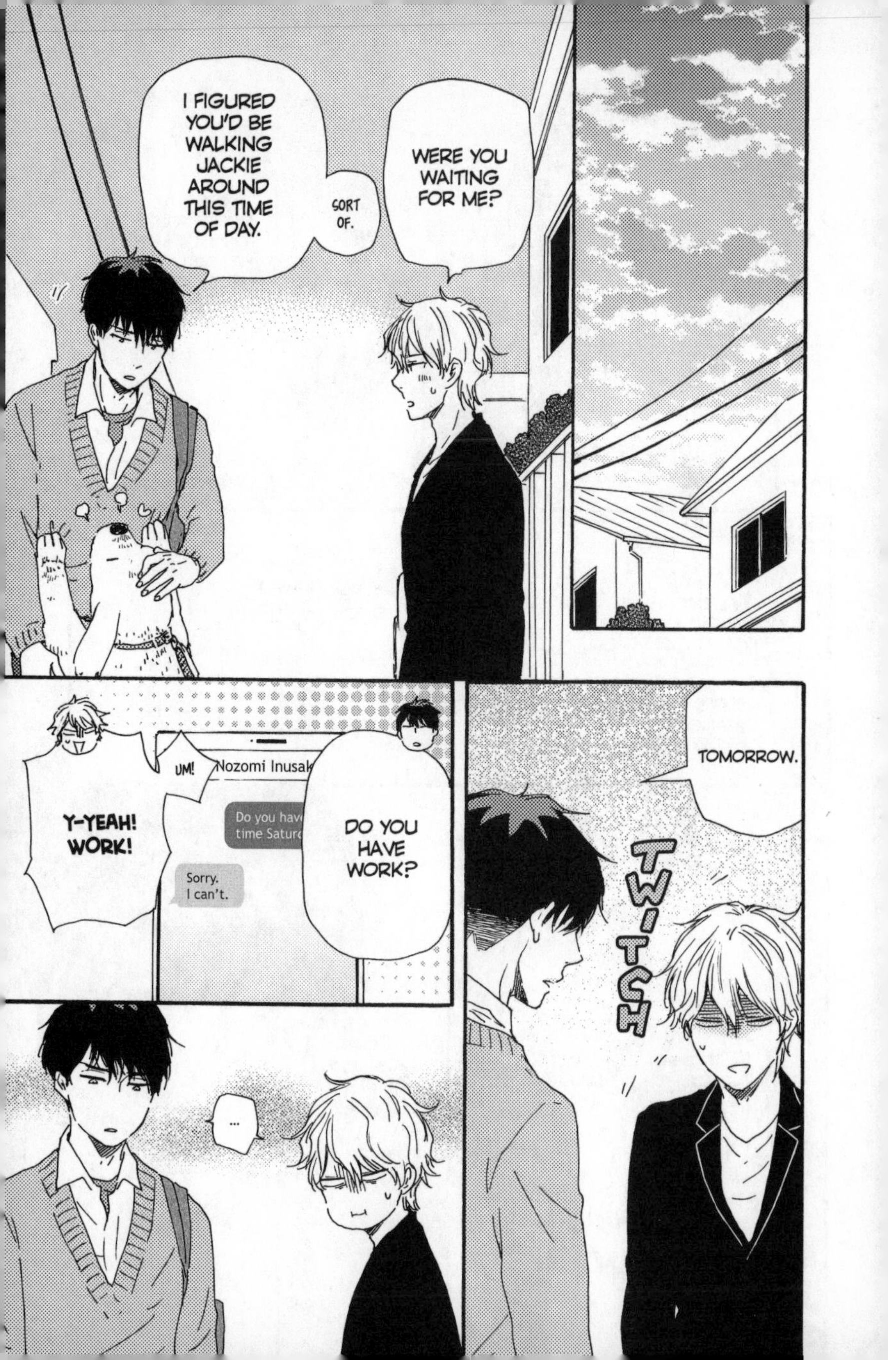
WERE YOU WAITING FOR ME?
SORT OF.
I FIGURED YOU'D BE WALKING JACKIE AROUND THIS TIME OF DAY.
TOMORROW.
TWITCH
DO YOU HAVE WORK?
Sorry. I can't.
UM!
Y-YEAH! WORK!
...

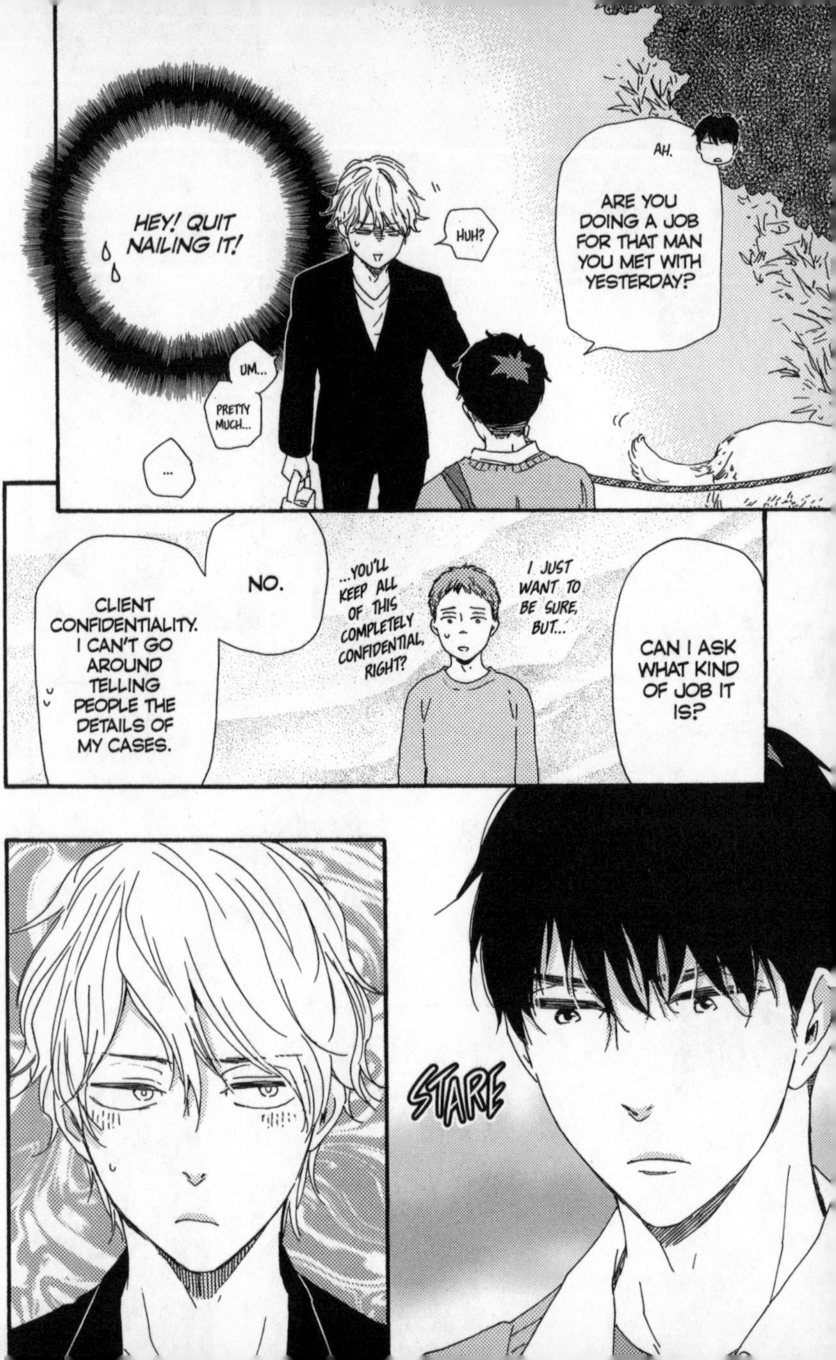
AH.
ARE YOU DOING A JOB FOR THAT MAN YOU MET WITH YESTERDAY?
HUH?
HEY! QUIT NAILING IT!
UM...
PRETTY MUCH...
...
CAN I ASK WHAT KIND OF JOB IT IS?
I JUST WANT TO BE SURE, BUT...
...YOU'LL KEEP ALL OF THIS COMPLETELY CONFIDENTIAL, RIGHT?
NO.
CLIENT CONFIDENTIALITY. I CAN'T GO AROUND TELLING PEOPLE THE DETAILS OF MY CASES.
STARE

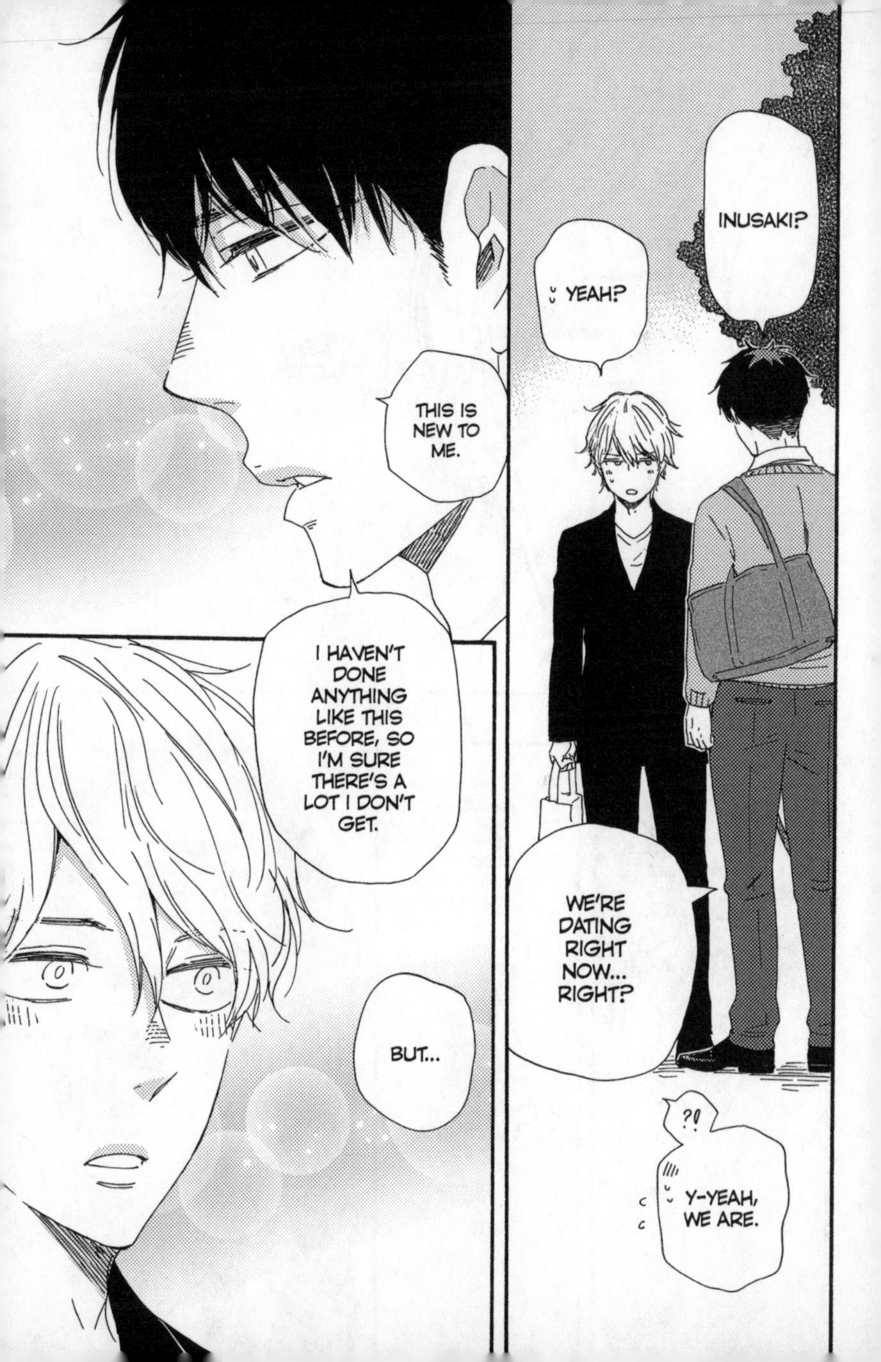
INUSAKI?
YEAH?
WE'RE DATING RIGHT NOW... RIGHT?
?!
Y-YEAH, WE ARE.
THIS IS NEW TO ME.
I HAVEN'T DONE ANYTHING LIKE THIS BEFORE, SO I'M SURE THERE'S A LOT I DON'T GET.
BUT...

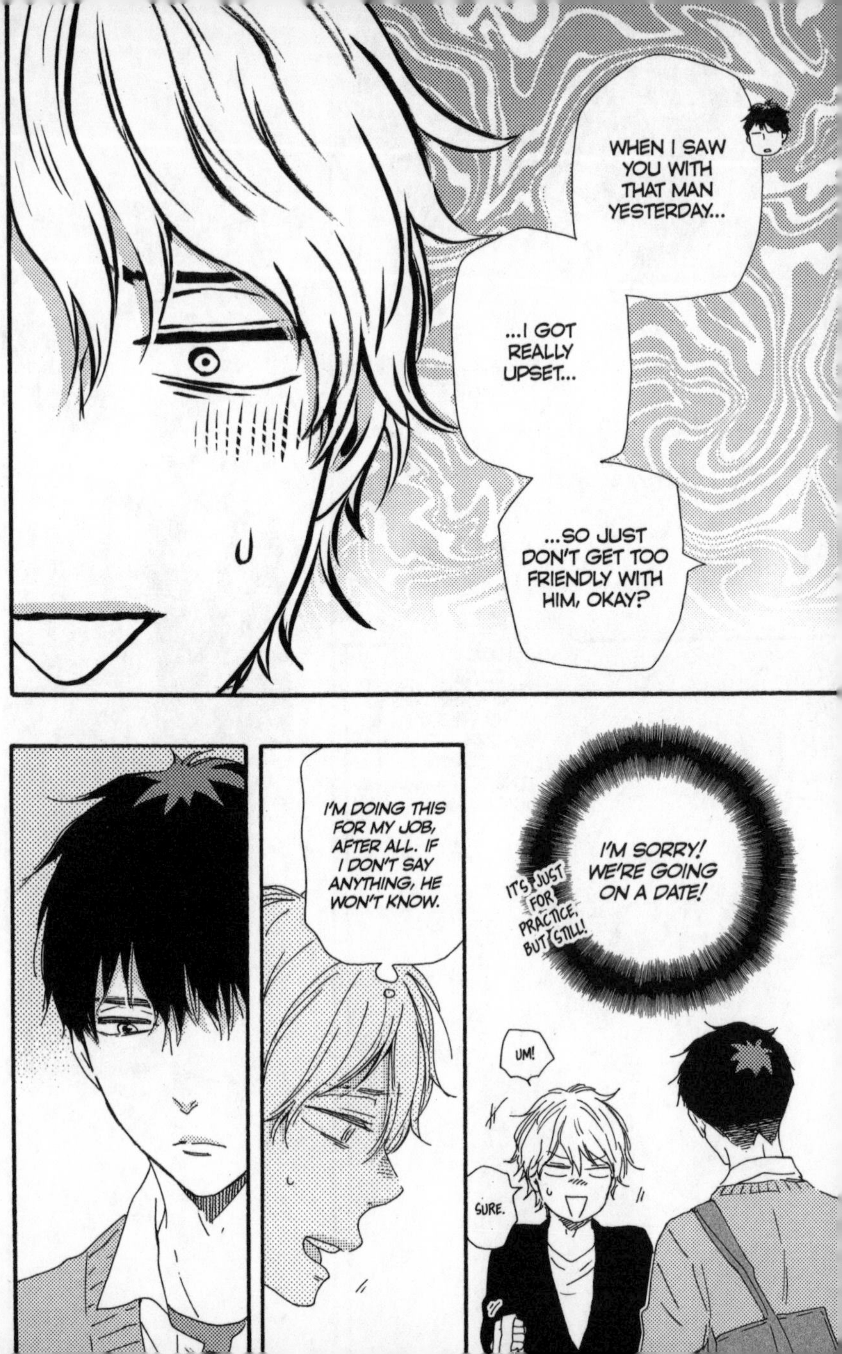
WHEN I SAW YOU WITH THAT MAN YESTERDAY...
...I GOT REALLY UPSET...
...SO JUST DON'T GET TOO FRIENDLY WITH HIM, OKAY?
I'M SORRY! WE'RE GOING ON A DATE!
IT'S JUST FOR PRACTICE, BUT STILL!
UM!
SURE.
I'M DOING THIS FOR MY JOB, AFTER ALL. IF I DON'T SAY ANYTHING, HE WON'T KNOW.

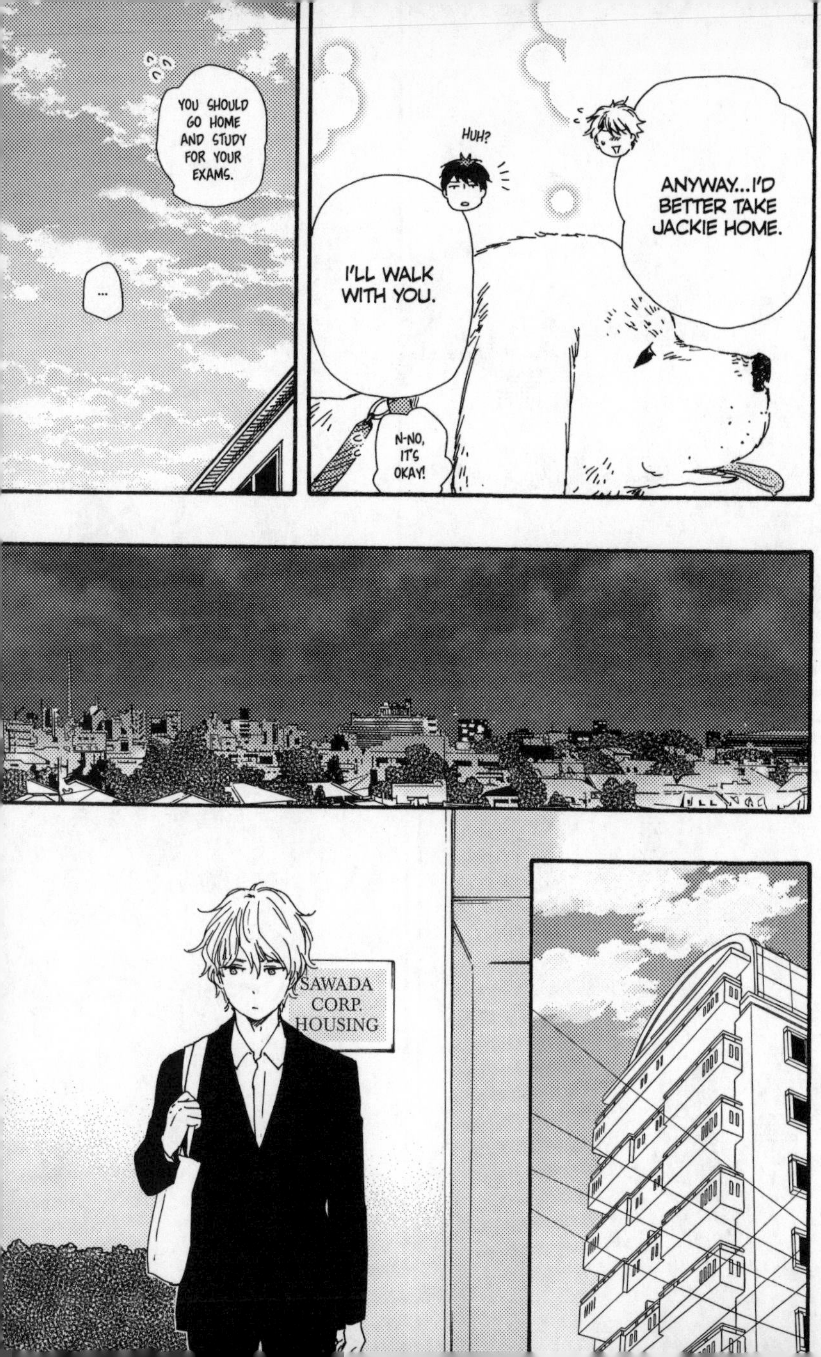
ANYWAY...I'D BETTER TAKE JACKIE HOME.
HUH?
I'LL WALK WITH YOU.
N-NO, IT'S OKAY!
YOU SHOULD GO HOME AND STUDY FOR YOUR EXAMS.
...
SAWADA CORP. HOUSING

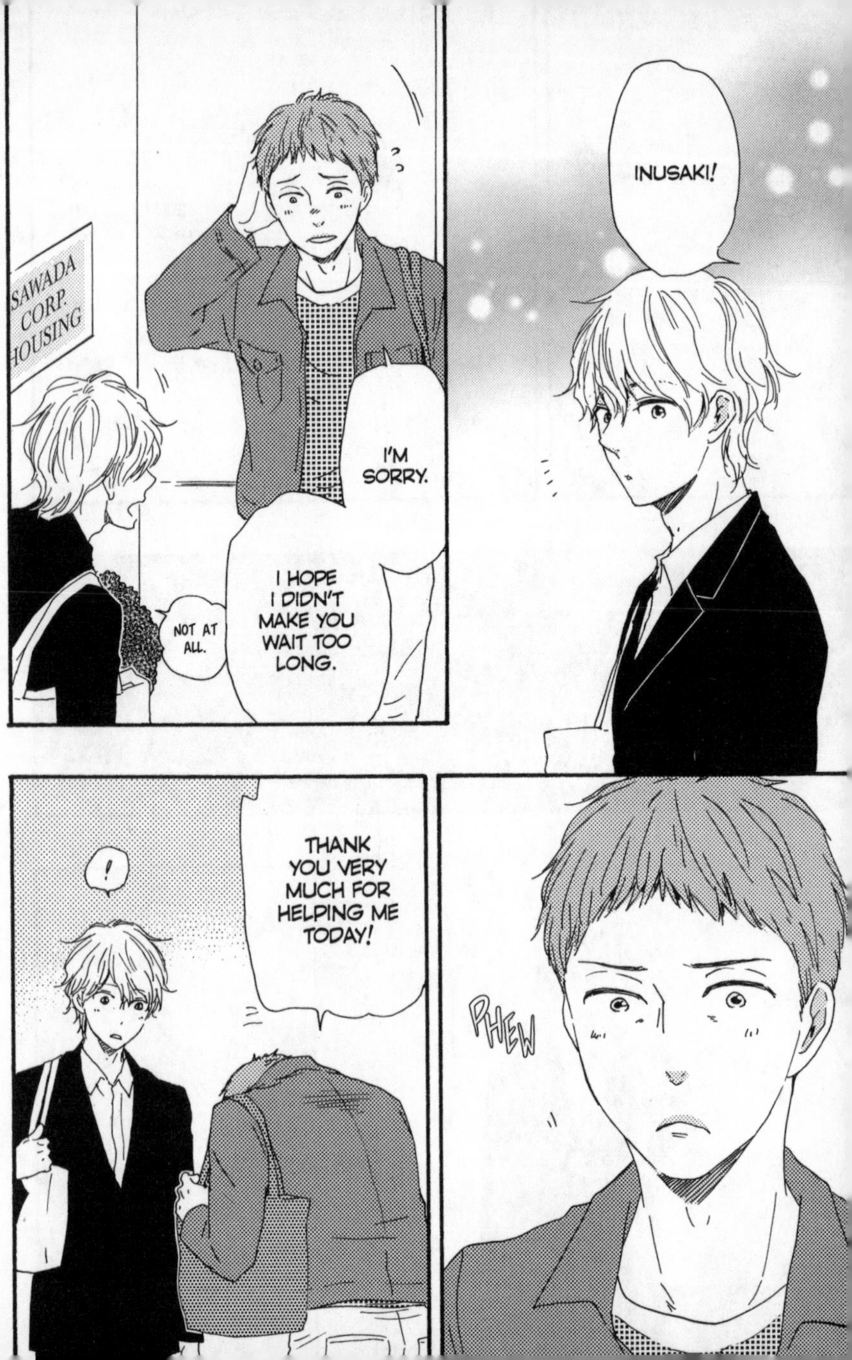
INUSAKI!
SAWADA CORP. HOUSING
I'M SORRY.
I HOPE I DIDN'T MAKE YOU WAIT TOO LONG.
NOT AT ALL.
PHEW
!
THANK YOU VERY MUCH FOR HELPING ME TODAY!

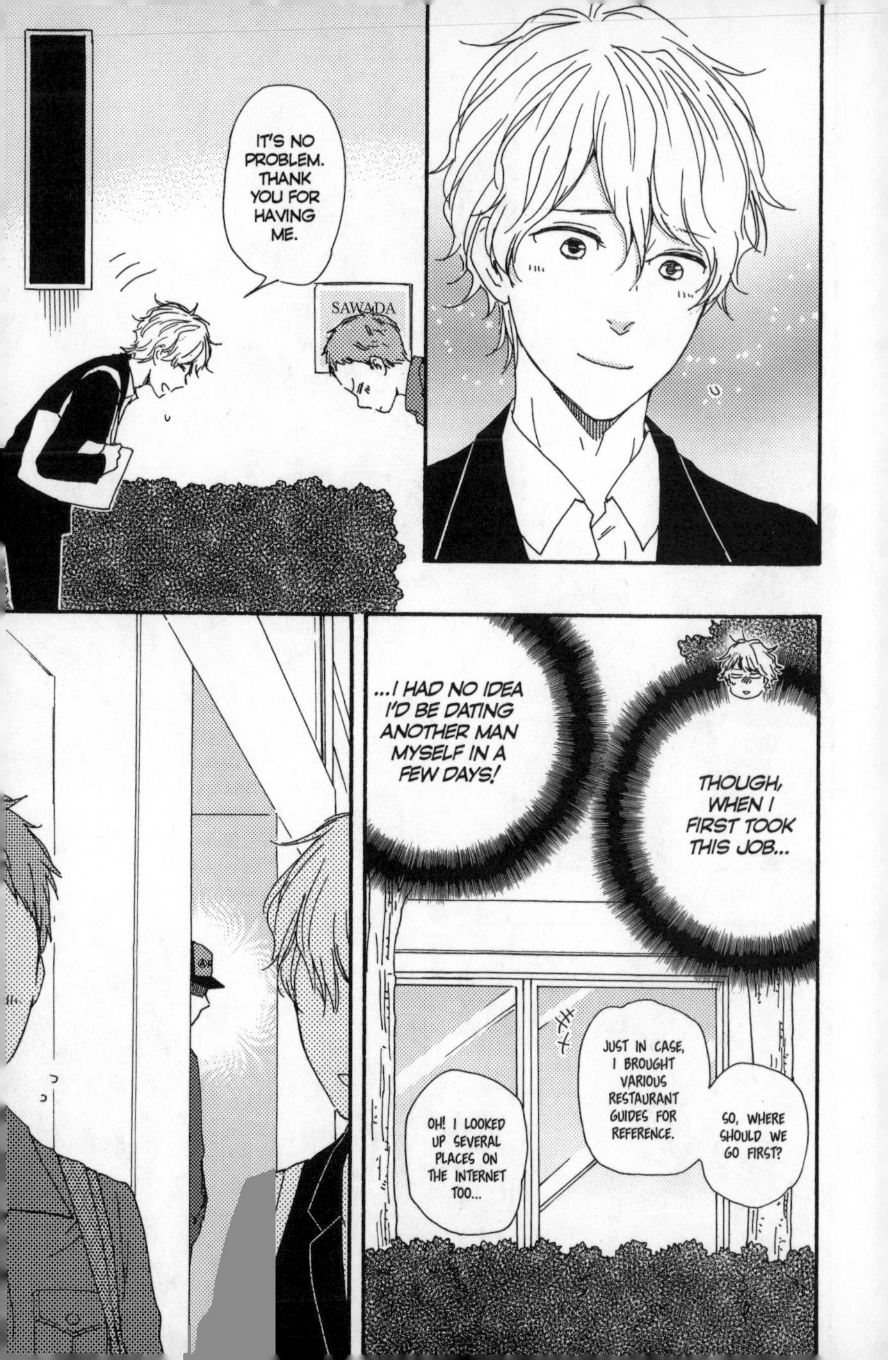
IT'S NO PROBLEM. THANK YOU FOR HAVING ME.
SAWADA
THOUGH, WHEN I FIRST TOOK THIS JOB...
...I HAD NO IDEA I'D BE DATING ANOTHER MAN MYSELF IN A FEW DAYS!
SO, WHERE SHOULD WE GO FIRST?
JUST IN CASE, I BROUGHT VARIOUS RESTAURANT GUIDES FOR REFERENCE.
OH! I LOOKED UP SEVERAL PLACES ON THE INTERNET TOO...

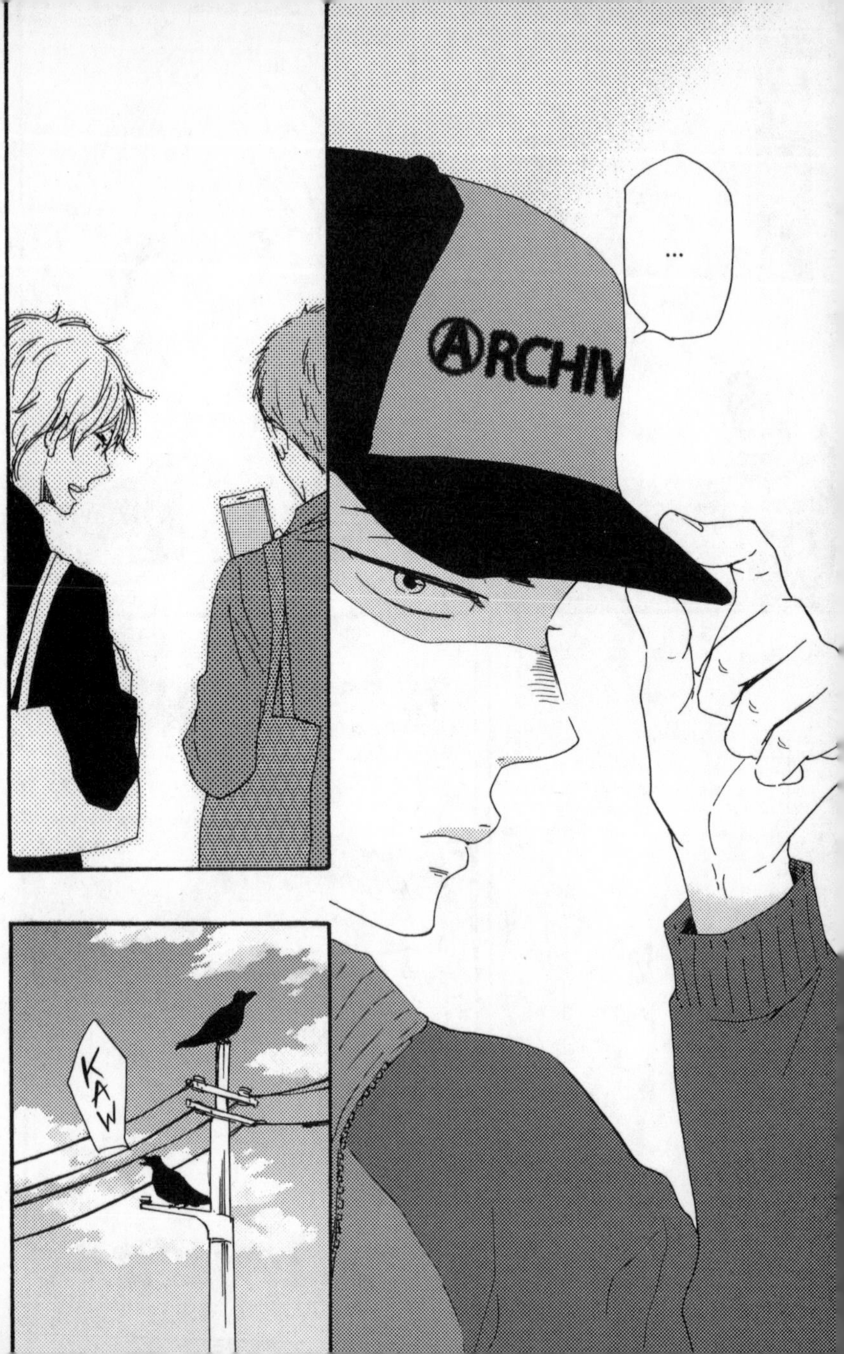
...
ARCHIV
KAW

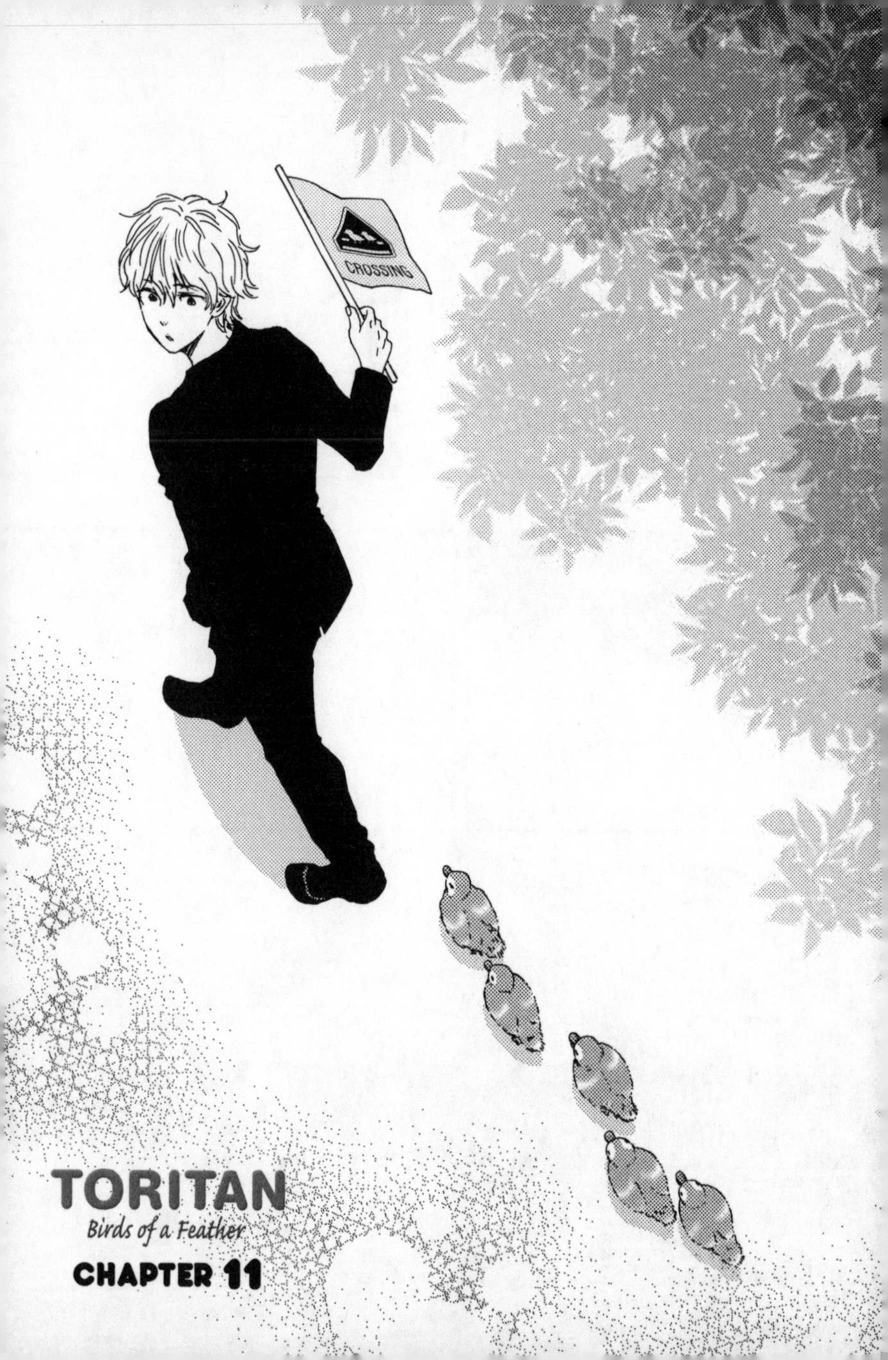
CROSSING

TORITAN

Birds of a Feather

CHAPTER 11

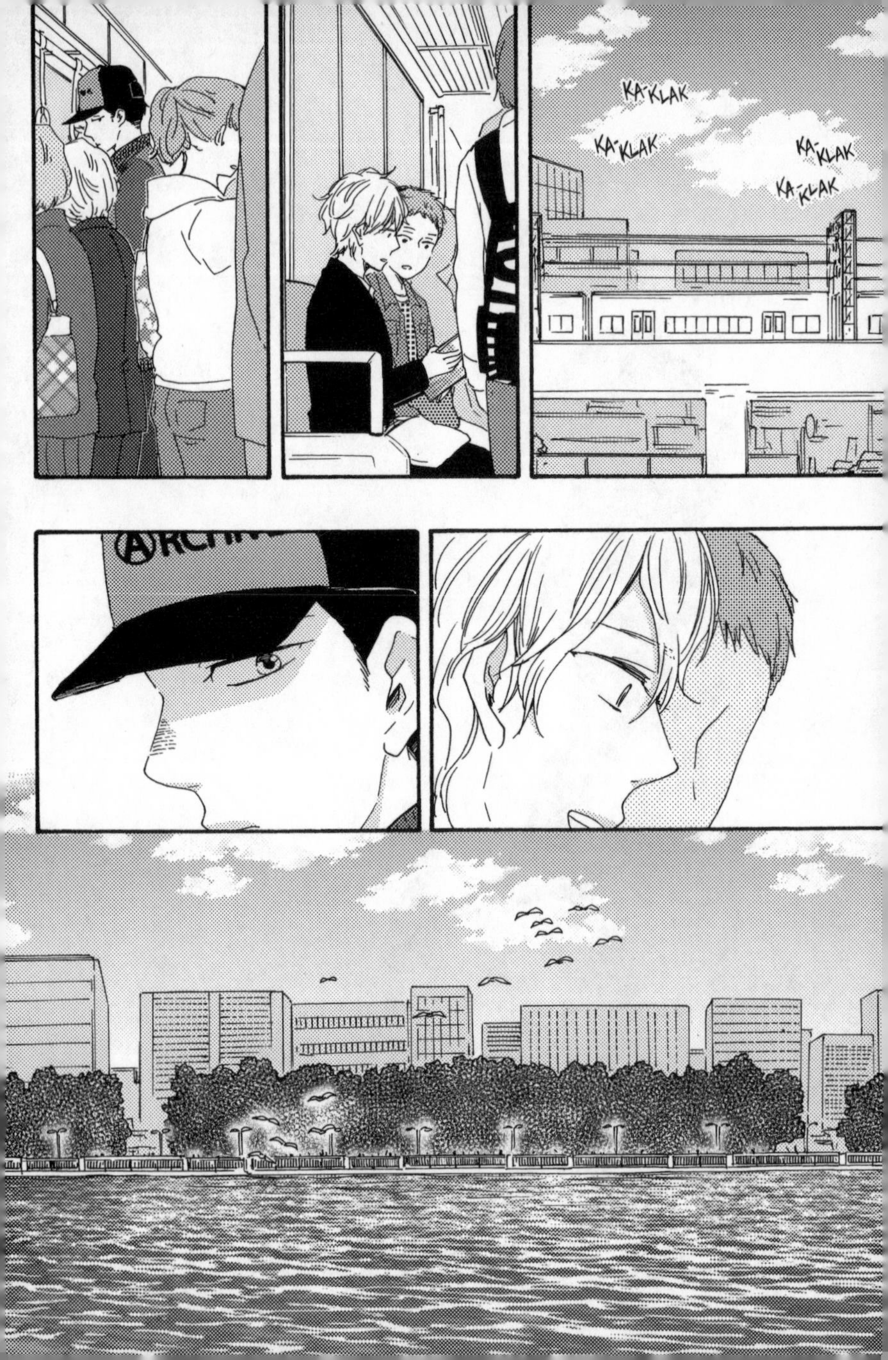
KA-KLAK
KA-KLAK
KA-KLAK
KA-KLAK

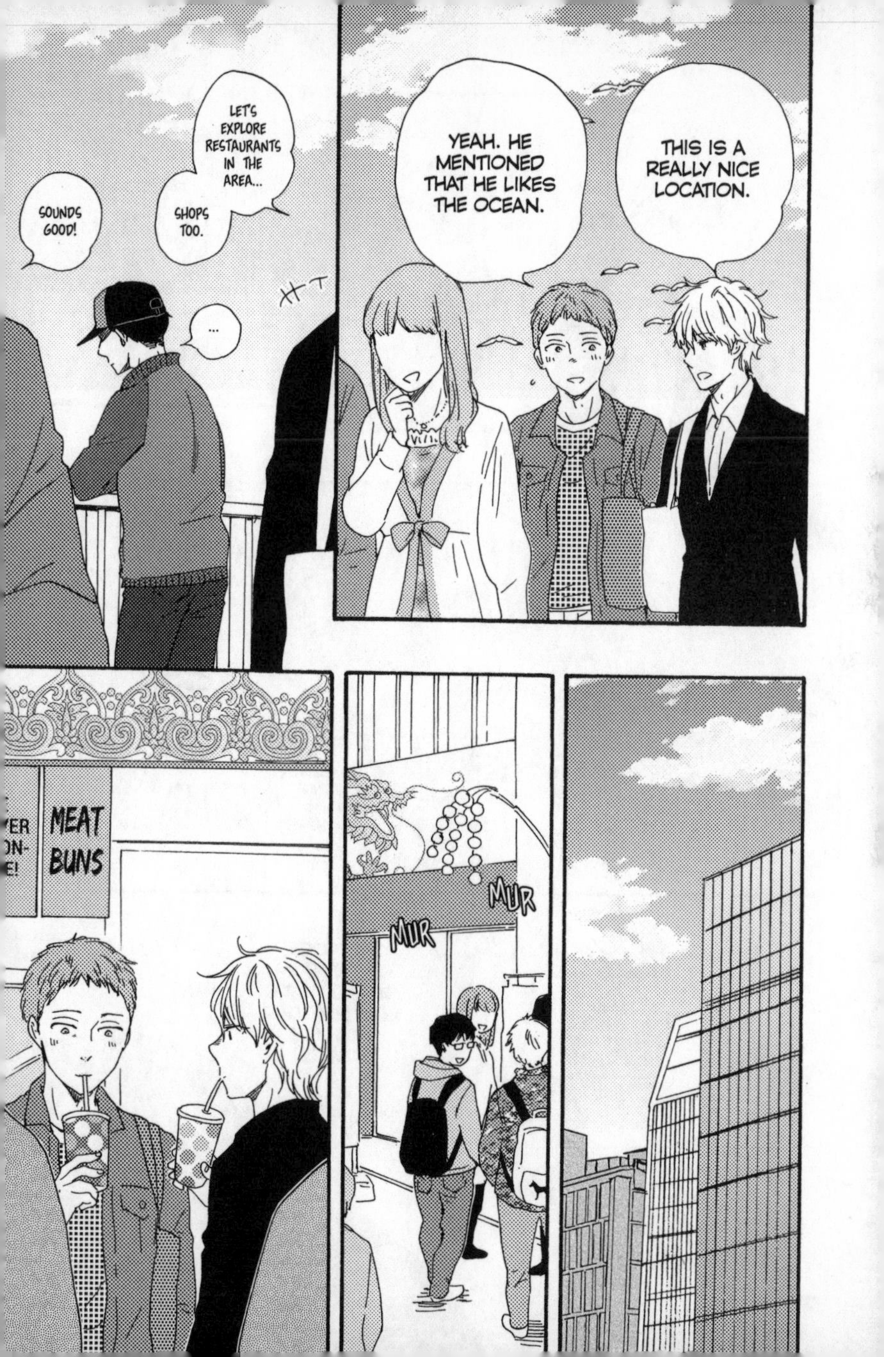
THIS IS A REALLY NICE LOCATION.
YEAH. HE MENTIONED THAT HE LIKES THE OCEAN.
LET'S EXPLORE RESTAURANTS IN THE AREA...
SHOPS TOO.
SOUNDS GOOD!
...
MUR
MUR
MEAT BUNS

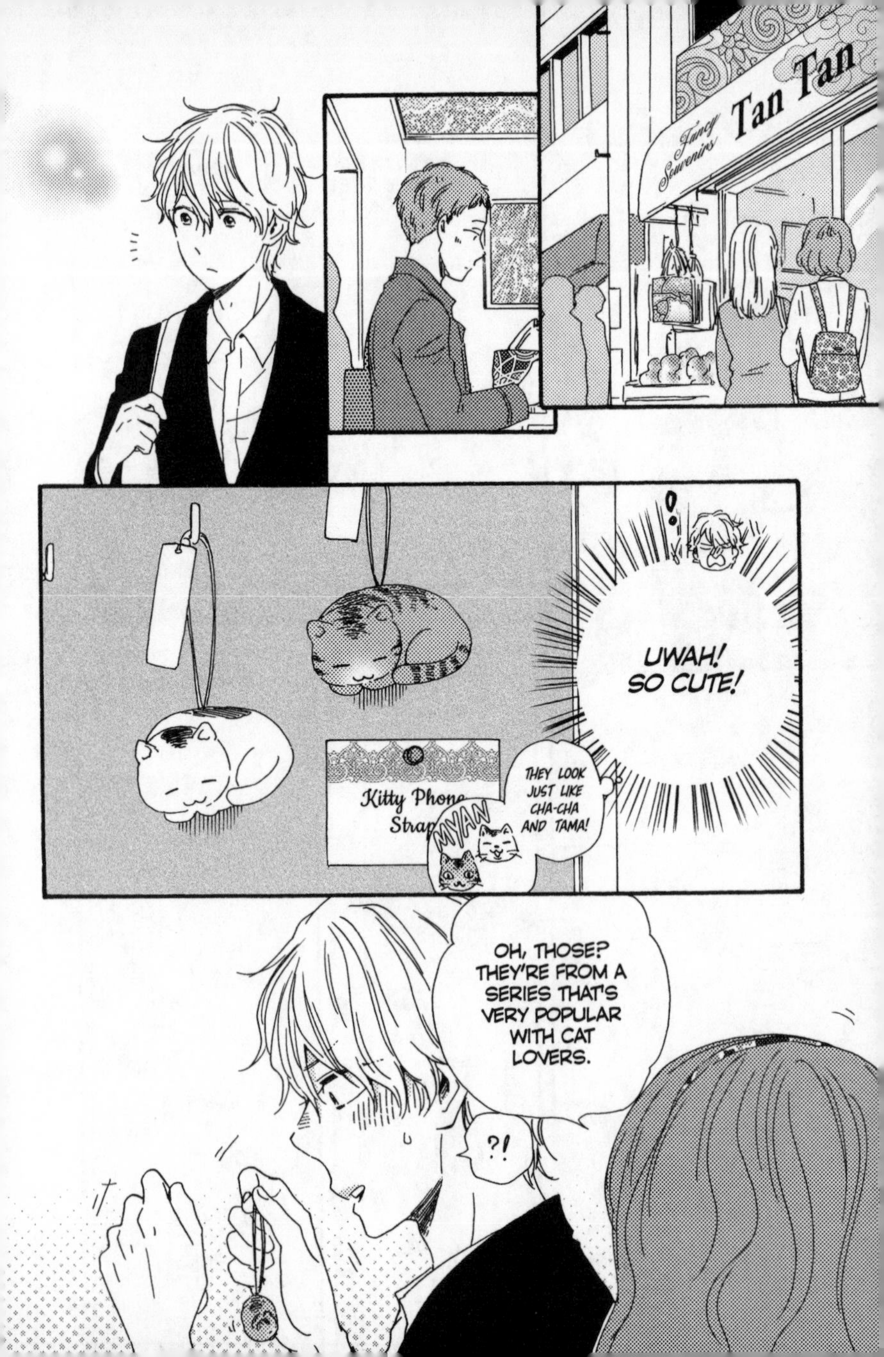
Fancy Souvenirs
Tan Tan
UWAH! SO CUTE!
THEY LOOK JUST LIKE CHA-CHA AND TAMA!
MYAN
Kitty Phone Strap
OH, THOSE? THEY'RE FROM A SERIES THAT'S VERY POPULAR WITH CAT LOVERS.
?!

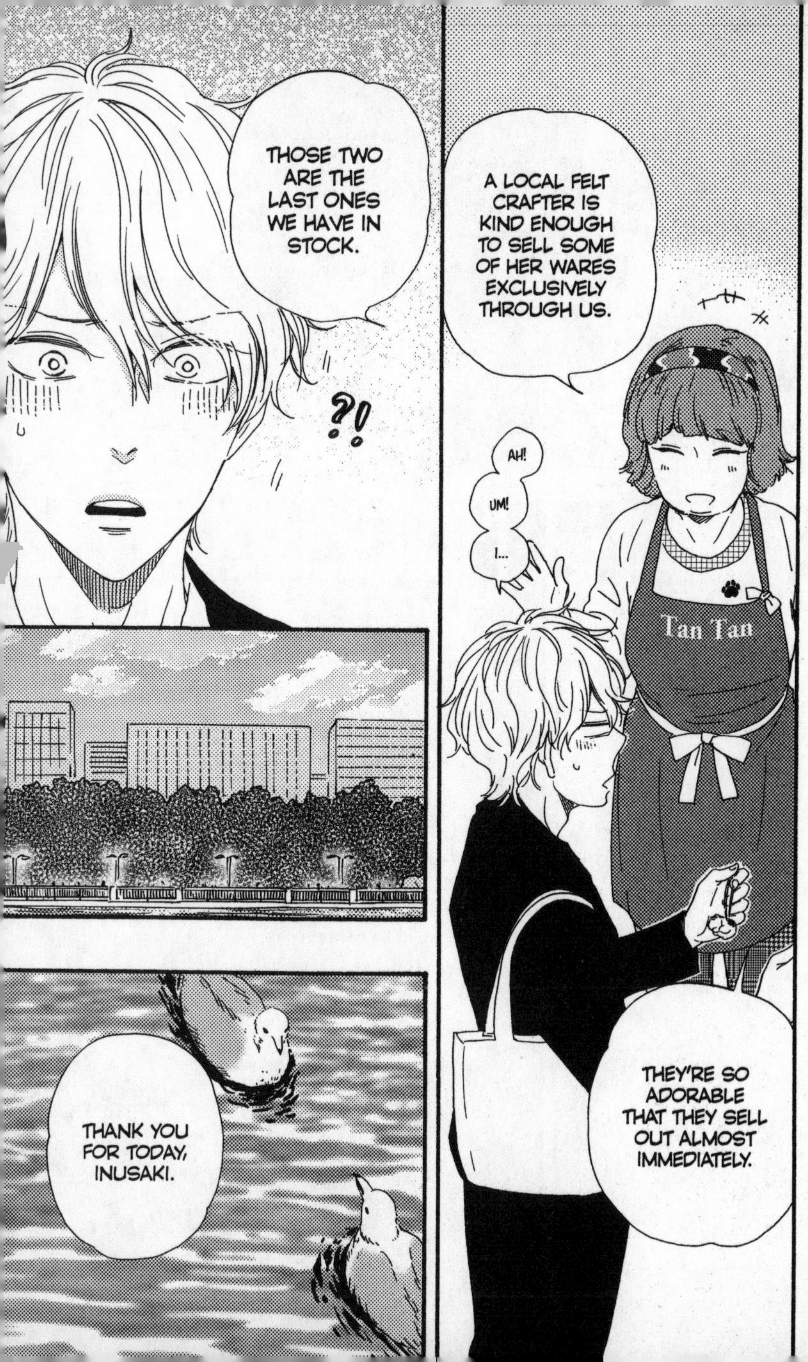
A LOCAL FELT CRAFTER IS KIND ENOUGH TO SELL SOME OF HER WARES EXCLUSIVELY THROUGH US.
AH!
UM!
I...
Tan Tan
THEY'RE SO ADORABLE THAT THEY SELL OUT ALMOST IMMEDIATELY.
THOSE TWO ARE THE LAST ONES WE HAVE IN STOCK.
?!
THANK YOU FOR TODAY, INUSAKI.

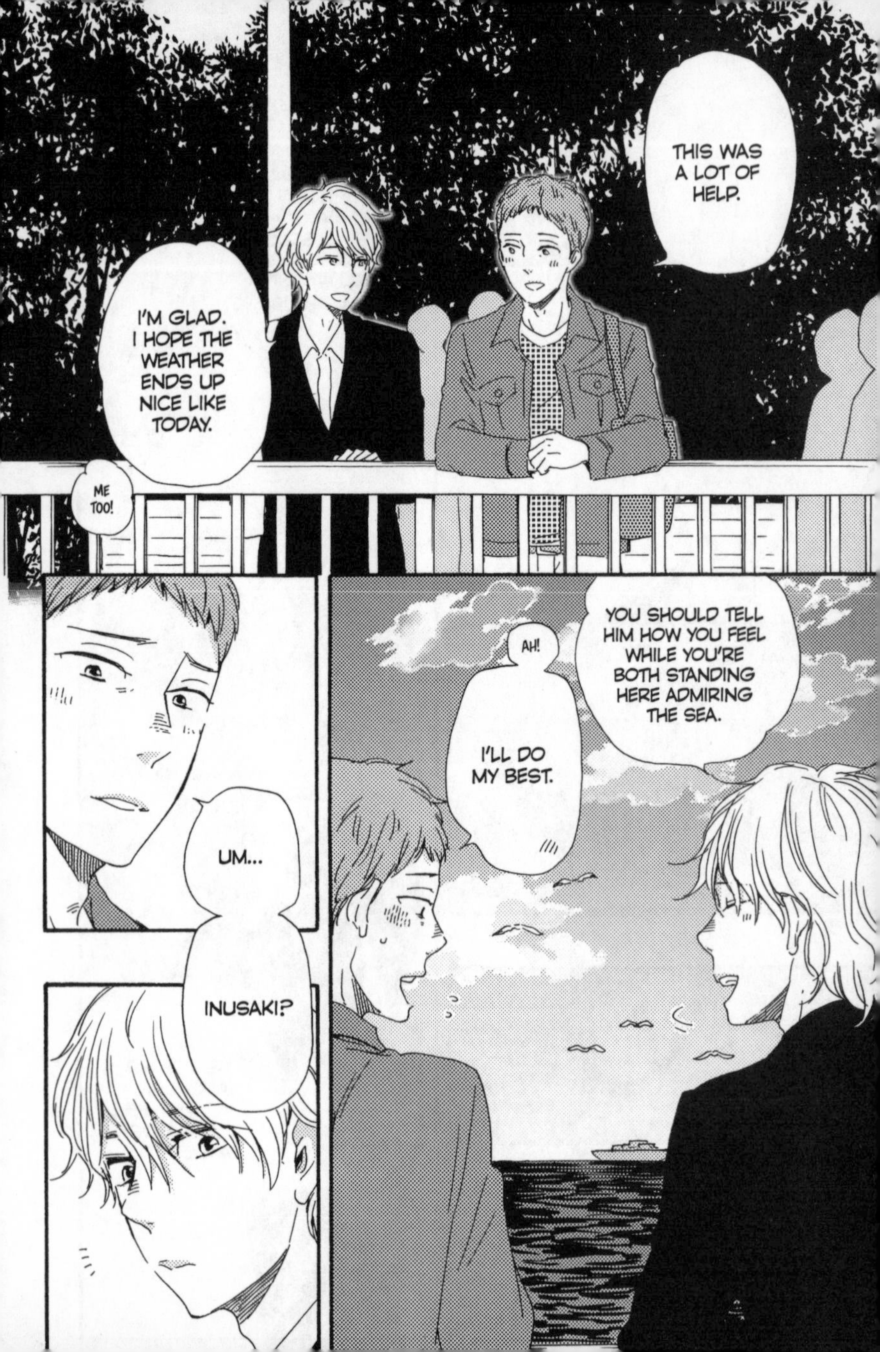
THIS WAS A LOT OF HELP.
I'M GLAD. I HOPE THE WEATHER ENDS UP NICE LIKE TODAY.
ME TOO!
YOU SHOULD TELL HIM HOW YOU FEEL WHILE YOU'RE BOTH STANDING HERE ADMIRING THE SEA.
AH!
I'LL DO MY BEST.
UM...
INUSAKI?

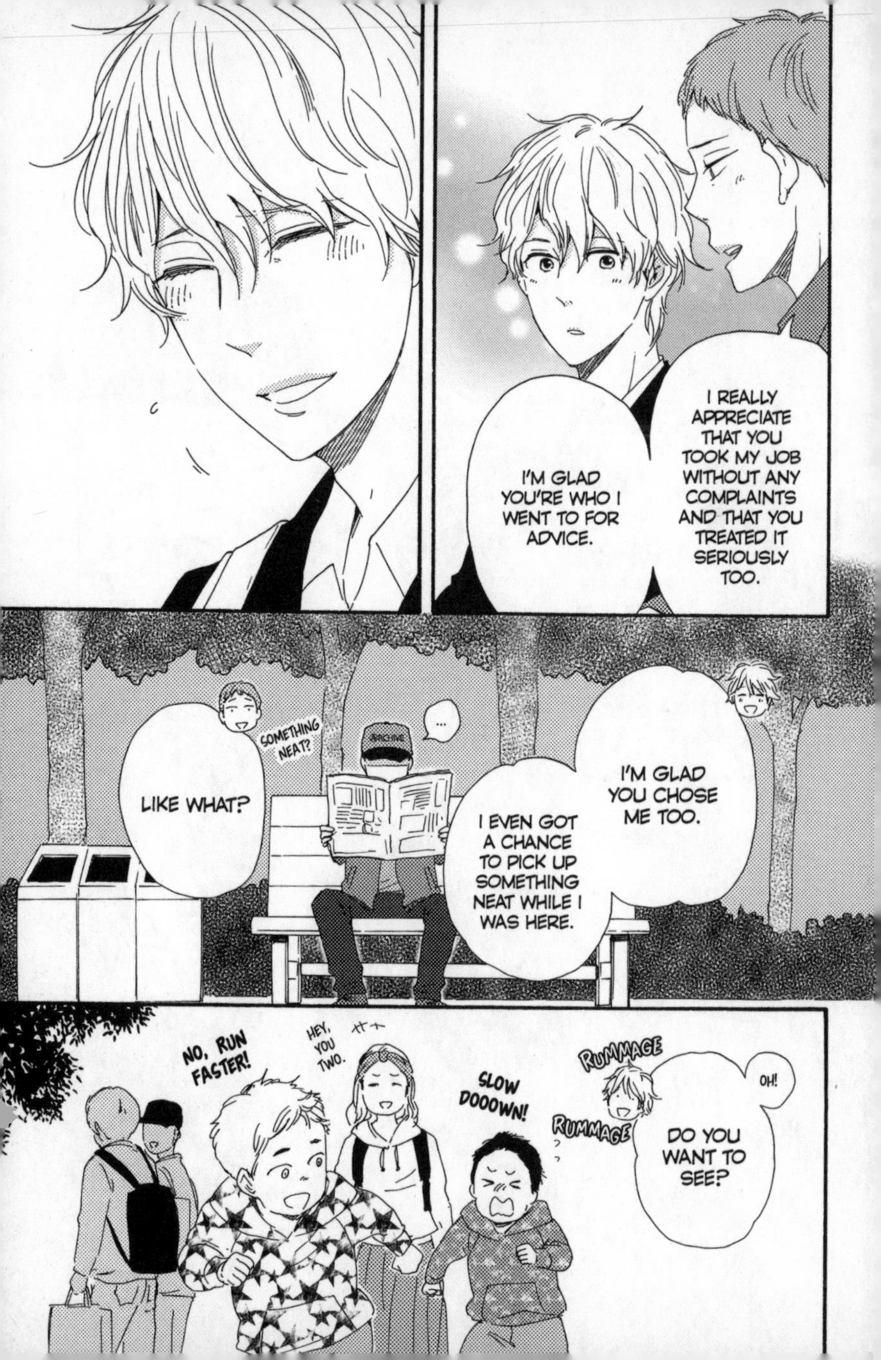
I REALLY APPRECIATE THAT YOU TOOK MY JOB WITHOUT ANY COMPLAINTS AND THAT YOU TREATED IT SERIOUSLY TOO.
I'M GLAD YOU'RE WHO I WENT TO FOR ADVICE.
I'M GLAD YOU CHOSE ME TOO.
I EVEN GOT A CHANCE TO PICK UP SOMETHING NEAT WHILE I WAS HERE.
...
SOMETHING NEAT?
LIKE WHAT?
OH!
DO YOU WANT TO SEE?
RUMMAGE
RUMMAGE
SLOW DOOOWN!
HEY, YOU TWO.
NO, RUN FASTER!

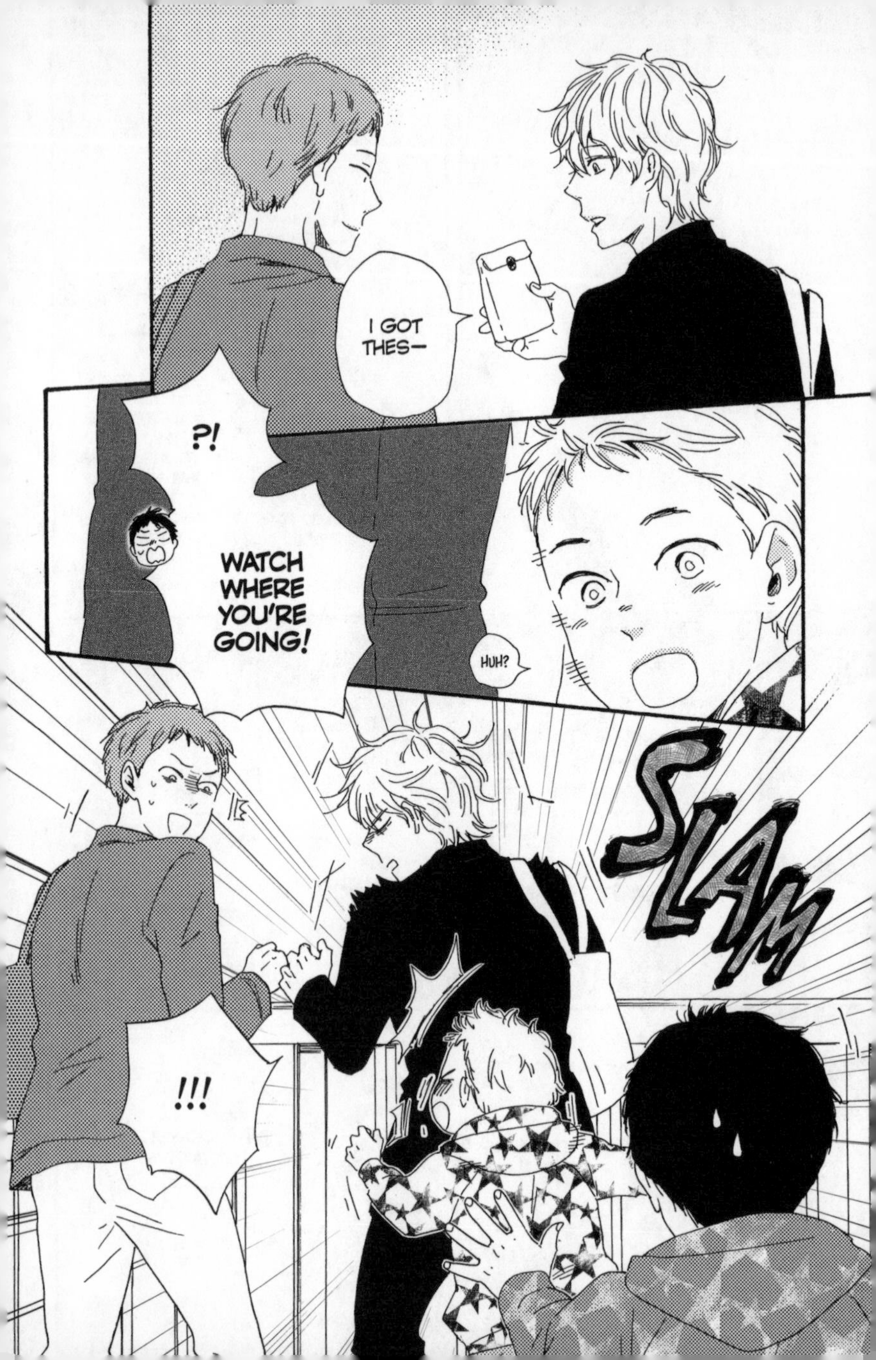
I GOT THES—
HUH?
?!
WATCH WHERE YOU'RE GOING!
SLAM
!!!

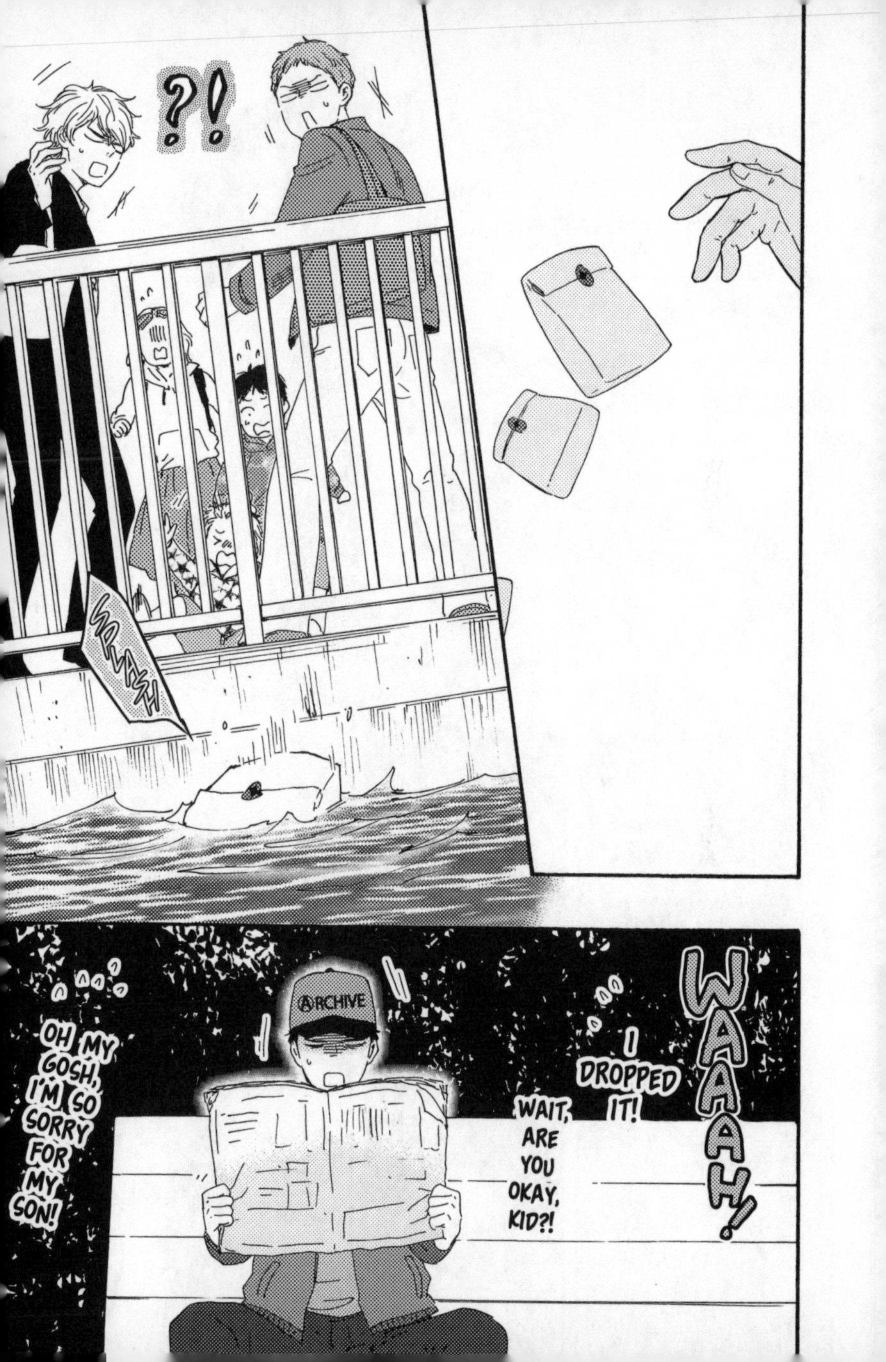
?!
SPLASH
WAAAH!
I DROPPED IT!
WAIT, ARE YOU OKAY, KID?!
OH MY GOSH, I'M SO SORRY FOR MY SON!

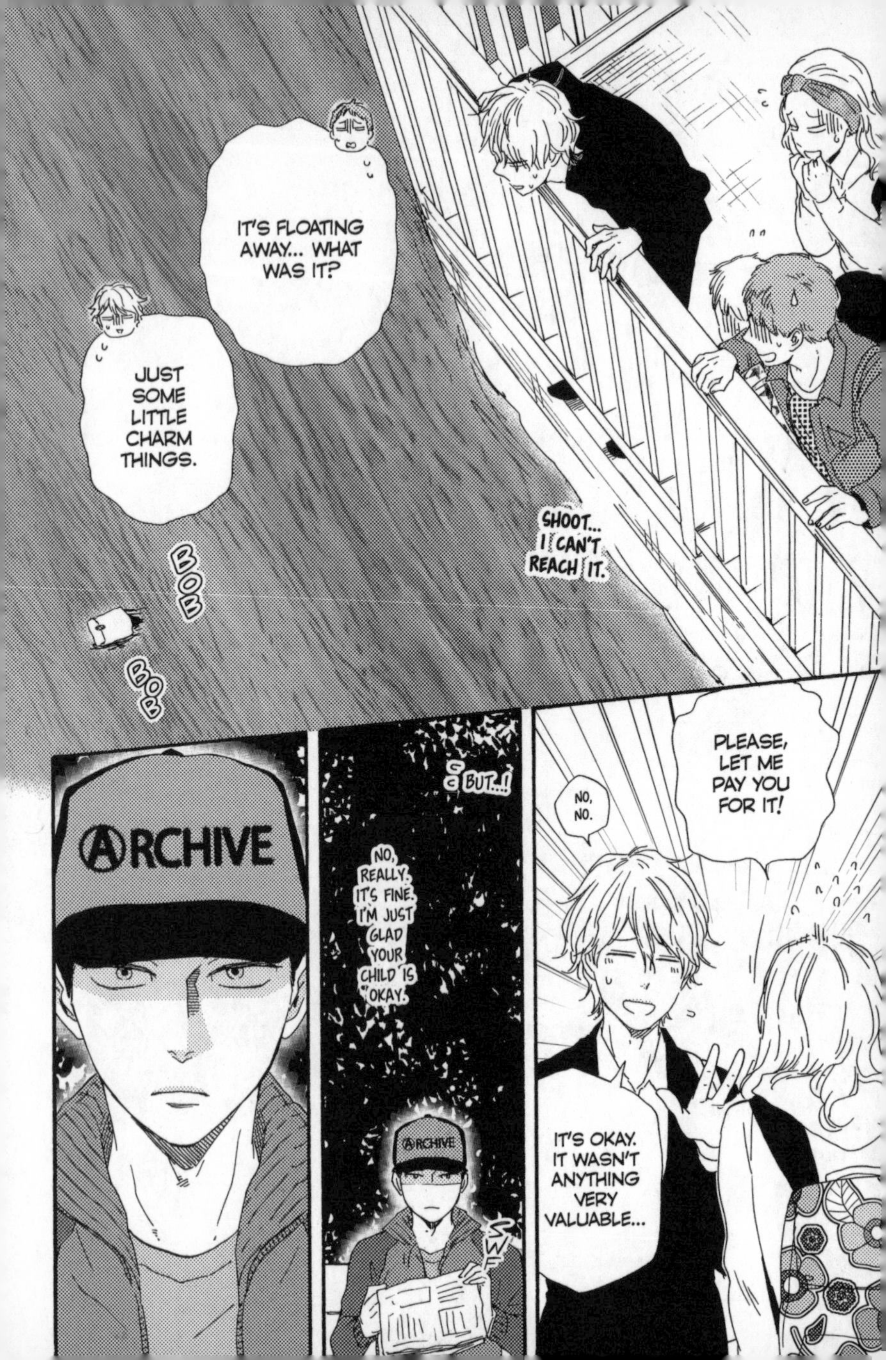
SHOOT... I CAN'T REACH IT.
IT'S FLOATING AWAY... WHAT WAS IT?
JUST SOME LITTLE CHARM THINGS.
BOB
BOB
PLEASE, LET ME PAY YOU FOR IT!
NO, NO.
IT'S OKAY. IT WASN'T ANYTHING VERY VALUABLE...
BUT...!
NO, REALLY. IT'S FINE. I'M JUST GLAD YOUR CHILD IS OKAY.
ARCHIVE
SWF
ARCHIVE

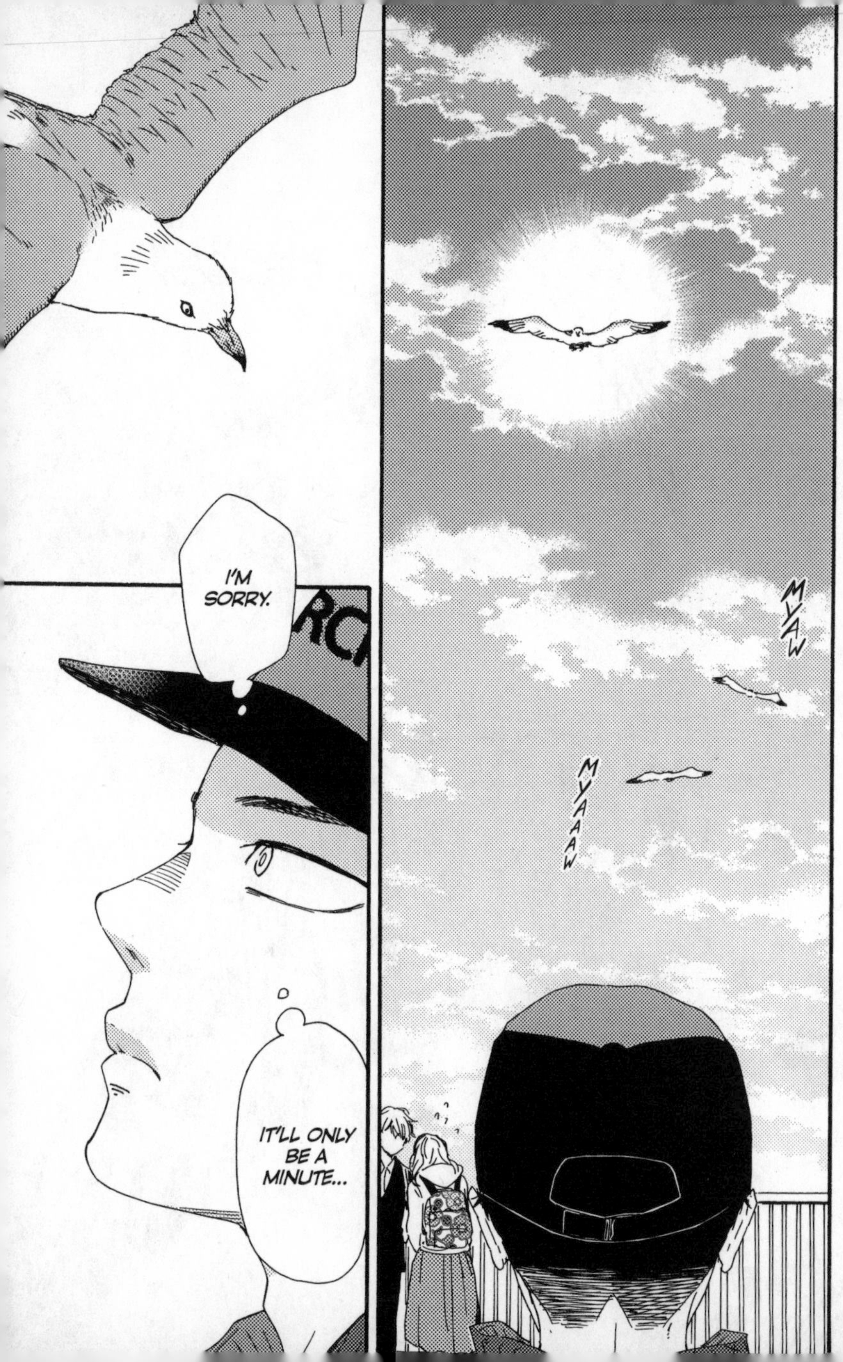
MYAAW
MYAAAAW
I'M SORRY.
IT'LL ONLY BE A MINUTE...

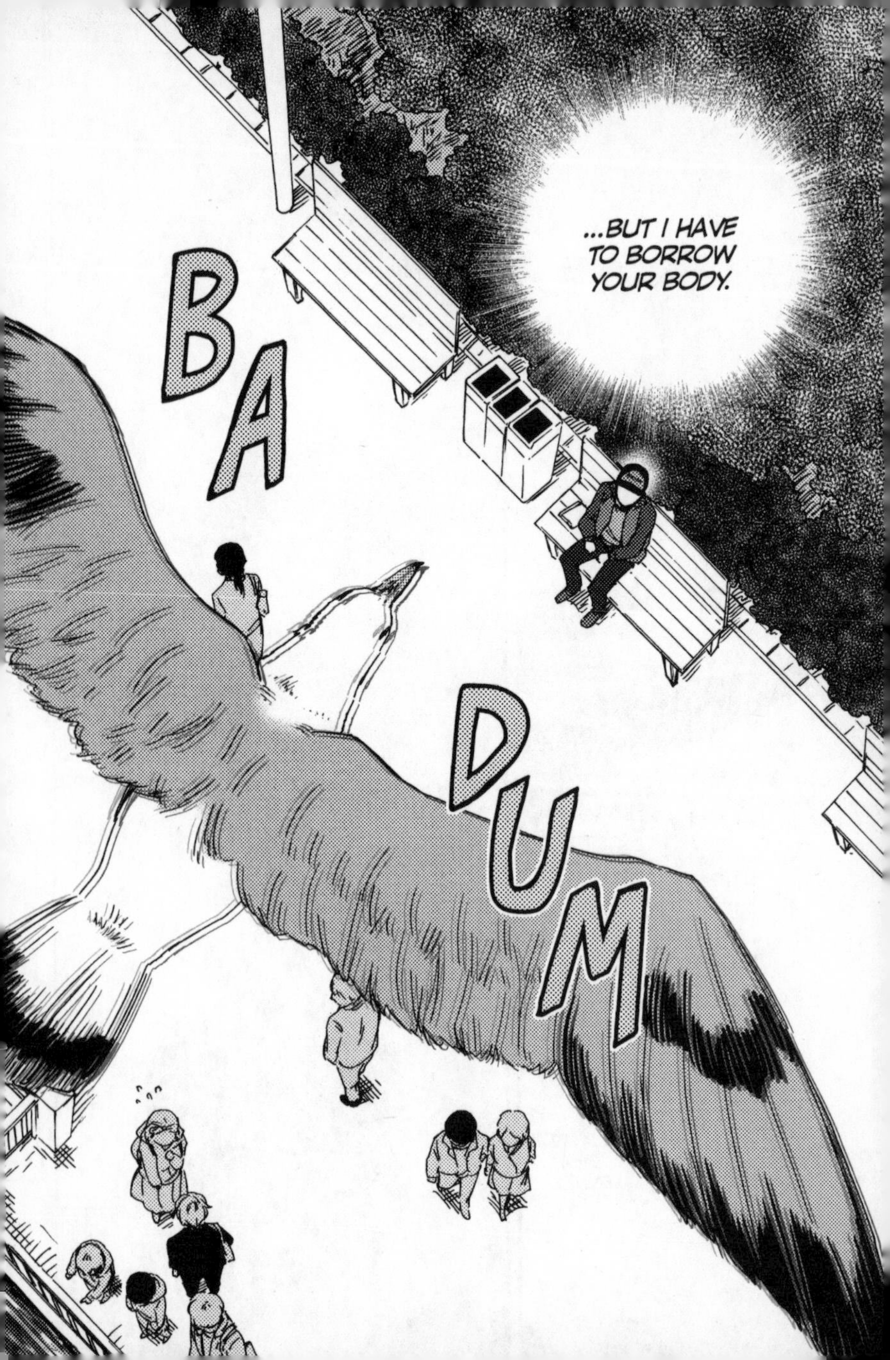
...BUT I HAVE TO BORROW YOUR BODY.
BA
DUM

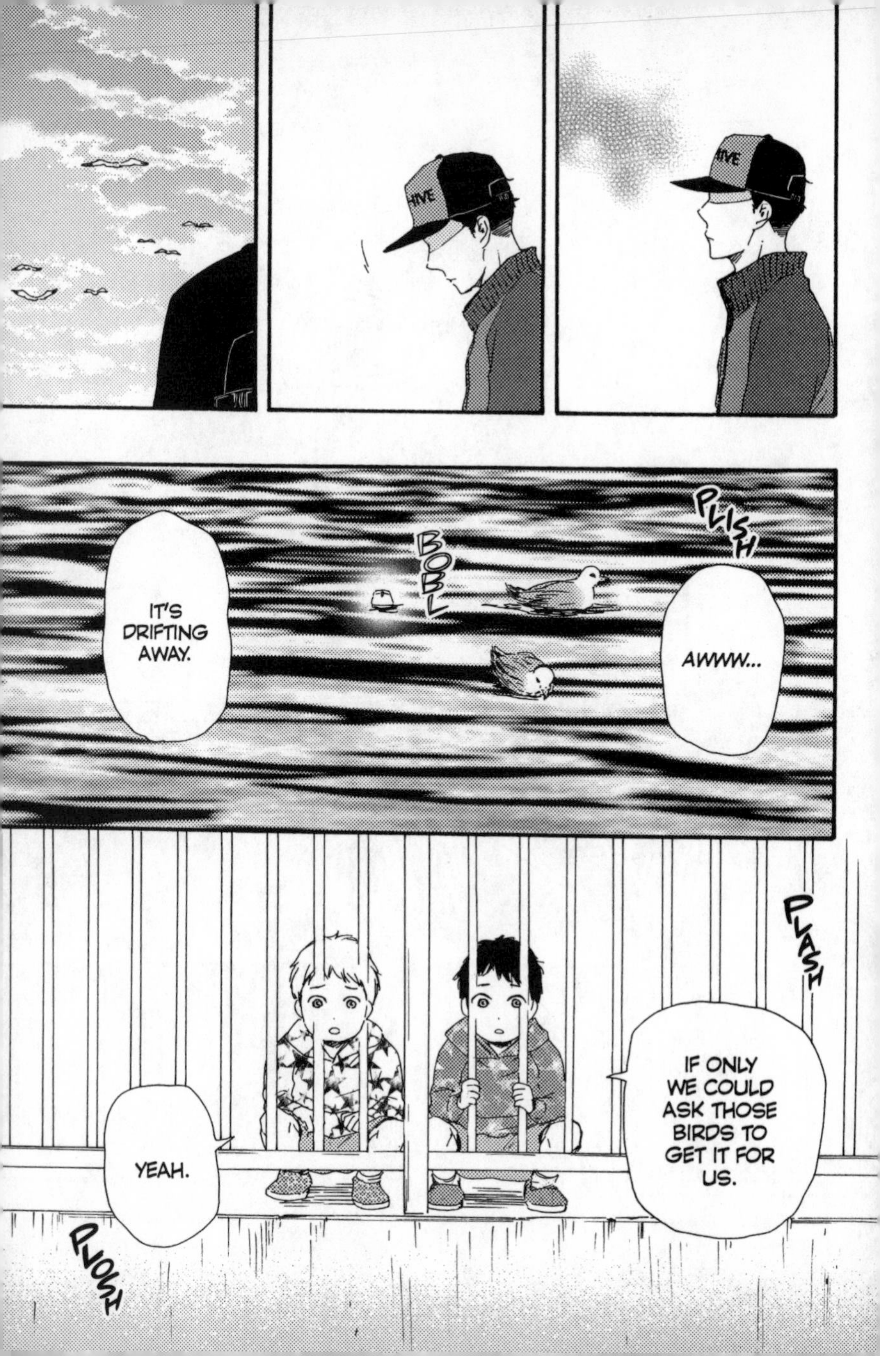
HIVE
HIVE
PLISH
AWWW...
BOBL
IT'S DRIFTING AWAY.
PLASH
IF ONLY WE COULD ASK THOSE BIRDS TO GET IT FOR US.
YEAH.
PLOSH

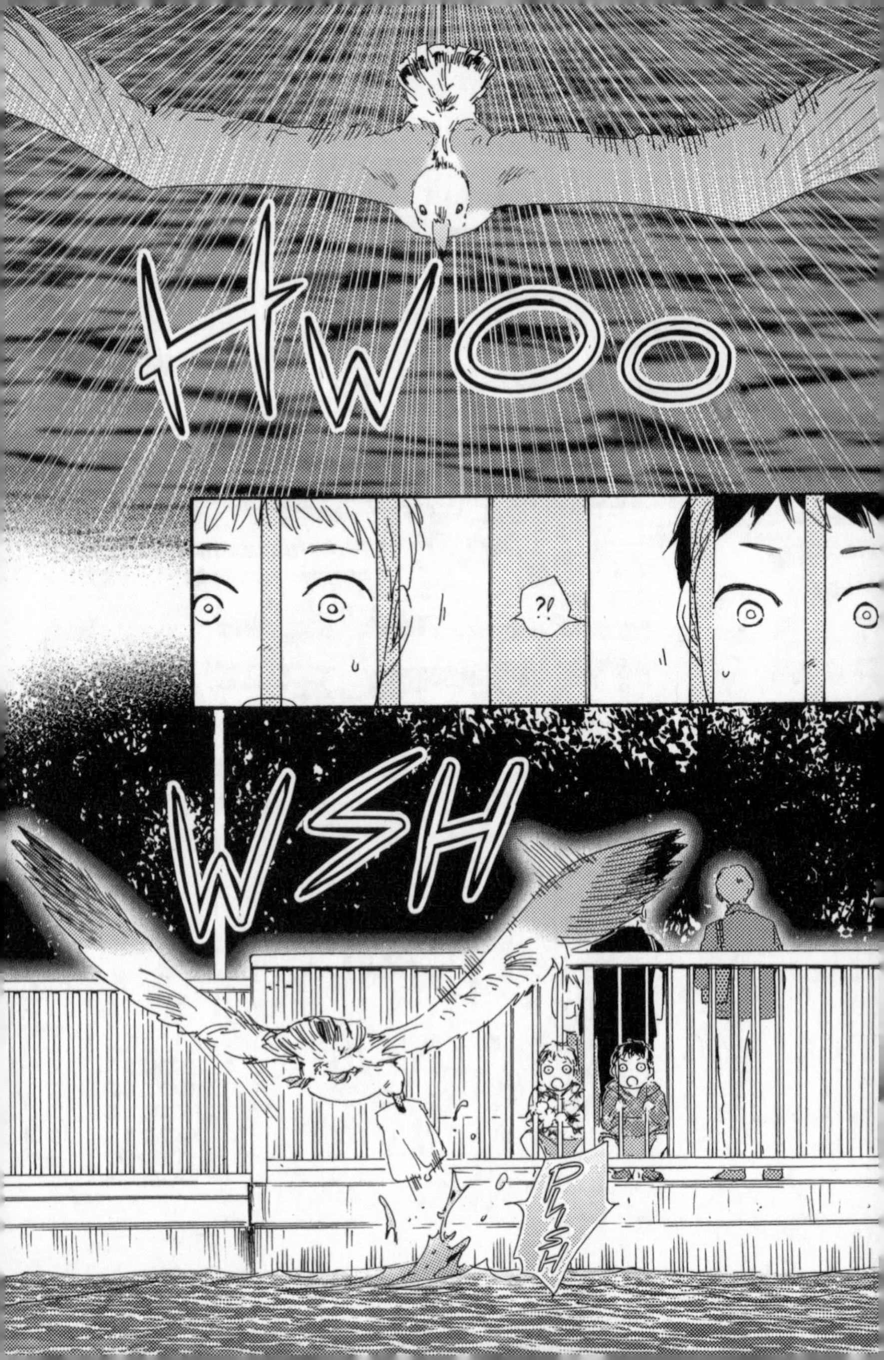
HWOO
?!
WSH
PLISH

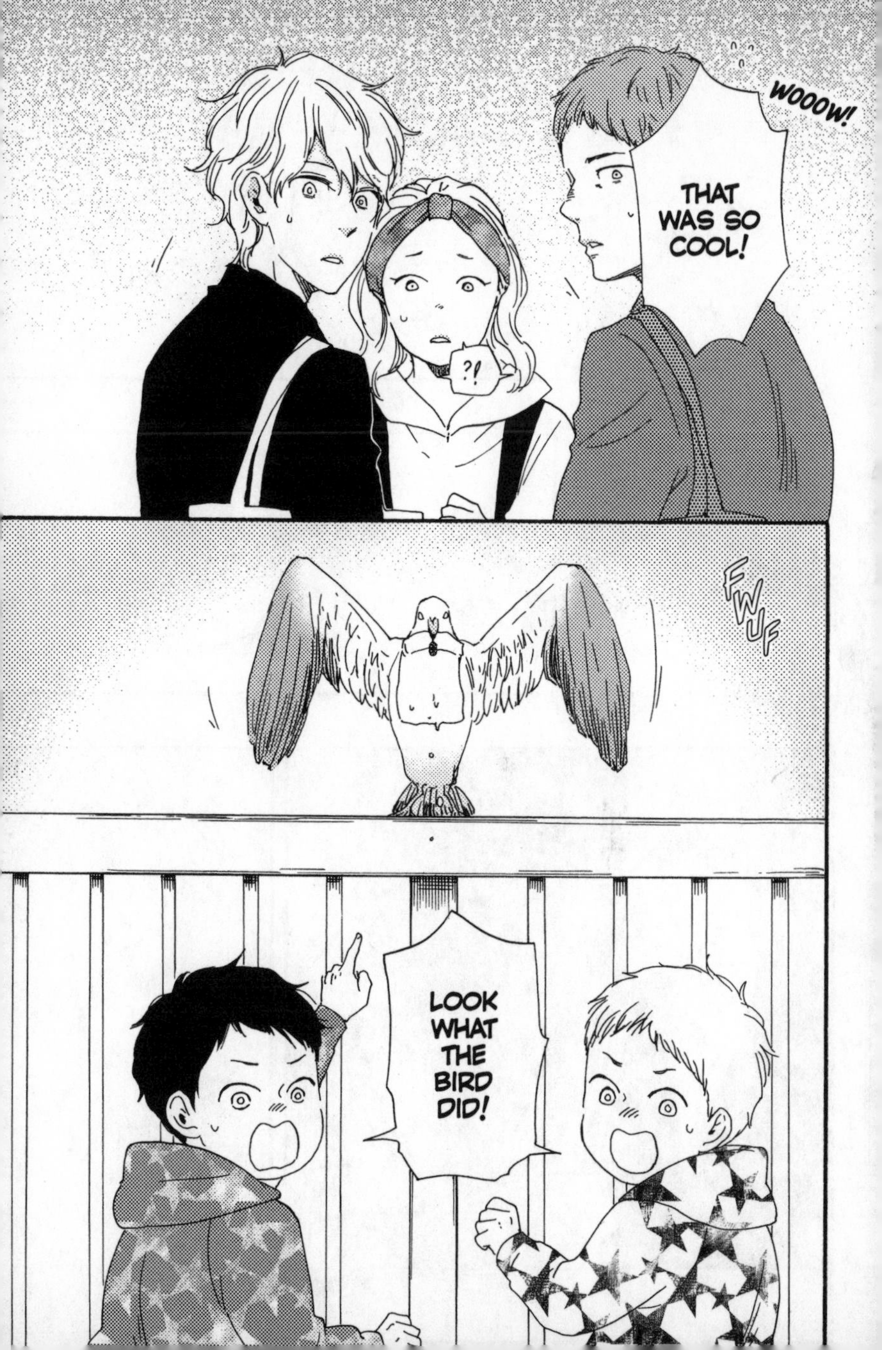
WOOOW!
THAT WAS SO COOL!
?!
FWUF
LOOK WHAT THE BIRD DID!

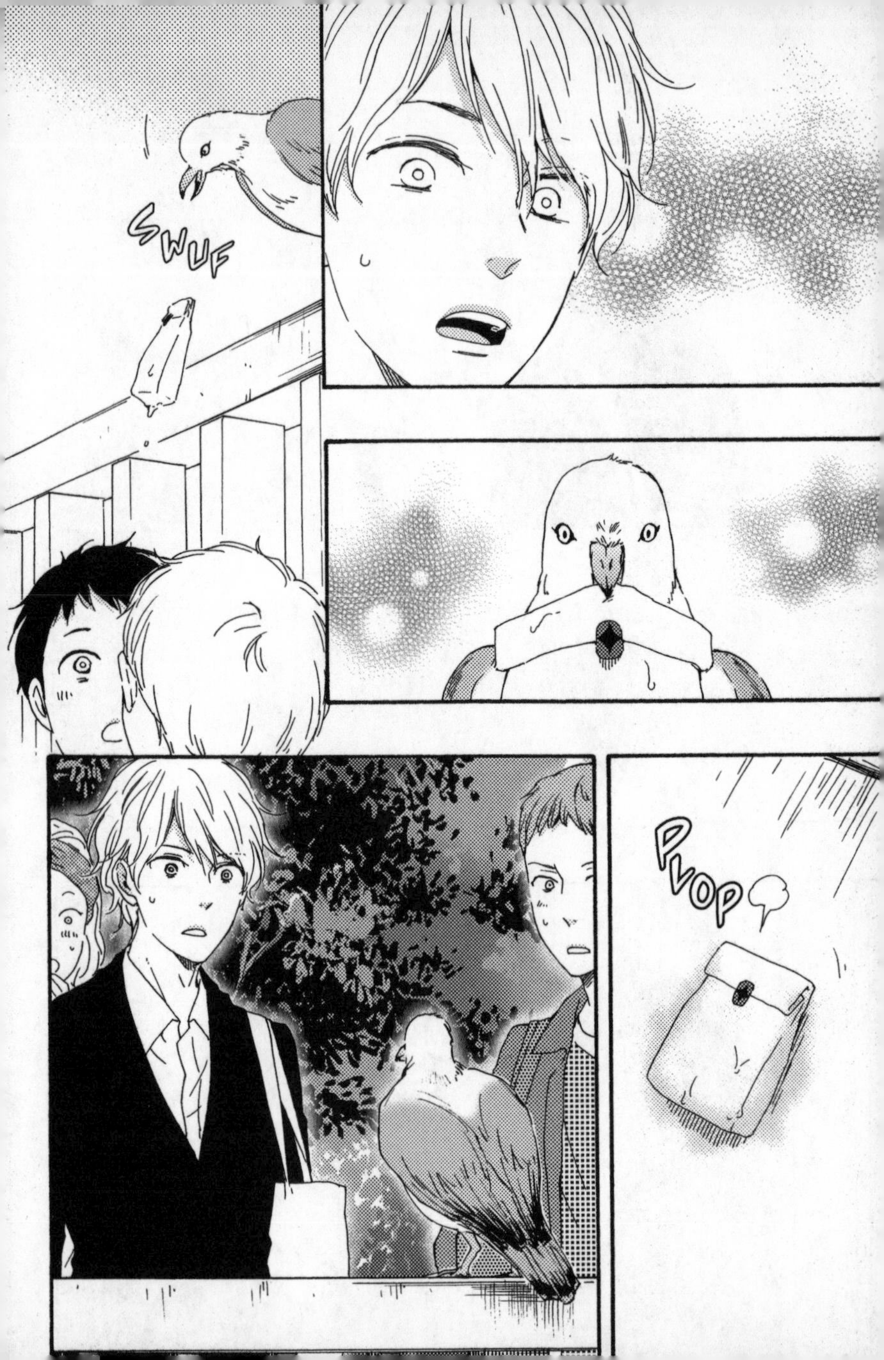
SWUF
PVOP

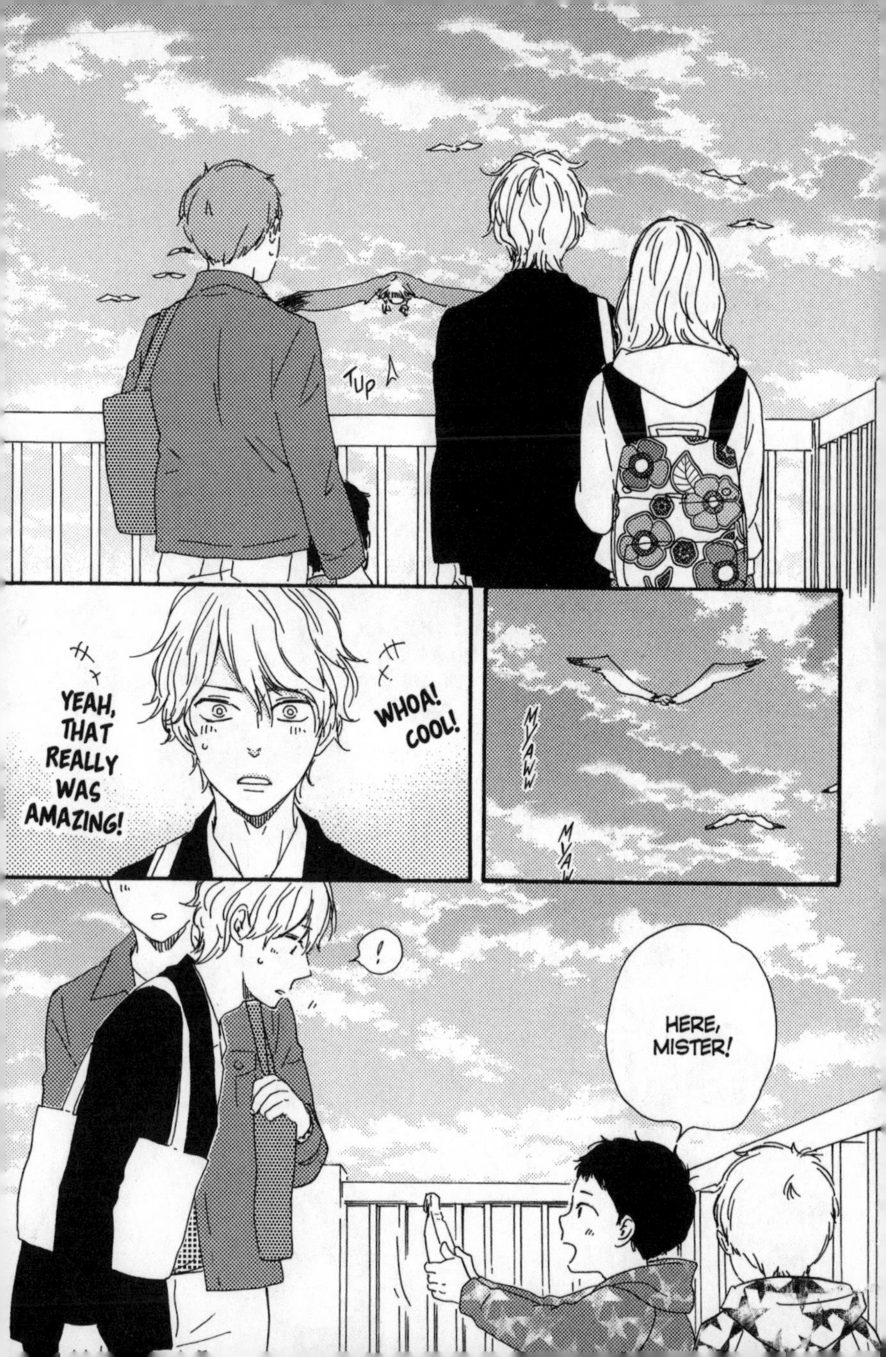
TUP
MYAWW
MYAW
WHOA! COOL!
YEAH, THAT REALLY WAS AMAZING!
HERE, MISTER!
!

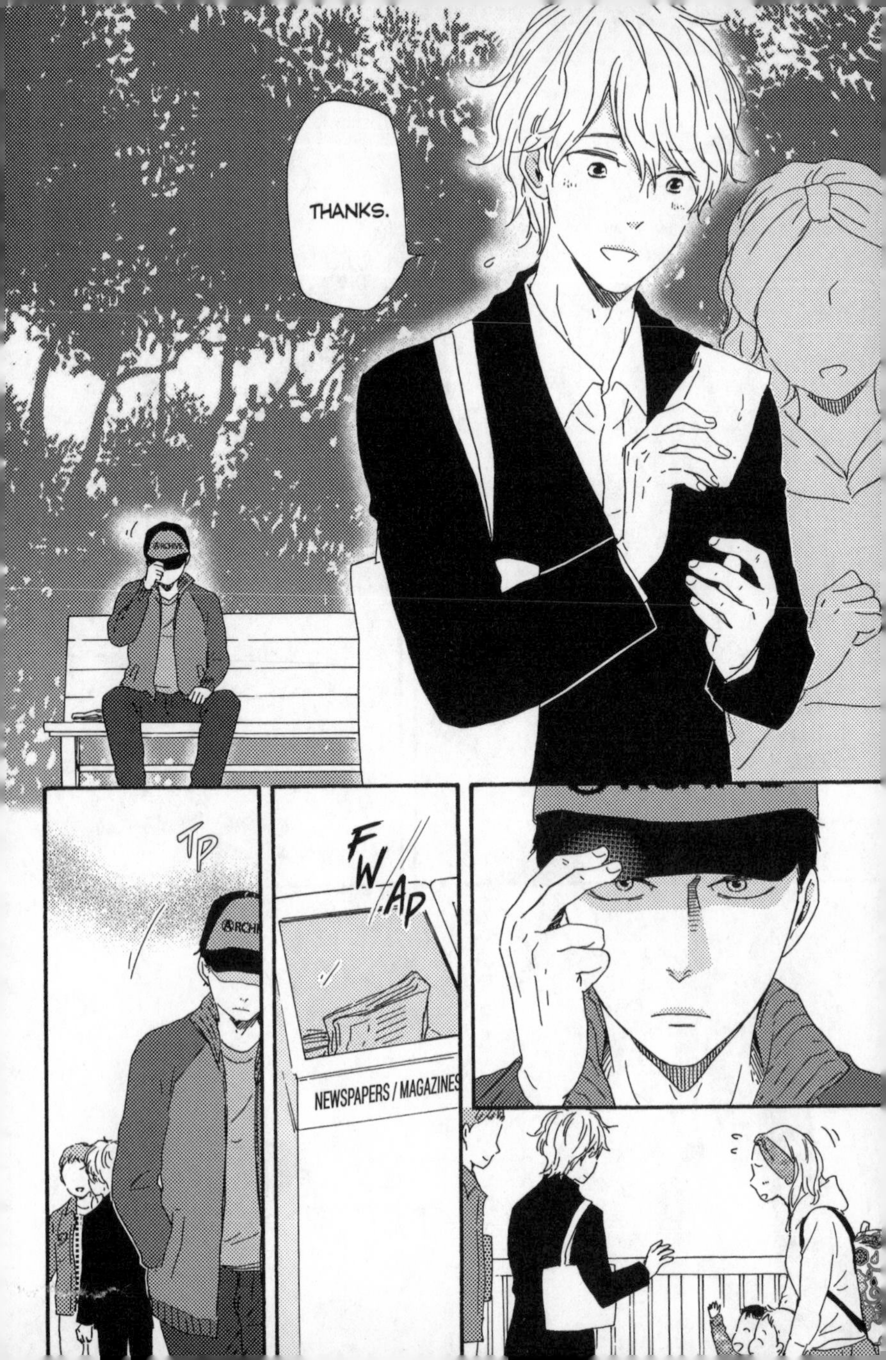
THANKS.
ARCHIVE
FWAP
NEWSPAPERS / MAGAZINES
TP

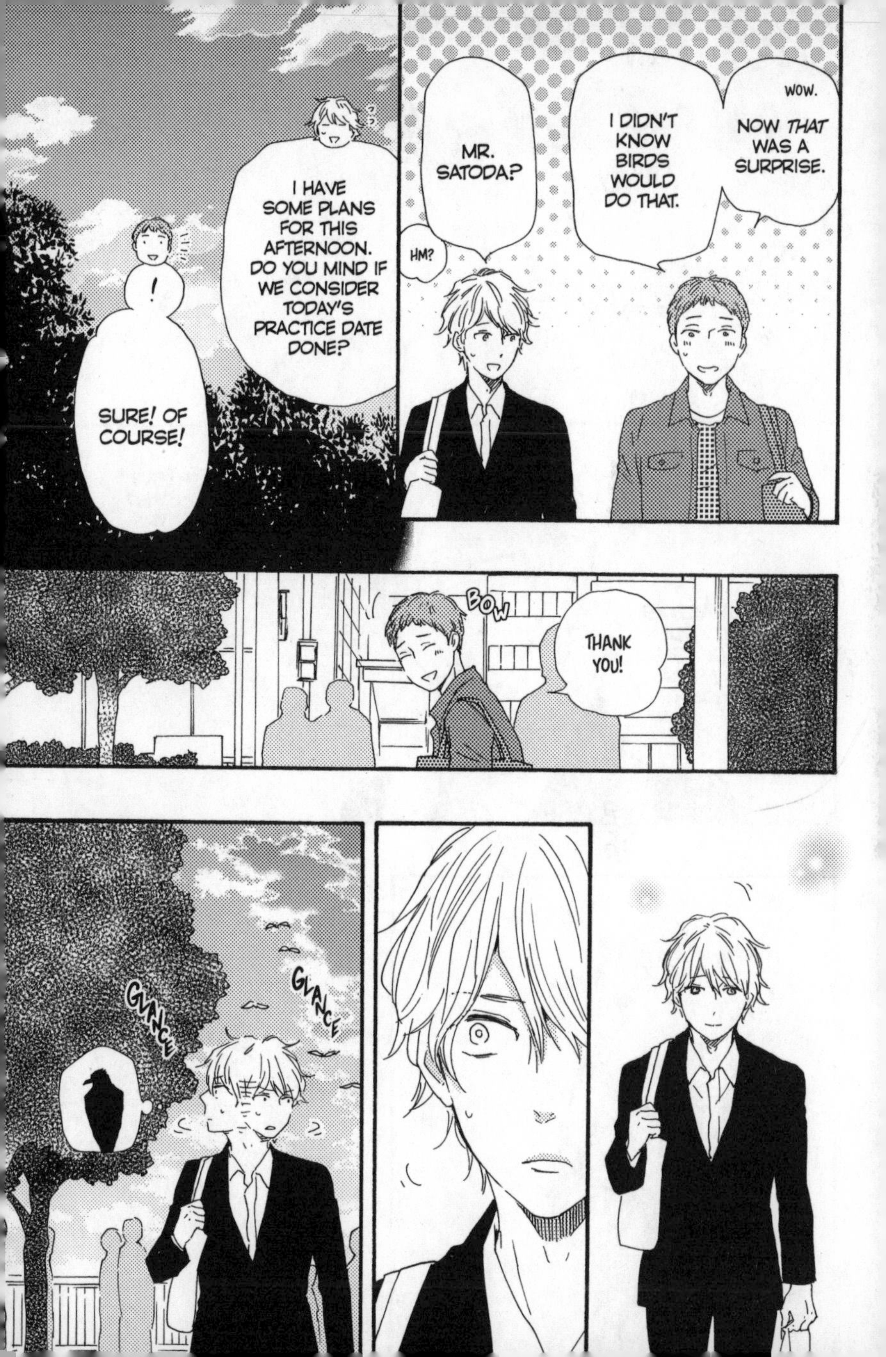

WOW.
NOW THAT WAS A SURPRISE.
I DIDN'T KNOW BIRDS WOULD DO THAT.
MR. SATODA?
HM?
I HAVE SOME PLANS FOR THIS AFTERNOON. DO YOU MIND IF WE CONSIDER TODAY'S PRACTICE DATE DONE?
SURE! OF COURSE!
BOW
THANK YOU!
GLANCE
GLANCE

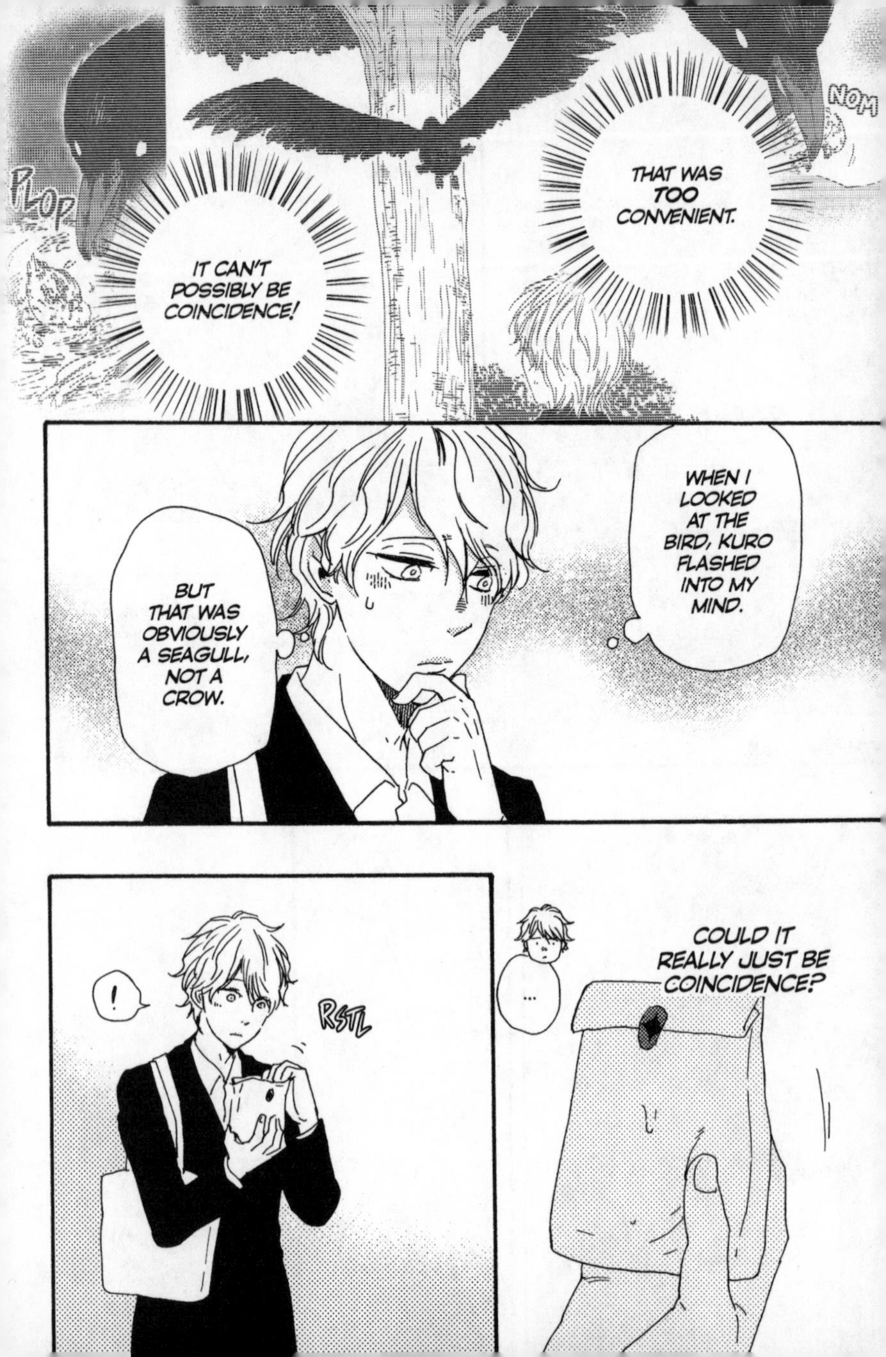
NOM
THAT WAS TOO CONVENIENT.
PLOP
IT CAN'T POSSIBLY BE COINCIDENCE!
WHEN I LOOKED AT THE BIRD, KURO FLASHED INTO MY MIND.
BUT THAT WAS OBVIOUSLY A SEAGULL, NOT A CROW.
COULD IT REALLY JUST BE COINCIDENCE?
...
!
RSTL

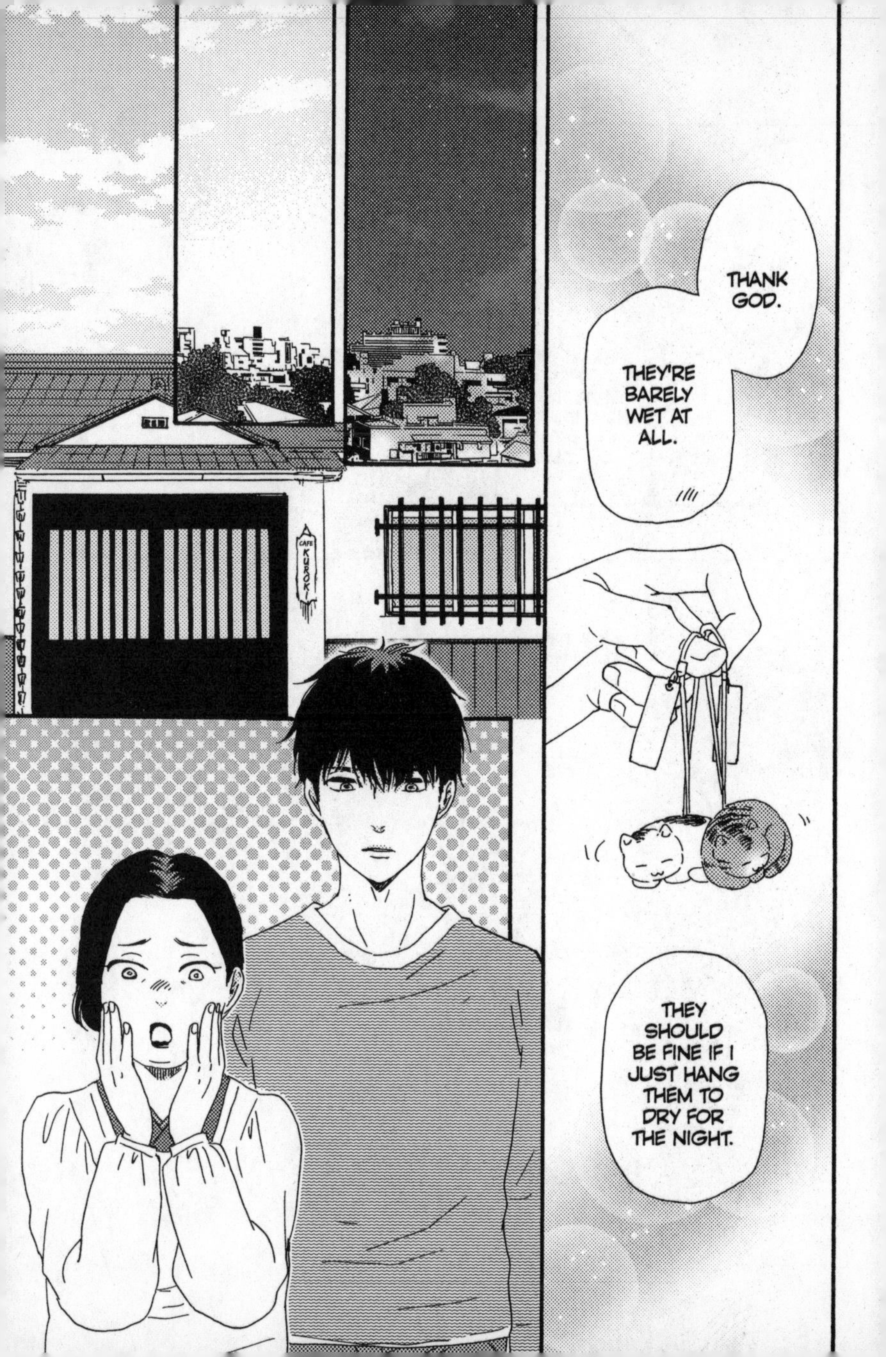
THANK GOD.
THEY'RE BARELY WET AT ALL.
THEY SHOULD BE FINE IF I JUST HANG THEM TO DRY FOR THE NIGHT.
CAFE KUROKI

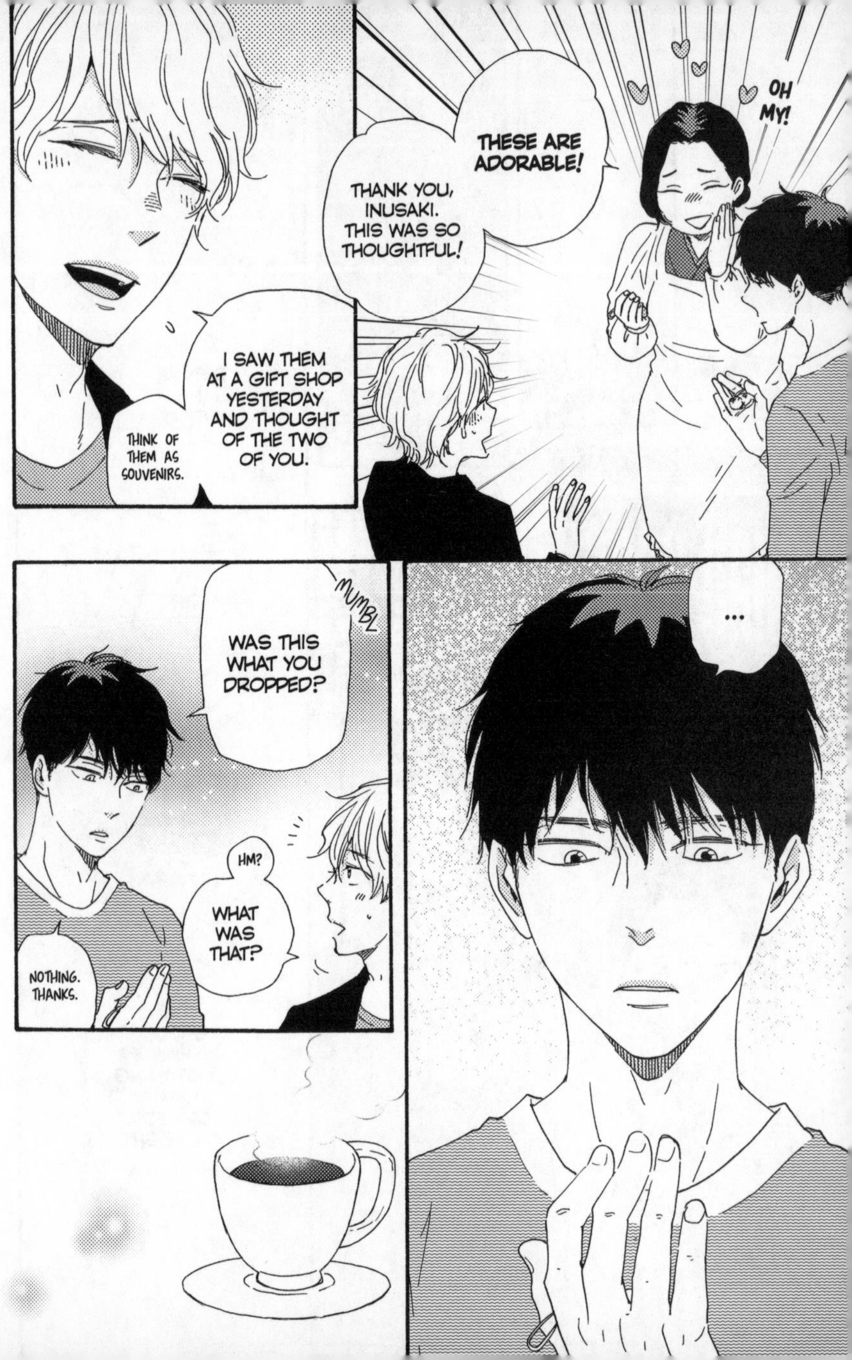
OH MY!
THESE ARE ADORABLE!
THANK YOU, INUSAKI. THIS WAS SO THOUGHTFUL!
I SAW THEM AT A GIFT SHOP YESTERDAY AND THOUGHT OF THE TWO OF YOU.
THINK OF THEM AS SOUVENIRS.
...
MUMBL
WAS THIS WHAT YOU DROPPED?
HM?
WHAT WAS THAT?
NOTHING. THANKS.

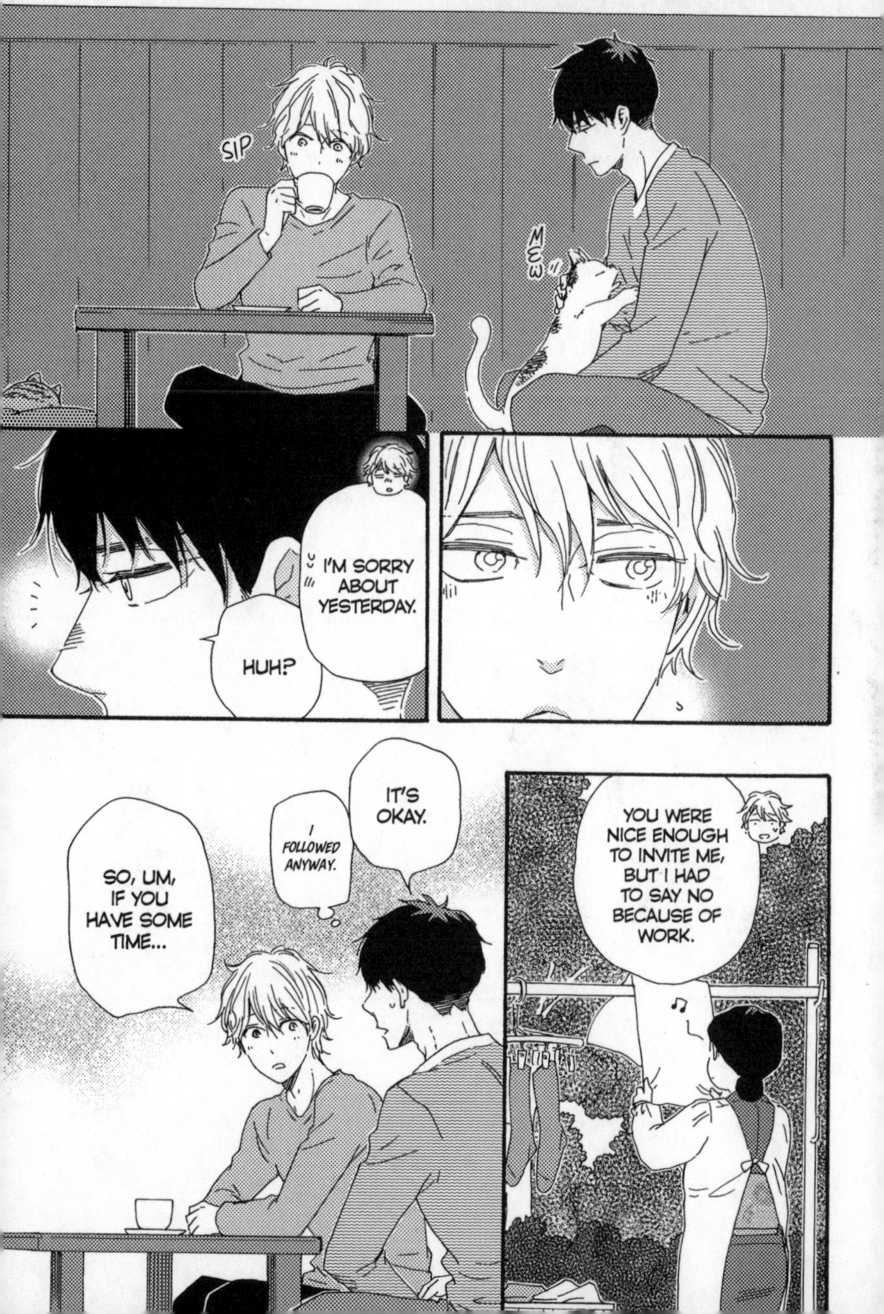
MEW
SIP
I'M SORRY ABOUT YESTERDAY.
HUH?
YOU WERE NICE ENOUGH TO INVITE ME, BUT I HAD TO SAY NO BECAUSE OF WORK.
IT'S OKAY.
I FOLLOWED ANYWAY.
SO, UM, IF YOU HAVE SOME TIME...

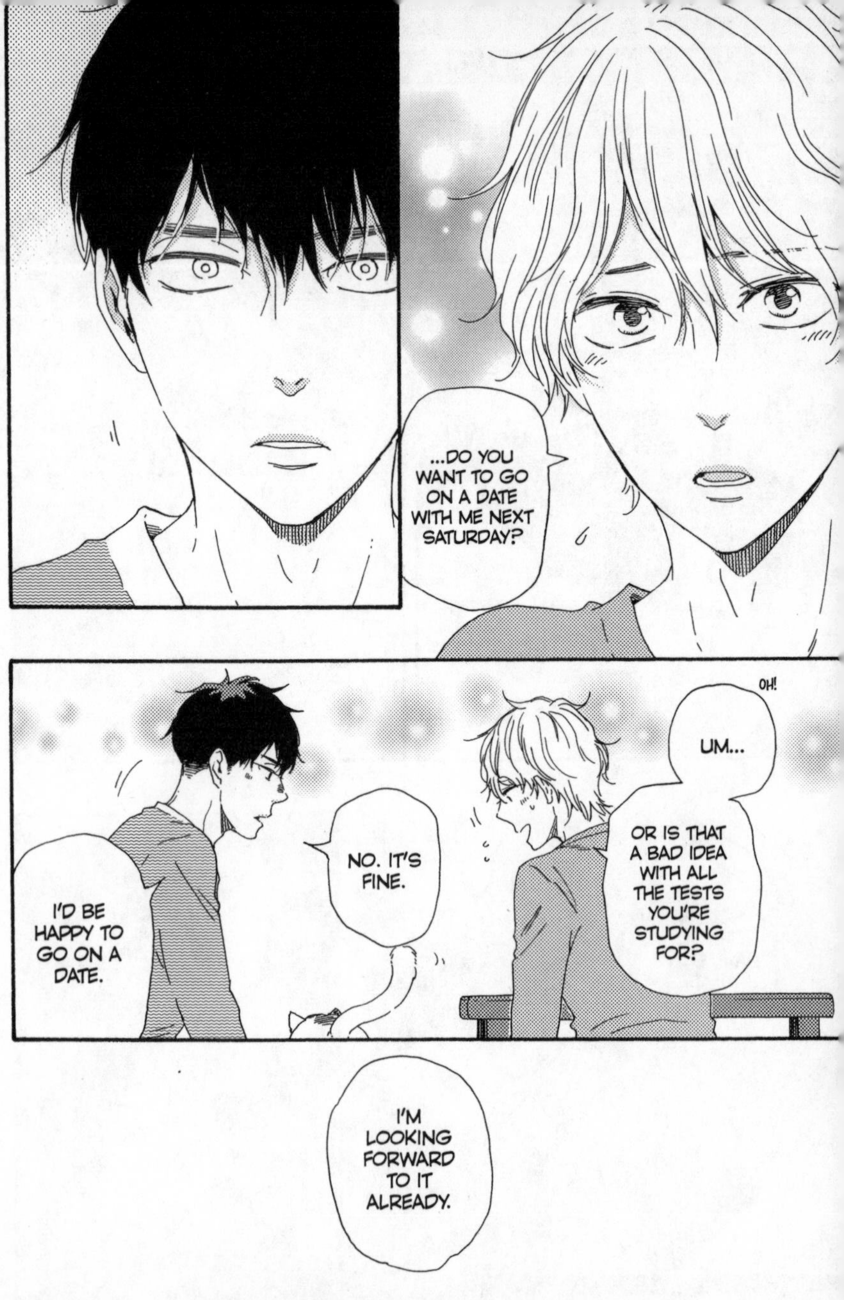
...DO YOU WANT TO GO ON A DATE WITH ME NEXT SATURDAY?
OH!
UM...
OR IS THAT A BAD IDEA WITH ALL THE TESTS YOU'RE STUDYING FOR?
NO. IT'S FINE.
I'D BE HAPPY TO GO ON A DATE.
I'M LOOKING FORWARD TO IT ALREADY.

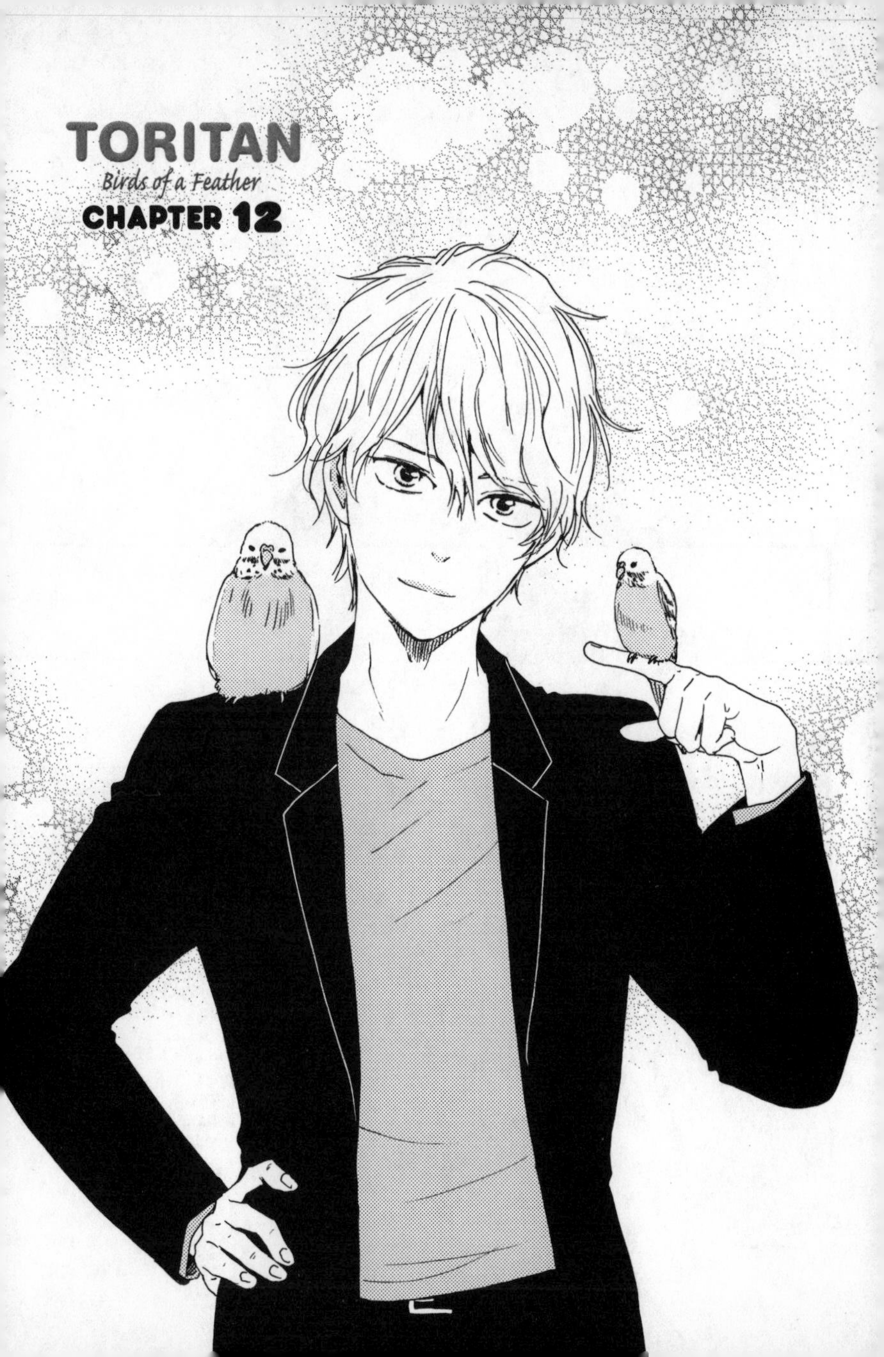
TORITAN
Birds of a Feather
CHAPTER 12

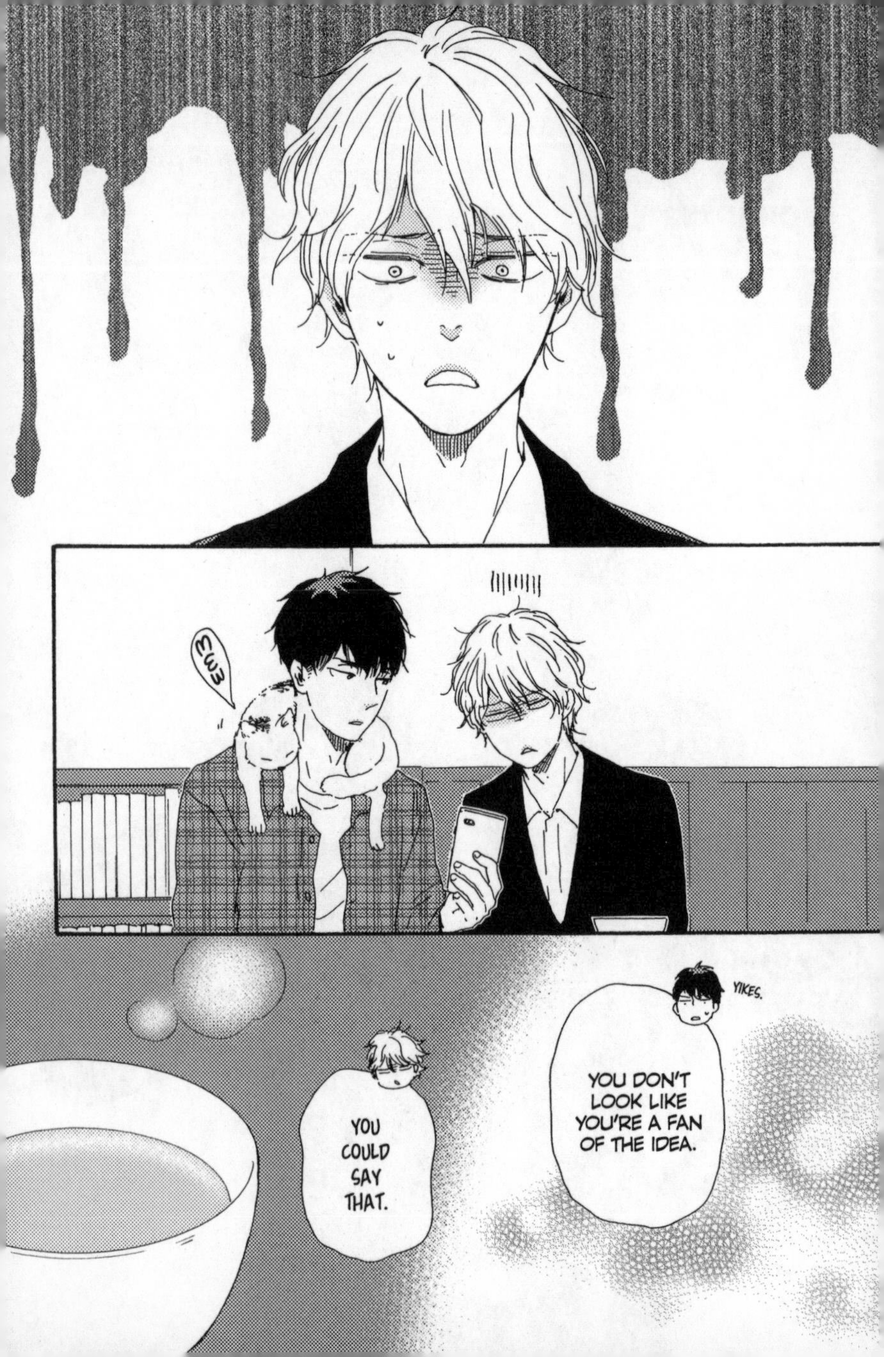
MEW
YIKES.
YOU DON'T LOOK LIKE YOU'RE A FAN OF THE IDEA.
YOU COULD SAY THAT.

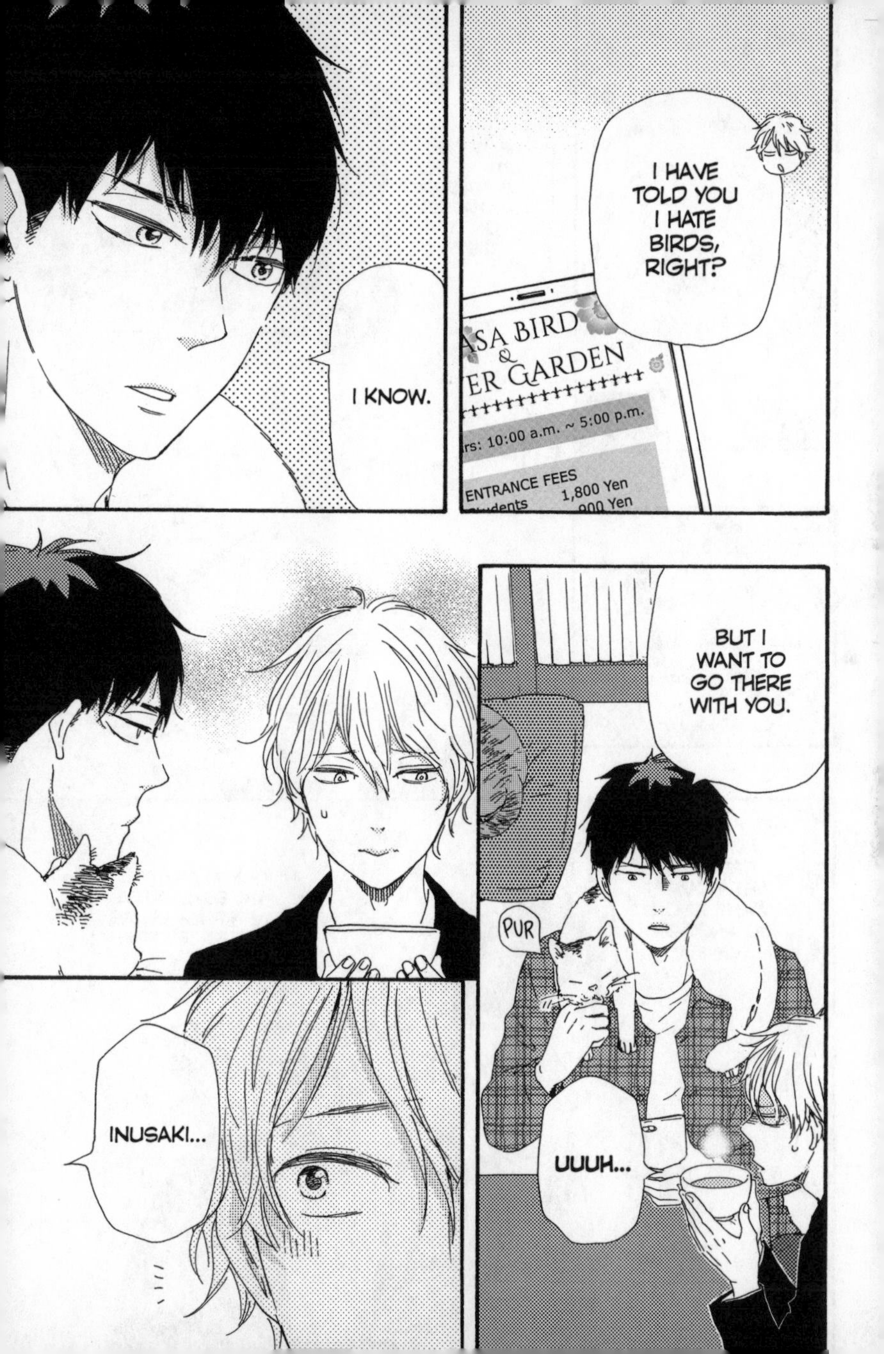
I HAVE TOLD YOU I HATE BIRDS, RIGHT?
ASA BIRD
&
ER GARDEN
rs: 10:00 a.m. ~ 5:00 p.m.
ENTRANCE FEES
1,800 Yen
I KNOW.
BUT I WANT TO GO THERE WITH YOU.
PUR
UUUH...
INUSAKI...

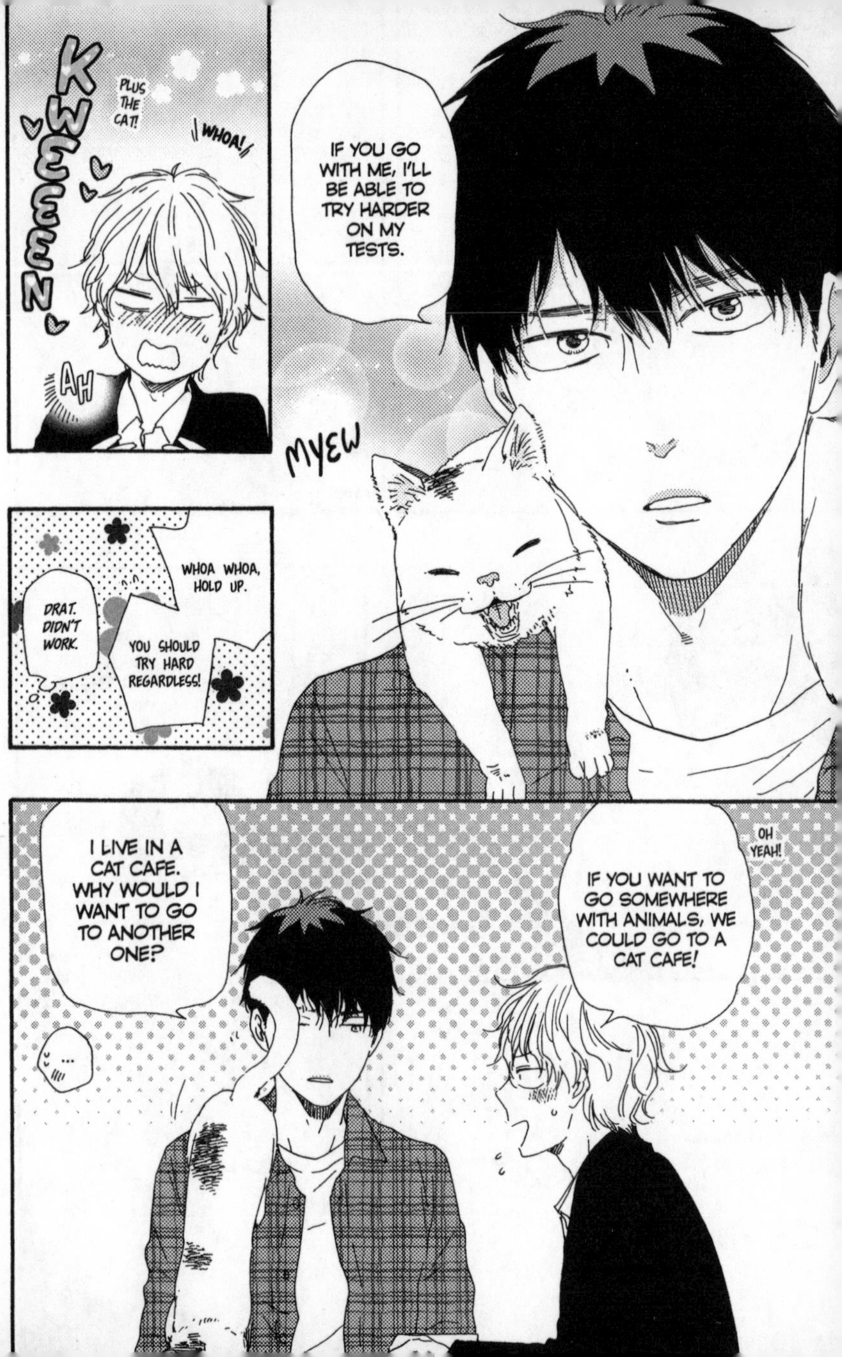
IF YOU GO WITH ME, I'LL BE ABLE TO TRY HARDER ON MY TESTS.
MYEW
PLUS THE CAT!
WHOA!
KWEEEEN
AH
WHOA WHOA, HOLD UP.
YOU SHOULD TRY HARD REGARDLESS!
DRAT. DIDN'T WORK.
OH YEAH!
IF YOU WANT TO GO SOMEWHERE WITH ANIMALS, WE COULD GO TO A CAT CAFE!
I LIVE IN A CAT CAFE. WHY WOULD I WANT TO GO TO ANOTHER ONE?
...

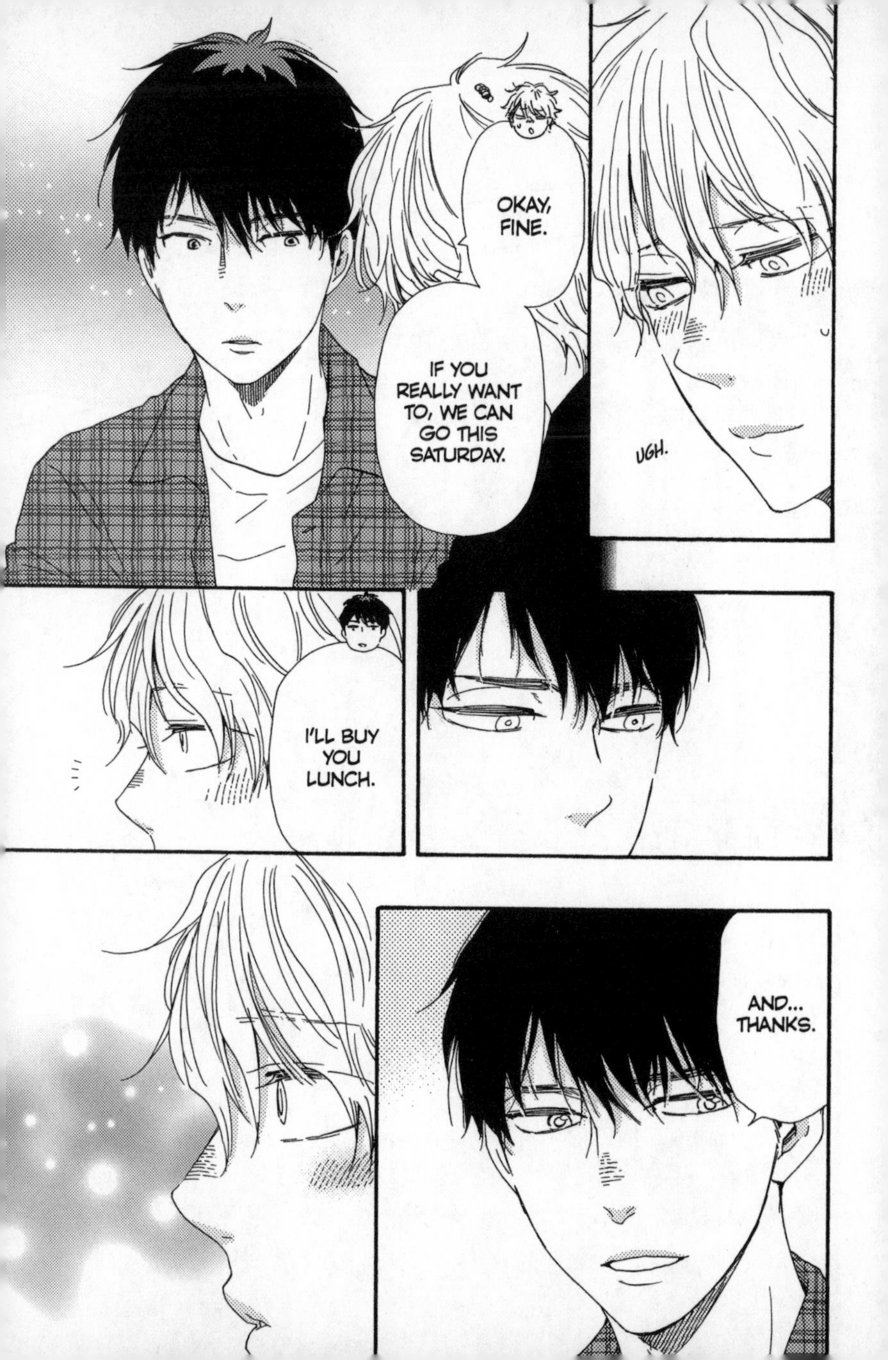
UGH.
OKAY, FINE.
IF YOU REALLY WANT TO, WE CAN GO THIS SATURDAY.
I'LL BUY YOU LUNCH.
AND... THANKS.

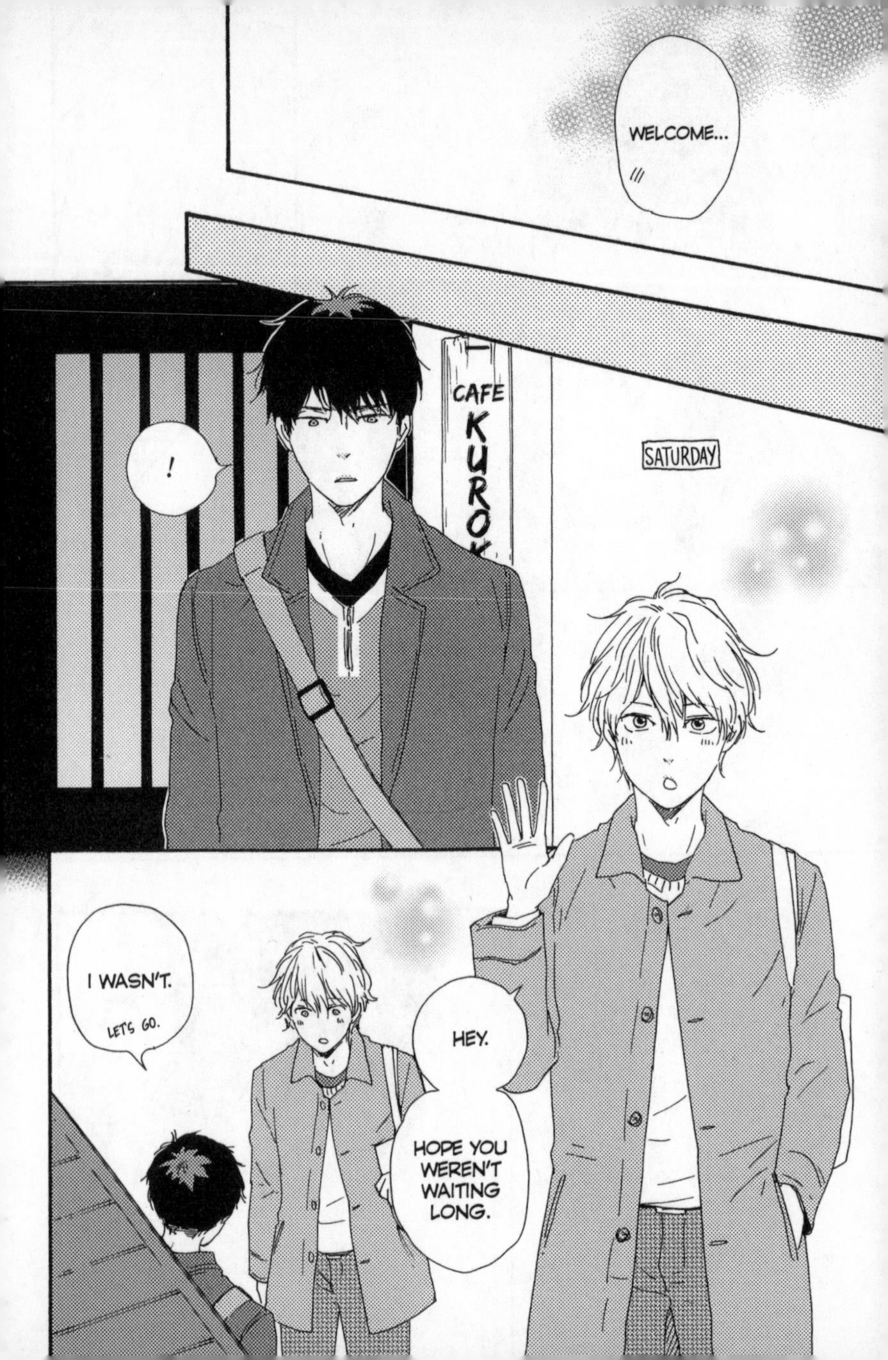
WELCOME...
SATURDAY
CAFE KUROK
!
HEY.
HOPE YOU WEREN'T WAITING LONG.
I WASN'T.
LET'S GO.

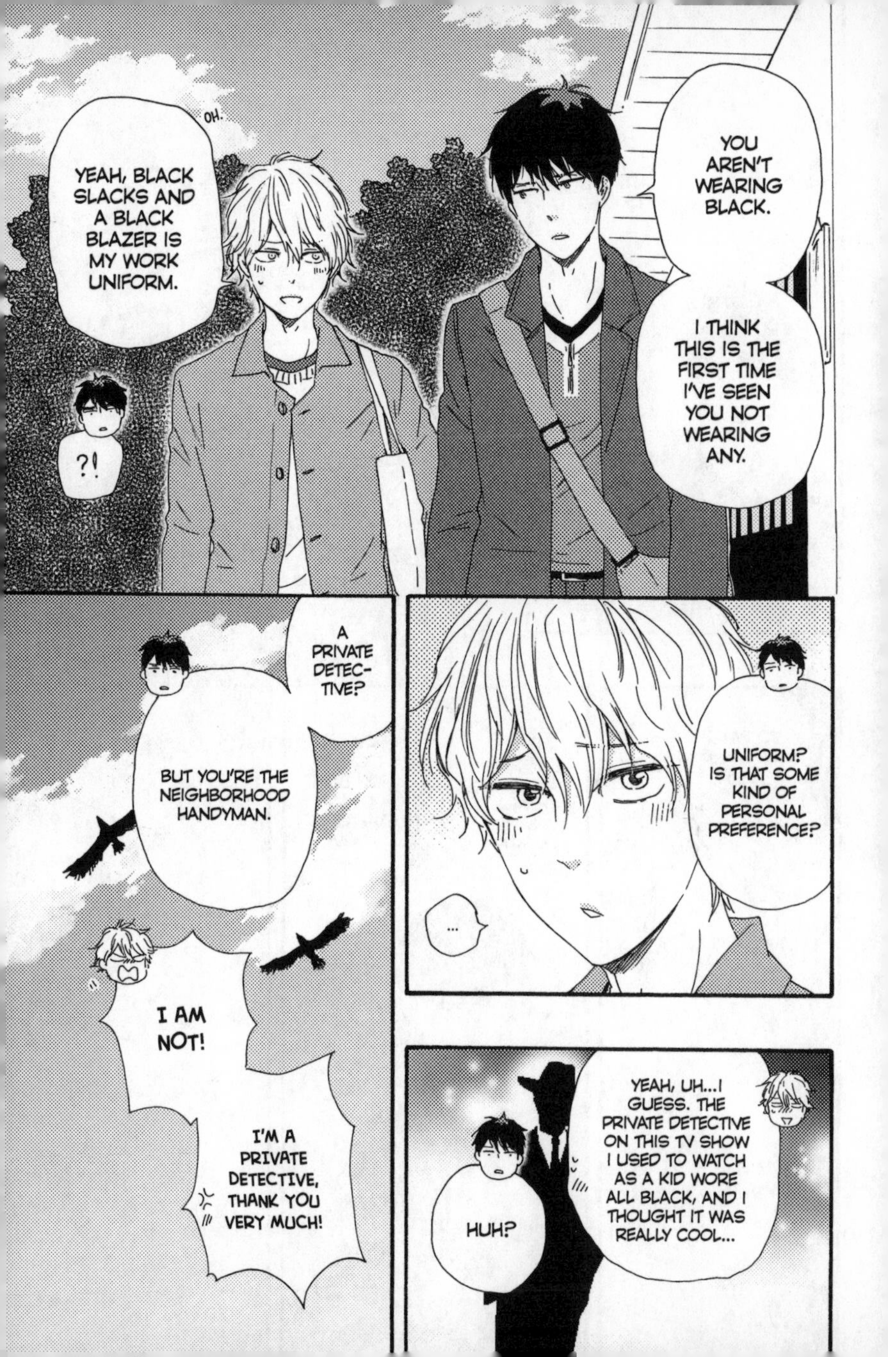
YOU AREN'T WEARING BLACK.
I THINK THIS IS THE FIRST TIME I'VE SEEN YOU NOT WEARING ANY.
OH.
YEAH, BLACK SLACKS AND A BLACK BLAZER IS MY WORK UNIFORM.
?!
UNIFORM? IS THAT SOME KIND OF PERSONAL PREFERENCE?
...
YEAH, UH...I GUESS. THE PRIVATE DETECTIVE ON THIS TV SHOW I USED TO WATCH AS A KID WORE ALL BLACK, AND I THOUGHT IT WAS REALLY COOL...
HUH?
A PRIVATE DETEC-TIVE?
BUT YOU'RE THE NEIGHBORHOOD HANDYMAN.
I AM NOT!
I'M A PRIVATE DETECTIVE, THANK YOU VERY MUCH!

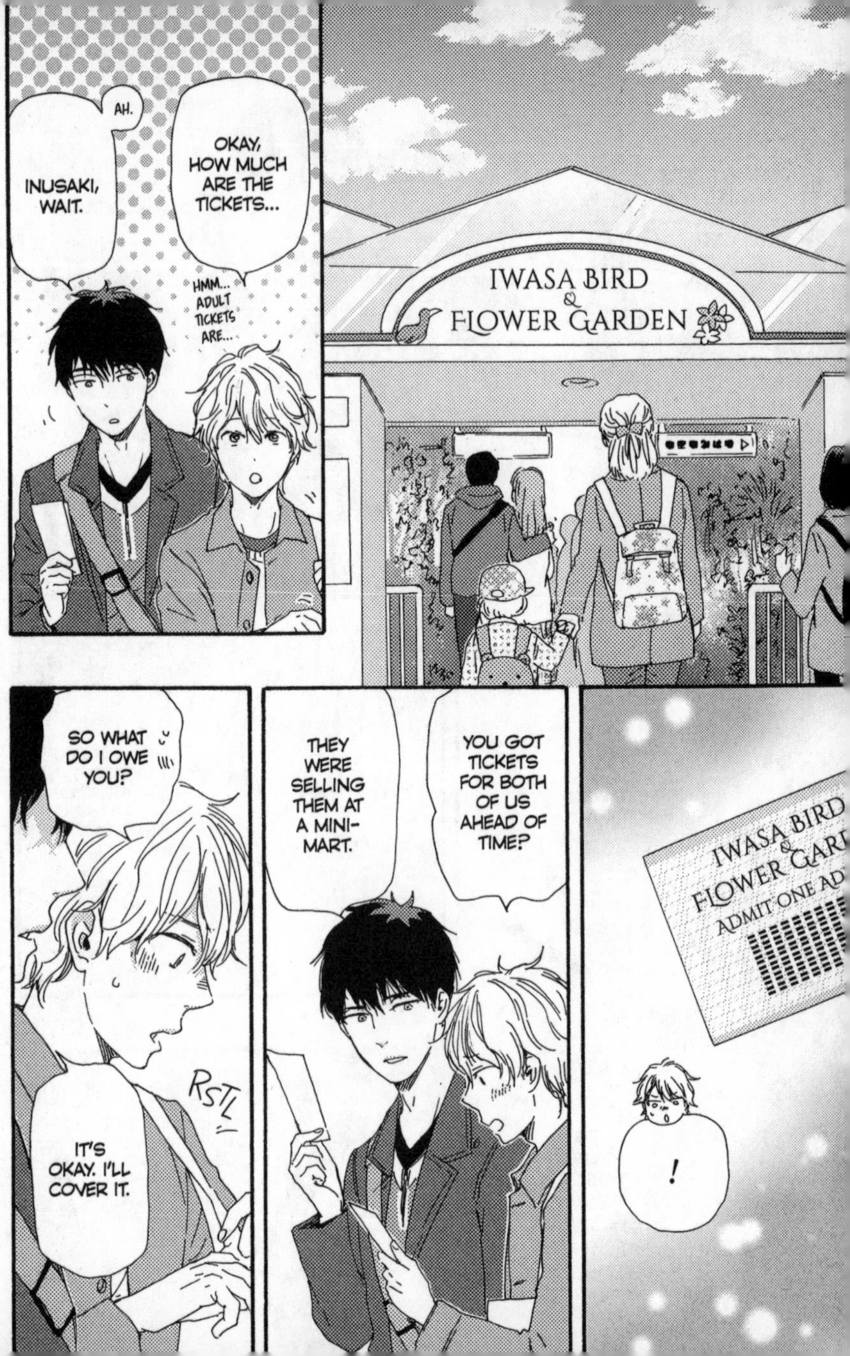
IWASA BIRD & FLOWER GARDEN
OKAY, HOW MUCH ARE THE TICKETS...
AH.
INUSAKI, WAIT.
HMM... ADULT TICKETS ARE...
IWASA BIRD &
FLOWER GAR
ADMIT ONE AD
!
YOU GOT TICKETS FOR BOTH OF US AHEAD OF TIME?
THEY WERE SELLING THEM AT A MINI-MART.
SO WHAT DO I OWE YOU?
RSTL
IT'S OKAY. I'LL COVER IT.

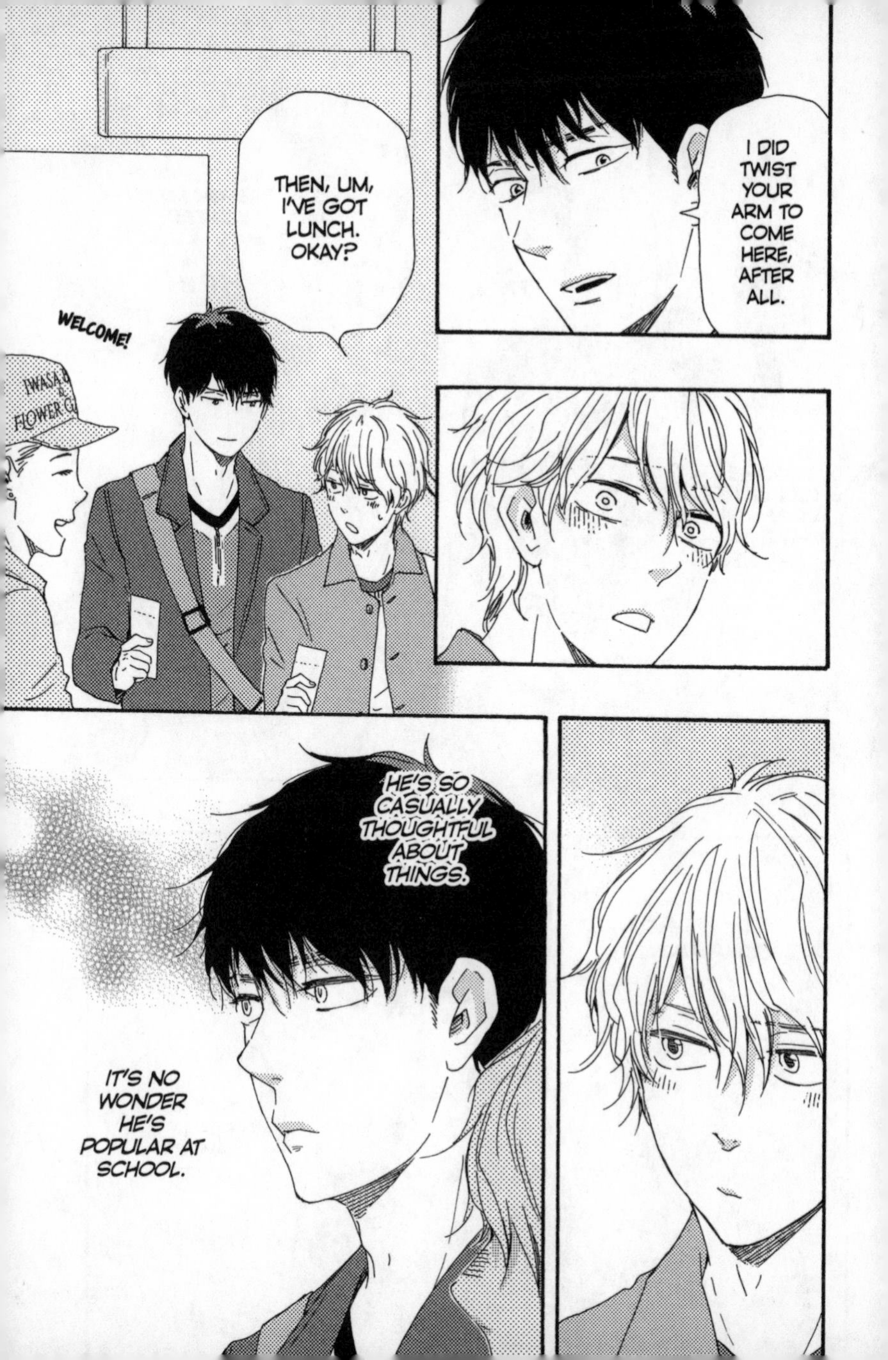
I DID TWIST YOUR ARM TO COME HERE, AFTER ALL.
THEN, UM, I'VE GOT LUNCH. OKAY?
WELCOME!
HE'S SO CASUALLY THOUGHTFUL ABOUT THINGS.
IT'S NO WONDER HE'S POPULAR AT SCHOOL.

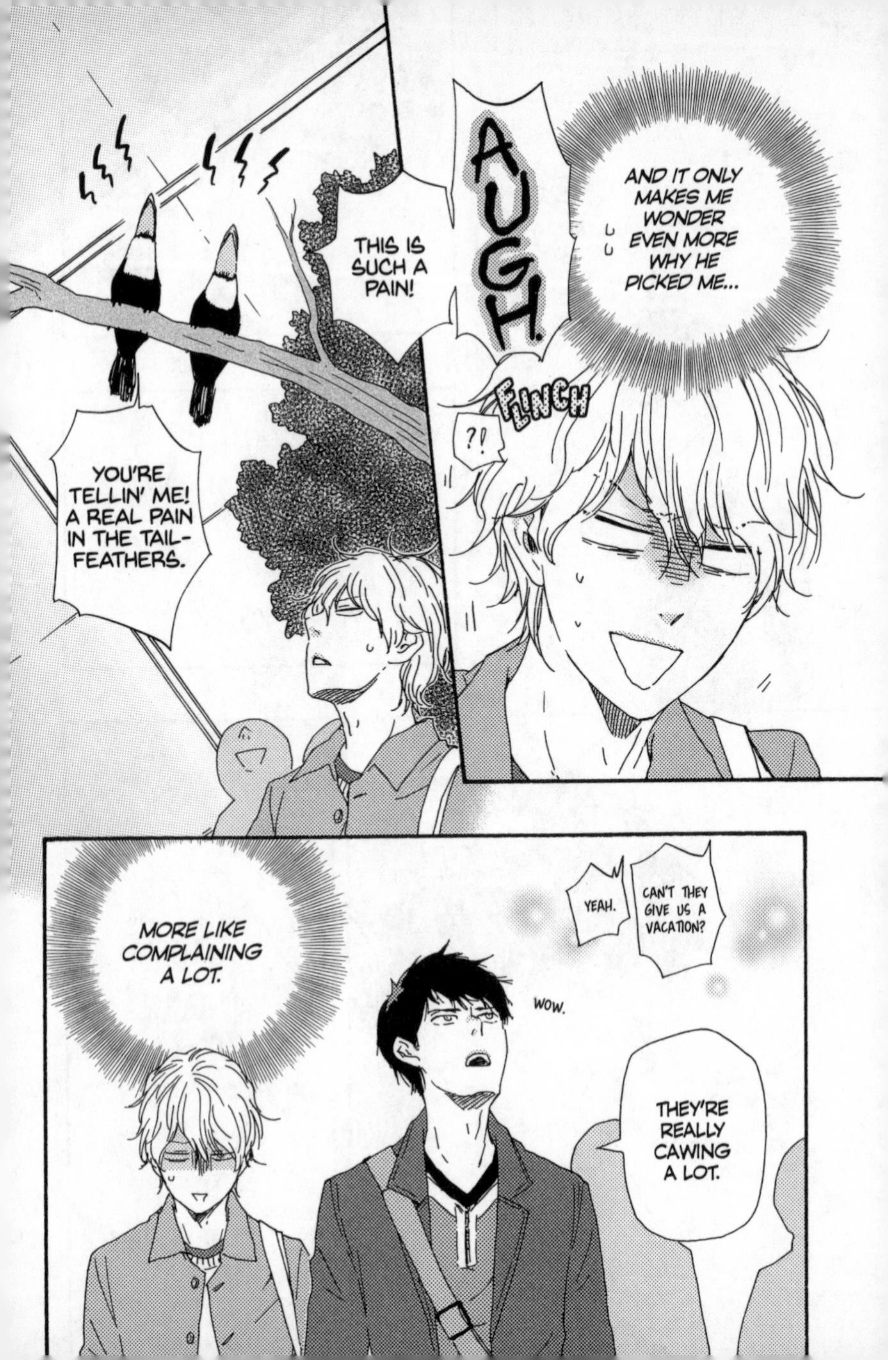
AND IT ONLY MAKES ME WONDER EVEN MORE WHY HE PICKED ME...
AUGH.
FLINCH
?!
THIS IS SUCH A PAIN!
YOU'RE TELLIN' ME! A REAL PAIN IN THE TAIL-FEATHERS.
CAN'T THEY GIVE US A VACATION?
YEAH.
THEY'RE REALLY CAWING A LOT.
WOW.
MORE LIKE COMPLAINING A LOT.

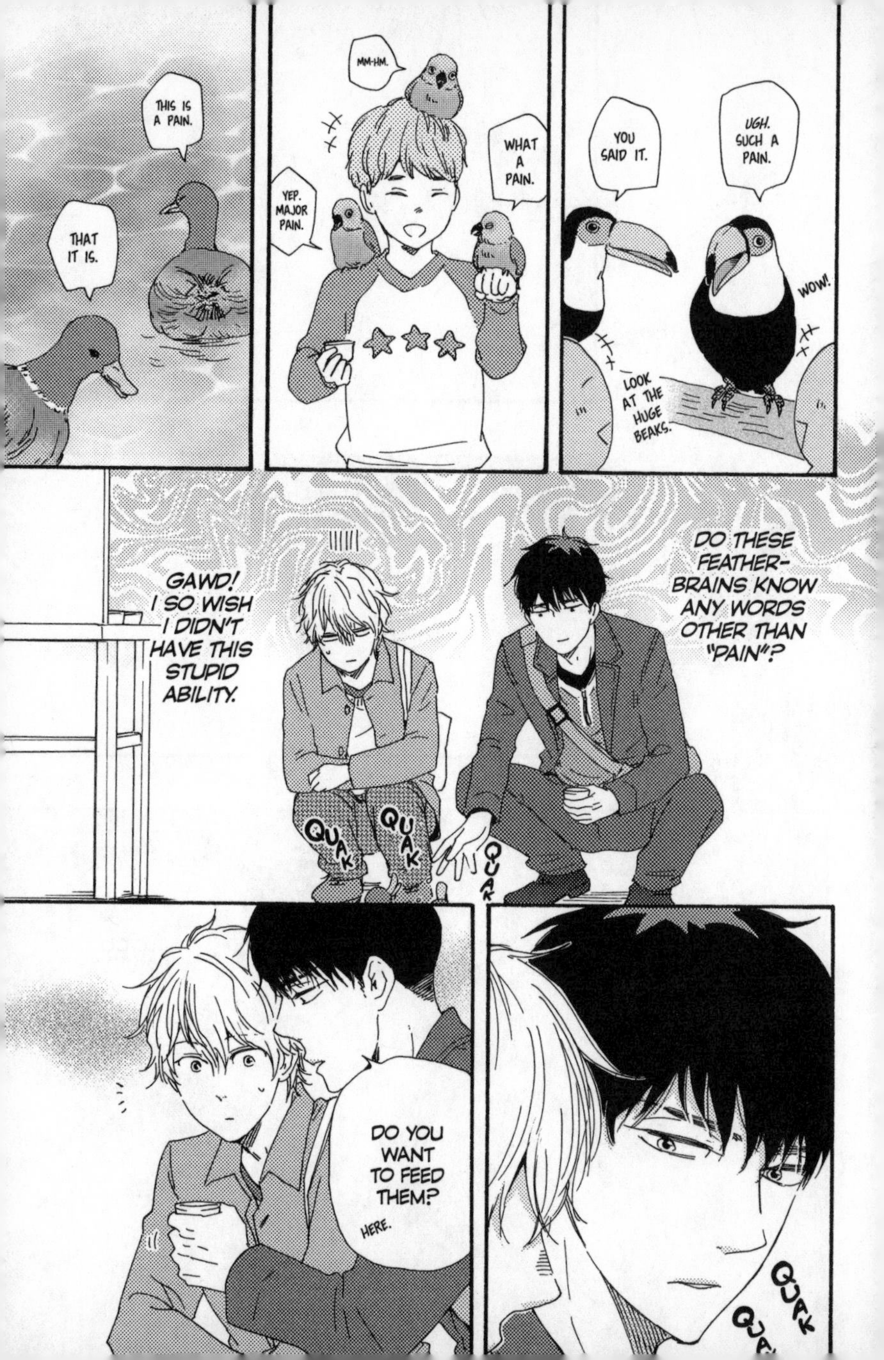
UGH. SUCH A PAIN.
YOU SAID IT.
WOW!
LOOK AT THE HUGE BEAKS.
MM-HM.
WHAT A PAIN.
YEP. MAJOR PAIN.
THIS IS A PAIN.
THAT IT IS.
DO THESE FEATHER-BRAINS KNOW ANY WORDS OTHER THAN "PAIN"?
GAWD! I SO WISH I DIDN'T HAVE THIS STUPID ABILITY.
QUAK
QUAK
QUAK
QUAK
DO YOU WANT TO FEED THEM?
HERE.

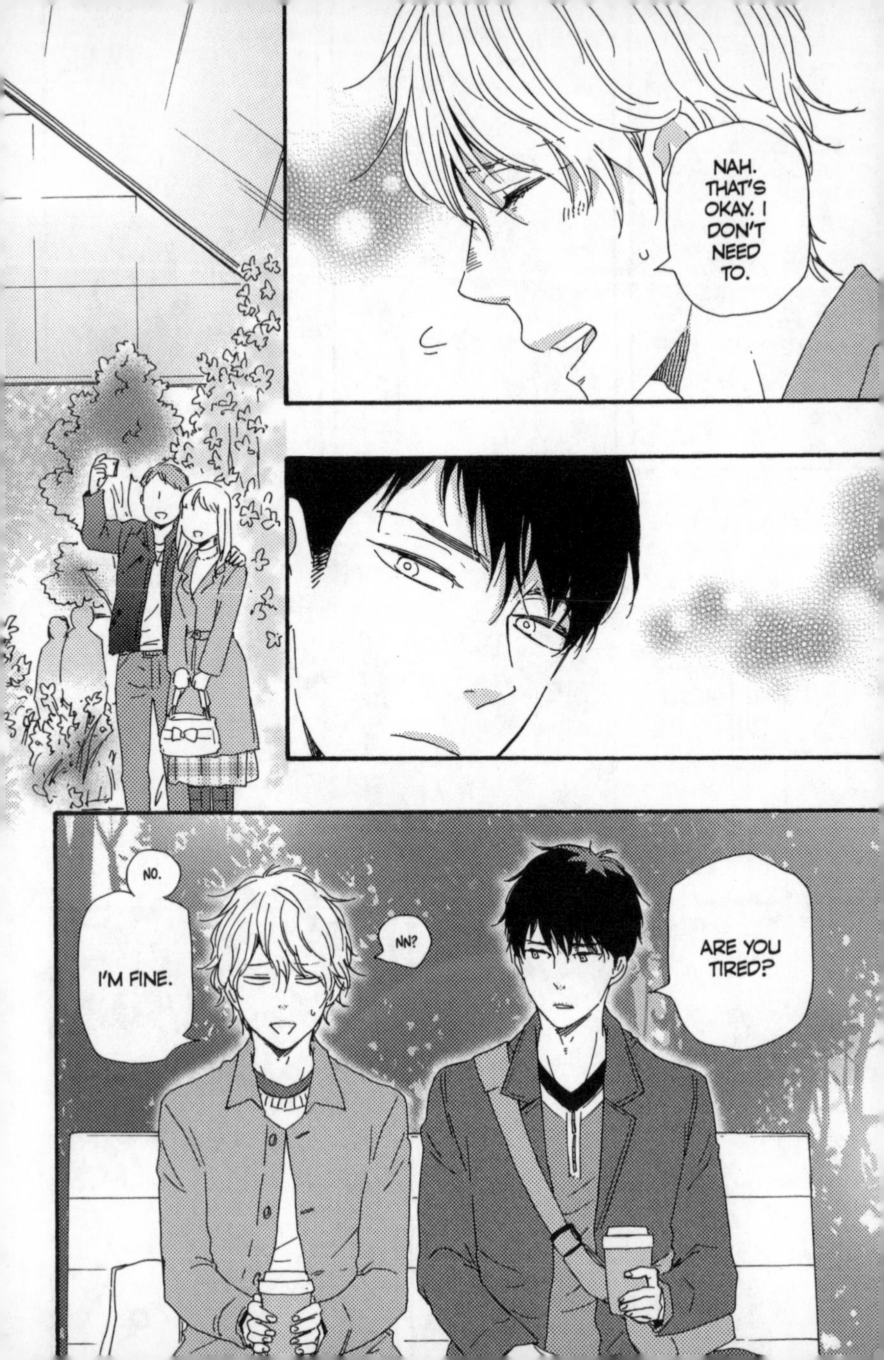
NAH. THAT'S OKAY. I DON'T NEED TO.
ARE YOU TIRED?
NN?
NO.
I'M FINE.

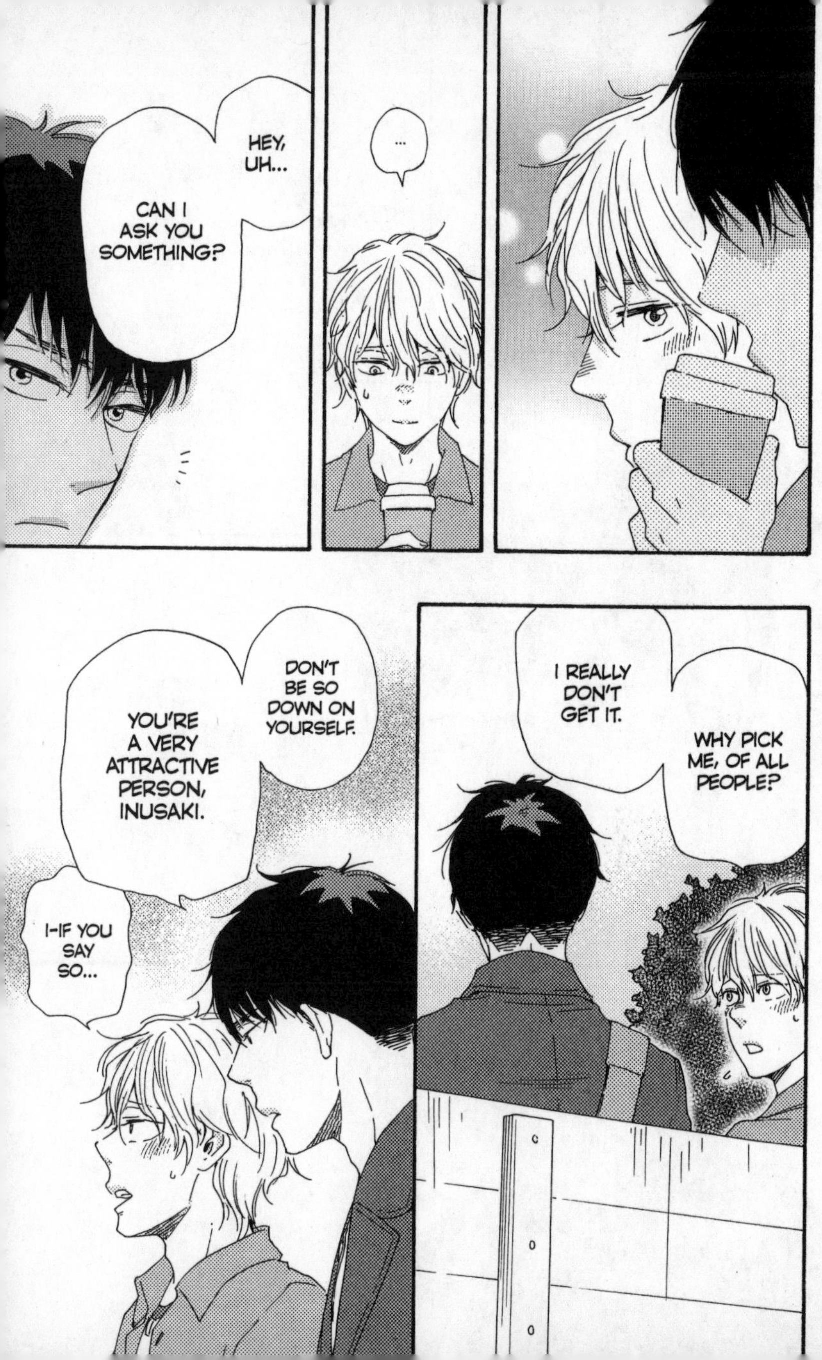
...
HEY, UH...
CAN I ASK YOU SOMETHING?
I REALLY DON'T GET IT.
WHY PICK ME, OF ALL PEOPLE?
DON'T BE SO DOWN ON YOURSELF.
YOU'RE A VERY ATTRACTIVE PERSON, INUSAKI.
I-IF YOU SAY SO...

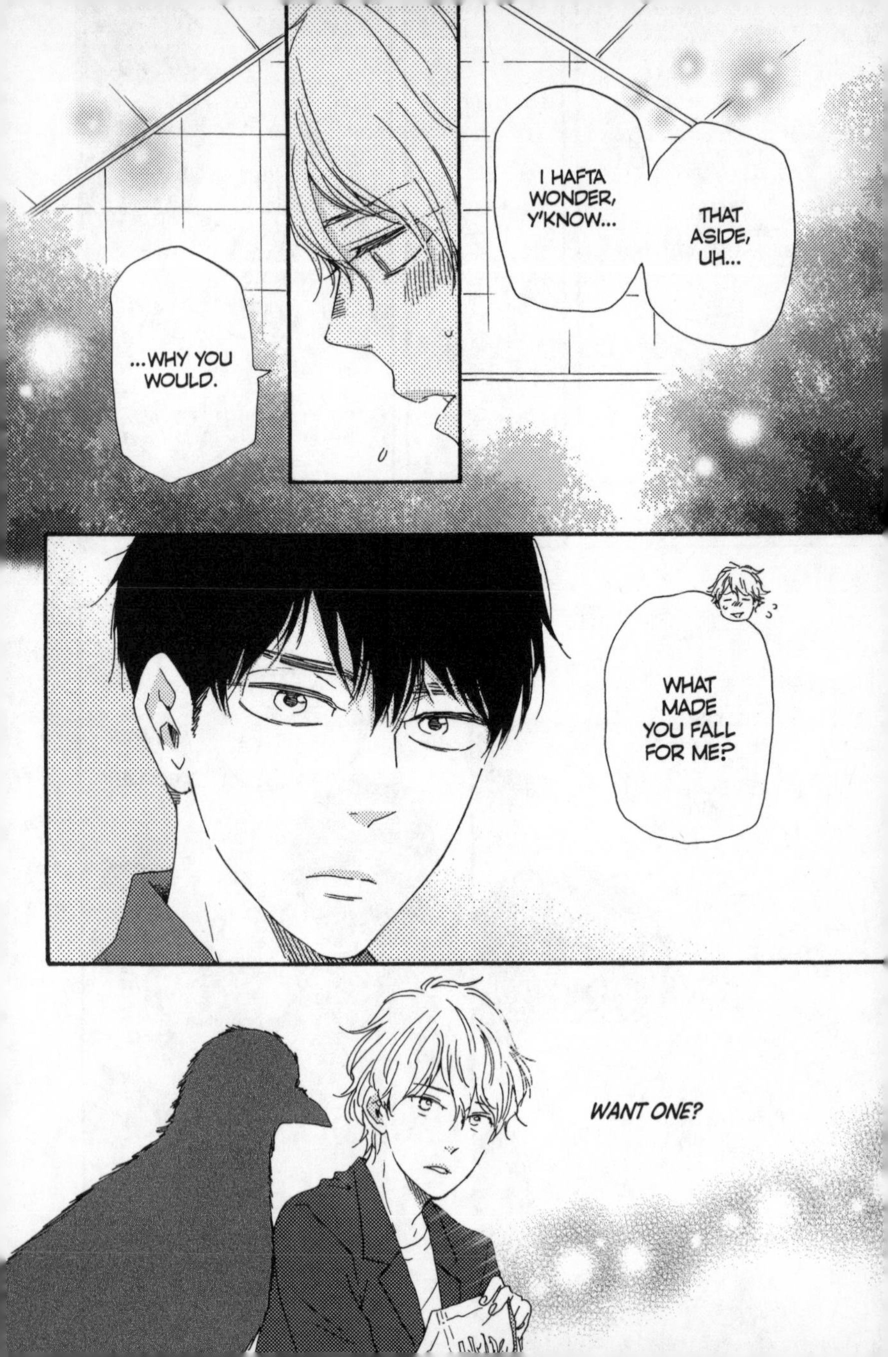
THAT ASIDE, UH...
I HAFTA WONDER, Y'KNOW...
...WHY YOU WOULD.
WHAT MADE YOU FALL FOR ME?
WANT ONE?

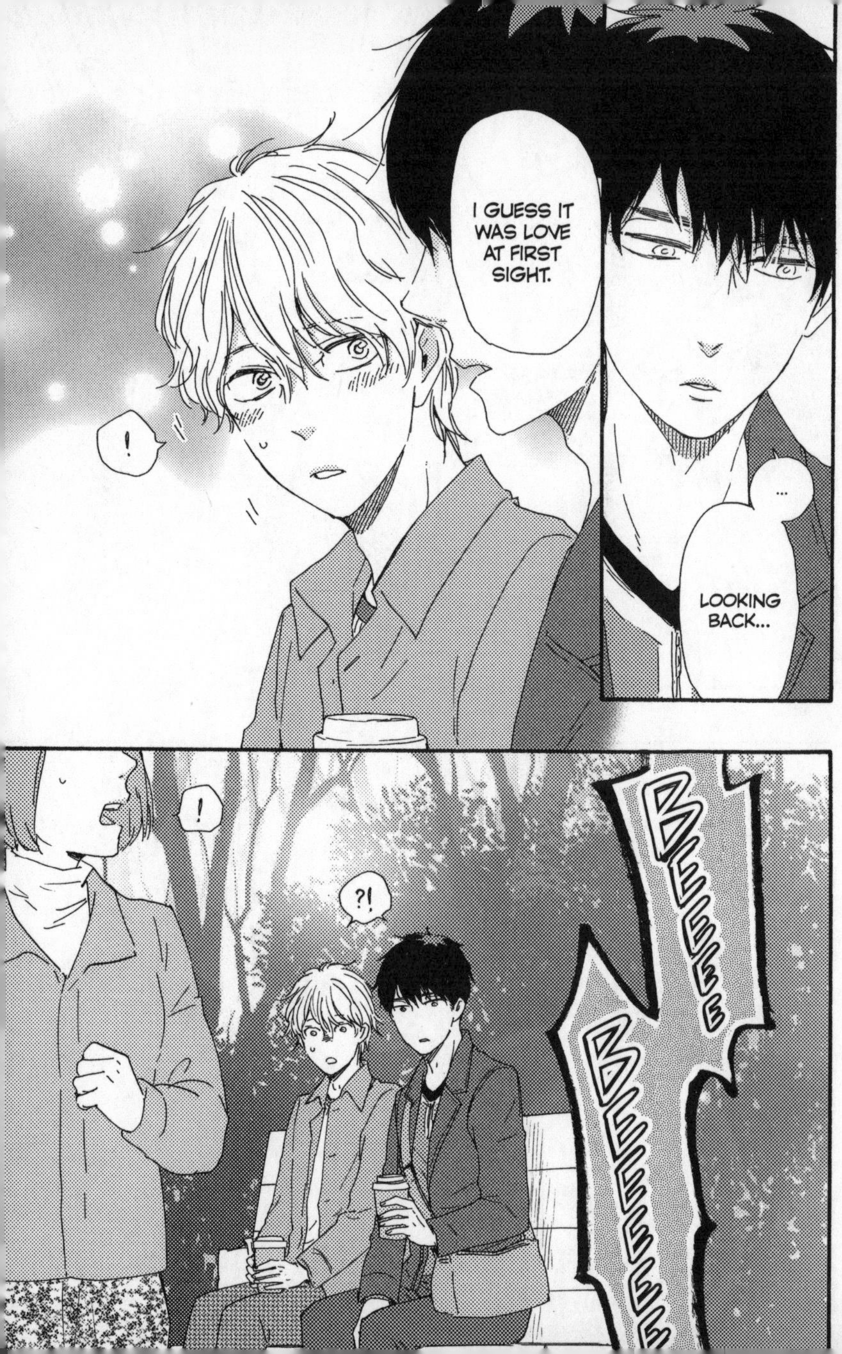
...
LOOKING BACK...
I GUESS IT WAS LOVE AT FIRST SIGHT.
!
BEEEEEE
BEEEEEEEE
!
?!

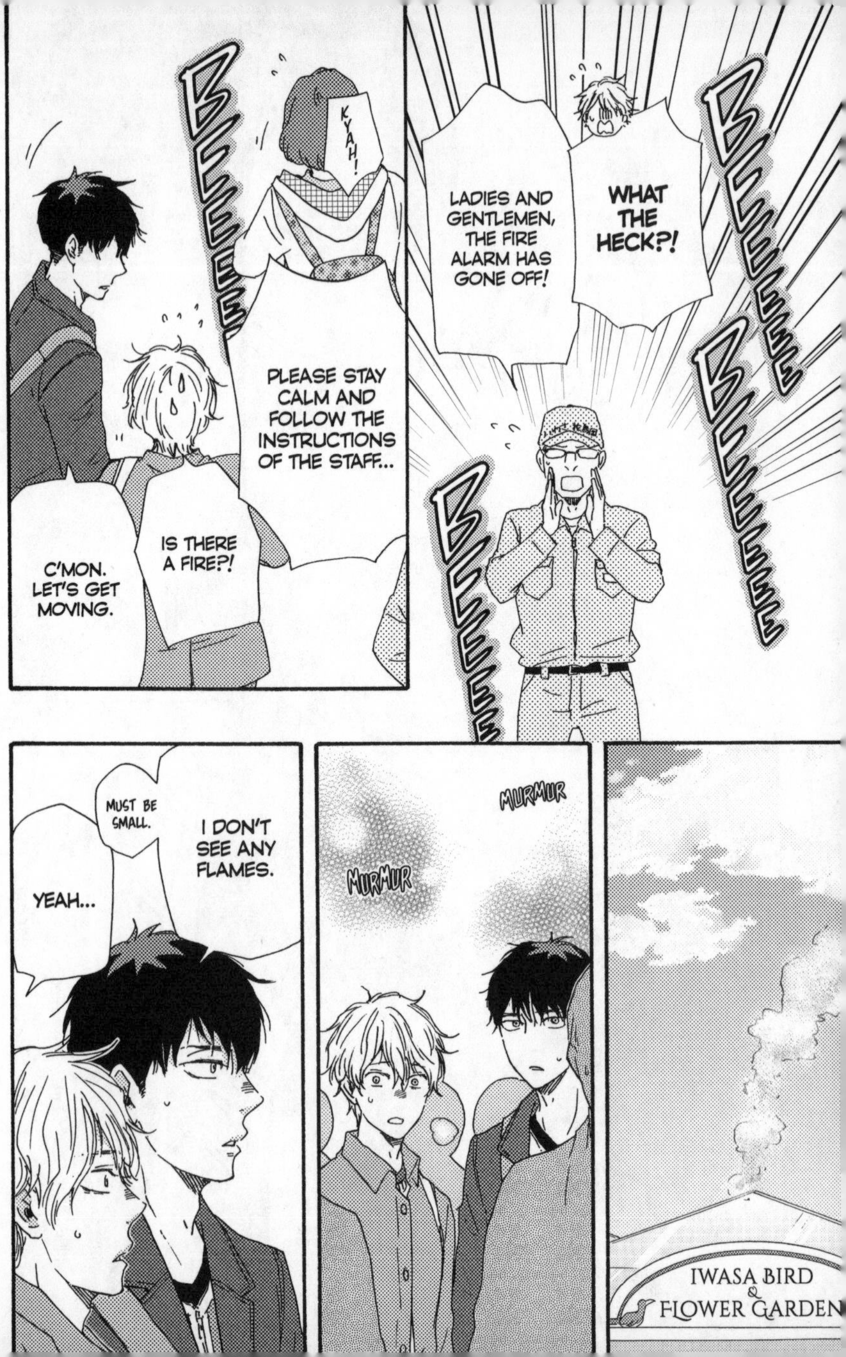
WHAT THE HECK?!
LADIES AND GENTLEMEN, THE FIRE ALARM HAS GONE OFF!
KYAH!
PLEASE STAY CALM AND FOLLOW THE INSTRUCTIONS OF THE STAFF...
IS THERE A FIRE?!
C'MON. LET'S GET MOVING.
IWASA BIRD & FLOWER GARDEN
MURMUR
MURMUR
I DON'T SEE ANY FLAMES.
MUST BE SMALL.
YEAH...

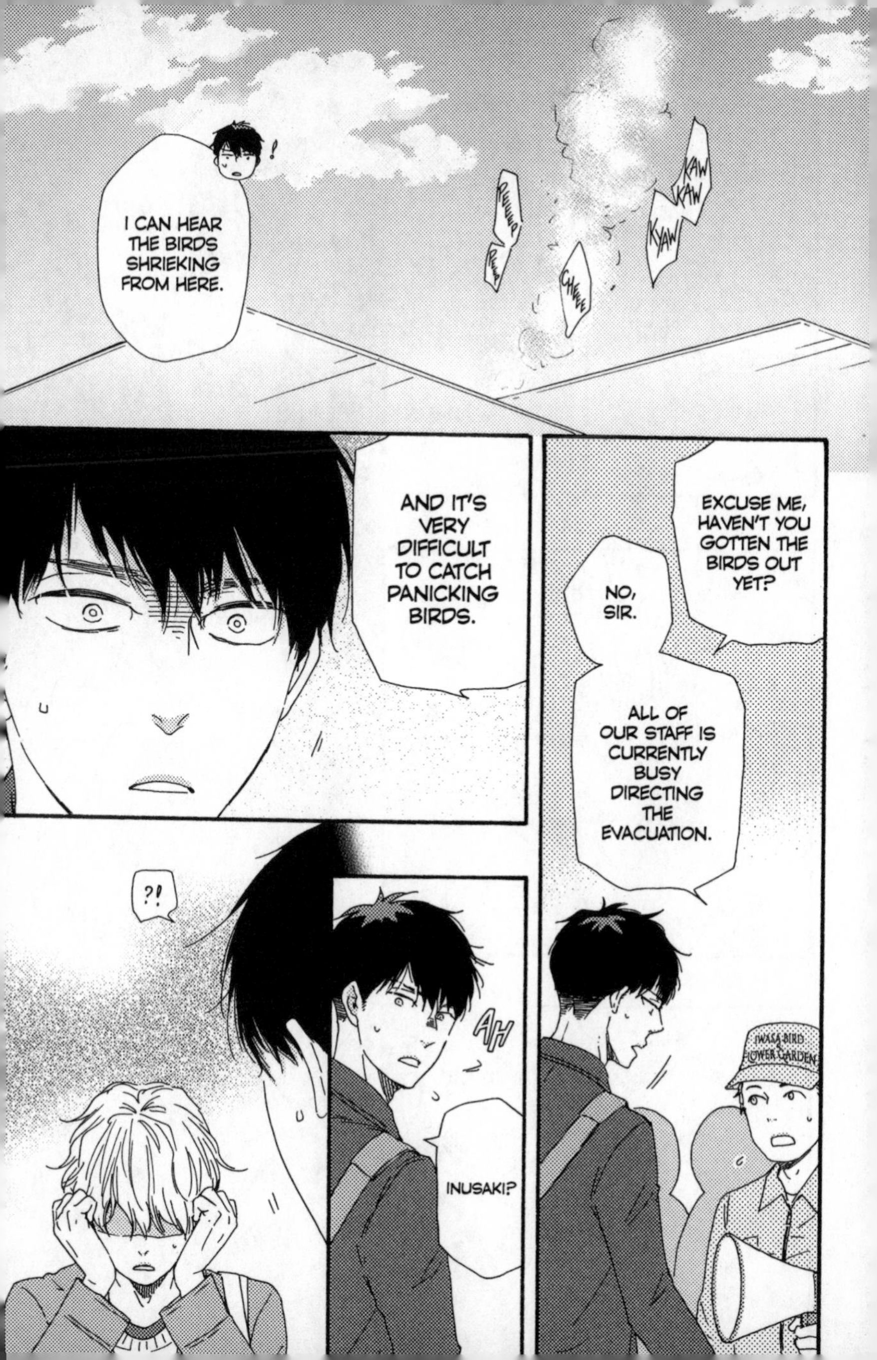
KAW
KAW
KYAW
CHEEEE
!
I CAN HEAR THE BIRDS SHRIEKING FROM HERE.
EXCUSE ME, HAVEN'T YOU GOTTEN THE BIRDS OUT YET?
NO, SIR.
ALL OF OUR STAFF IS CURRENTLY BUSY DIRECTING THE EVACUATION.
AND IT'S VERY DIFFICULT TO CATCH PANICKING BIRDS.
IWASA BIRD
LOWER GARDEN
AH
INUSAKI?
?!

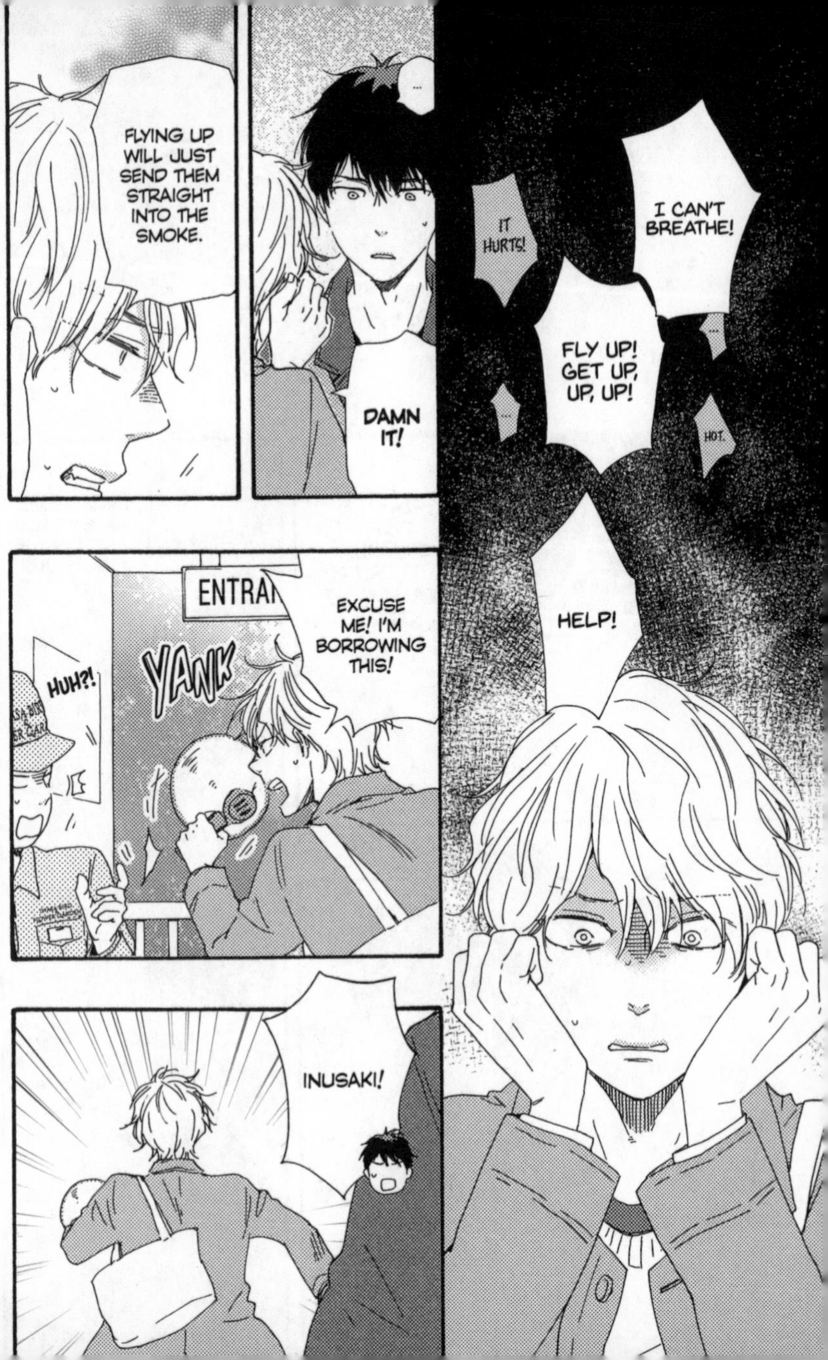
I CAN'T BREATHE!
IT HURTS!
...
FLY UP! GET UP, UP, UP!
...
HOT.
HELP!
...
DAMN IT!
FLYING UP WILL JUST SEND THEM STRAIGHT INTO THE SMOKE.
ENTRAN
EXCUSE ME! I'M BORROWING THIS!
YANK
HUH?!
INUSAKI!

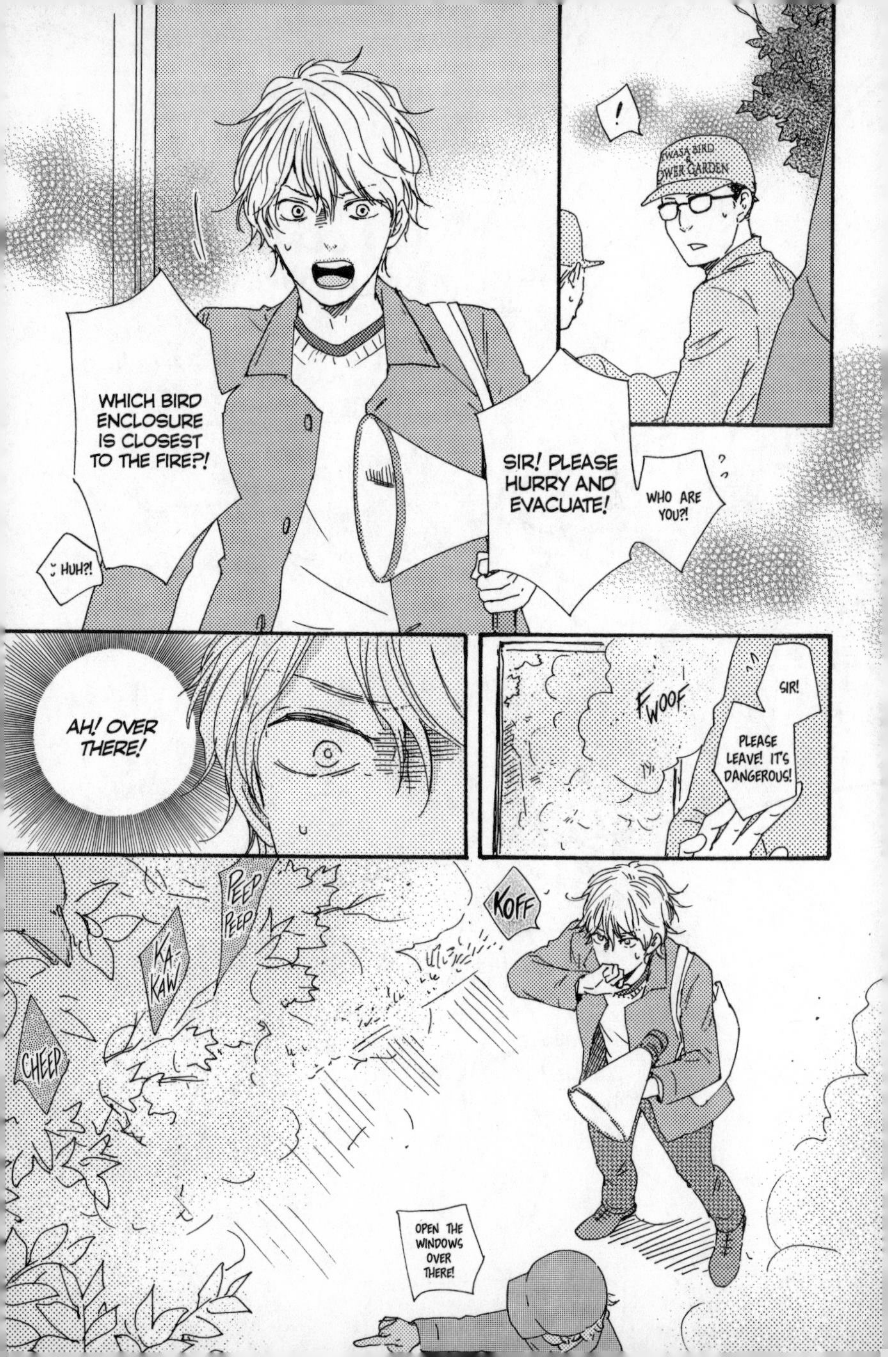
!
SIR! PLEASE HURRY AND EVACUATE!
WHO ARE YOU?!
WHICH BIRD ENCLOSURE IS CLOSEST TO THE FIRE?!
HUH?!
FWOOF
SIR!
PLEASE LEAVE! IT'S DANGEROUS!
AH! OVER THERE!
KOFF
PEEP PEEP
KA-KAW
CHEEP
OPEN THE WINDOWS OVER THERE!

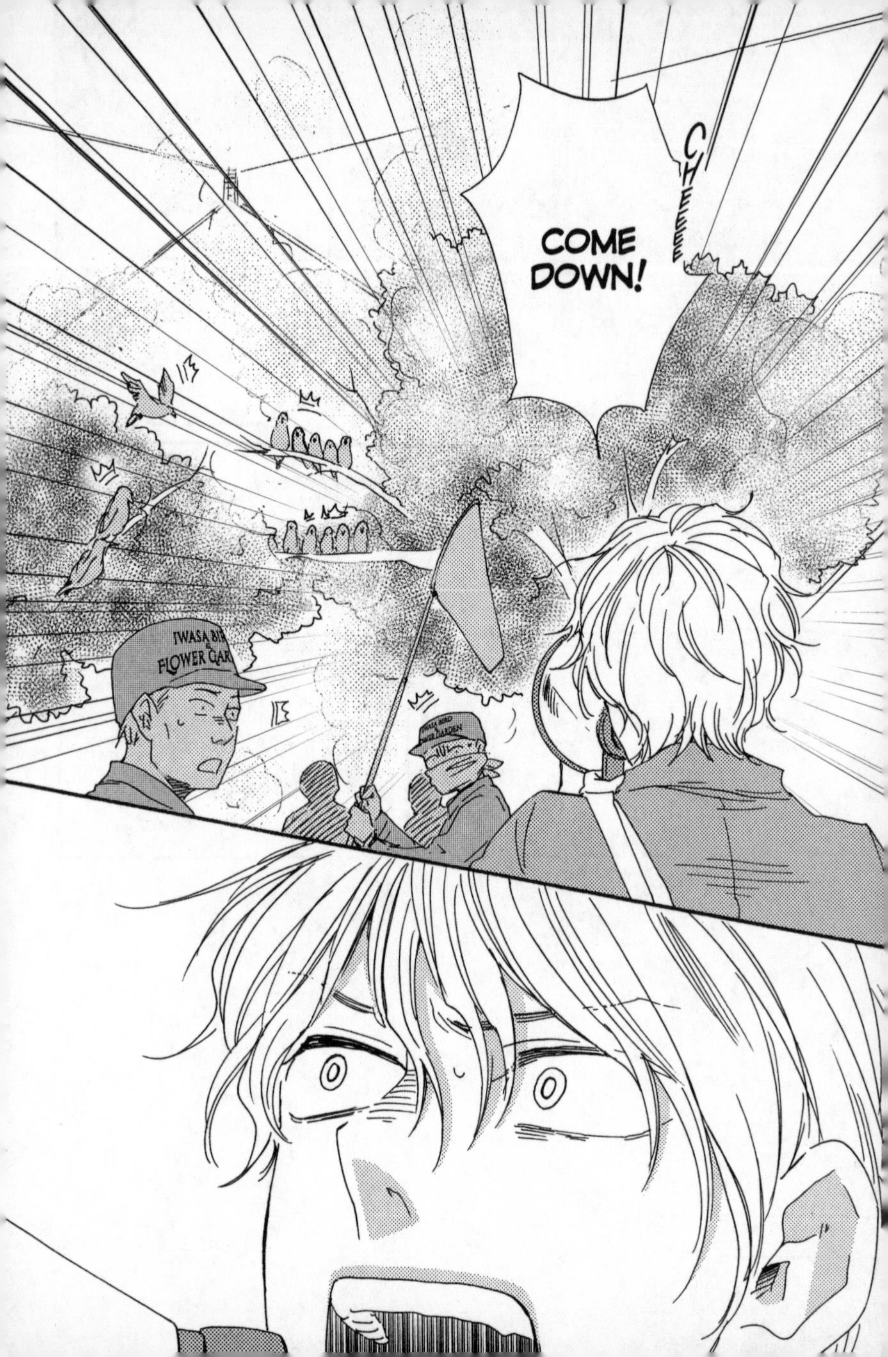
COME DOWN!
CHEEEE

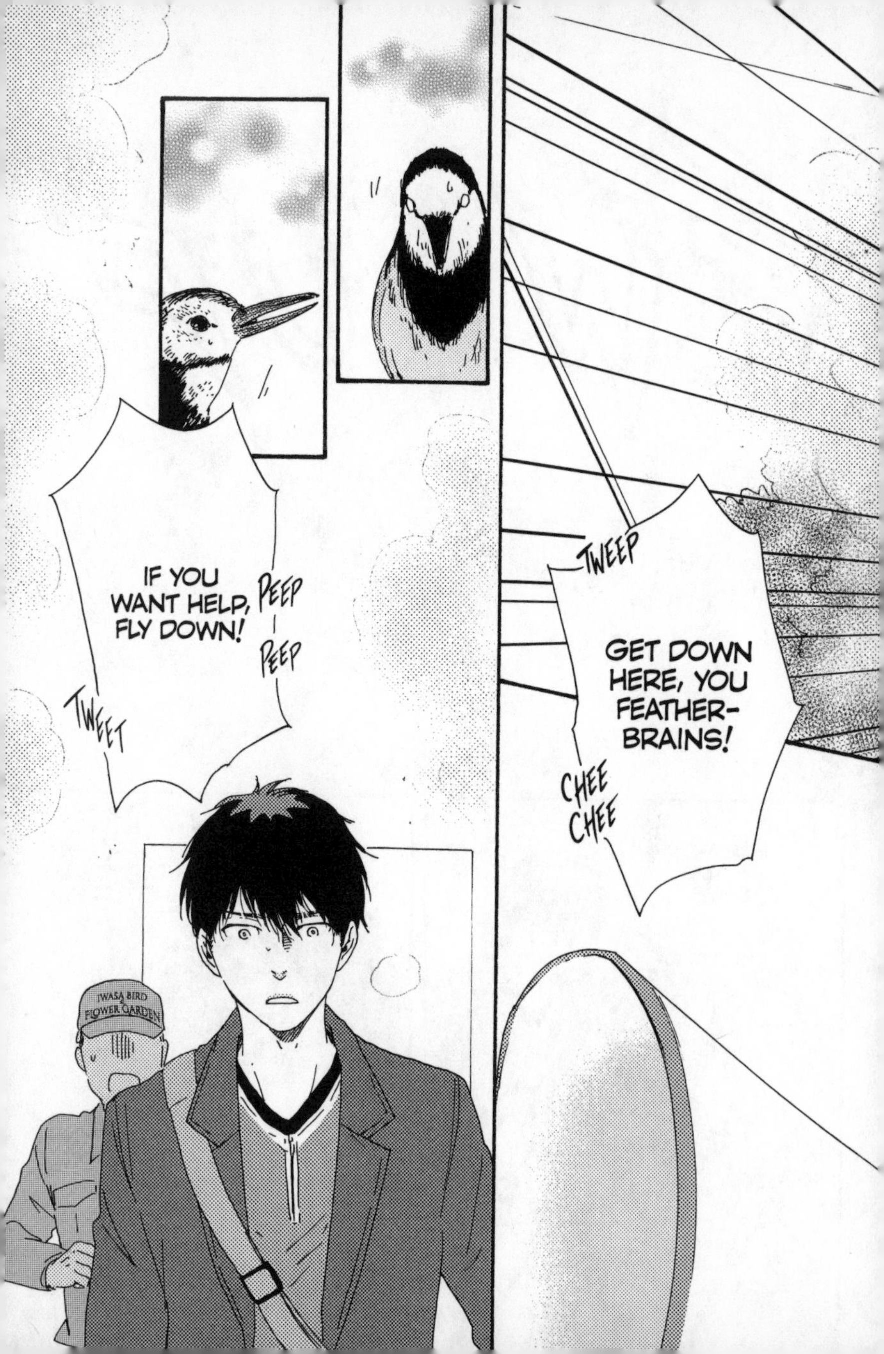
TWEEP
GET DOWN HERE, YOU FEATHER-BRAINS!
CHEE CHEE
IF YOU WANT HELP, FLY DOWN!
PEEP
PEEP
TWEET
IWASA BIRD & FLOWER GARDEN

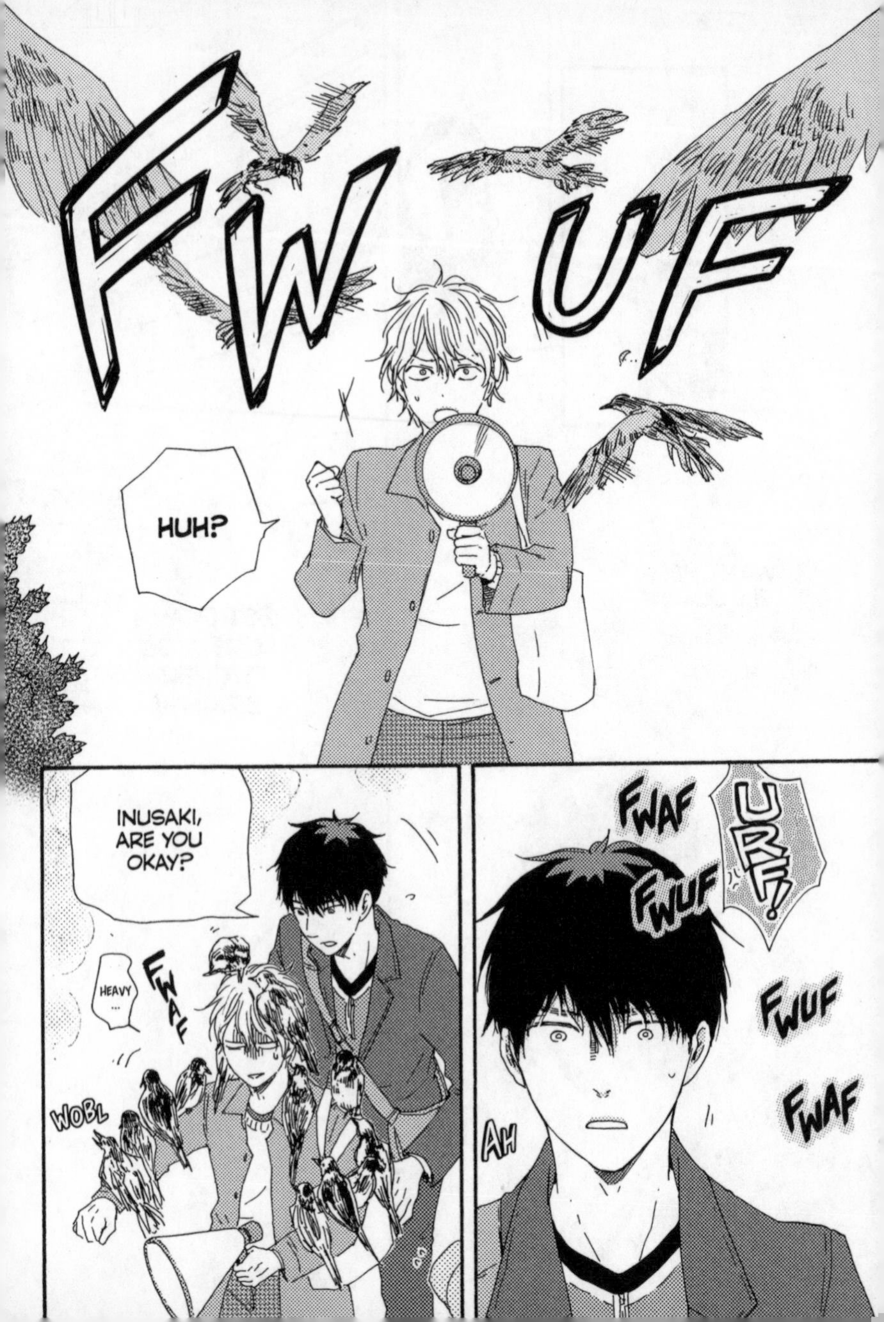
FWUF
HUH?
FWAF
URFF!
FWUF
FWUF
FWAF
AH
INUSAKI, ARE YOU OKAY?
FWAF
HEAVY...
WOBL

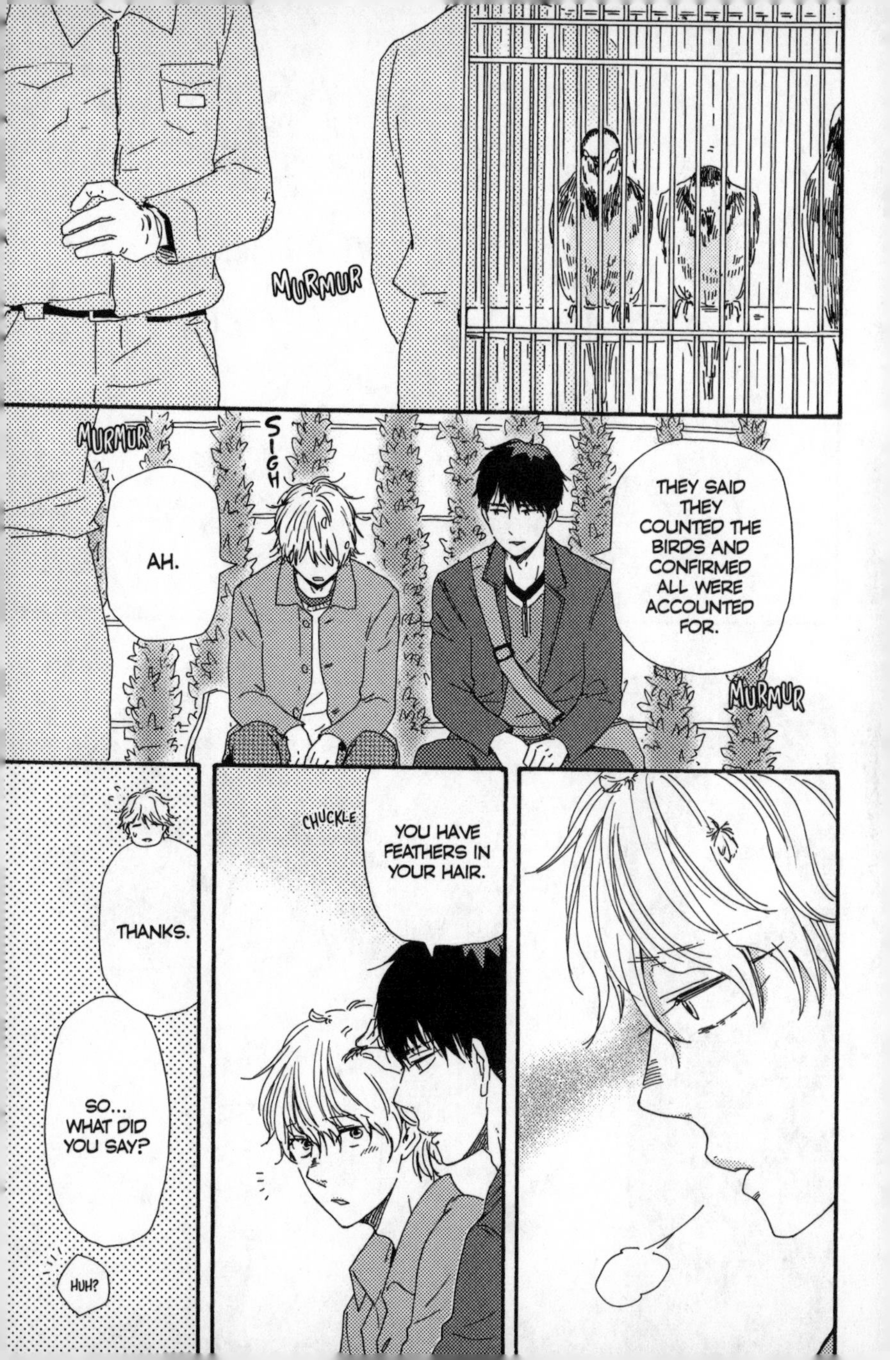
MURMUR
THEY SAID THEY COUNTED THE BIRDS AND CONFIRMED ALL WERE ACCOUNTED FOR.
SIGH
MURMUR
AH.
MURMUR
YOU HAVE FEATHERS IN YOUR HAIR.
CHUCKLE
THANKS.
SO... WHAT DID YOU SAY?
HUH?

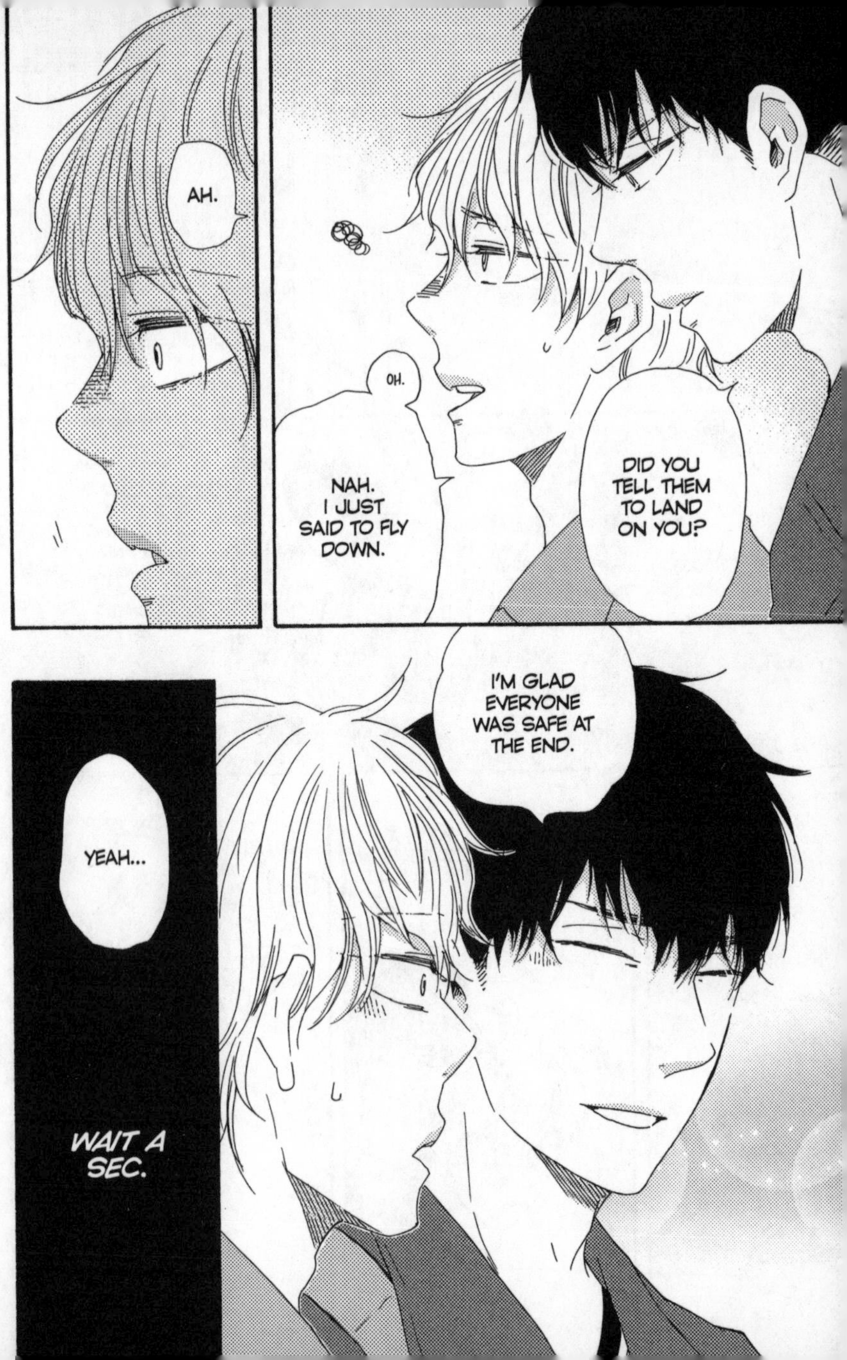
DID YOU TELL THEM TO LAND ON YOU?
NAH. I JUST SAID TO FLY DOWN.
OH.
AH.
I'M GLAD EVERYONE WAS SAFE AT THE END.
YEAH...
WAIT A SEC.

TORITAN
Birds of a Feather
CHAPTER 13

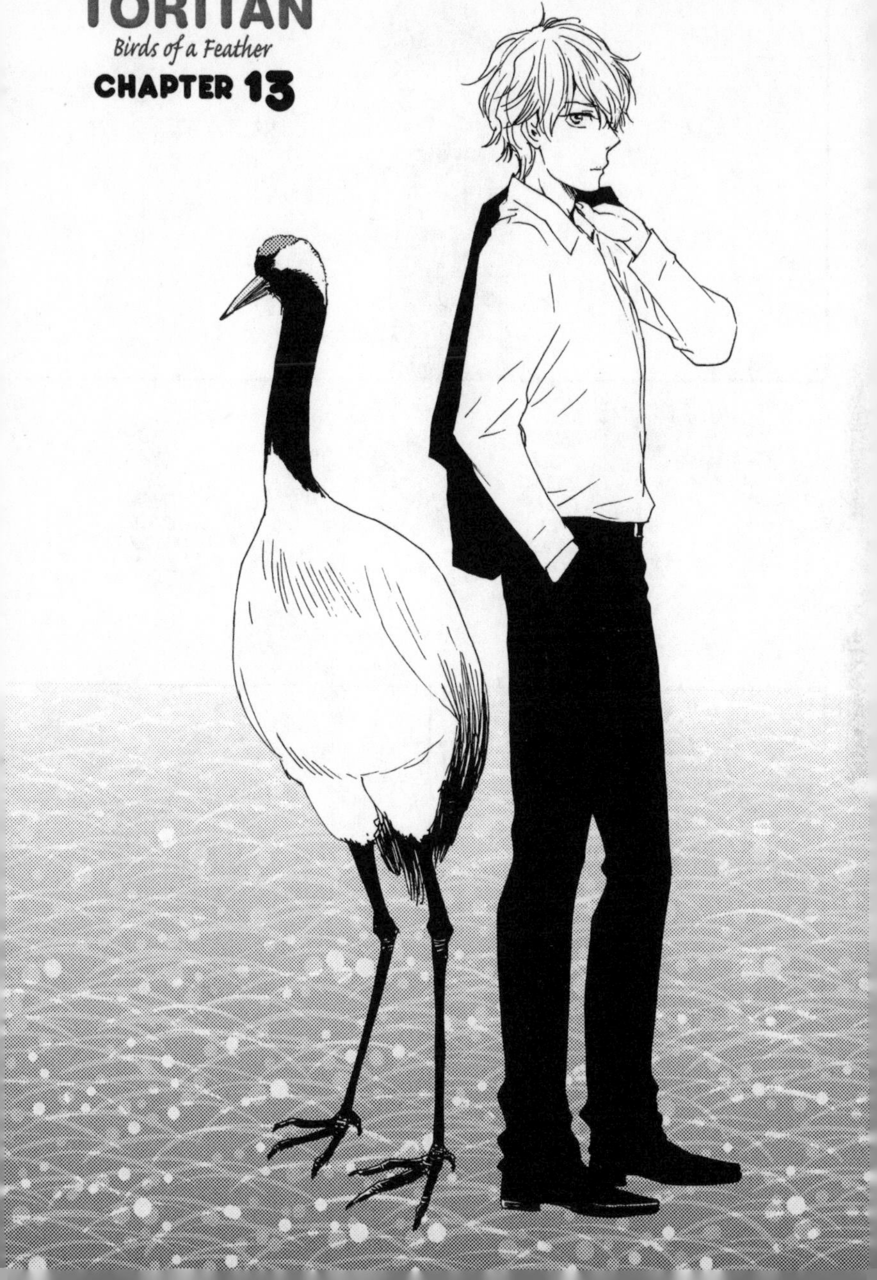

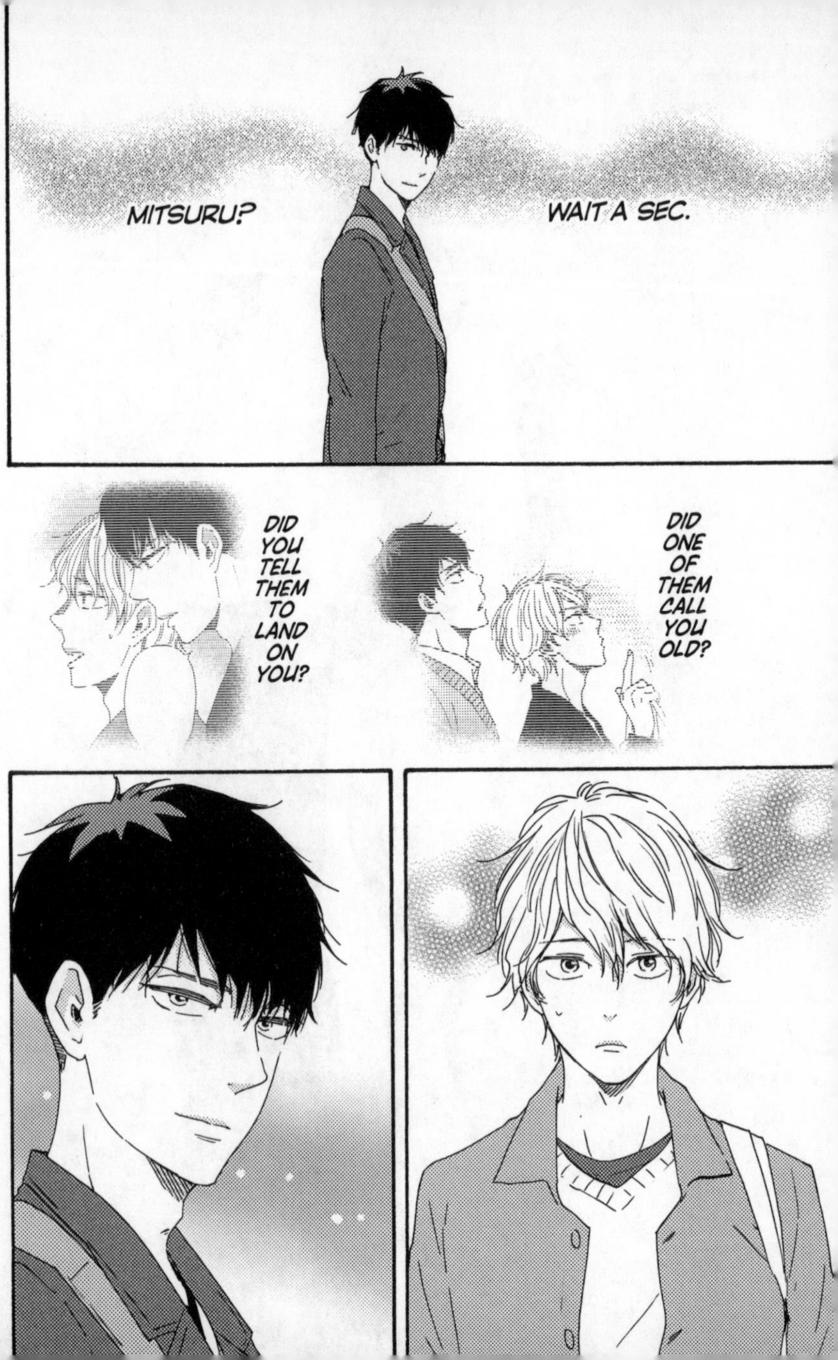
WAIT A SEC.
MITSURU?
DID ONE OF THEM CALL YOU OLD?
DID YOU TELL THEM TO LAND ON YOU?

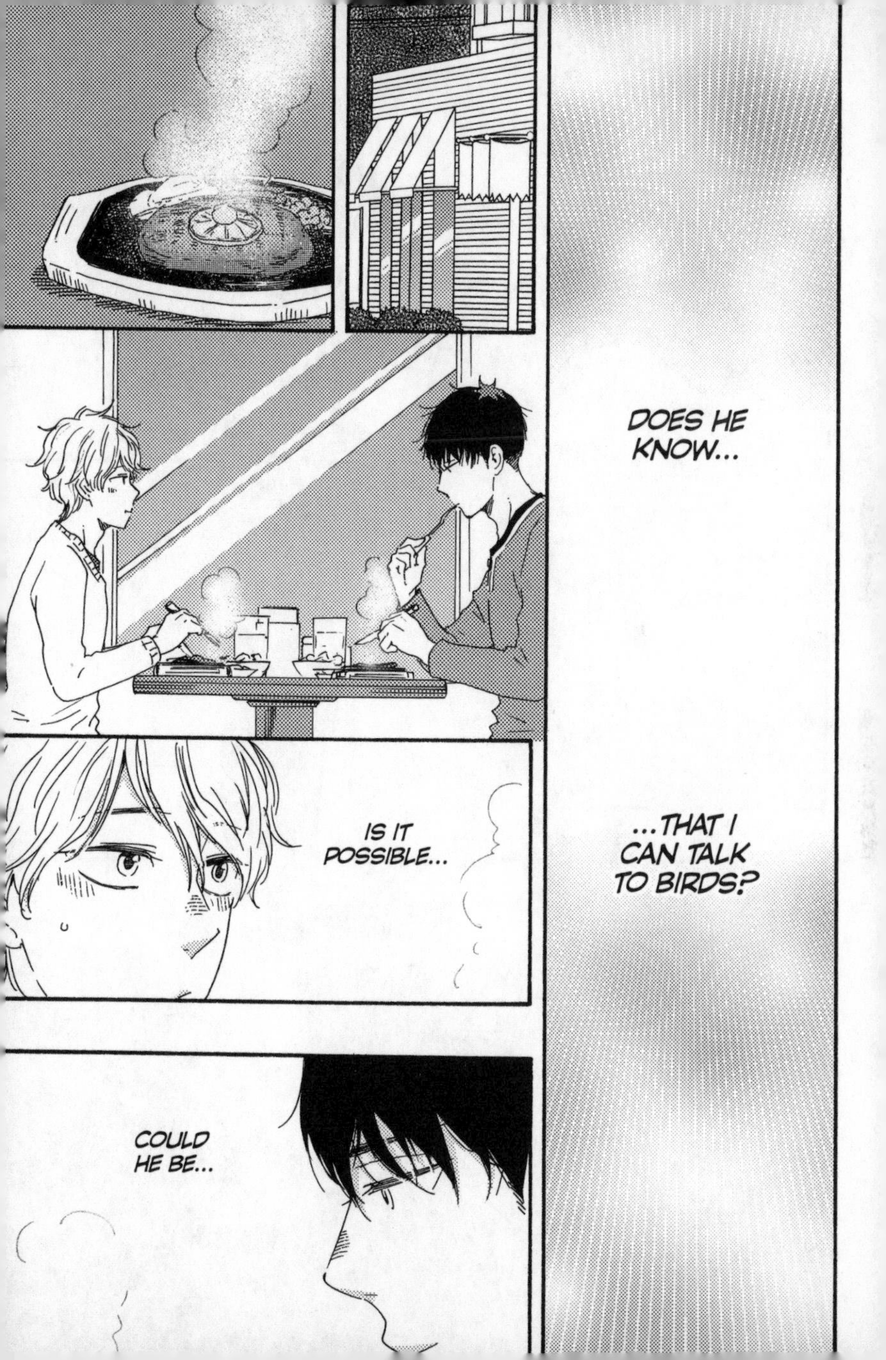

DOES HE KNOW...
...THAT I CAN TALK TO BIRDS?
IS IT POSSIBLE...
COULD HE BE...

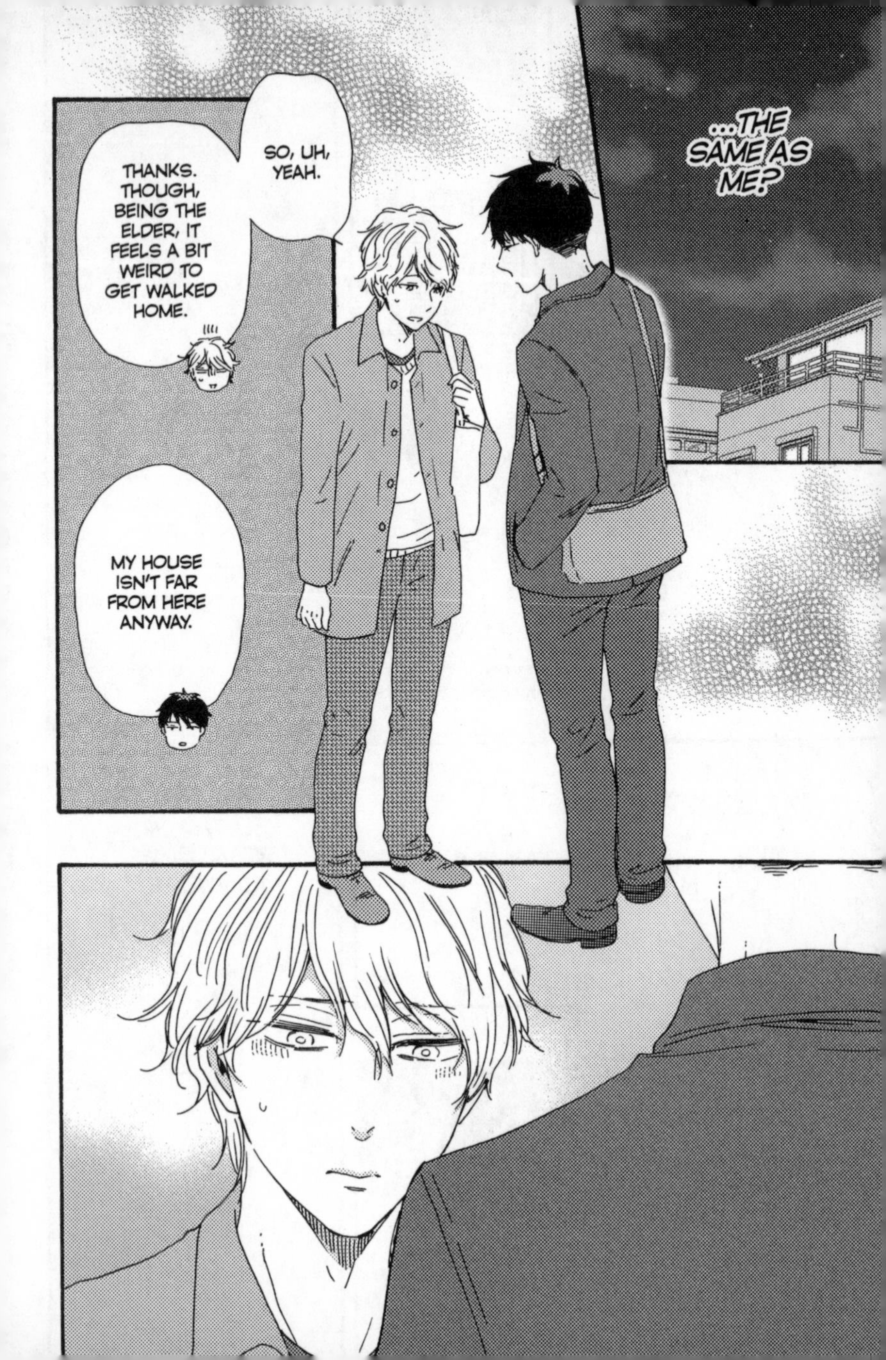
...THE SAME AS ME?
SO, UH, YEAH.
THANKS. THOUGH, BEING THE ELDER, IT FEELS A BIT WEIRD TO GET WALKED HOME.
MY HOUSE ISN'T FAR FROM HERE ANYWAY.

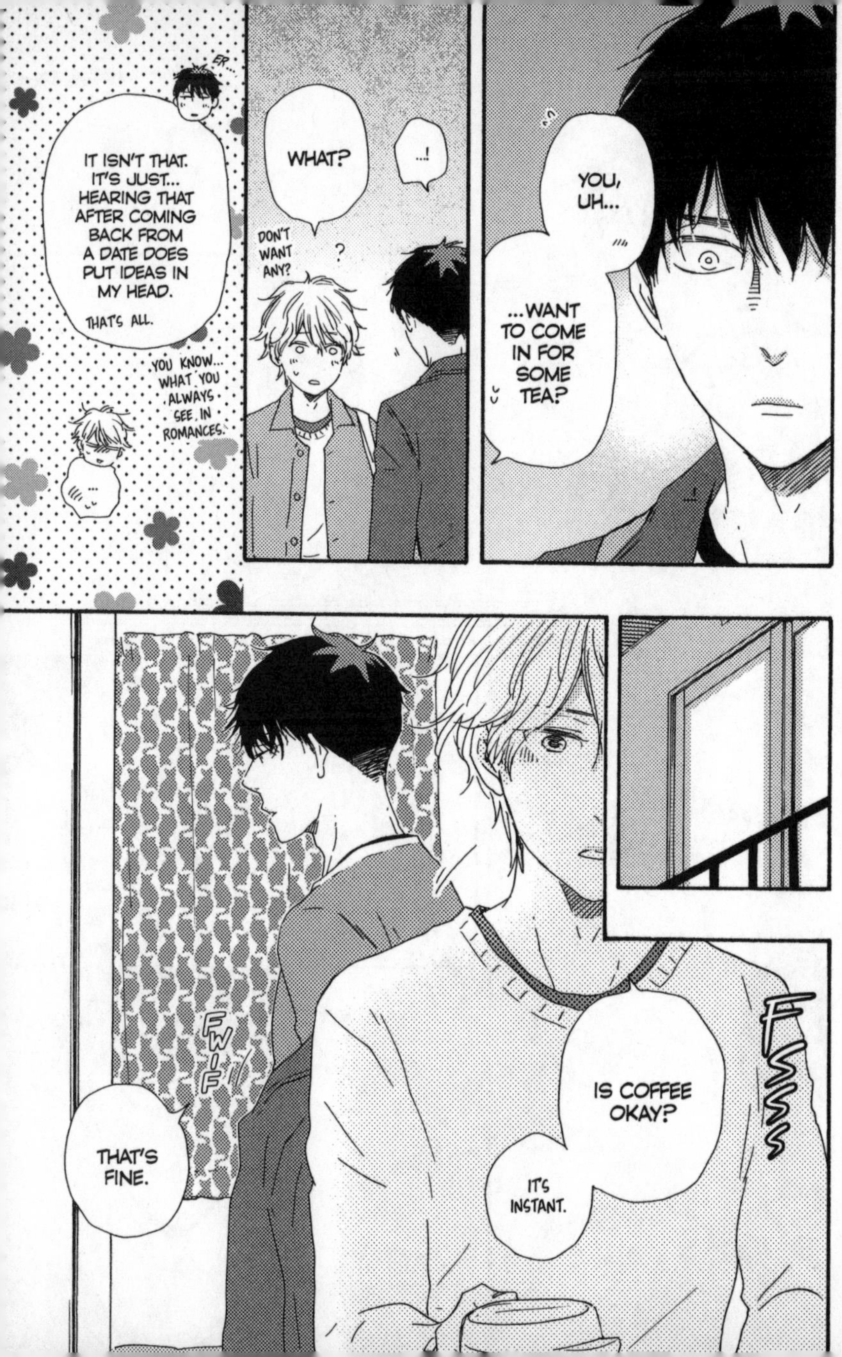
YOU, UH...
...WANT TO COME IN FOR SOME TEA?
...!
WHAT?
DON'T WANT ANY?
?
ER...
IT ISN'T THAT. IT'S JUST... HEARING THAT AFTER COMING BACK FROM A DATE DOES PUT IDEAS IN MY HEAD.
THAT'S ALL.
YOU KNOW... WHAT YOU ALWAYS SEE IN ROMANCES.
...
FSSS
IS COFFEE OKAY?
IT'S INSTANT.
FWIF
THAT'S FINE.

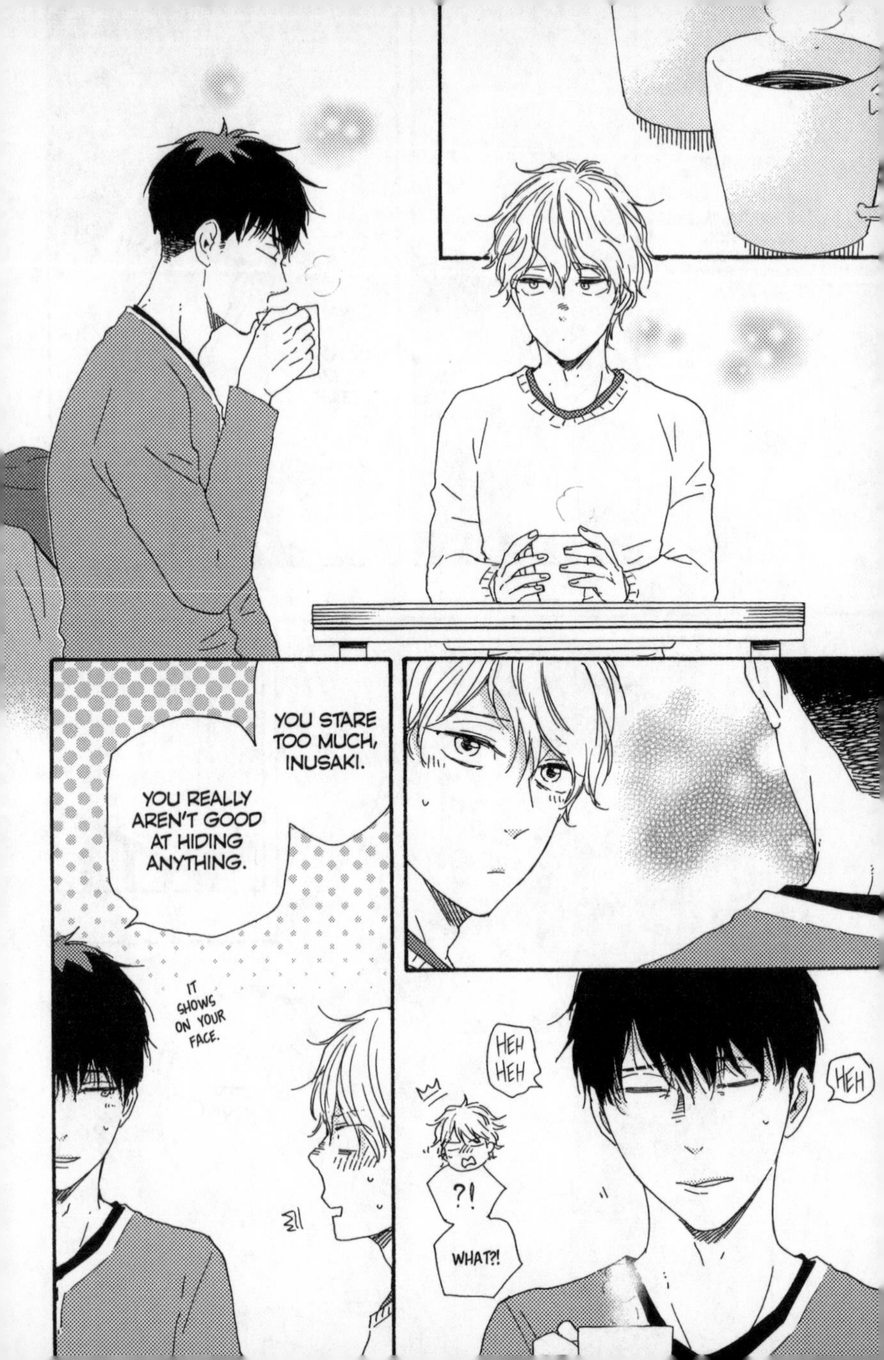
HEH HEH
HEH
?!
WHAT?!
YOU STARE TOO MUCH, INUSAKI.
YOU REALLY AREN'T GOOD AT HIDING ANYTHING.
IT SHOWS ON YOUR FACE.

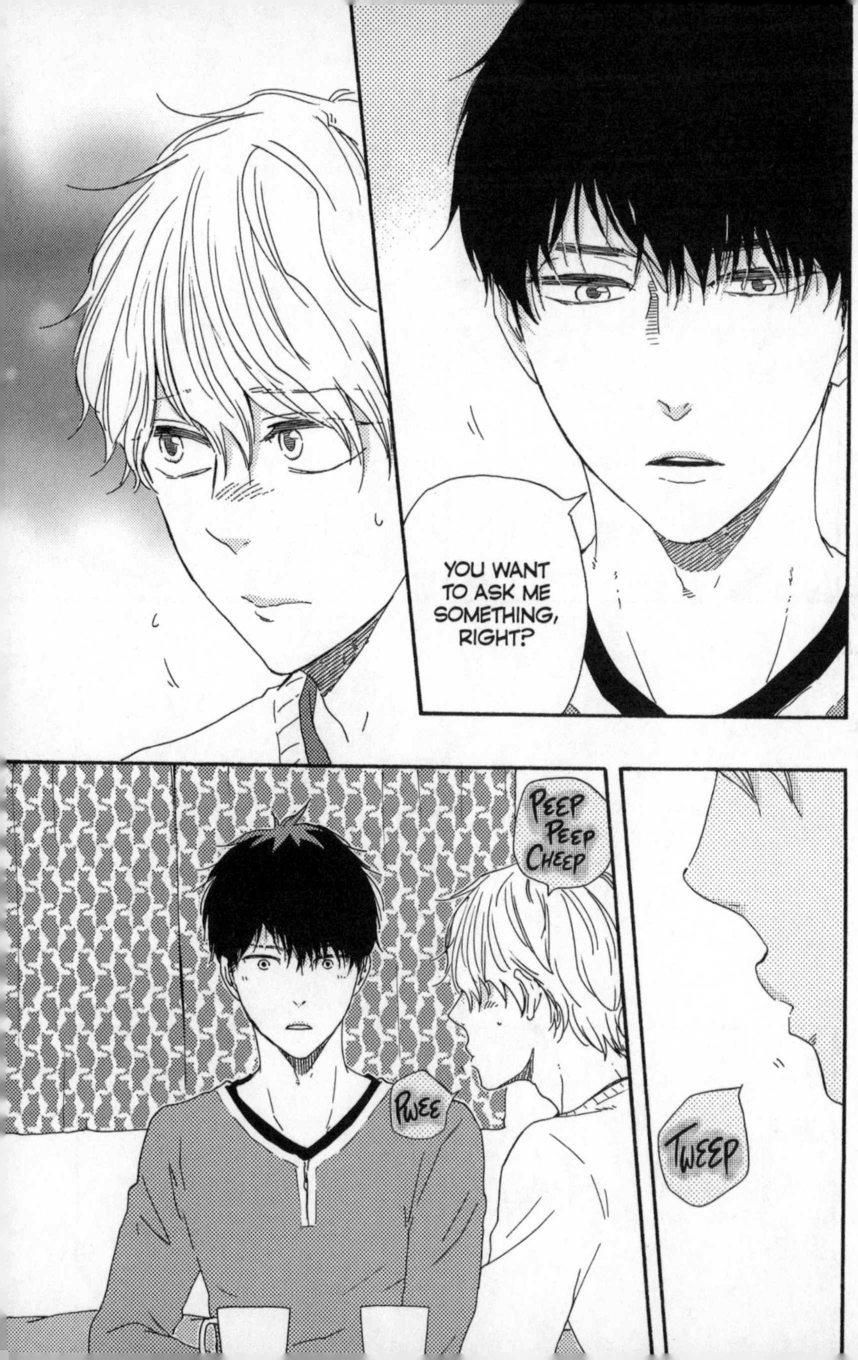
YOU WANT TO ASK ME SOMETHING, RIGHT?
TWEEP
PEEP PEEP CHEEP
PWEE

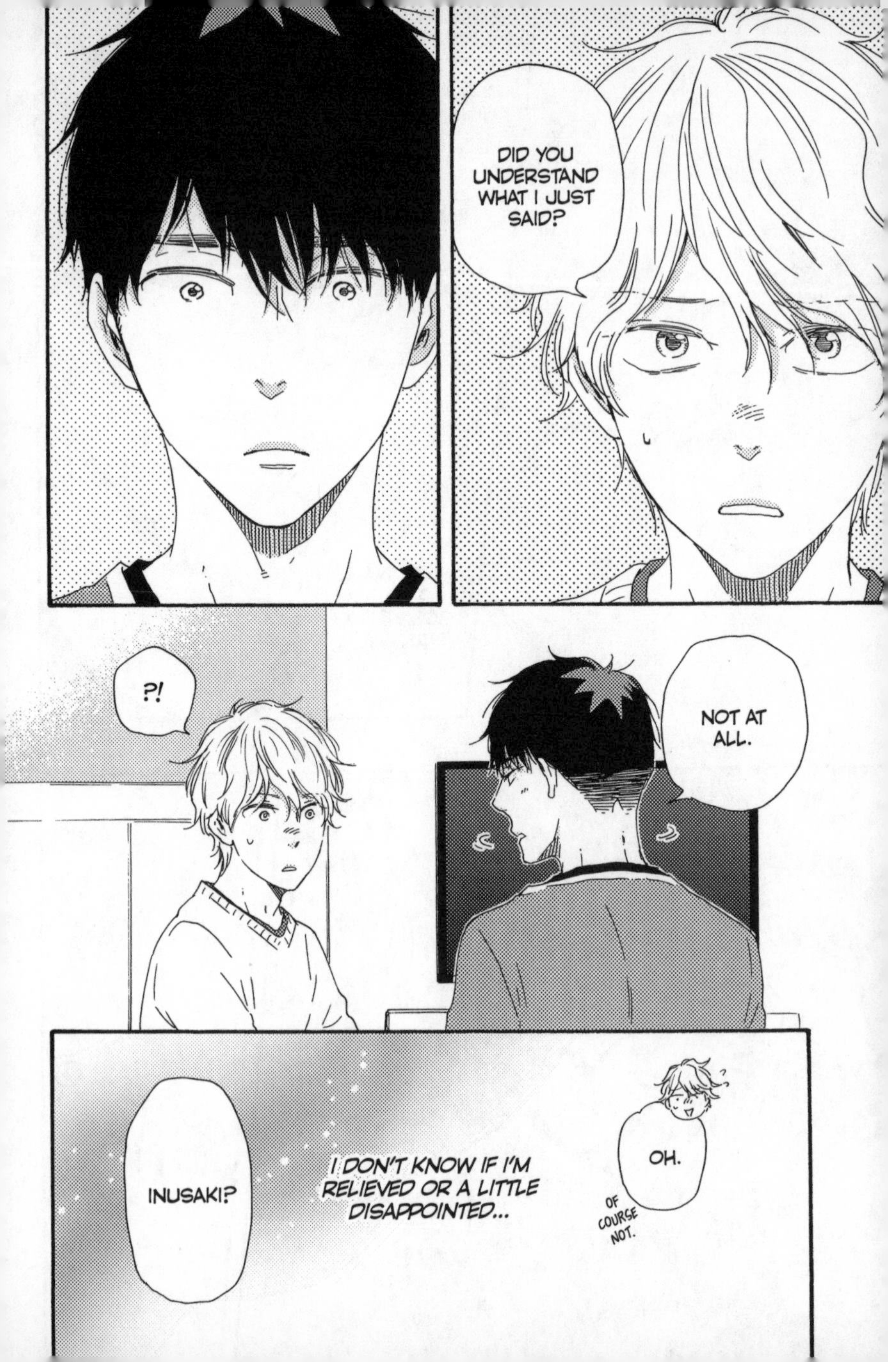
DID YOU UNDERSTAND WHAT I JUST SAID?
NOT AT ALL.
?!
OH.
OF COURSE NOT.
I DON'T KNOW IF I'M RELIEVED OR A LITTLE DISAPPOINTED...
INUSAKI?

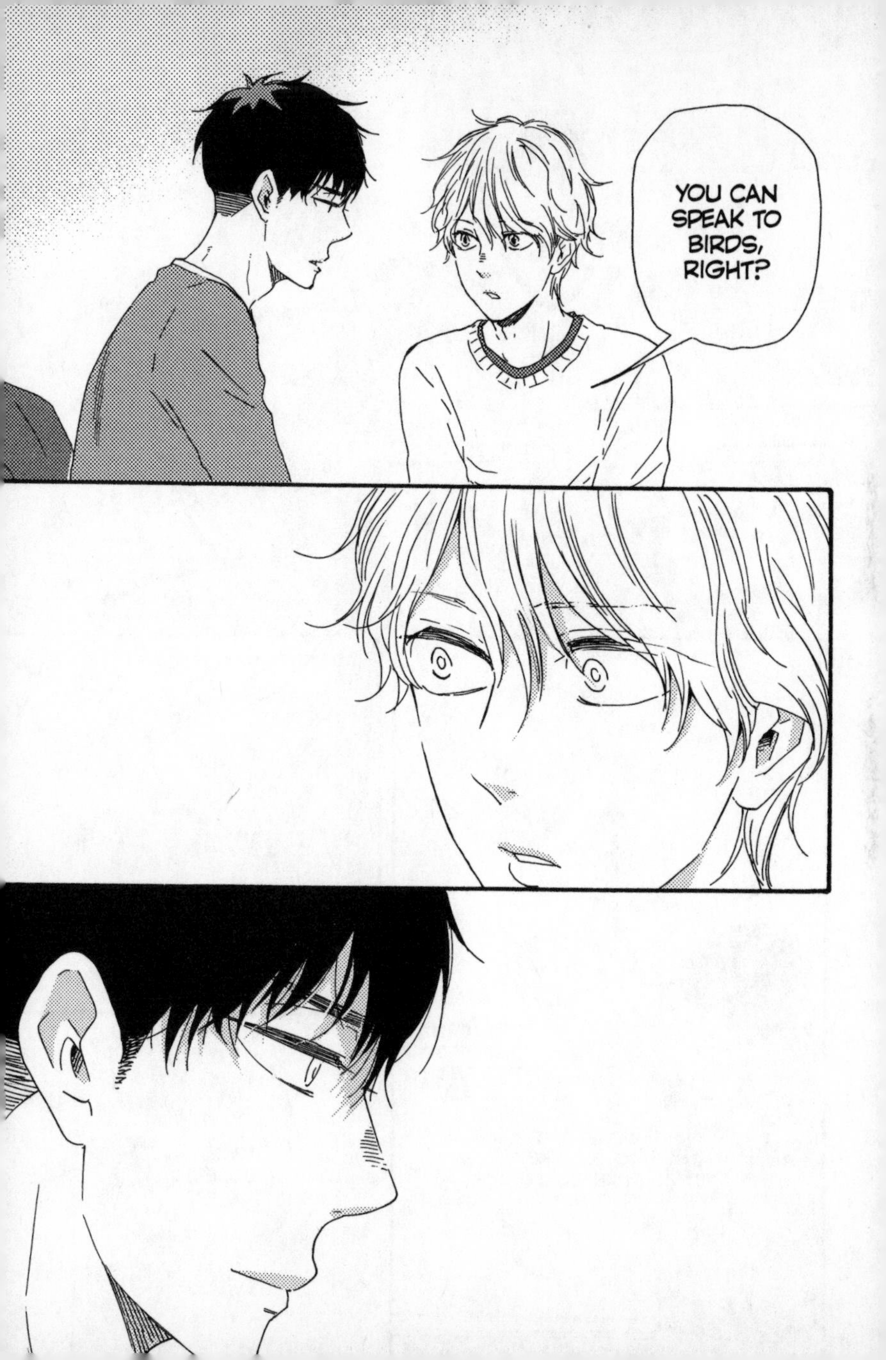
YOU CAN SPEAK TO BIRDS, RIGHT?

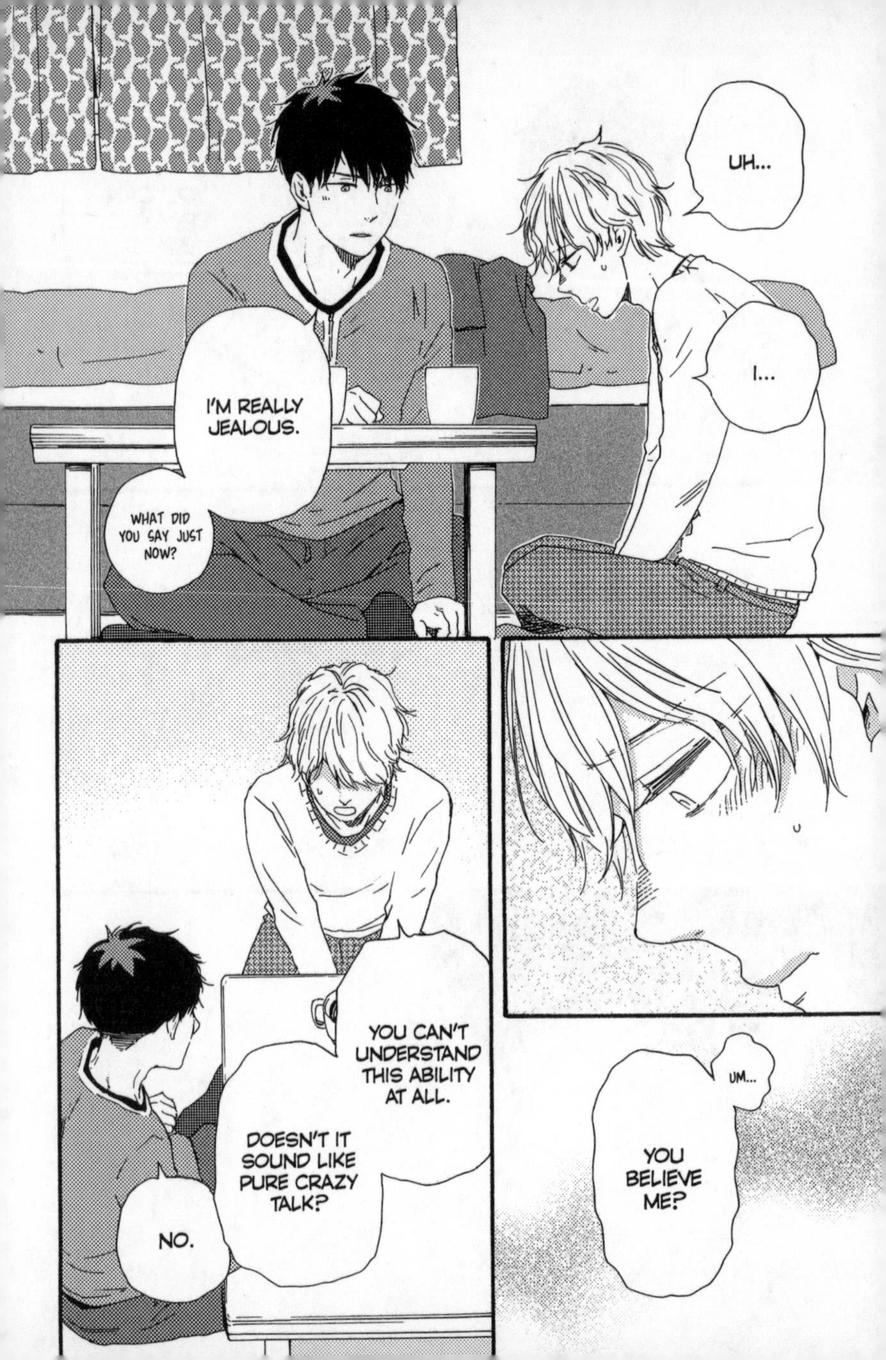
UH...
I...
I'M REALLY JEALOUS.
WHAT DID YOU SAY JUST NOW?
UM...
YOU BELIEVE ME?
YOU CAN'T UNDERSTAND THIS ABILITY AT ALL.
DOESN'T IT SOUND LIKE PURE CRAZY TALK?
NO.

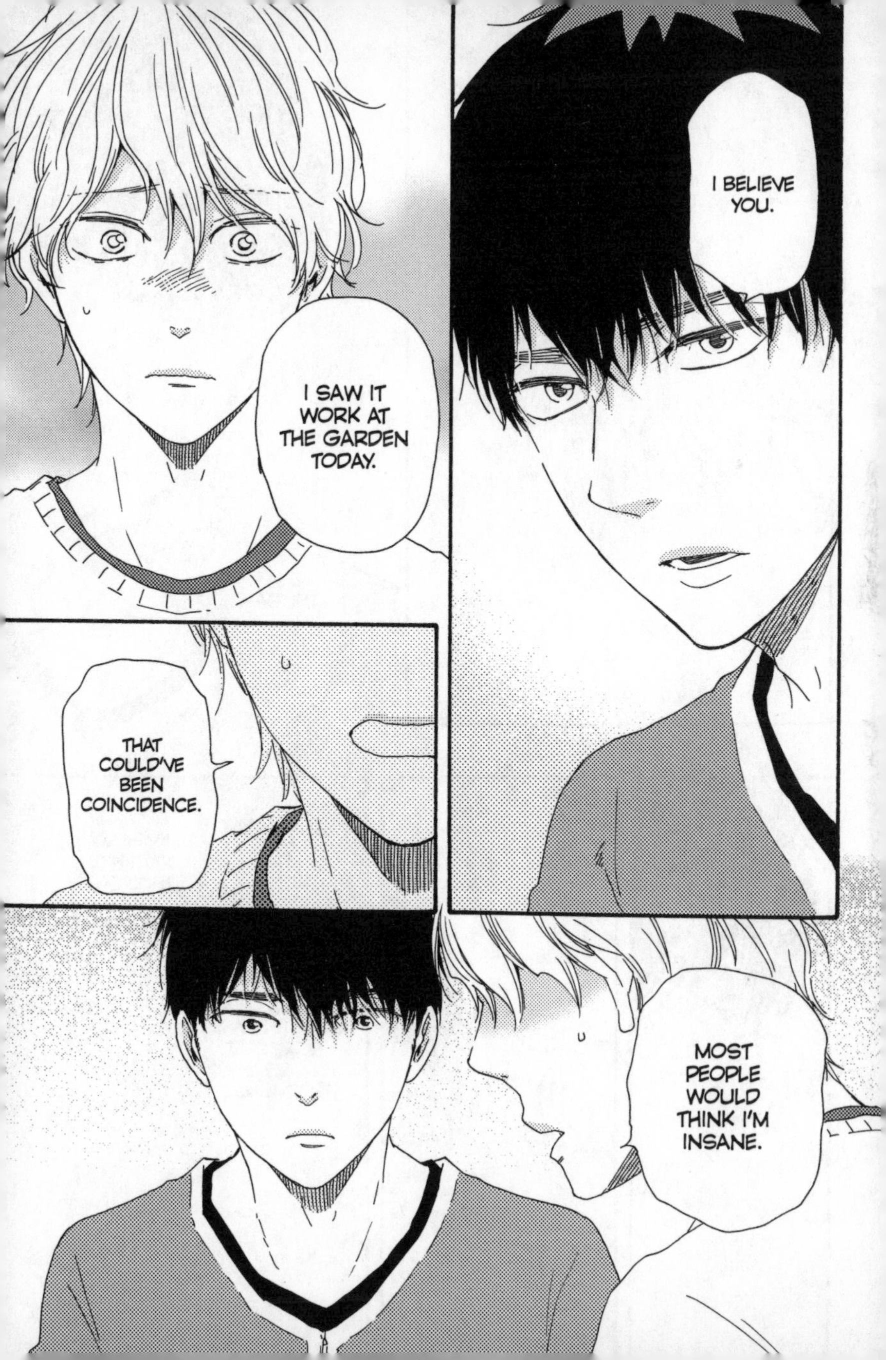
I BELIEVE YOU.
I SAW IT WORK AT THE GARDEN TODAY.
THAT COULD'VE BEEN COINCIDENCE.
MOST PEOPLE WOULD THINK I'M INSANE.

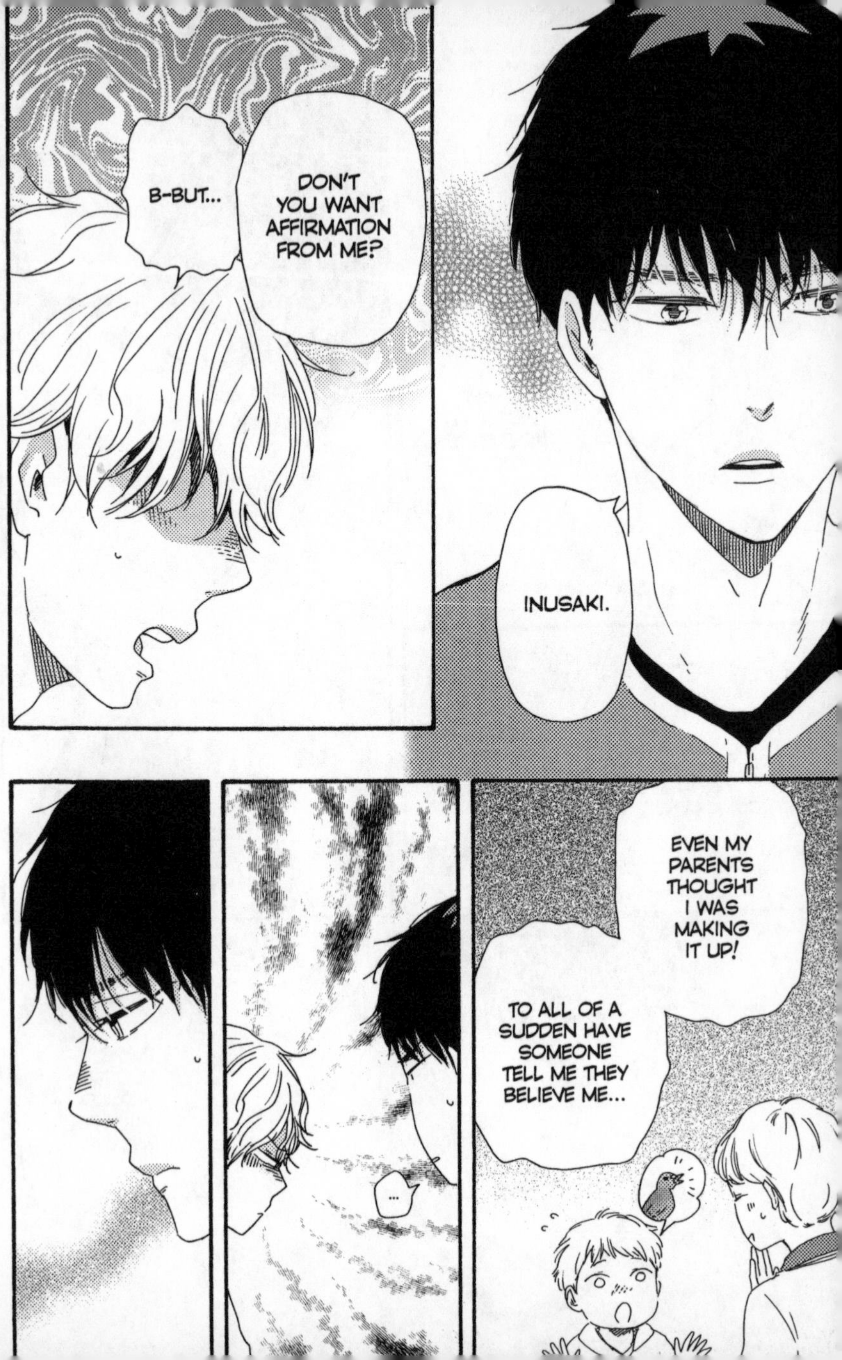
INUSAKI.
DON'T YOU WANT AFFIRMATION FROM ME?
B-BUT...
EVEN MY PARENTS THOUGHT I WAS MAKING IT UP!
TO ALL OF A SUDDEN HAVE SOMEONE TELL ME THEY BELIEVE ME...
...

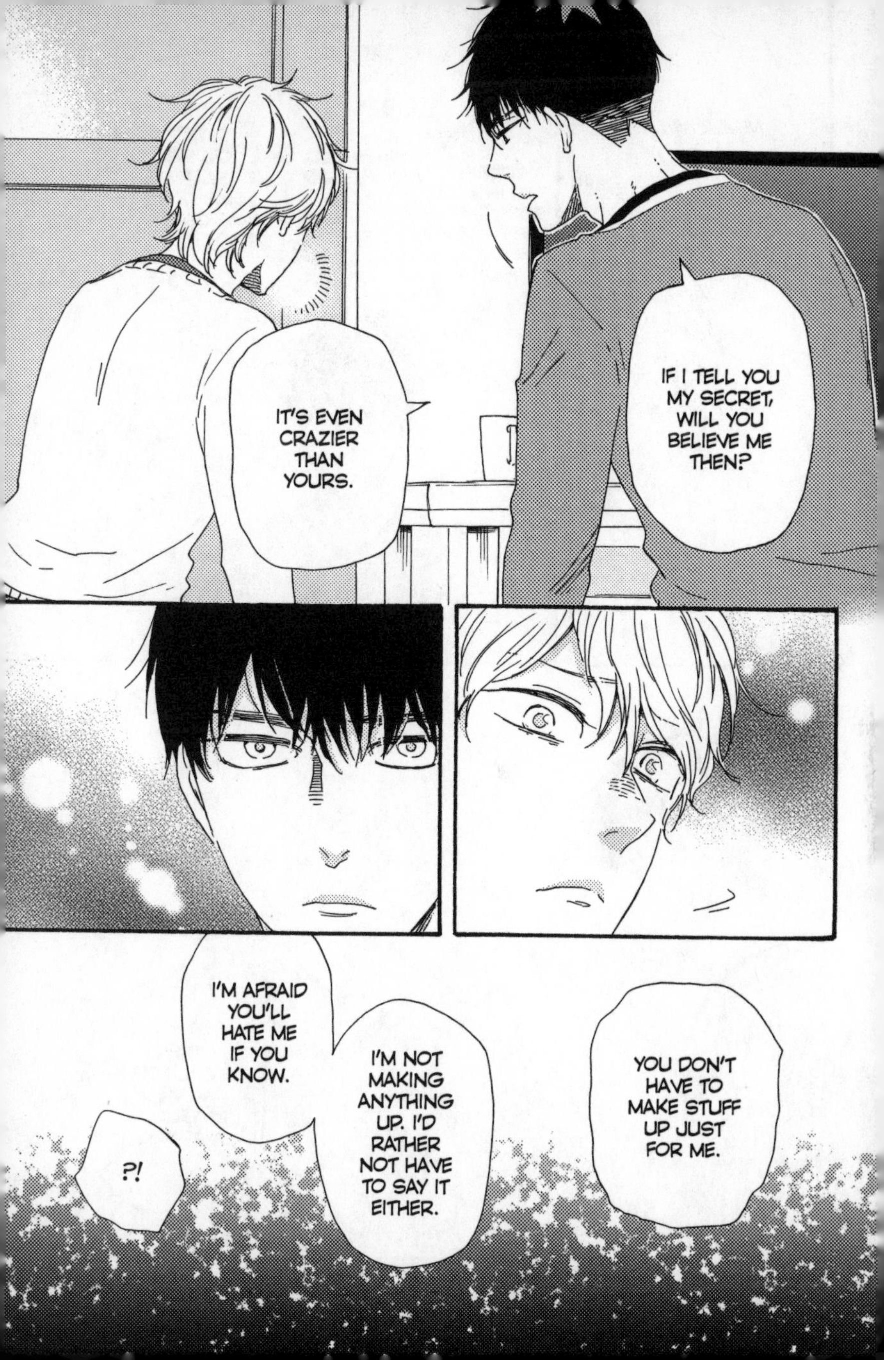

IF I TELL YOU MY SECRET, WILL YOU BELIEVE ME THEN?
IT'S EVEN CRAZIER THAN YOURS.
YOU DON'T HAVE TO MAKE STUFF UP JUST FOR ME.
I'M NOT MAKING ANYTHING UP. I'D RATHER NOT HAVE TO SAY IT EITHER.
I'M AFRAID YOU'LL HATE ME IF YOU KNOW.
?!

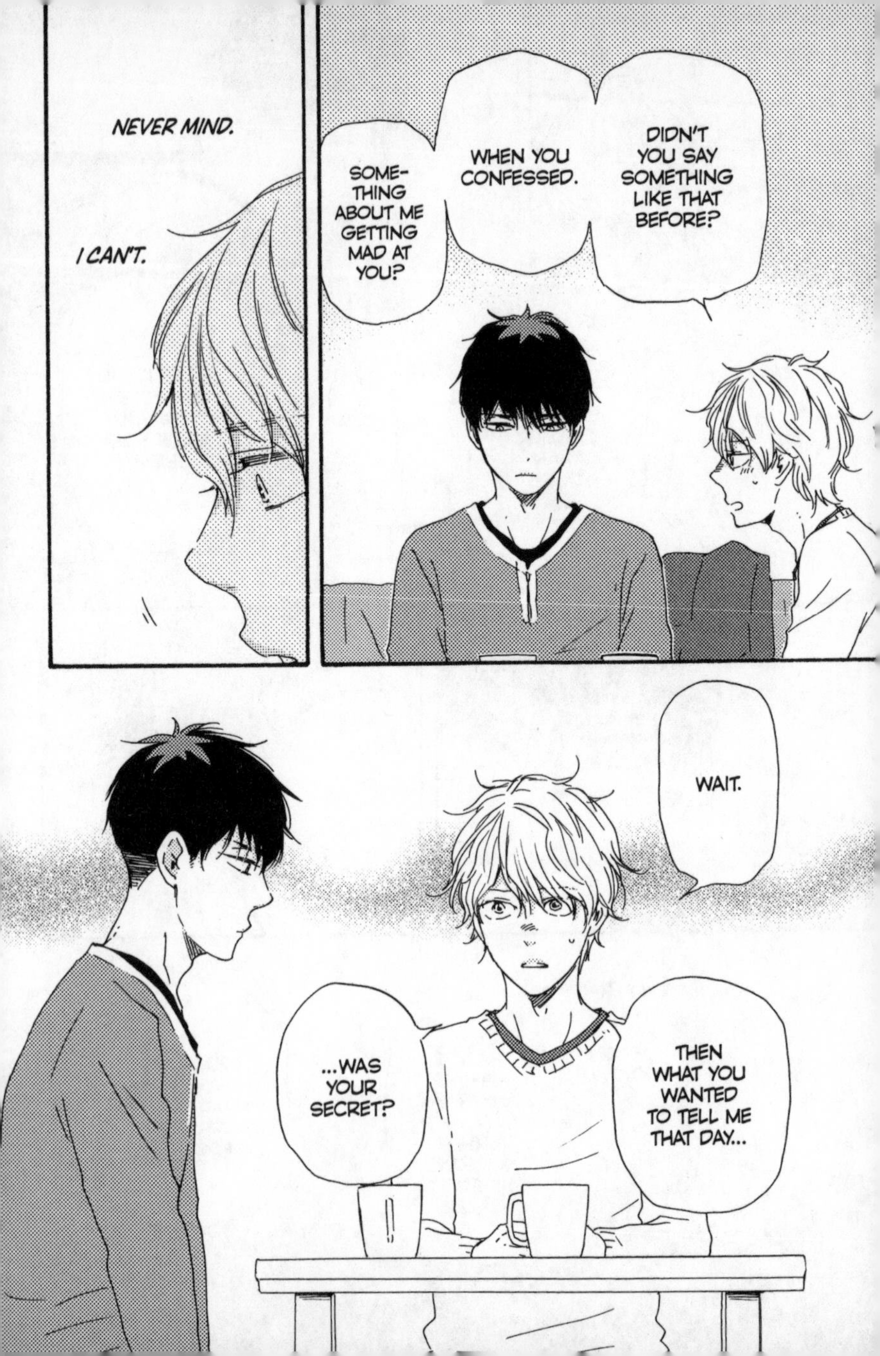
DIDN'T YOU SAY SOMETHING LIKE THAT BEFORE?
WHEN YOU CONFESSED.
SOME-THING ABOUT ME GETTING MAD AT YOU?
NEVER MIND.
I CAN'T.
WAIT.
THEN WHAT YOU WANTED TO TELL ME THAT DAY...
...WAS YOUR SECRET?

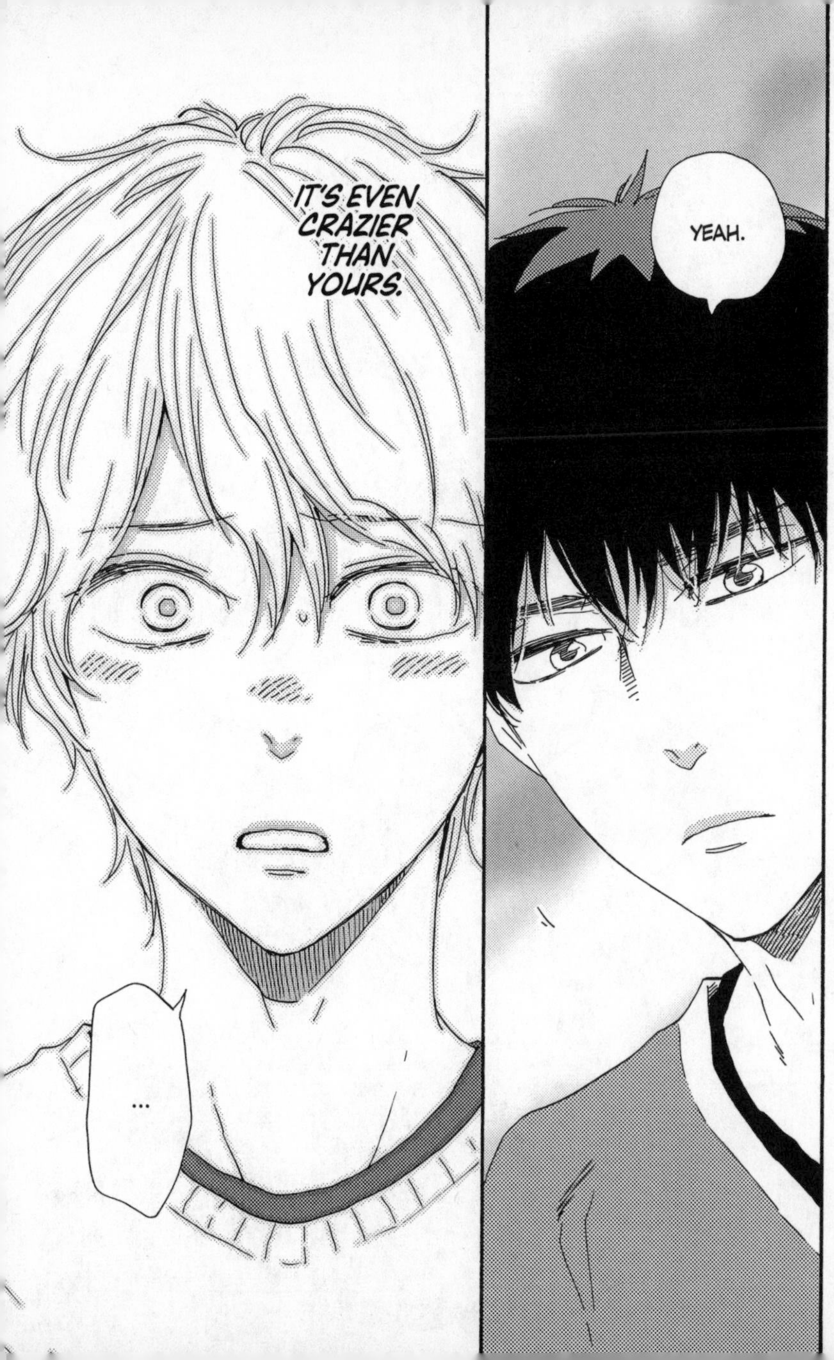
YEAH.
IT'S EVEN CRAZIER THAN YOURS.
...

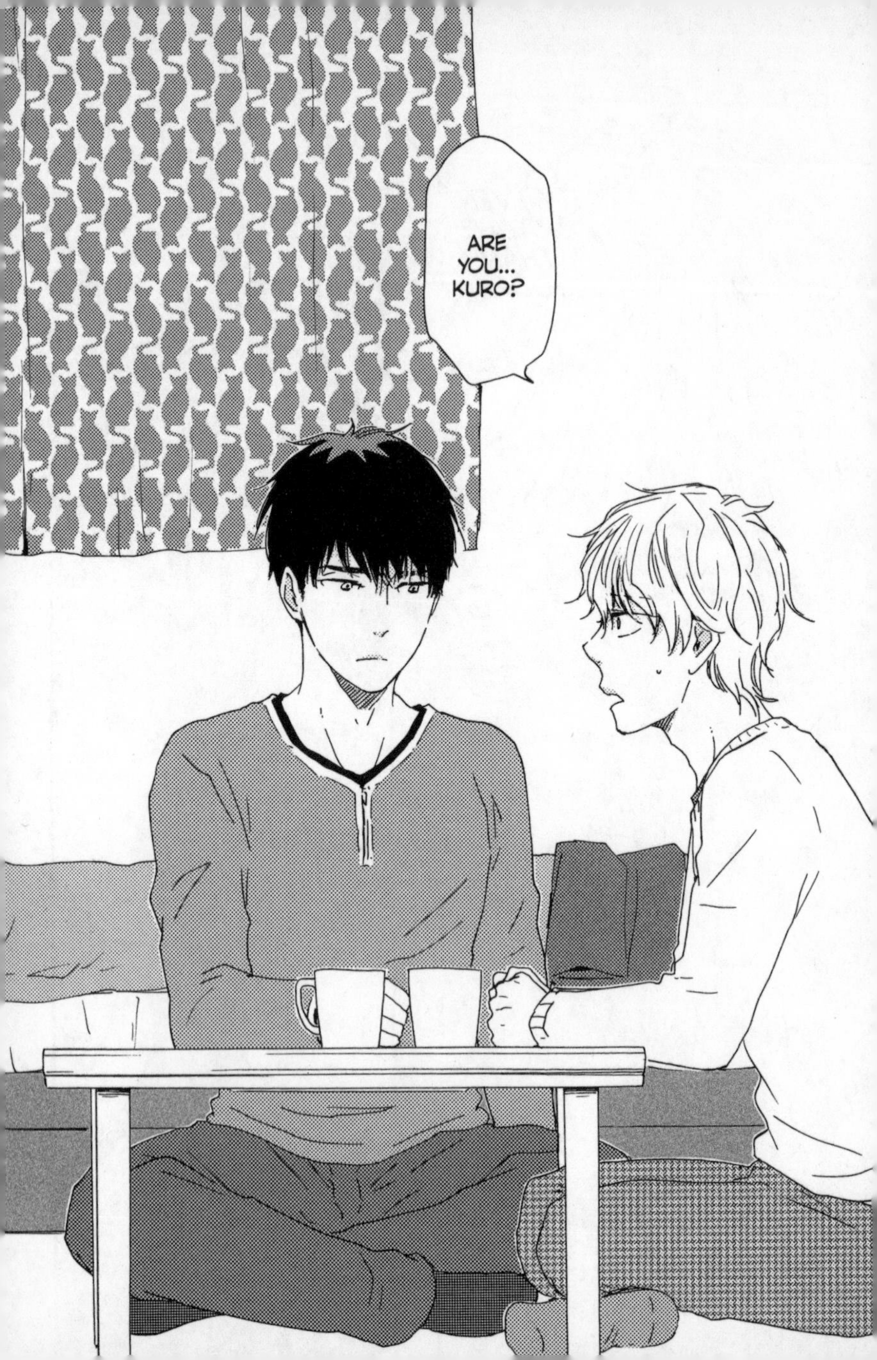
ARE YOU... KURO?

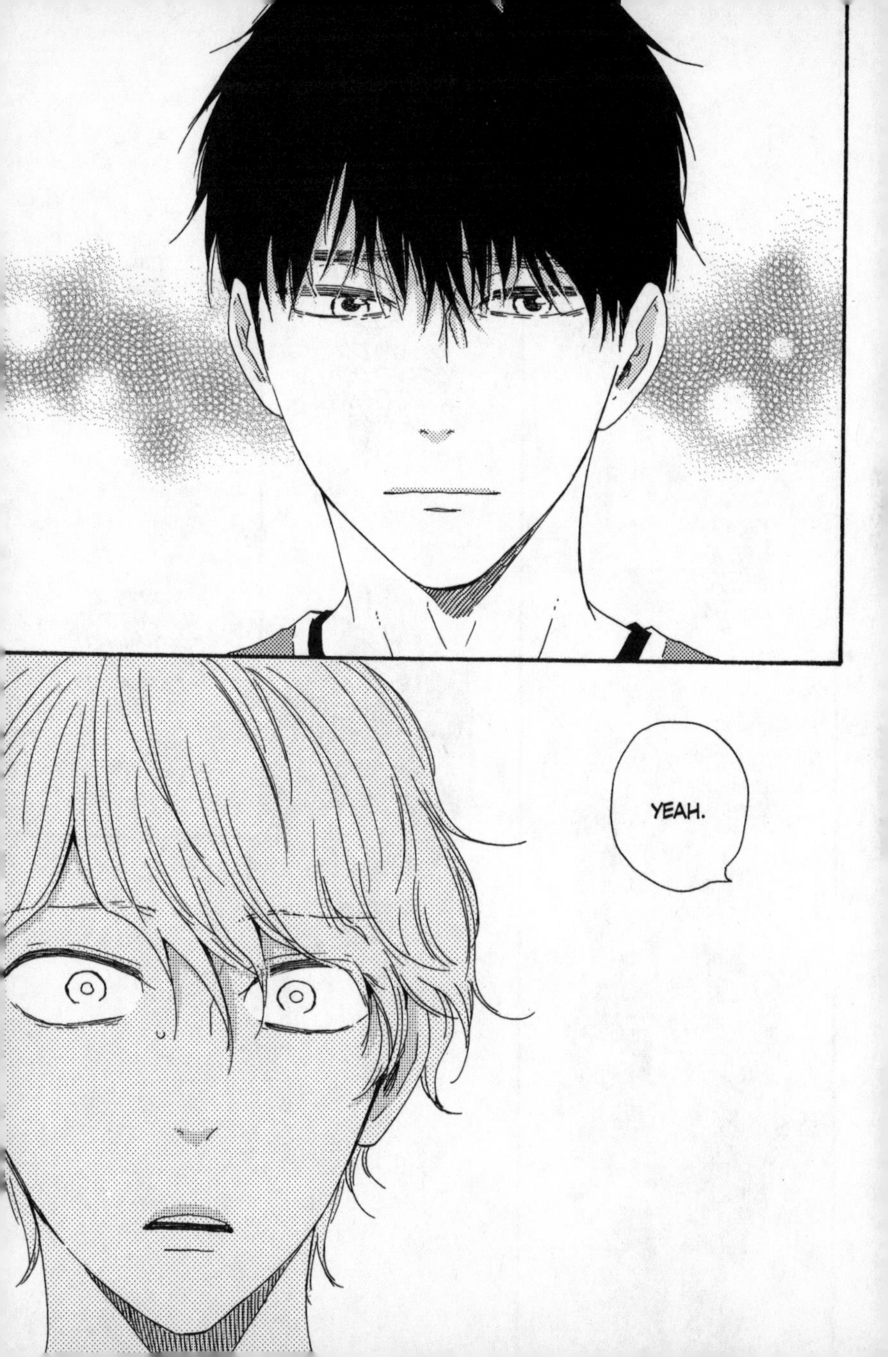
YEAH.

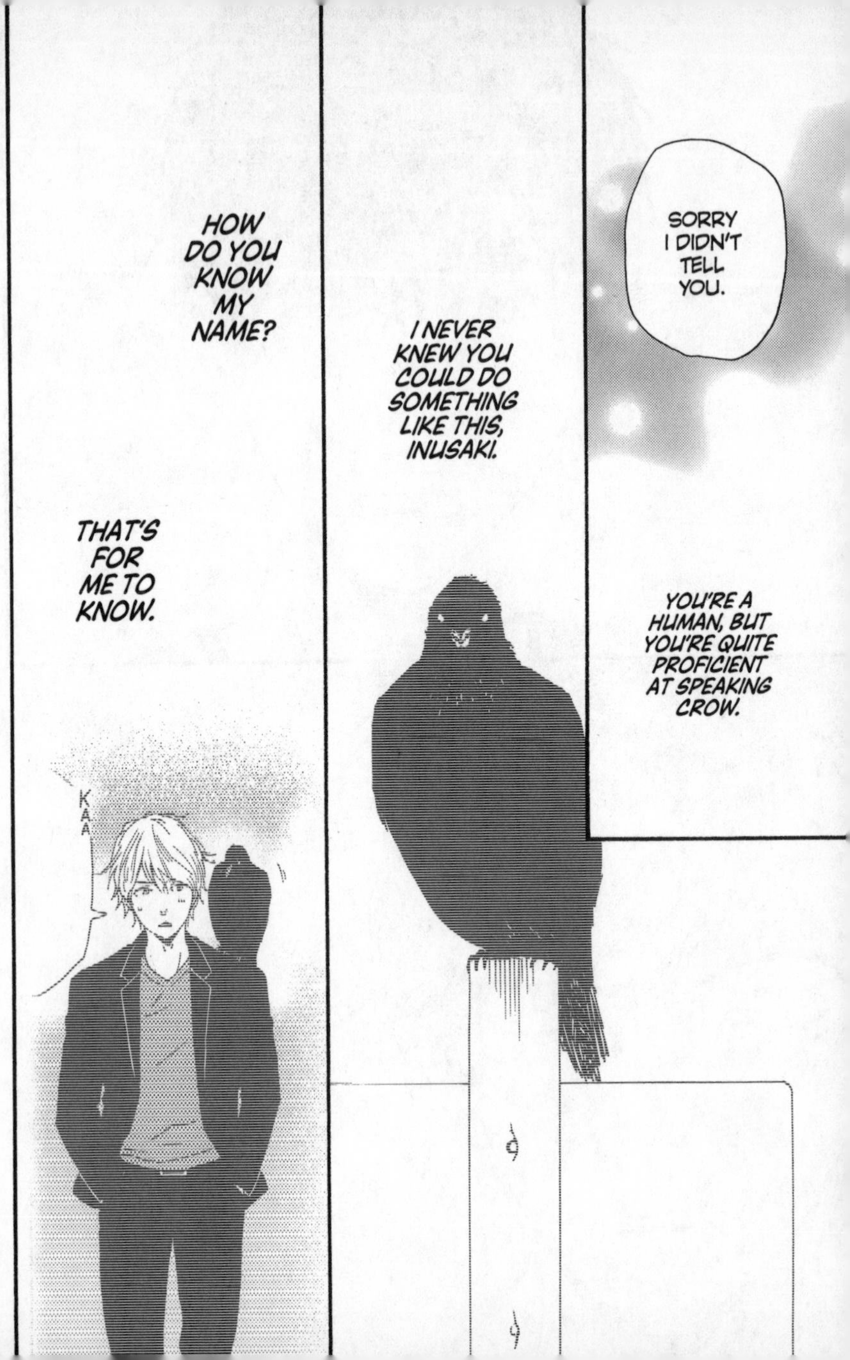
SORRY I DIDN'T TELL YOU.
YOU'RE A HUMAN, BUT YOU'RE QUITE PROFICIENT AT SPEAKING CROW.
I NEVER KNEW YOU COULD DO SOMETHING LIKE THIS, INUSAKI.
HOW DO YOU KNOW MY NAME?
THAT'S FOR ME TO KNOW.
KAA

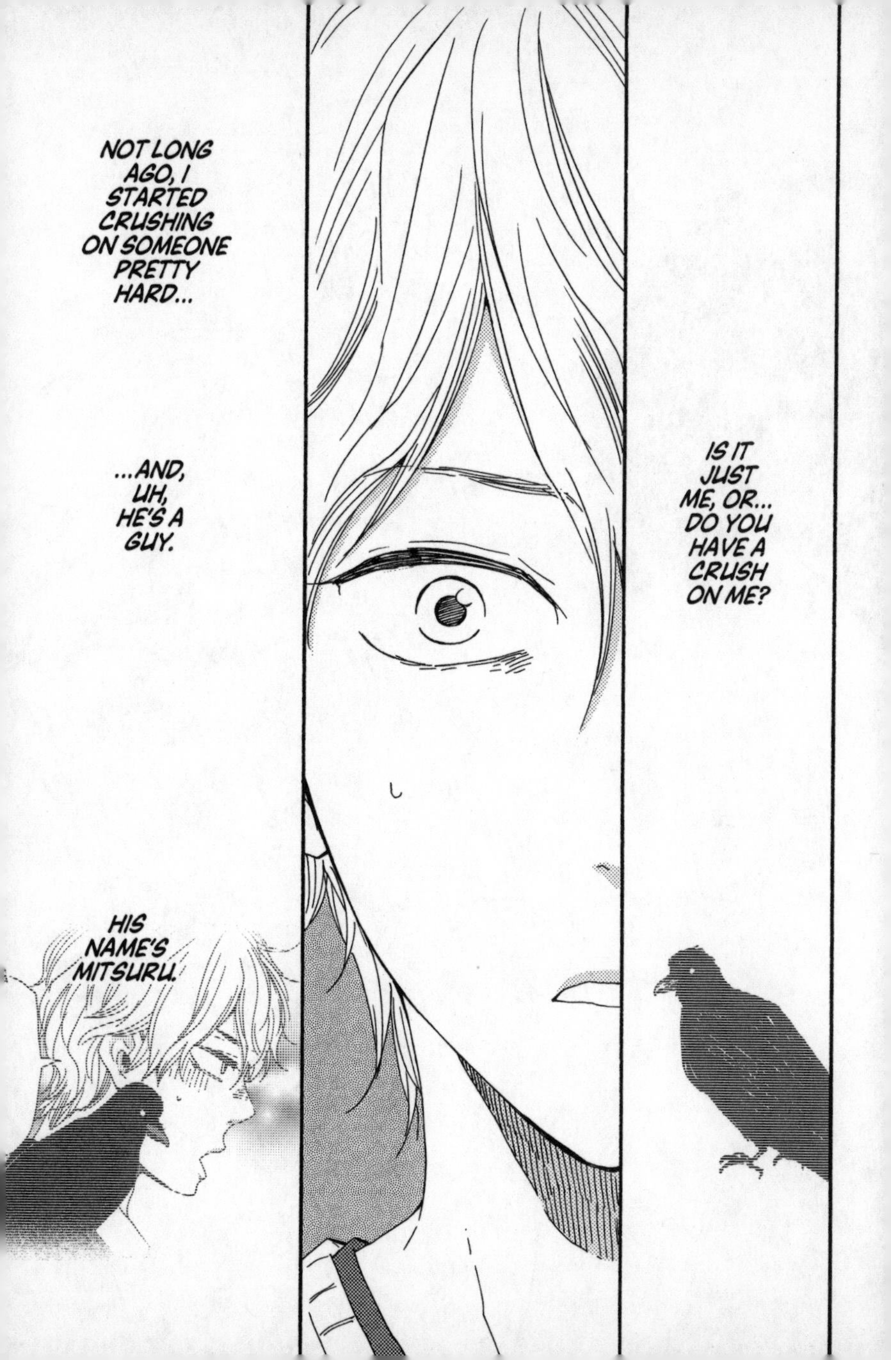
IS IT JUST ME, OR... DO YOU HAVE A CRUSH ON ME?
NOT LONG AGO, I STARTED CRUSHING ON SOMEONE PRETTY HARD...
...AND, UH, HE'S A GUY.
HIS NAME'S MITSURU.

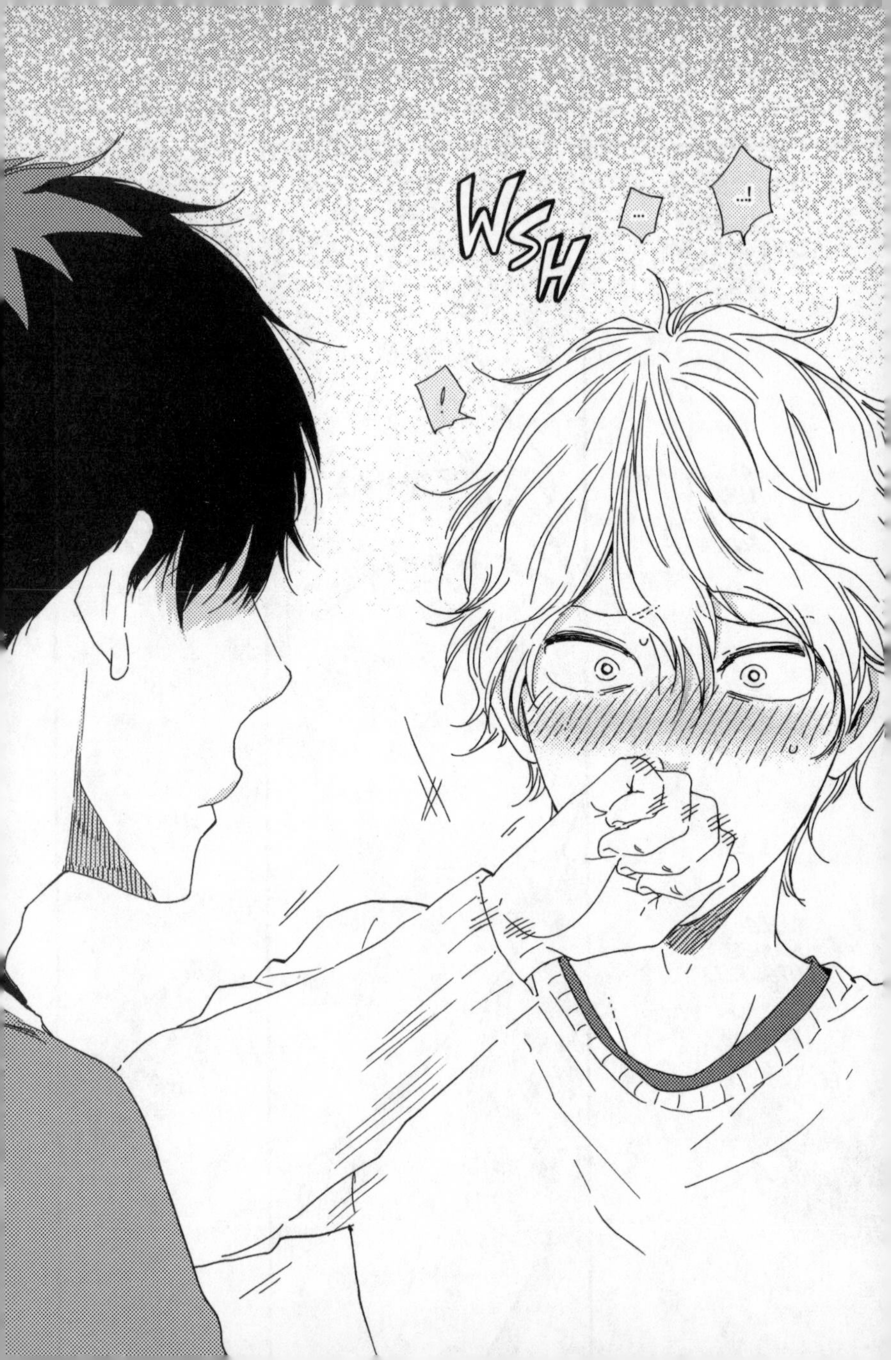
...!
...
WSH
!

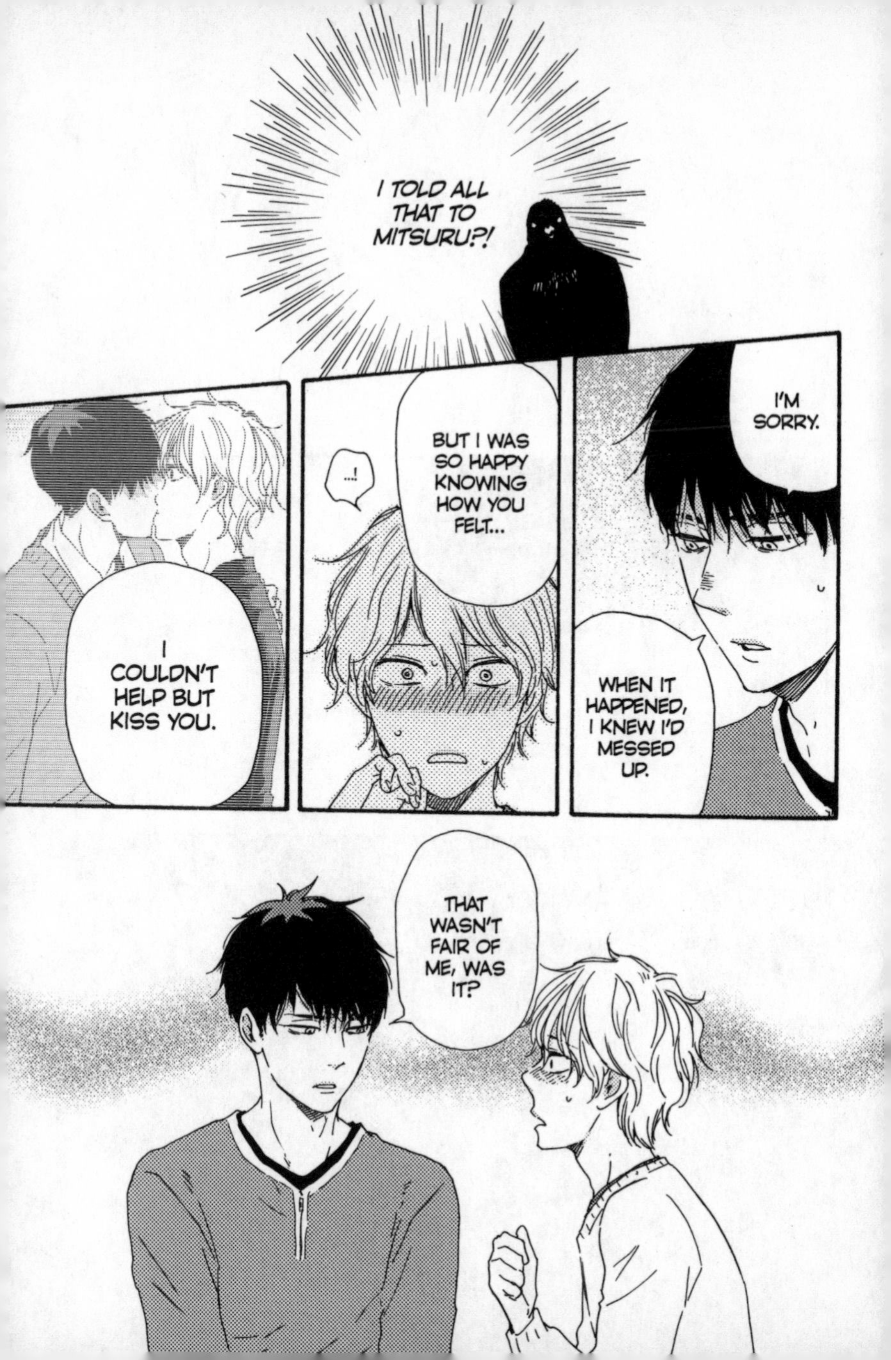
I TOLD ALL THAT TO MITSURU?!
I'M SORRY.
WHEN IT HAPPENED, I KNEW I'D MESSED UP.
BUT I WAS SO HAPPY KNOWING HOW YOU FELT...
...!
I COULDN'T HELP BUT KISS YOU.
THAT WASN'T FAIR OF ME, WAS IT?

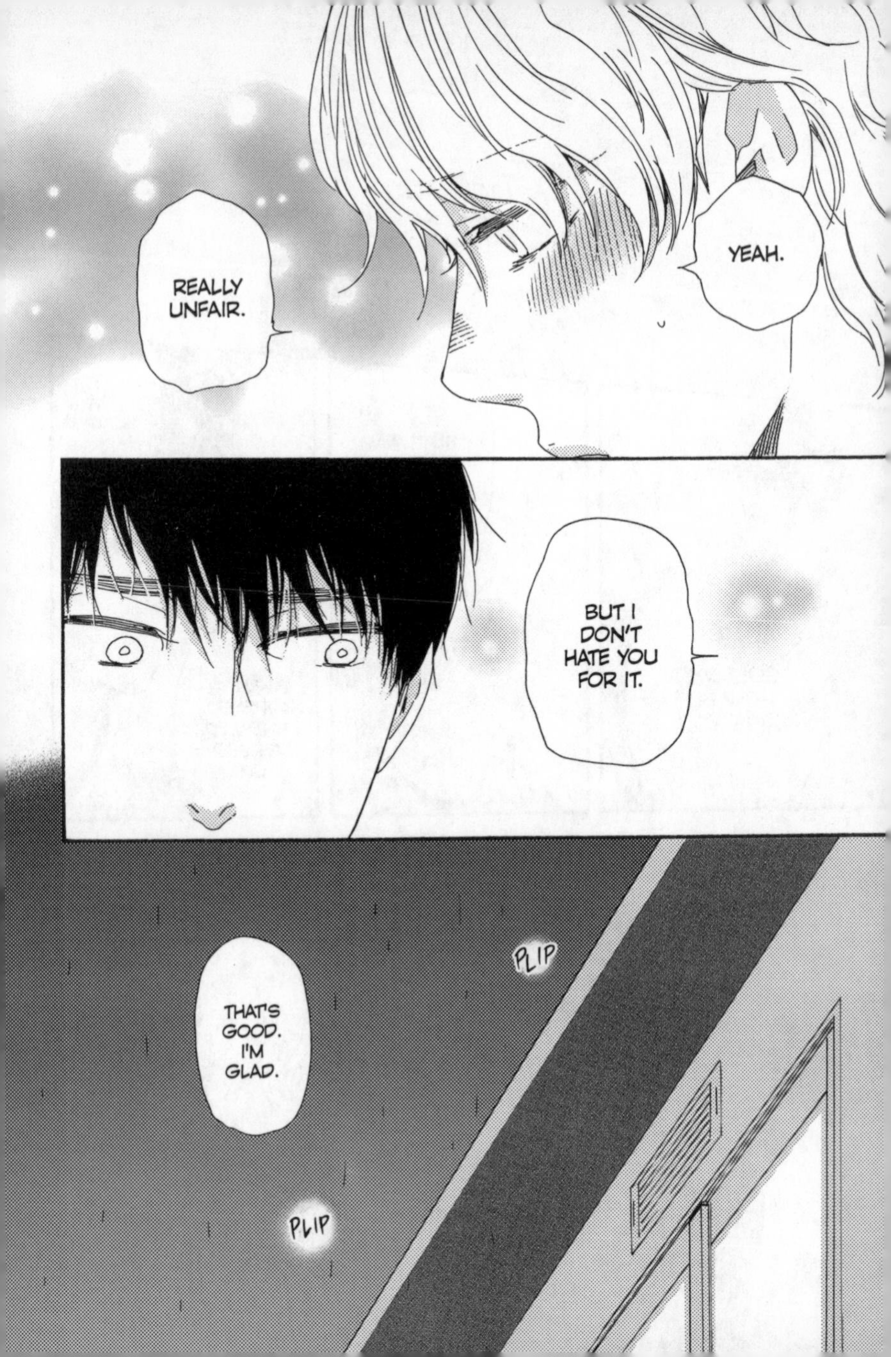
YEAH.
REALLY UNFAIR.
BUT I DON'T HATE YOU FOR IT.
PLIP
THAT'S GOOD. I'M GLAD.
PLIP

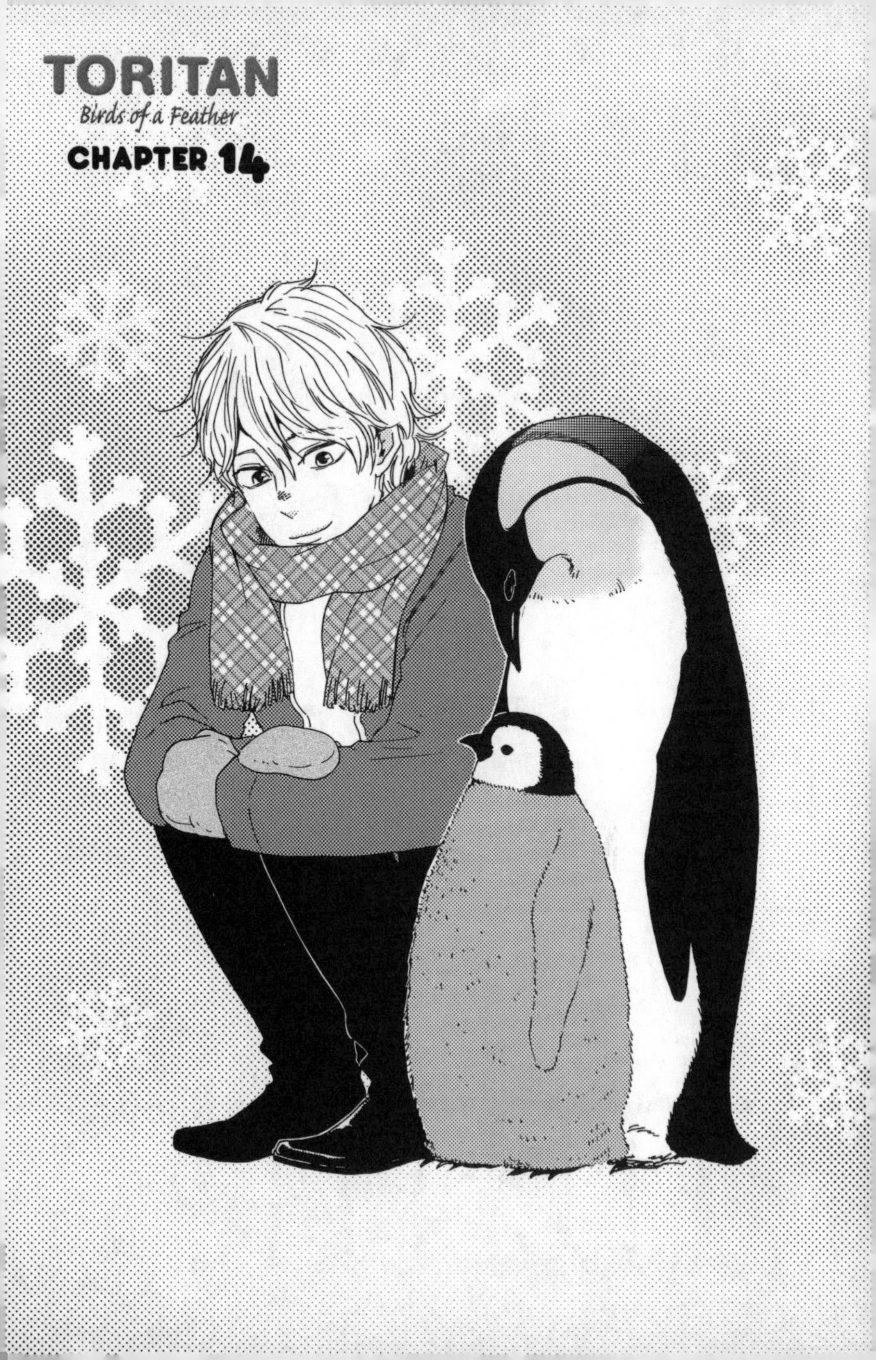
TORITAN
Birds of a Feather
CHAPTER 14

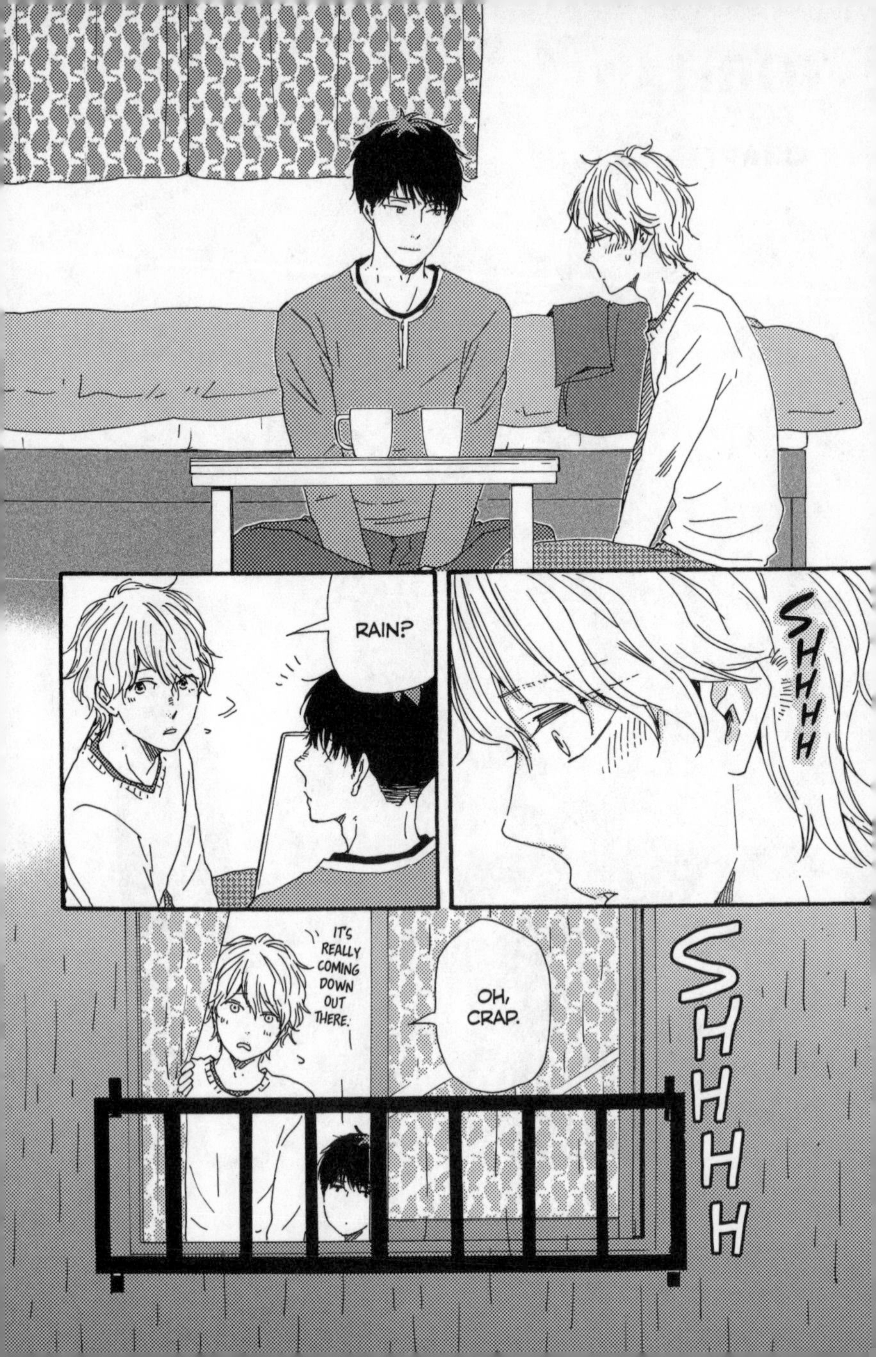
SHHHH
RAIN?
SHHHH
OH, CRAP.
IT'S REALLY COMING DOWN OUT THERE.

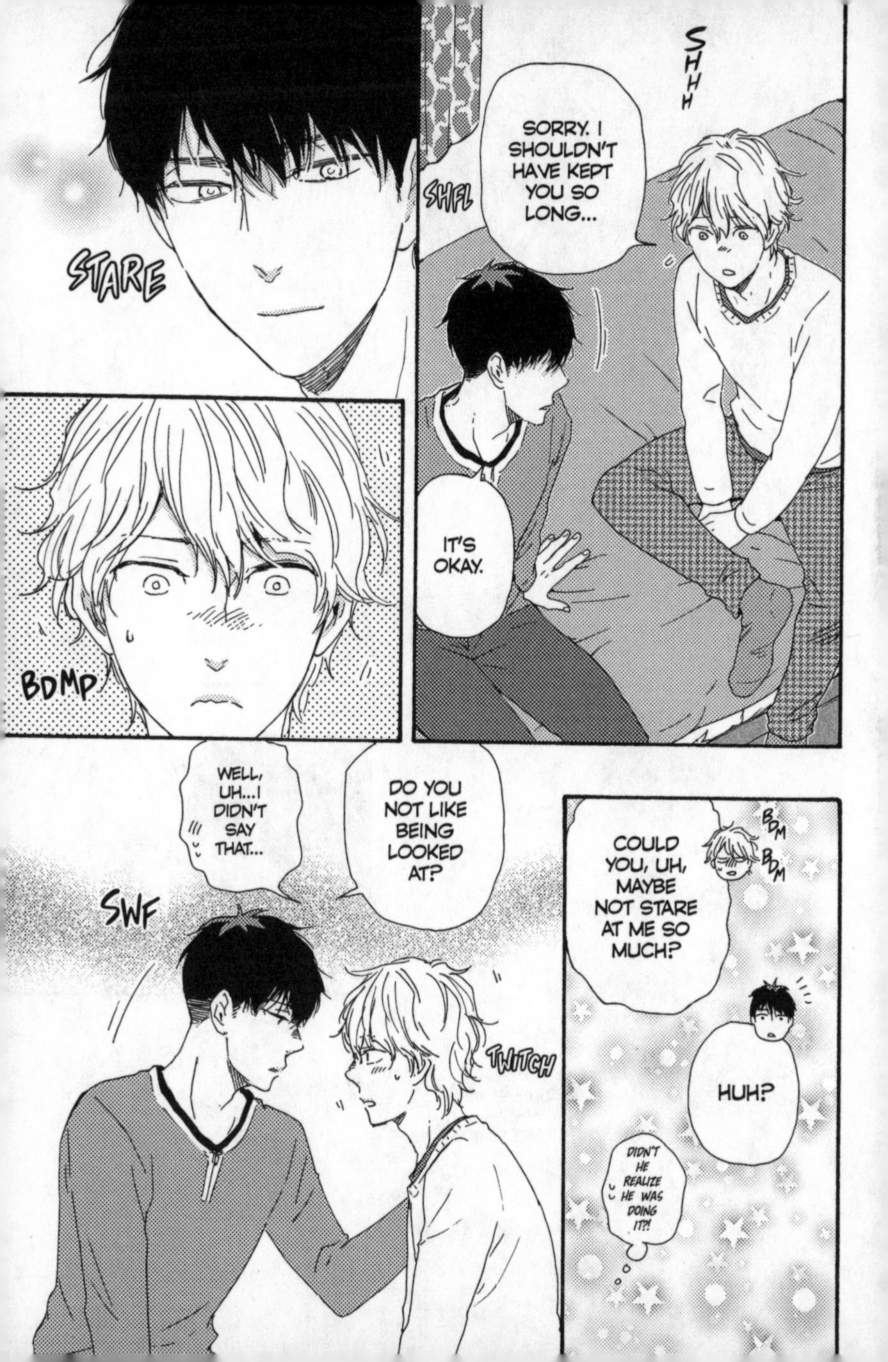
SHHH
SORRY. I SHOULDN'T HAVE KEPT YOU SO LONG...
SHFL
IT'S OKAY.
STARE
BDMP
BDM BDM
COULD YOU, UH, MAYBE NOT STARE AT ME SO MUCH?
HUH?
DIDN'T HE REALIZE HE WAS DOING IT?!
DO YOU NOT LIKE BEING LOOKED AT?
WELL, UH...I DIDN'T SAY THAT...
SWF
TWITCH

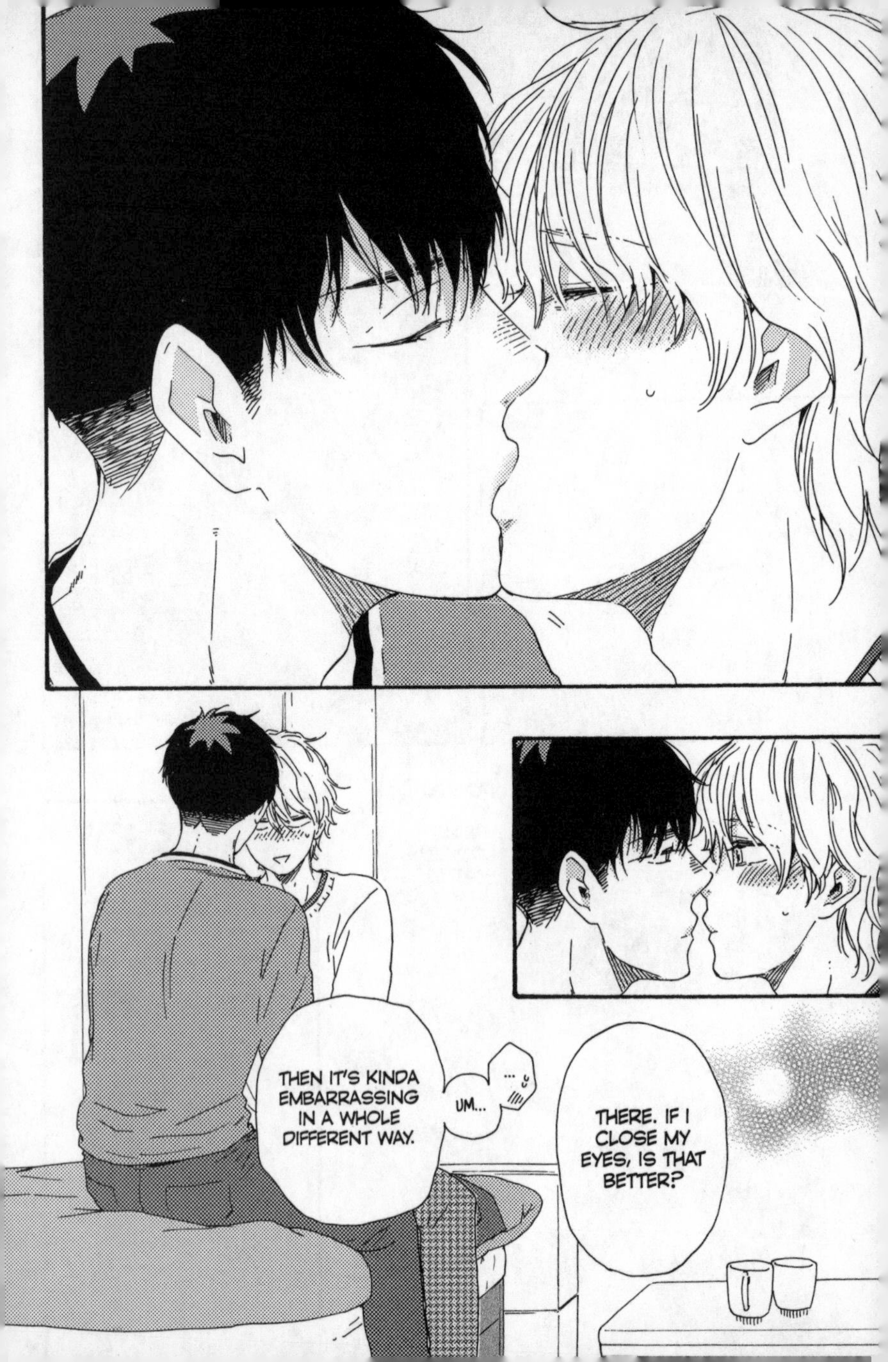
THERE. IF I CLOSE MY EYES, IS THAT BETTER?
UM...
THEN IT'S KINDA EMBARRASSING IN A WHOLE DIFFERENT WAY.

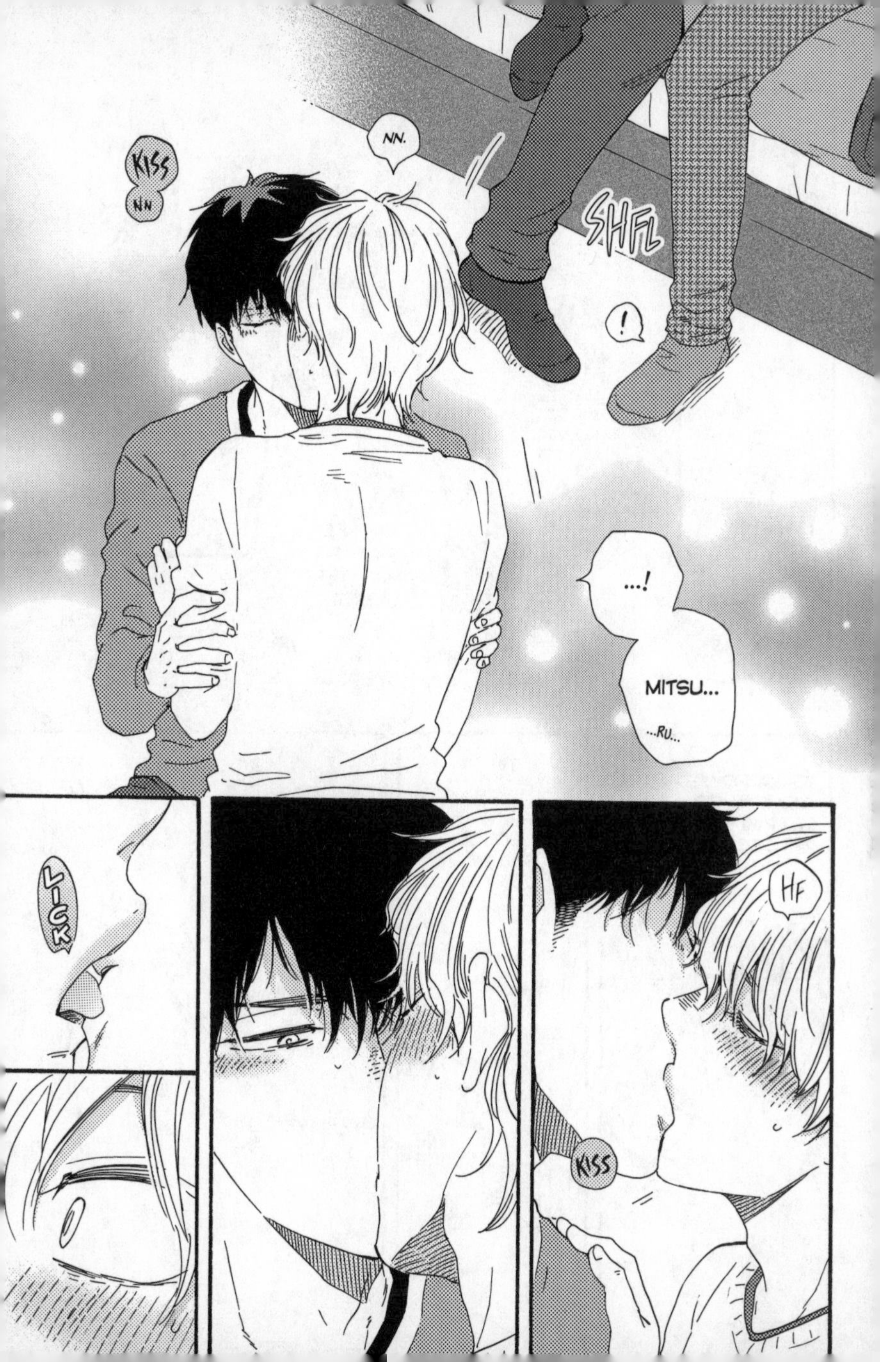
SHFL
NN.
KISS
NN
!
...!
MITSU...
...RU...
HF
KISS
LICK

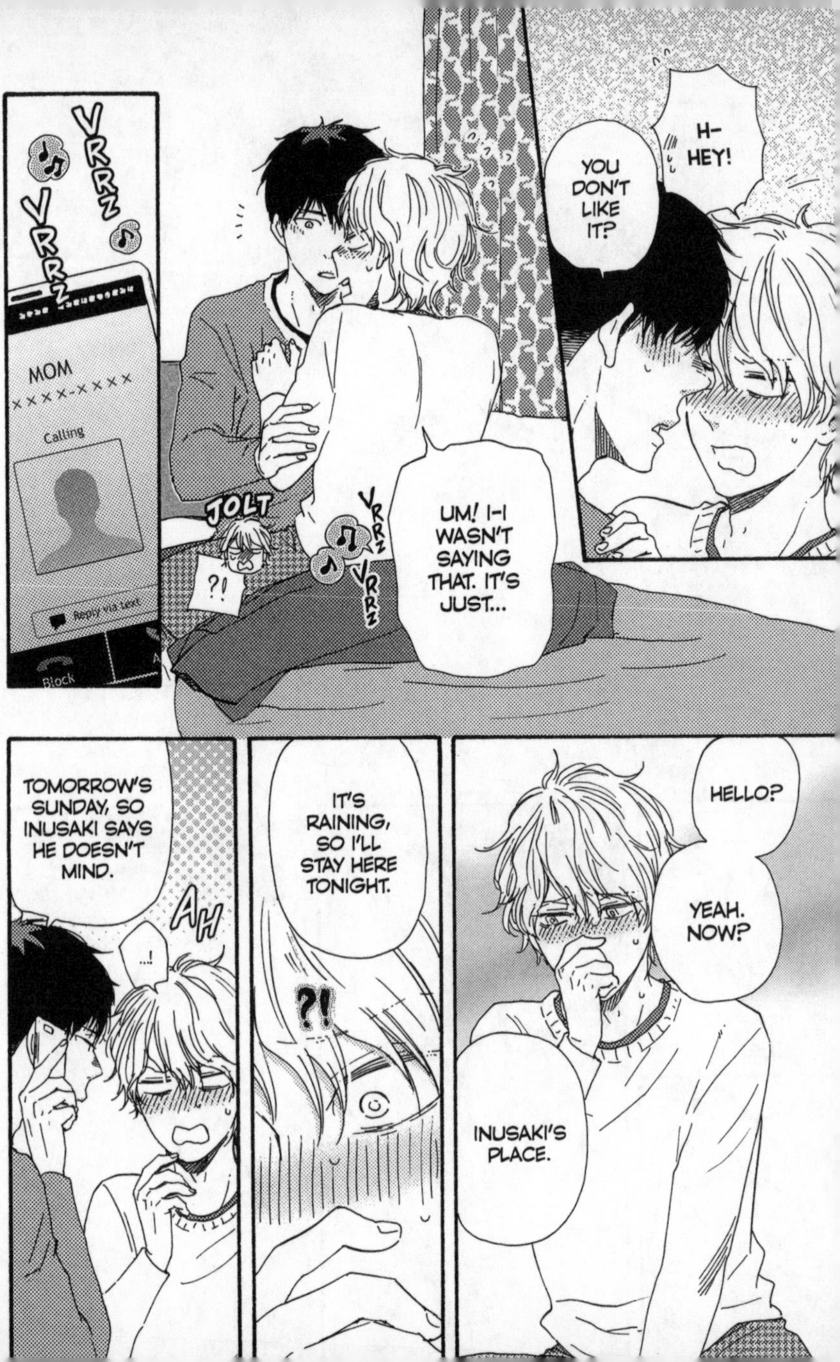
H- HEY!
YOU DON'T LIKE IT?
UM! I-I WASN'T SAYING THAT. IT'S JUST...
VRRZ
VRRZ
JOLT
?!
VRRZ
VRRZ
MOM
××××-××××
Calling
Reply via text
Block
HELLO?
YEAH. NOW?
INUSAKI'S PLACE.
IT'S RAINING, SO I'LL STAY HERE TONIGHT.
?!
TOMORROW'S SUNDAY, SO INUSAKI SAYS HE DOESN'T MIND.
AH
...!

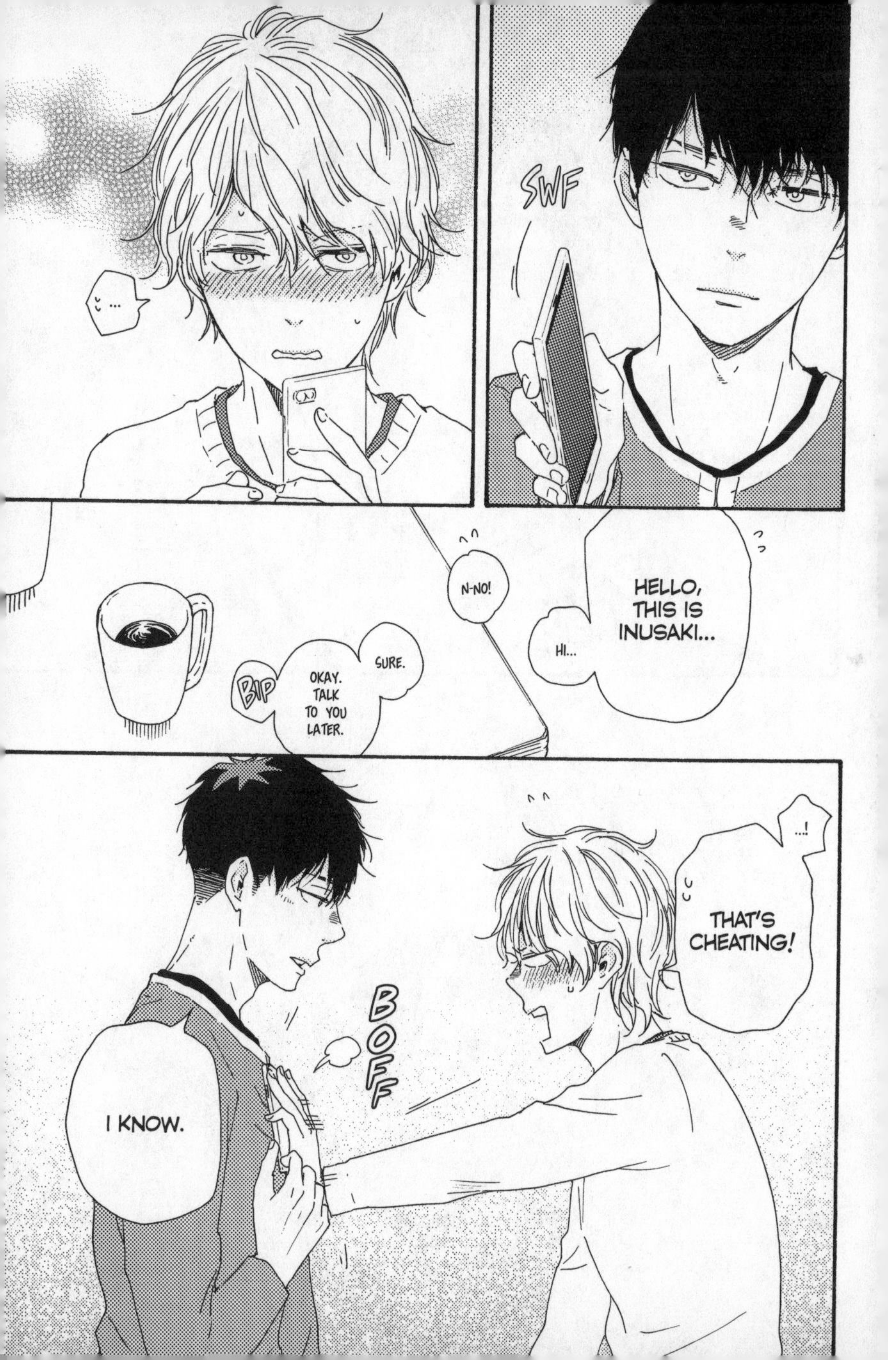
SWF
...
HELLO, THIS IS INUSAKI...
HI...
N-NO!
SURE.
OKAY. TALK TO YOU LATER.
BIP
...!
THAT'S CHEATING!
BOFF
I KNOW.

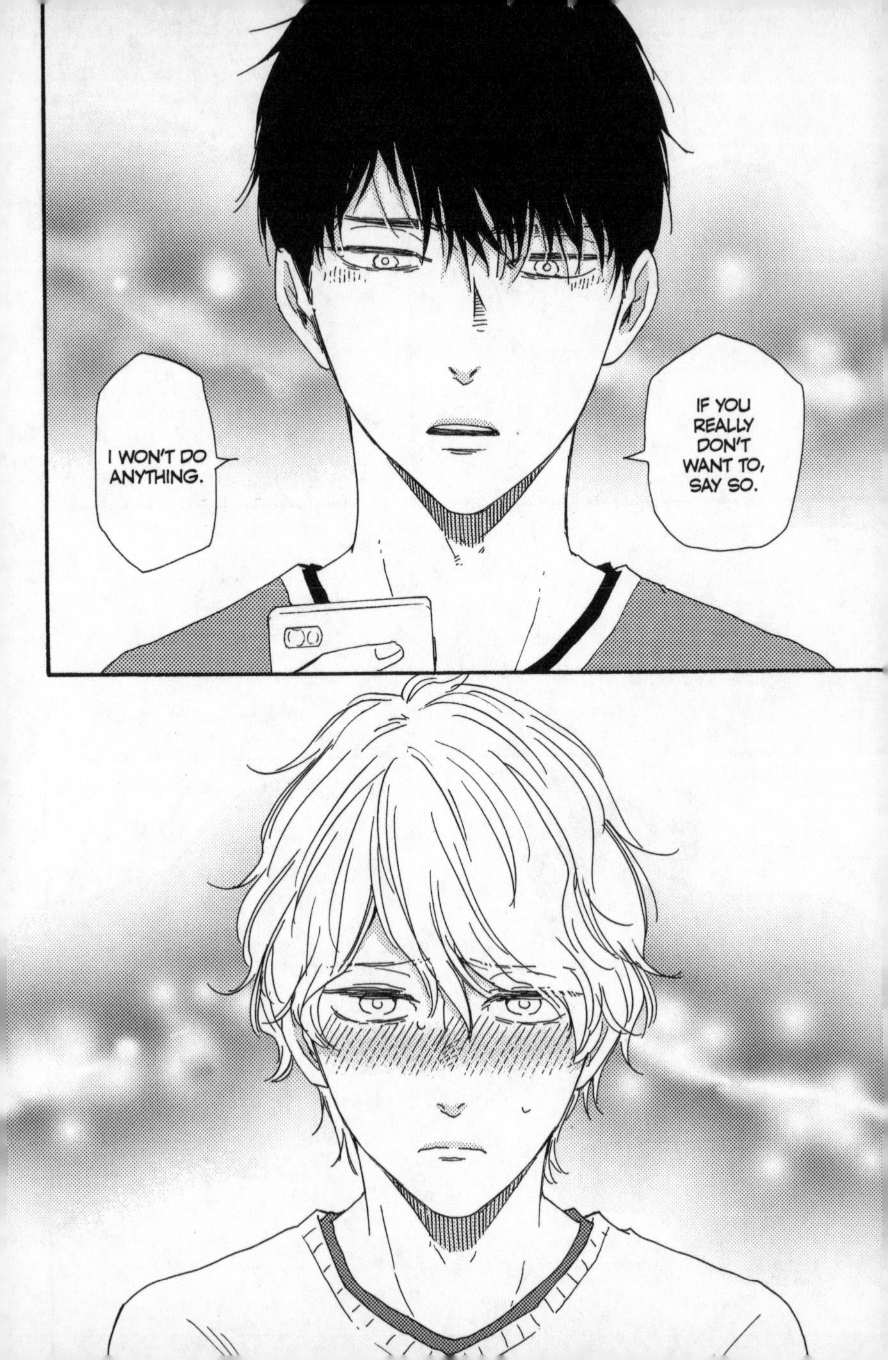
IF YOU REALLY DON'T WANT TO, SAY SO.
I WON'T DO ANYTHING.

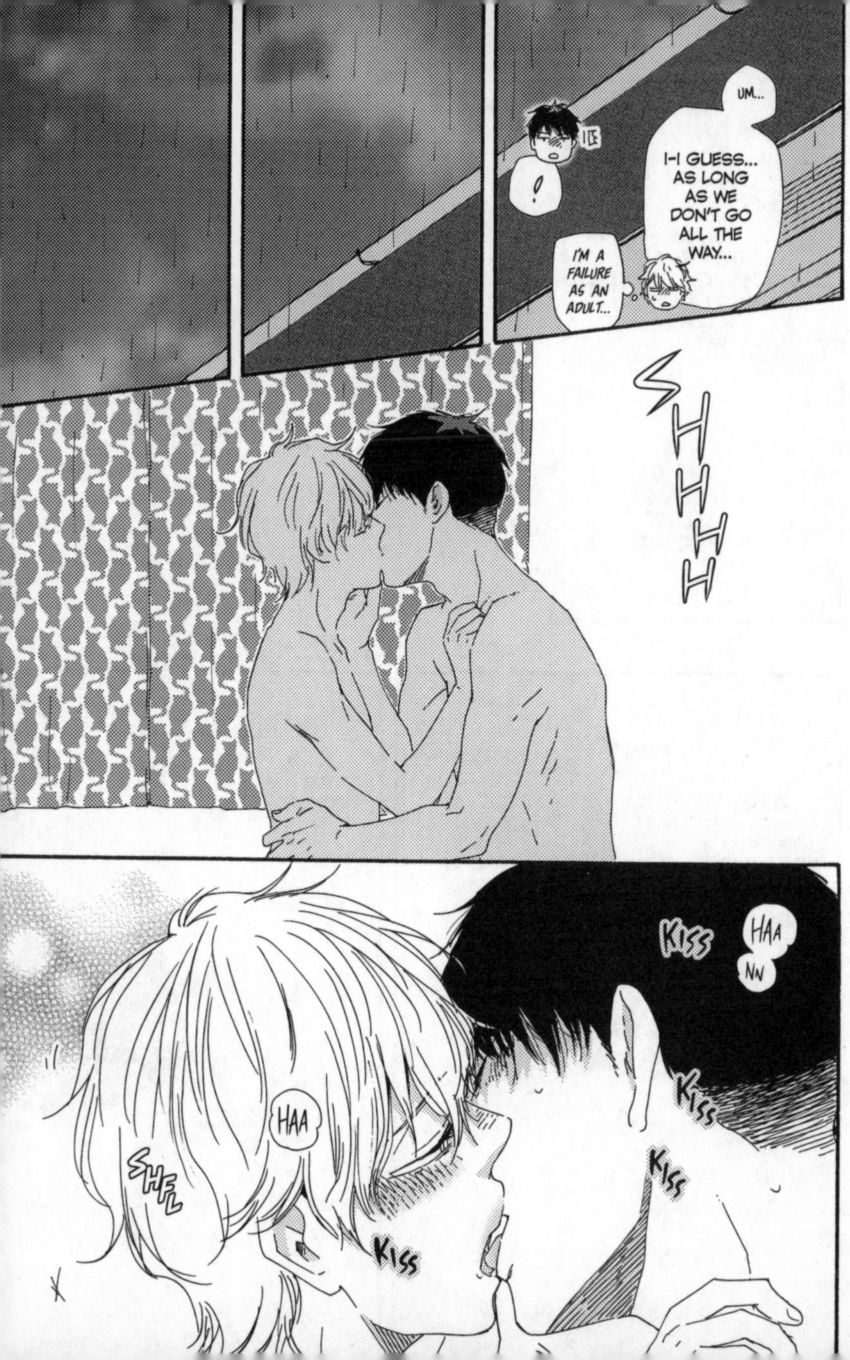
UM...
I-I GUESS... AS LONG AS WE DON'T GO ALL THE WAY...
!
I'M A FAILURE AS AN ADULT...
SHHHHH
KISS
HAA NN
KISS
KISS
HAA
SHFL
KISS

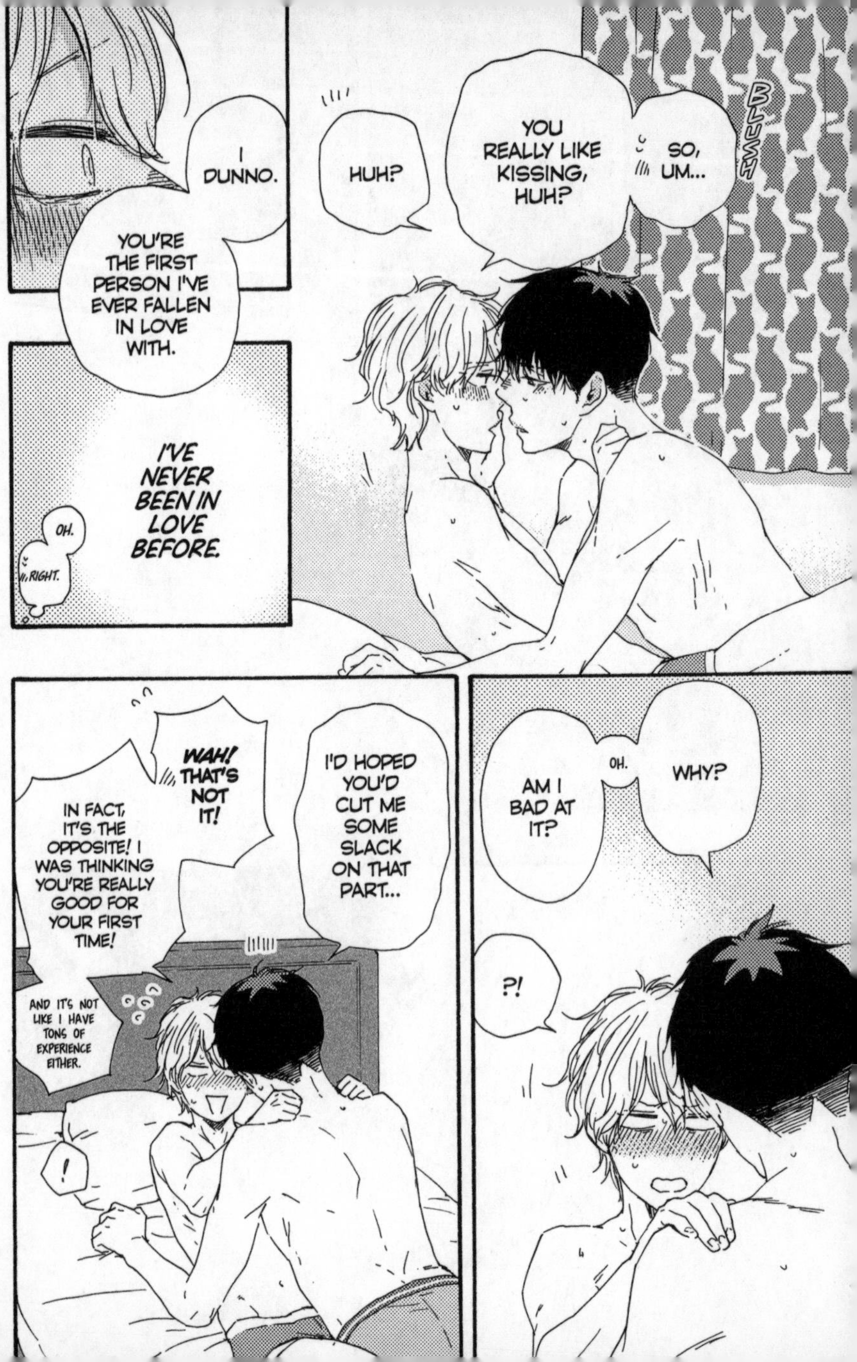
BLUSH
SO, UM...
YOU REALLY LIKE KISSING, HUH?
HUH?
I DUNNO.
YOU'RE THE FIRST PERSON I'VE EVER FALLEN IN LOVE WITH.
I'VE NEVER BEEN IN LOVE BEFORE.
OH.
RIGHT.
WHY?
OH.
AM I BAD AT IT?
?!
I'D HOPED YOU'D CUT ME SOME SLACK ON THAT PART...
WAH! THAT'S NOT IT!
IN FACT, IT'S THE OPPOSITE! I WAS THINKING YOU'RE REALLY GOOD FOR YOUR FIRST TIME!
AND IT'S NOT LIKE I HAVE TONS OF EXPERIENCE EITHER.
!

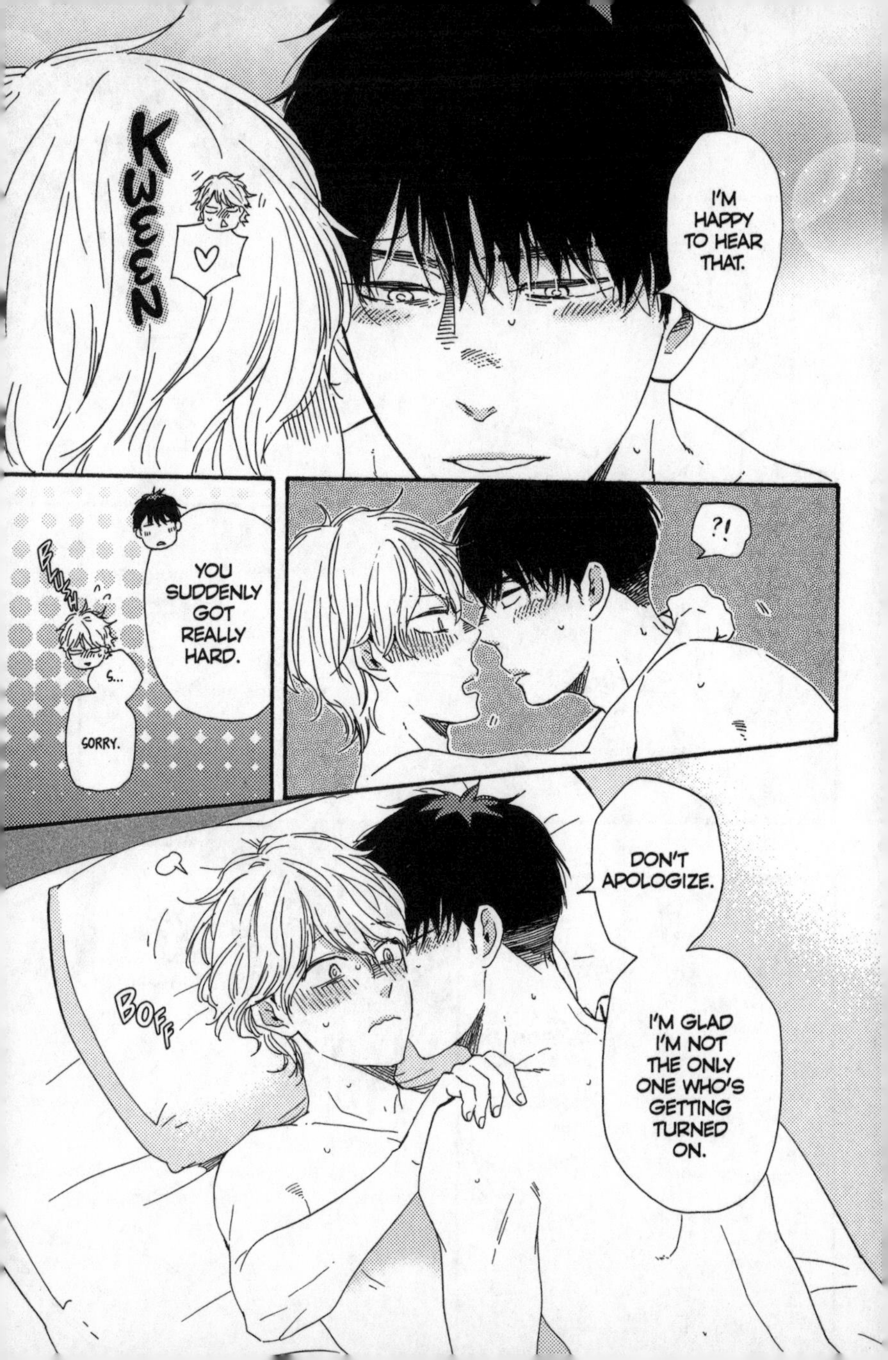

I'M HAPPY TO HEAR THAT.
KWEEN
?!
YOU SUDDENLY GOT REALLY HARD.
BLUSH
S...
SORRY.
DON'T APOLOGIZE.
I'M GLAD I'M NOT THE ONLY ONE WHO'S GETTING TURNED ON.
BOFF

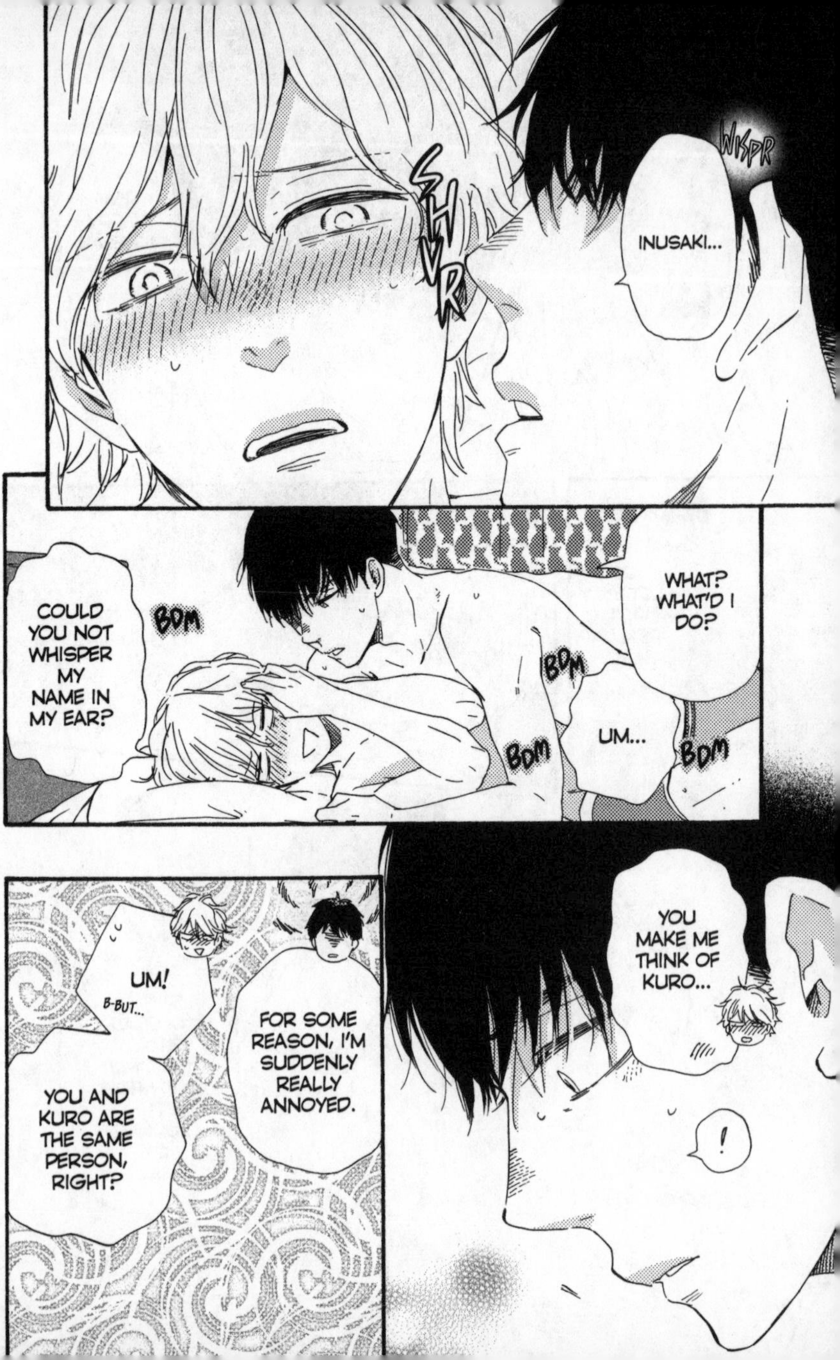
WISPR
INUSAKI...
SHVR
WHAT? WHAT'D I DO?
BDM
UM...
BDM
BDM
COULD YOU NOT WHISPER MY NAME IN MY EAR?
BDM
YOU MAKE ME THINK OF KURO...
!
FOR SOME REASON, I'M SUDDENLY REALLY ANNOYED.
UM!
B-BUT...
YOU AND KURO ARE THE SAME PERSON, RIGHT?

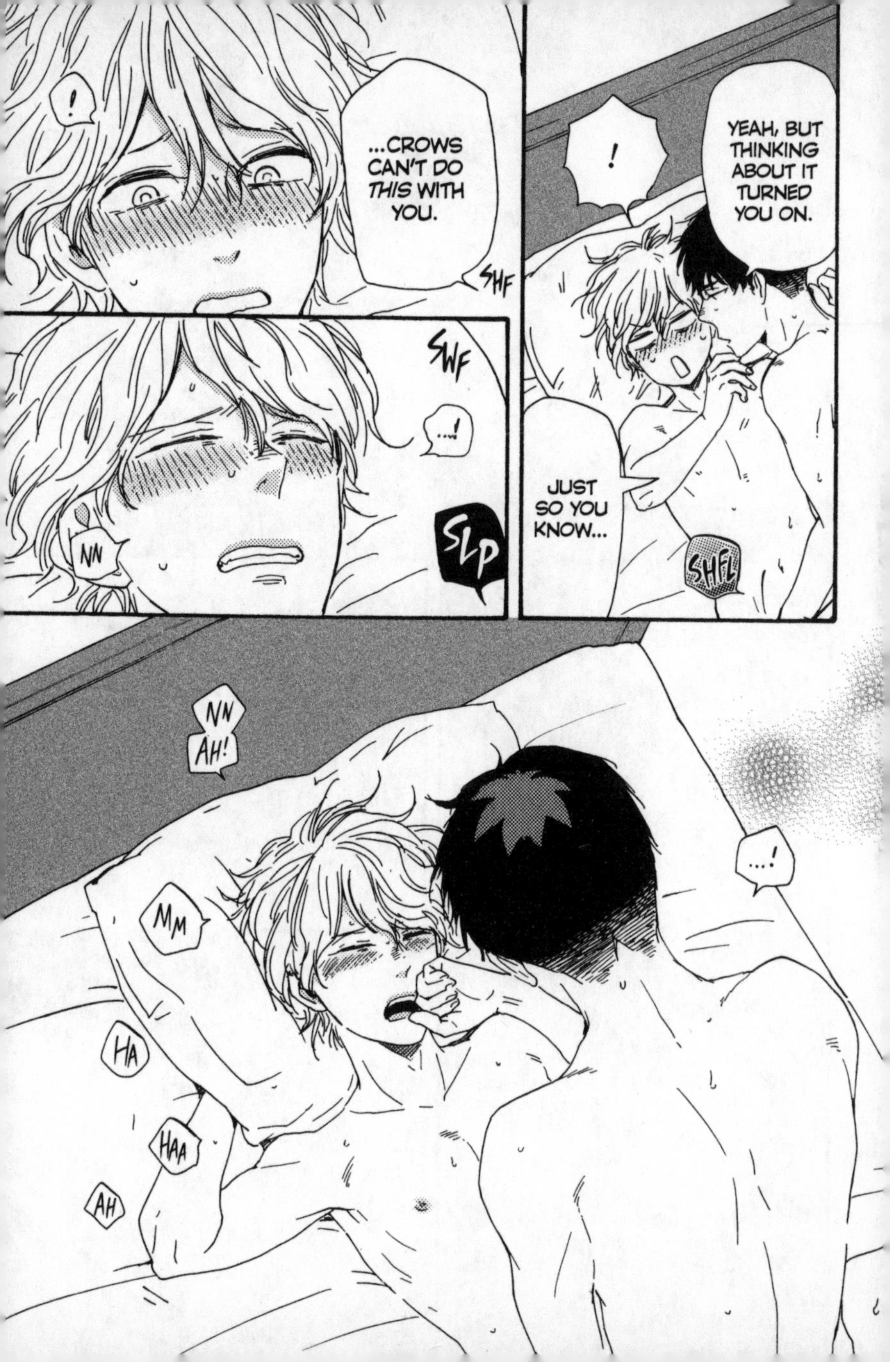
YEAH, BUT THINKING ABOUT IT TURNED YOU ON.
!
JUST SO YOU KNOW...
SHFL
...CROWS CAN'T DO *THIS* WITH YOU.
SHF
!
SWF
...!
SLP
NN
...!
NN AH!
MM
HA
HAA
AH

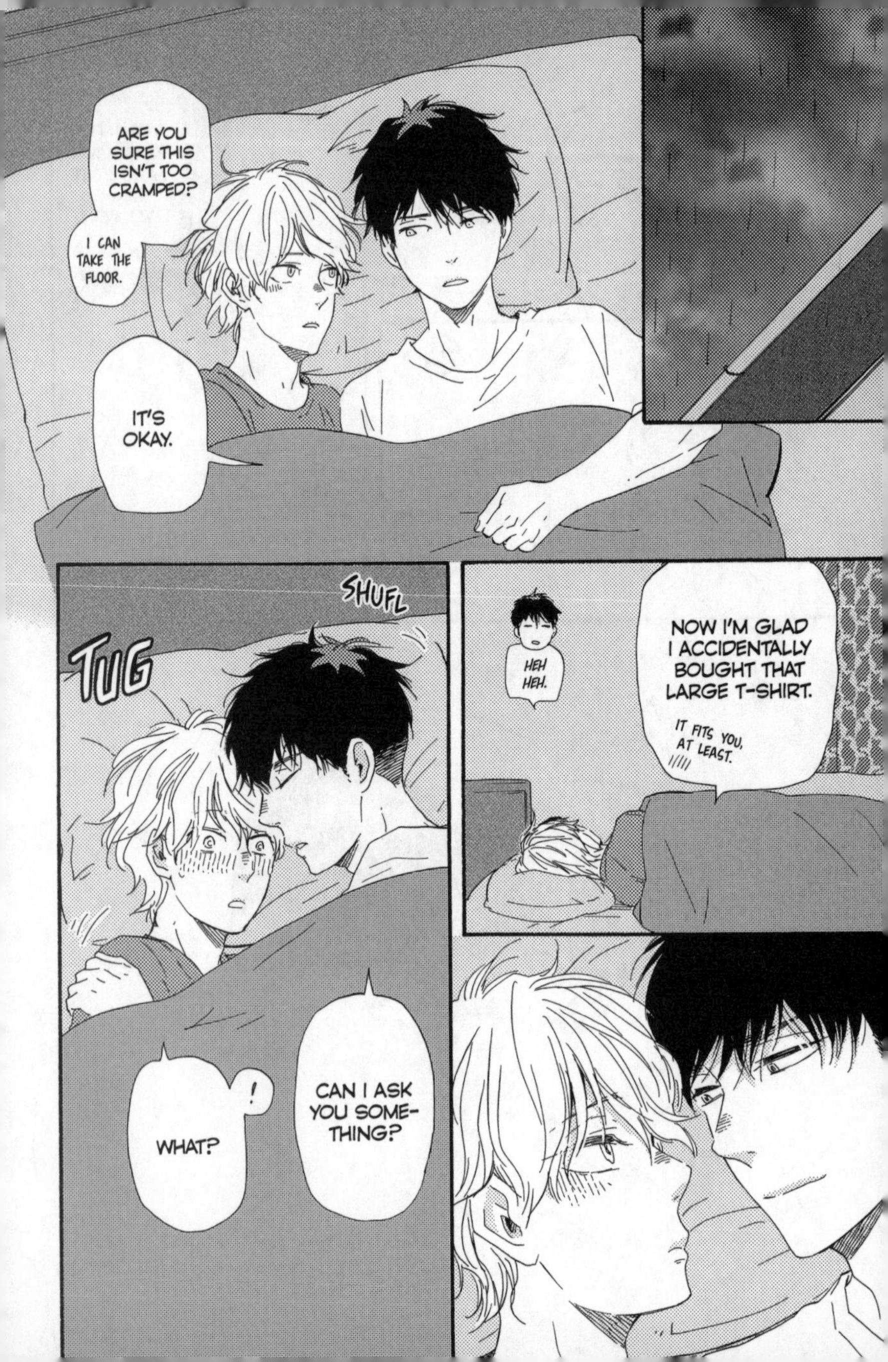
ARE YOU SURE THIS ISN'T TOO CRAMPED?
I CAN TAKE THE FLOOR.
IT'S OKAY.
NOW I'M GLAD I ACCIDENTALLY BOUGHT THAT LARGE T-SHIRT.
IT FITS YOU, AT LEAST.
HEH HEH.
SHUFL
TUG
CAN I ASK YOU SOME-THING?
!
WHAT?

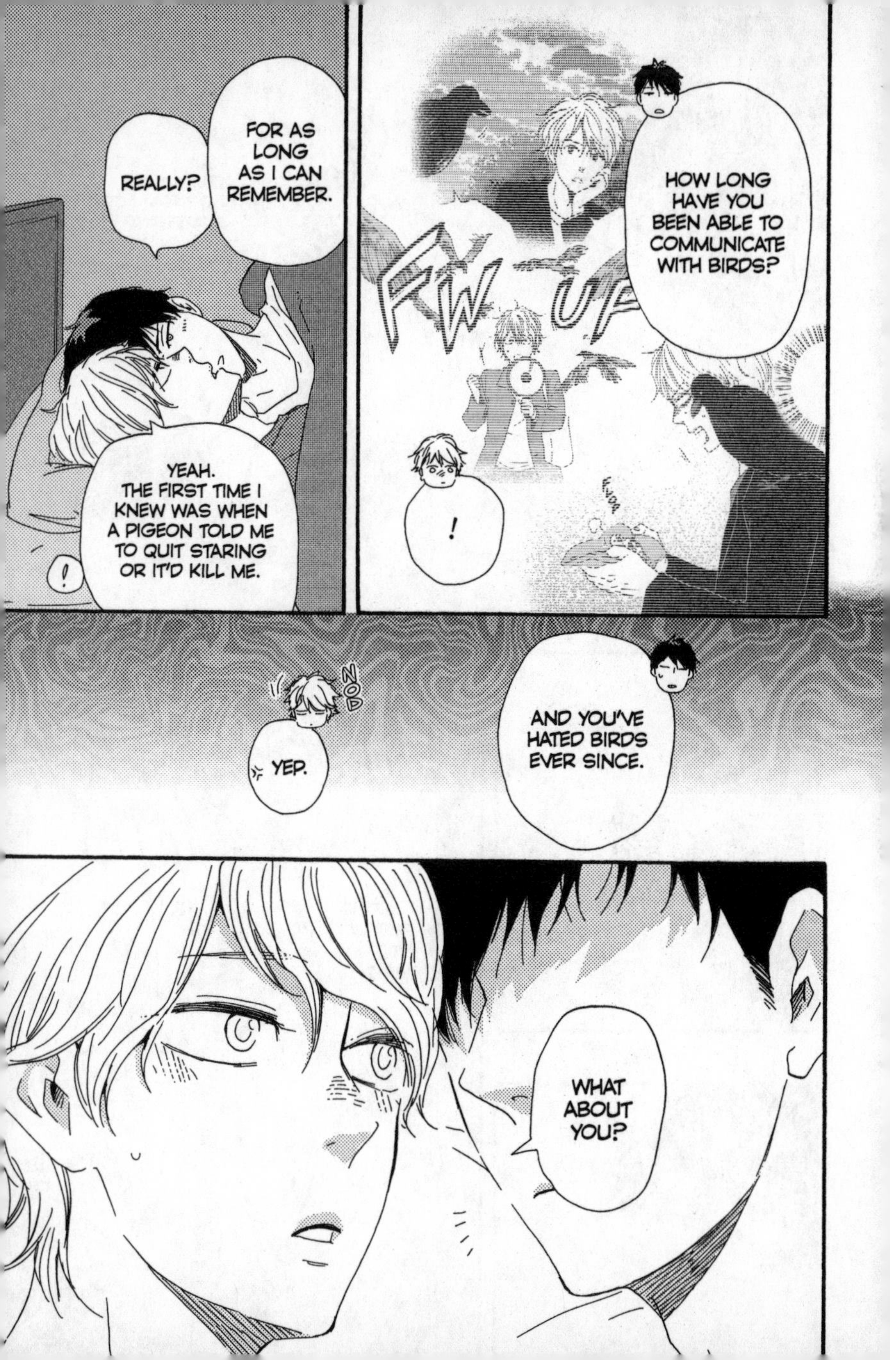
HOW LONG HAVE YOU BEEN ABLE TO COMMUNICATE WITH BIRDS?
FWUP
!
FOR AS LONG AS I CAN REMEMBER.
REALLY?
YEAH. THE FIRST TIME I KNEW WAS WHEN A PIGEON TOLD ME TO QUIT STARING OR IT'D KILL ME.
!
AND YOU'VE HATED BIRDS EVER SINCE.
NOD
YEP.
WHAT ABOUT YOU?

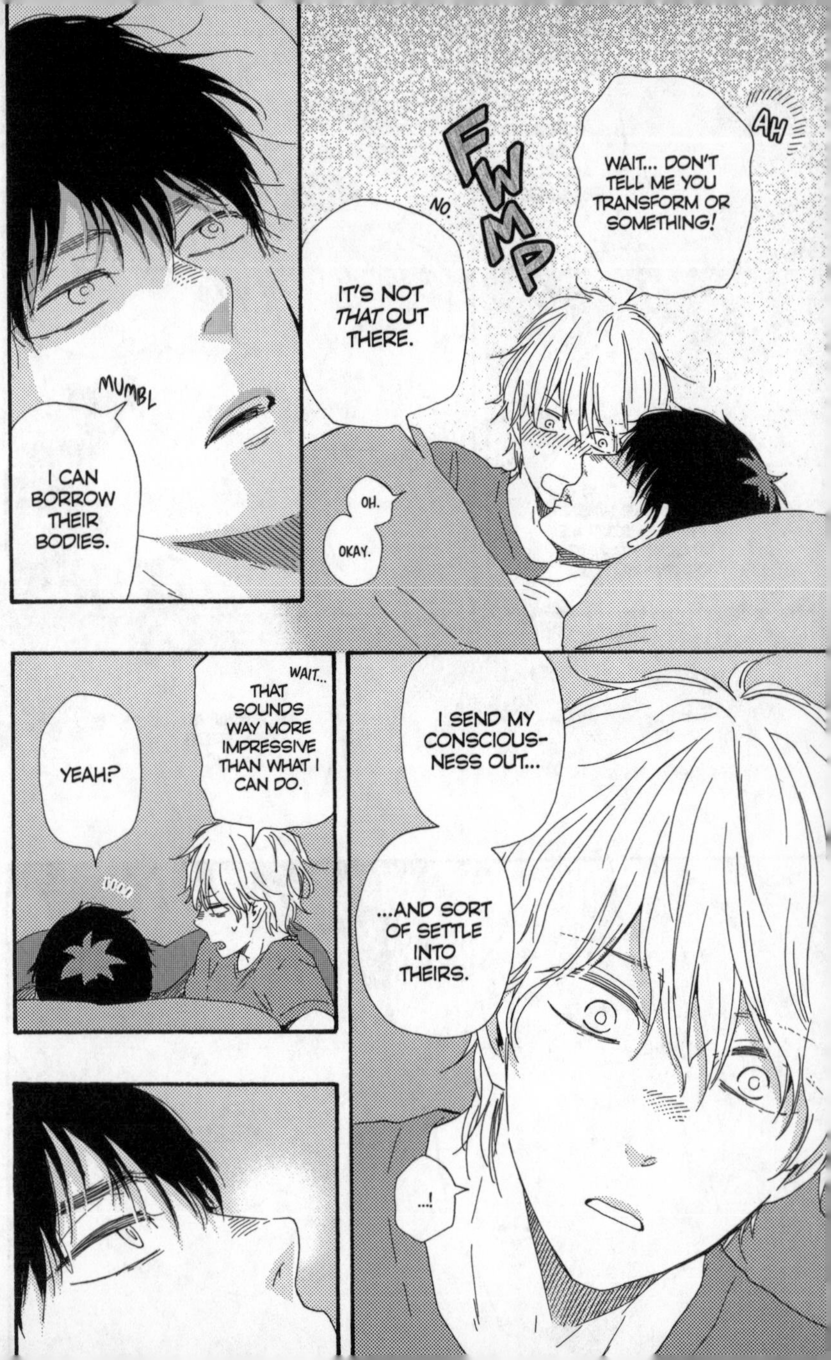
AH
WAIT... DON'T TELL ME YOU TRANSFORM OR SOMETHING!
FWMP
NO.
IT'S NOT *THAT* OUT THERE.
OH.
OKAY.
MUMBL
I CAN BORROW THEIR BODIES.
I SEND MY CONSCIOUS-NESS OUT...
...AND SORT OF SETTLE INTO THEIRS.
...!
WAIT... THAT SOUNDS WAY MORE IMPRESSIVE THAN WHAT I CAN DO.
YEAH?

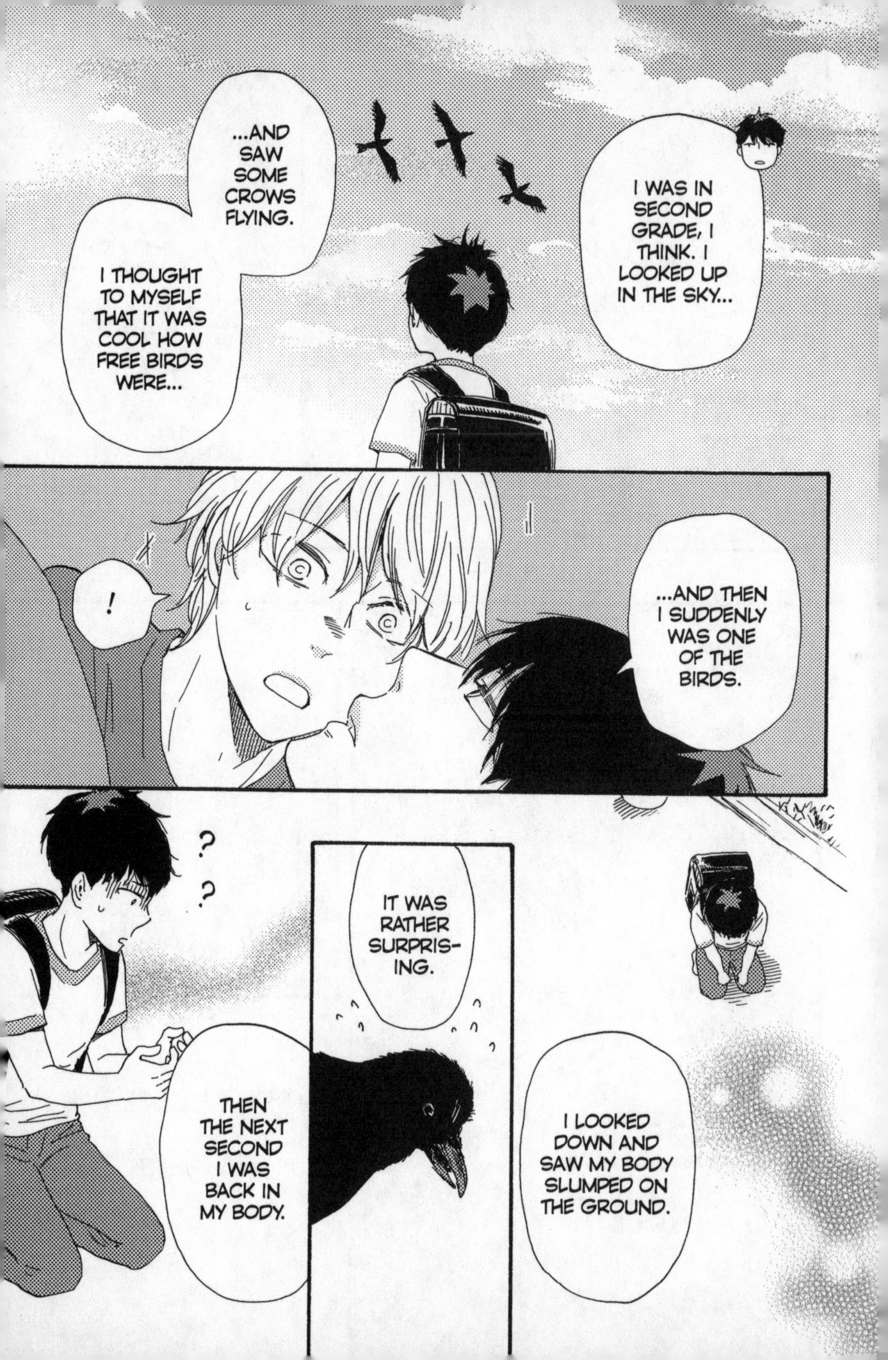
I WAS IN SECOND GRADE, I THINK. I LOOKED UP IN THE SKY...
...AND SAW SOME CROWS FLYING.
I THOUGHT TO MYSELF THAT IT WAS COOL HOW FREE BIRDS WERE...
...AND THEN I SUDDENLY WAS ONE OF THE BIRDS.
!
I LOOKED DOWN AND SAW MY BODY SLUMPED ON THE GROUND.
IT WAS RATHER SURPRIS-ING.
THEN THE NEXT SECOND I WAS BACK IN MY BODY.
? ?

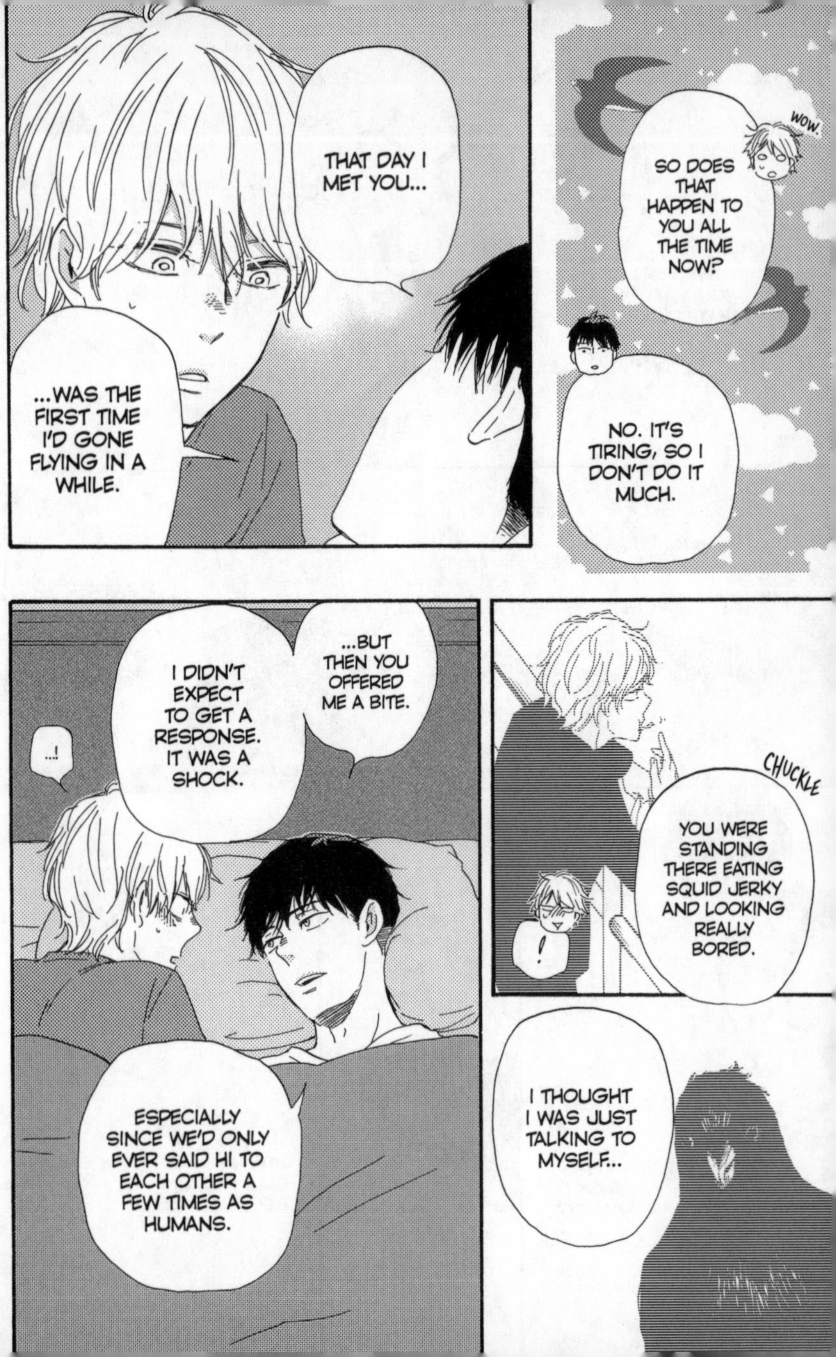
WOW.
SO DOES THAT HAPPEN TO YOU ALL THE TIME NOW?
NO. IT'S TIRING, SO I DON'T DO IT MUCH.
THAT DAY I MET YOU...
...WAS THE FIRST TIME I'D GONE FLYING IN A WHILE.
CHUCKLE
YOU WERE STANDING THERE EATING SQUID JERKY AND LOOKING REALLY BORED.
!
I THOUGHT I WAS JUST TALKING TO MYSELF...
...BUT THEN YOU OFFERED ME A BITE.
I DIDN'T EXPECT TO GET A RESPONSE. IT WAS A SHOCK.
...!
ESPECIALLY SINCE WE'D ONLY EVER SAID HI TO EACH OTHER A FEW TIMES AS HUMANS.

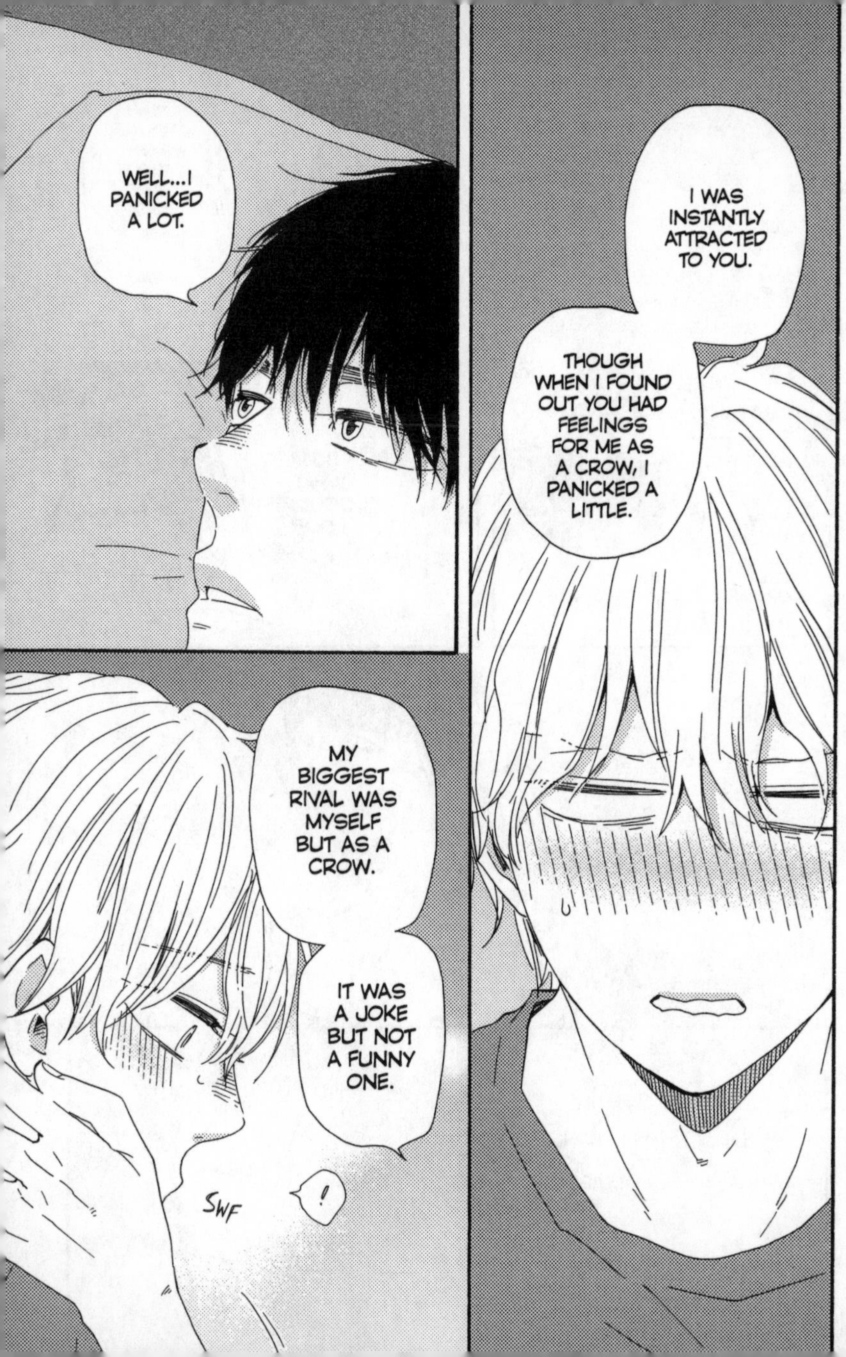
I WAS INSTANTLY ATTRACTED TO YOU.
THOUGH WHEN I FOUND OUT YOU HAD FEELINGS FOR ME AS A CROW, I PANICKED A LITTLE.
WELL...I PANICKED A LOT.
MY BIGGEST RIVAL WAS MYSELF BUT AS A CROW.
IT WAS A JOKE BUT NOT A FUNNY ONE.
!
SWF

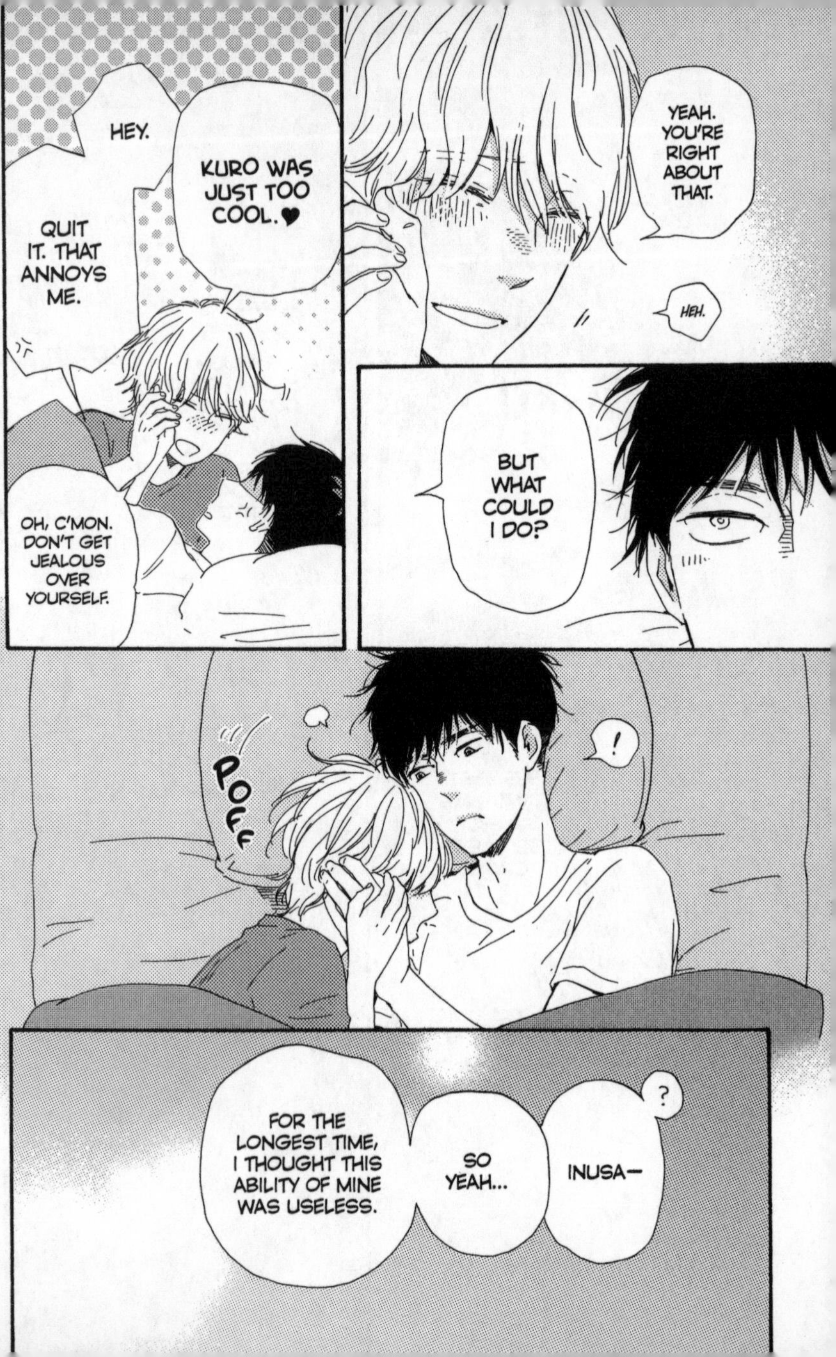
YEAH. YOU'RE RIGHT ABOUT THAT.
HEH.
BUT WHAT COULD I DO?
HEY.
KURO WAS JUST TOO COOL. ♥
QUIT IT. THAT ANNOYS ME.
OH, C'MON. DON'T GET JEALOUS OVER YOURSELF.
!
POFF
?
INUSA—
SO YEAH...
FOR THE LONGEST TIME, I THOUGHT THIS ABILITY OF MINE WAS USELESS.

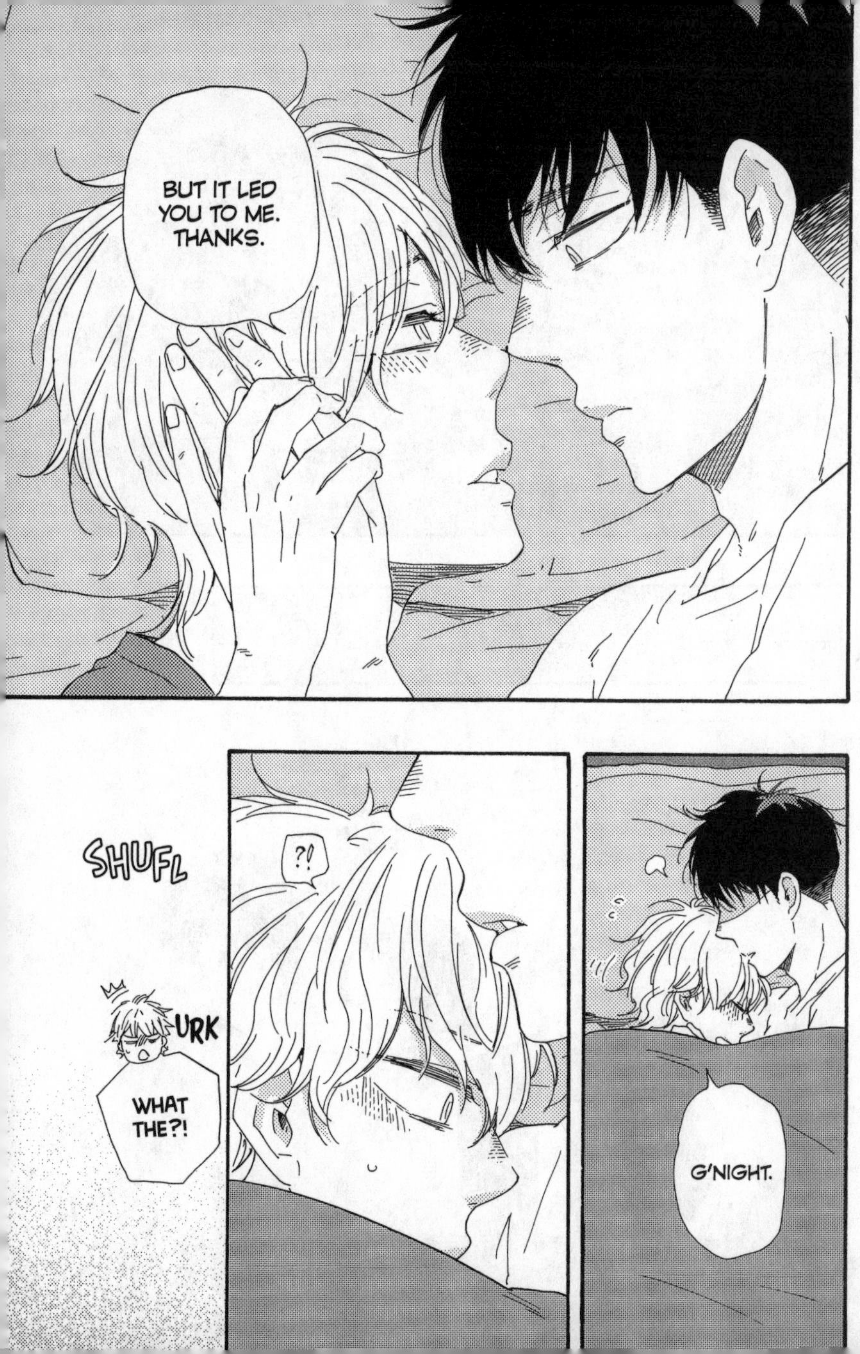
BUT IT LED YOU TO ME. THANKS.
G'NIGHT.
?!
SHUFL
URK
WHAT THE?!

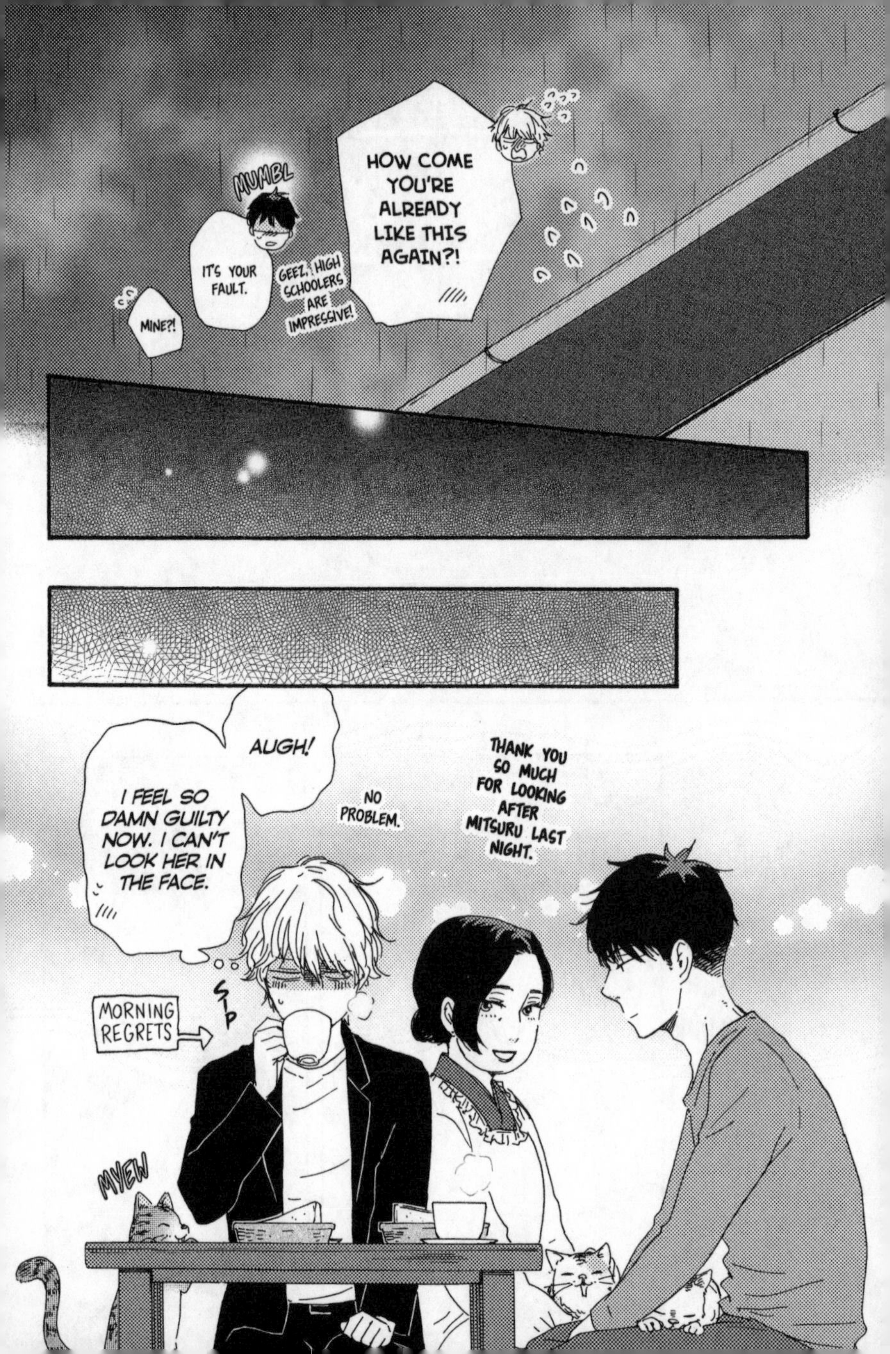
HOW COME YOU'RE ALREADY LIKE THIS AGAIN?!
GEEZ, HIGH SCHOOLERS ARE IMPRESSIVE!
MUMBL
IT'S YOUR FAULT.
MINE?!
THANK YOU SO MUCH FOR LOOKING AFTER MITSURU LAST NIGHT.
NO PROBLEM.
AUGH!
I FEEL SO DAMN GUILTY NOW. I CAN'T LOOK HER IN THE FACE.
SIP
MORNING REGRETS
MYEW

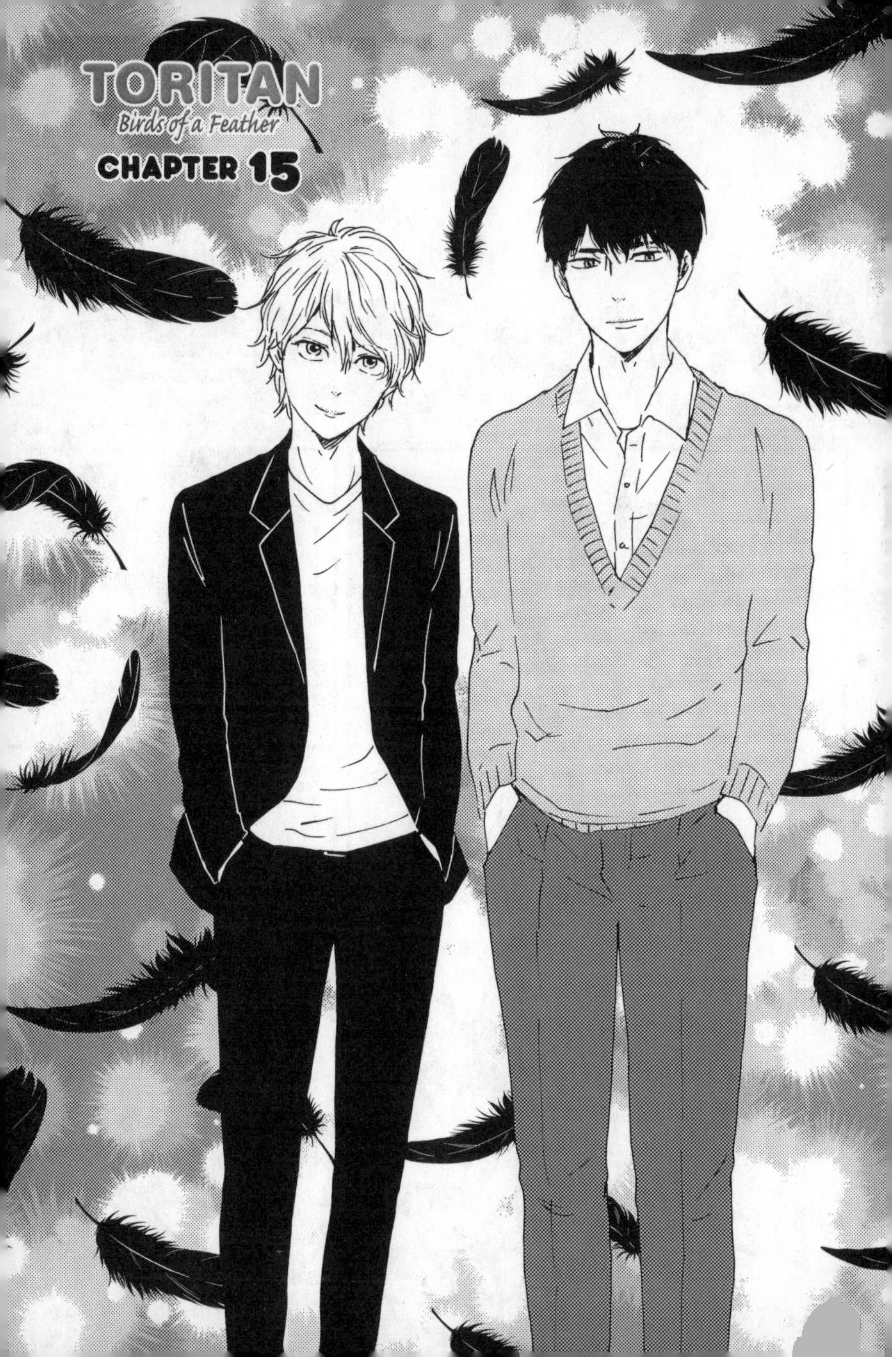
TORITAN
Birds of a Feather
CHAPTER 15

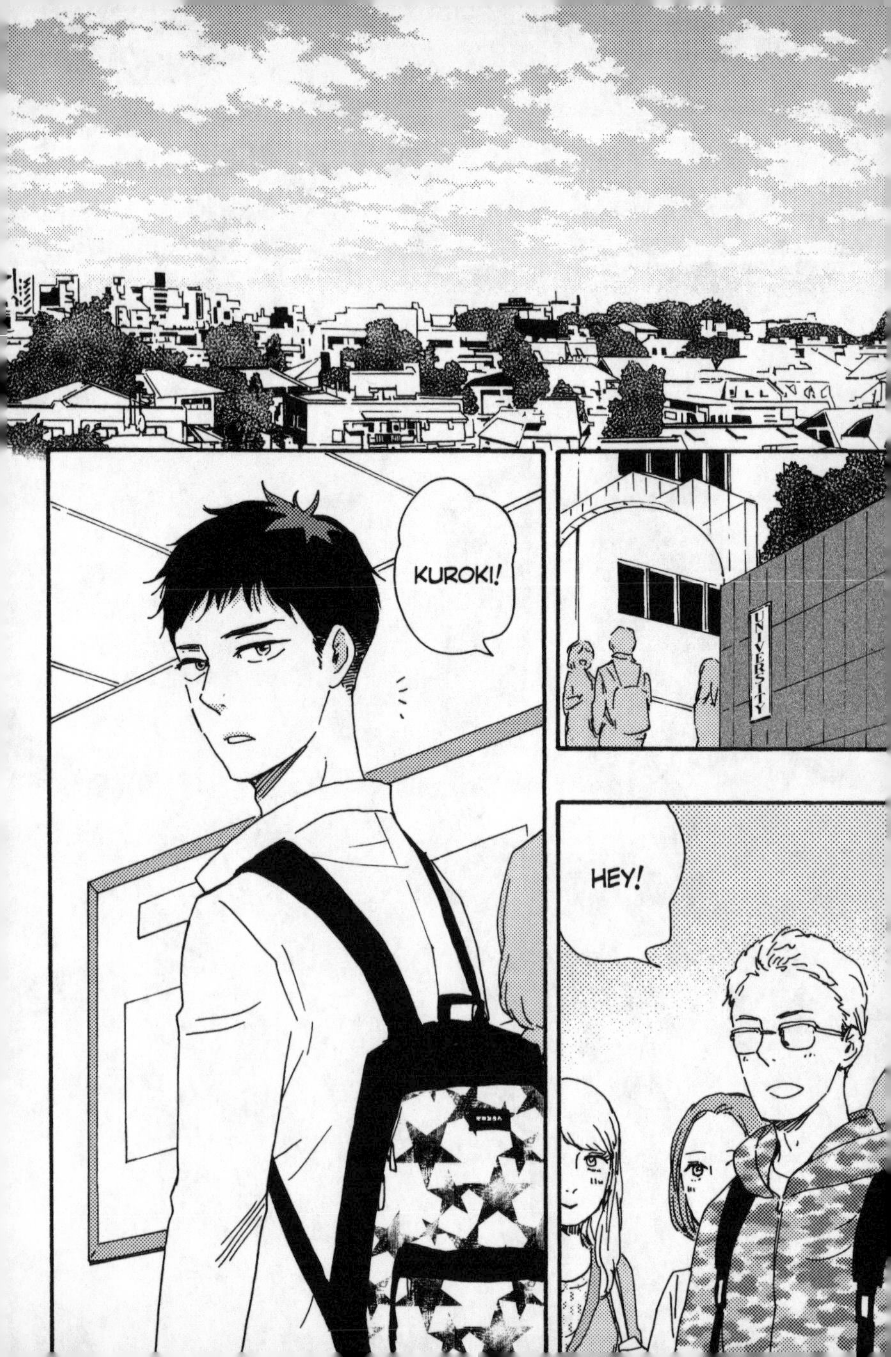
UNIVERSITY
HEY!
KUROKI!

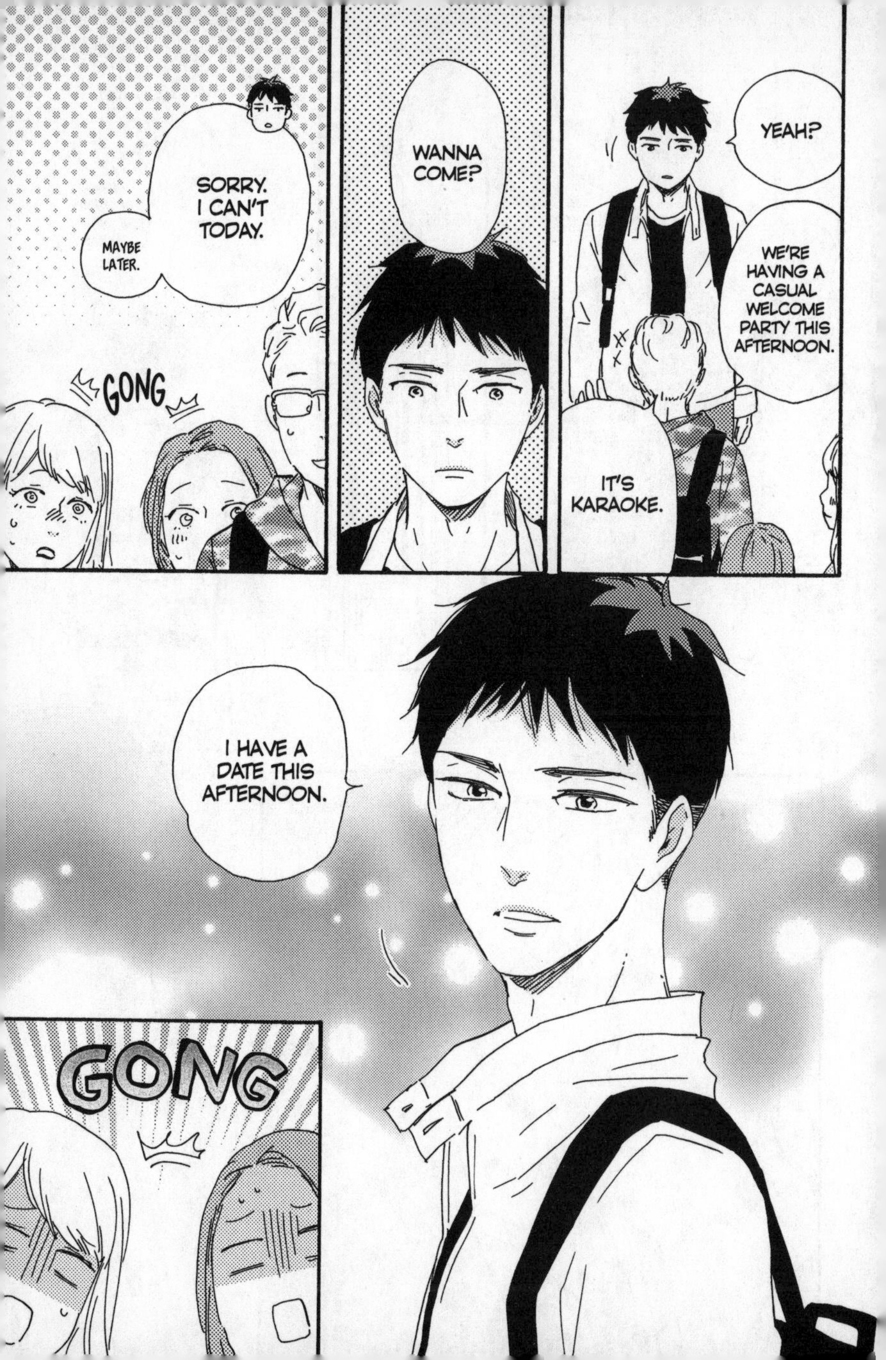
YEAH?
WE'RE HAVING A CASUAL WELCOME PARTY THIS AFTERNOON.
IT'S KARAOKE.
WANNA COME?
SORRY. I CAN'T TODAY.
MAYBE LATER.
GONG
I HAVE A DATE THIS AFTERNOON.
GONG

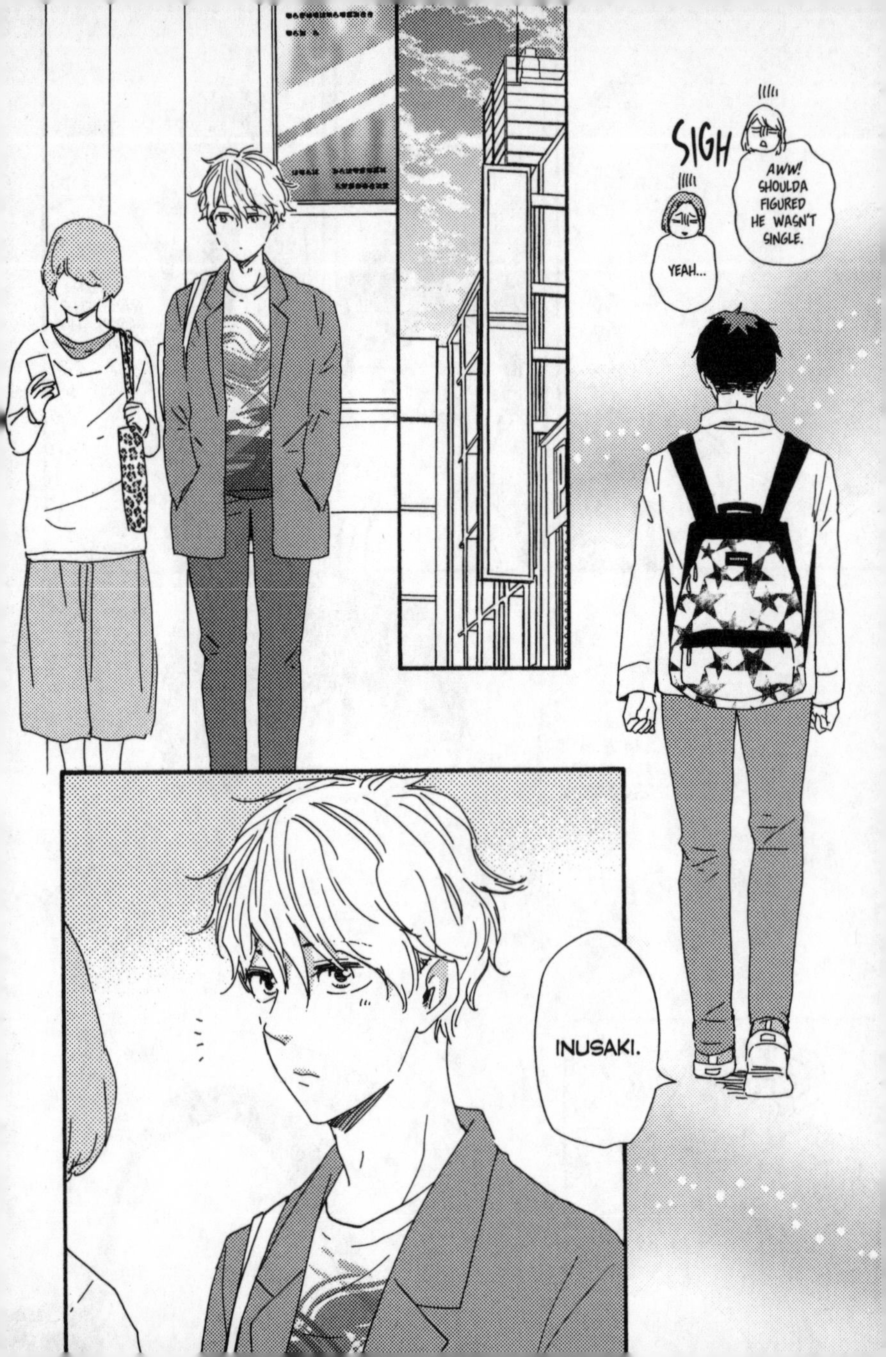
SIGH
AWW! SHOULDA FIGURED HE WASN'T SINGLE.
YEAH...
INUSAKI.

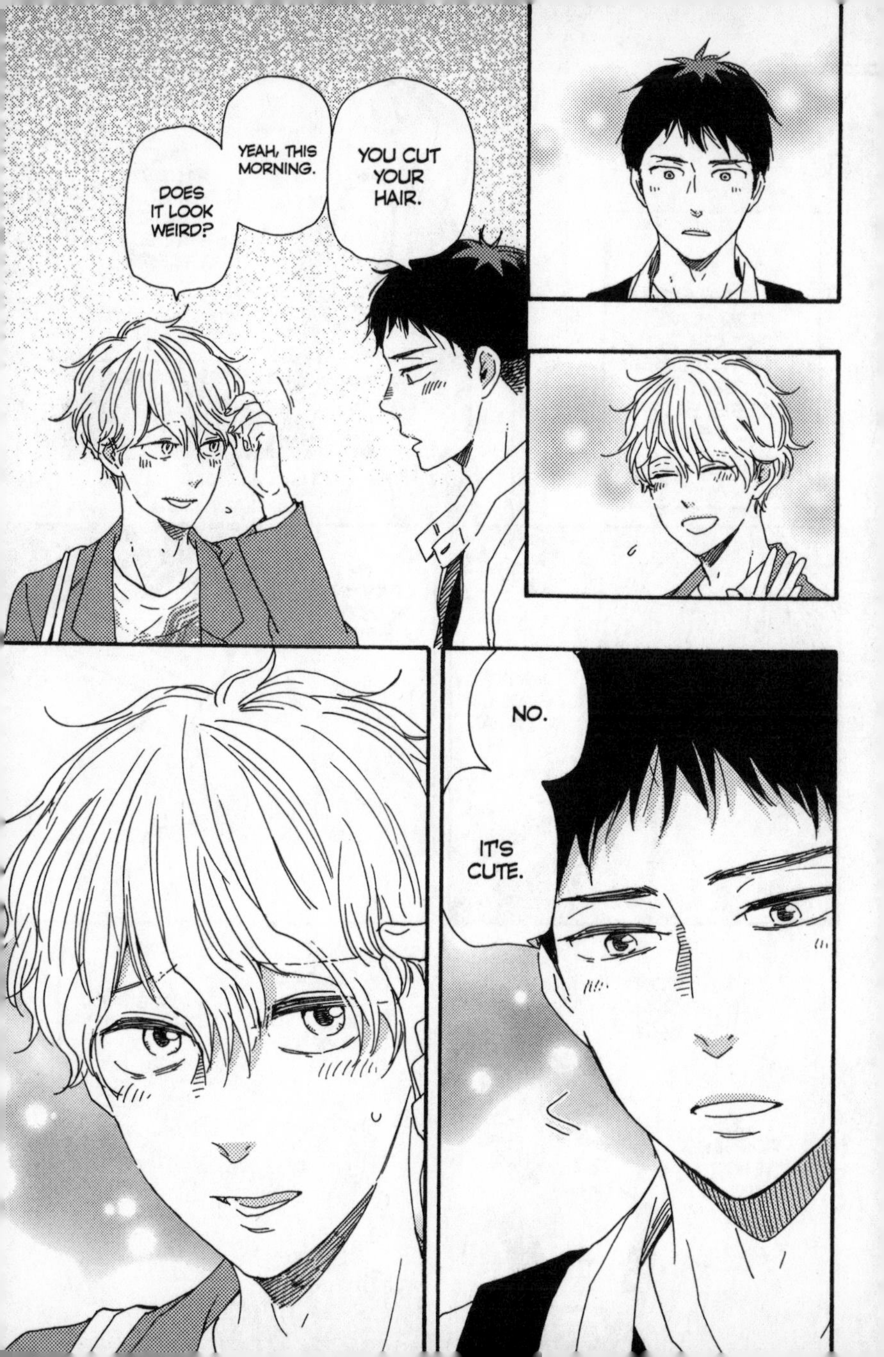
YOU CUT YOUR HAIR.
YEAH, THIS MORNING.
DOES IT LOOK WEIRD?
NO.
IT'S CUTE.

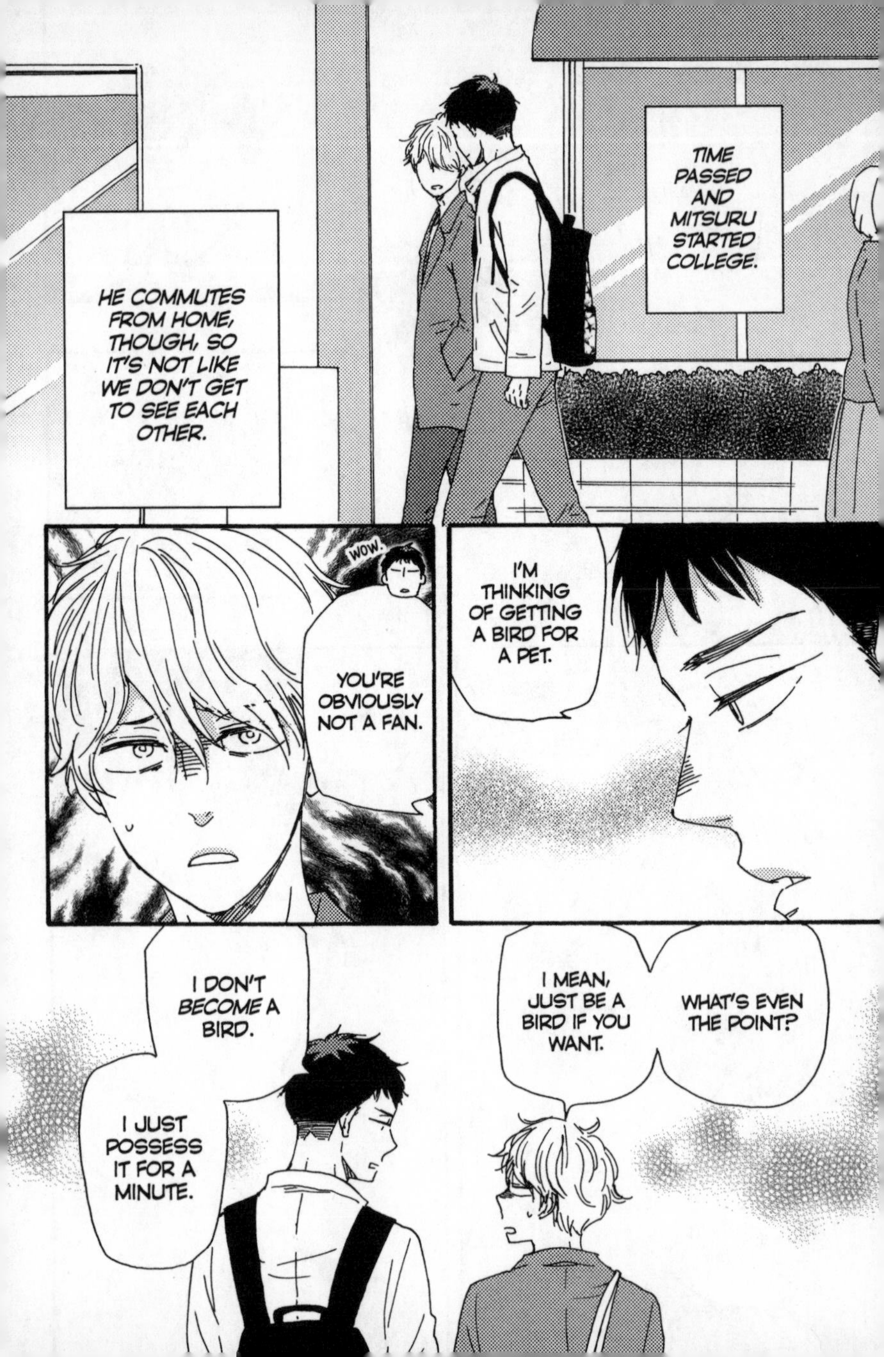
TIME PASSED AND MITSURU STARTED COLLEGE.
HE COMMUTES FROM HOME, THOUGH, SO IT'S NOT LIKE WE DON'T GET TO SEE EACH OTHER.
I'M THINKING OF GETTING A BIRD FOR A PET.
WOW.
YOU'RE OBVIOUSLY NOT A FAN.
WHAT'S EVEN THE POINT?
I MEAN, JUST BE A BIRD IF YOU WANT.
I DON'T BECOME A BIRD.
I JUST POSSESS IT FOR A MINUTE.

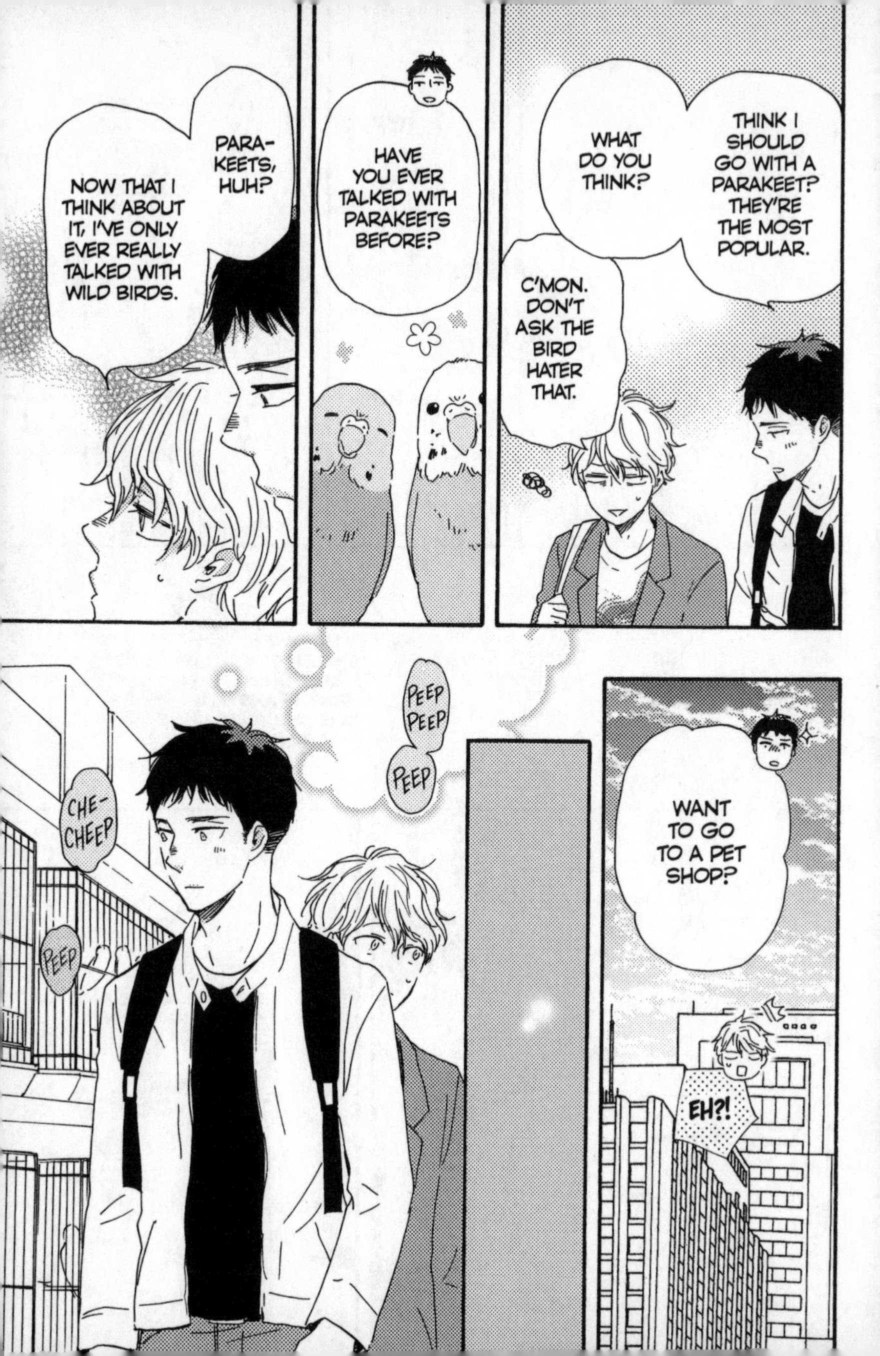
THINK I SHOULD GO WITH A PARAKEET? THEY'RE THE MOST POPULAR.
WHAT DO YOU THINK?
C'MON. DON'T ASK THE BIRD HATER THAT.
HAVE YOU EVER TALKED WITH PARAKEETS BEFORE?
PARA-KEETS, HUH?
NOW THAT I THINK ABOUT IT, I'VE ONLY EVER REALLY TALKED WITH WILD BIRDS.
WANT TO GO TO A PET SHOP?
EH?!
PEEP PEEP
PEEP
CHE-CHEEP
PEEP

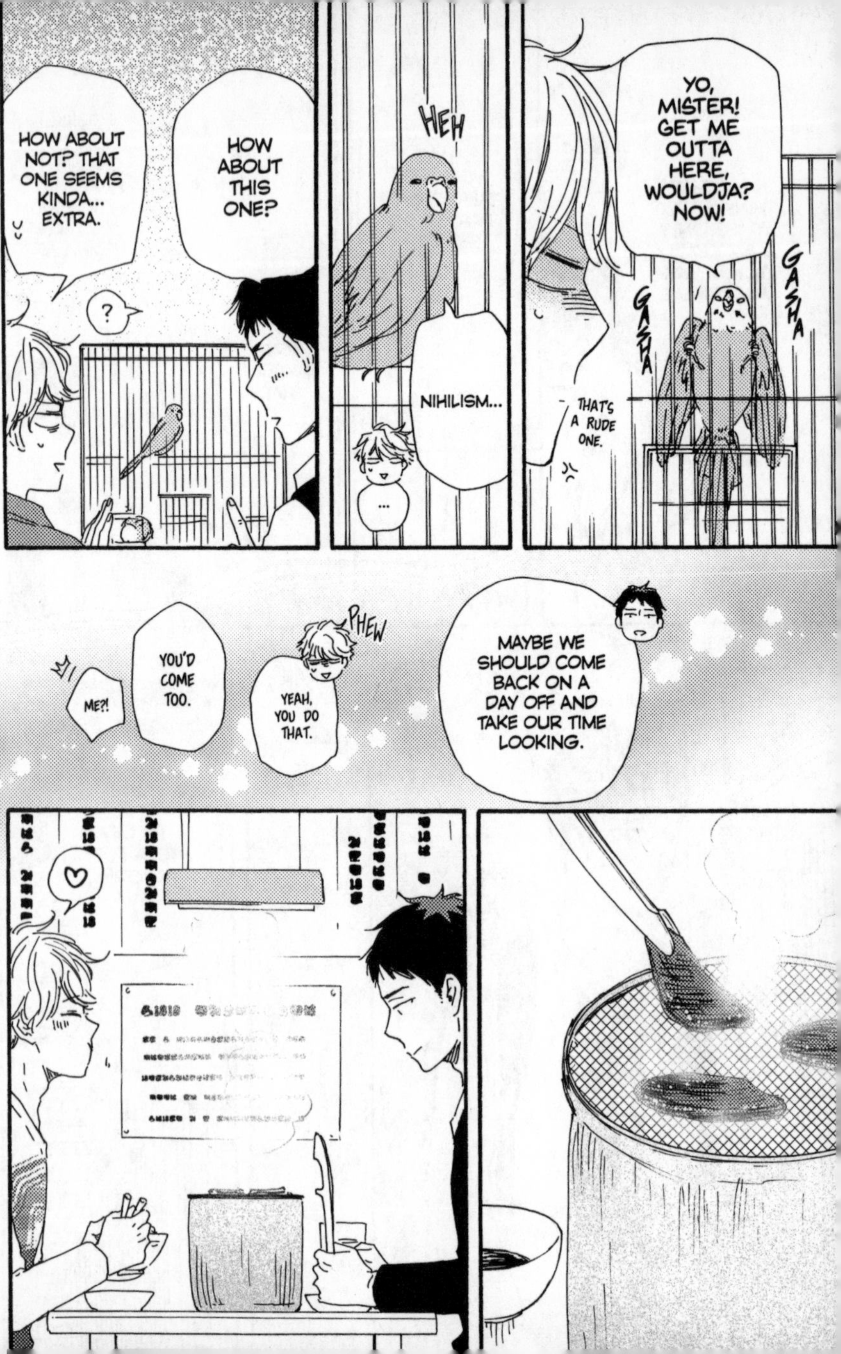
YO, MISTER! GET ME OUTTA HERE, WOULDJA? NOW!
GASHA
GASHA
THAT'S A RUDE ONE.
HEH
NIHILISM...
...
HOW ABOUT THIS ONE?
HOW ABOUT NOT? THAT ONE SEEMS KINDA... EXTRA.
?
MAYBE WE SHOULD COME BACK ON A DAY OFF AND TAKE OUR TIME LOOKING.
PHEW
YEAH, YOU DO THAT.
YOU'D COME TOO.
ME?!

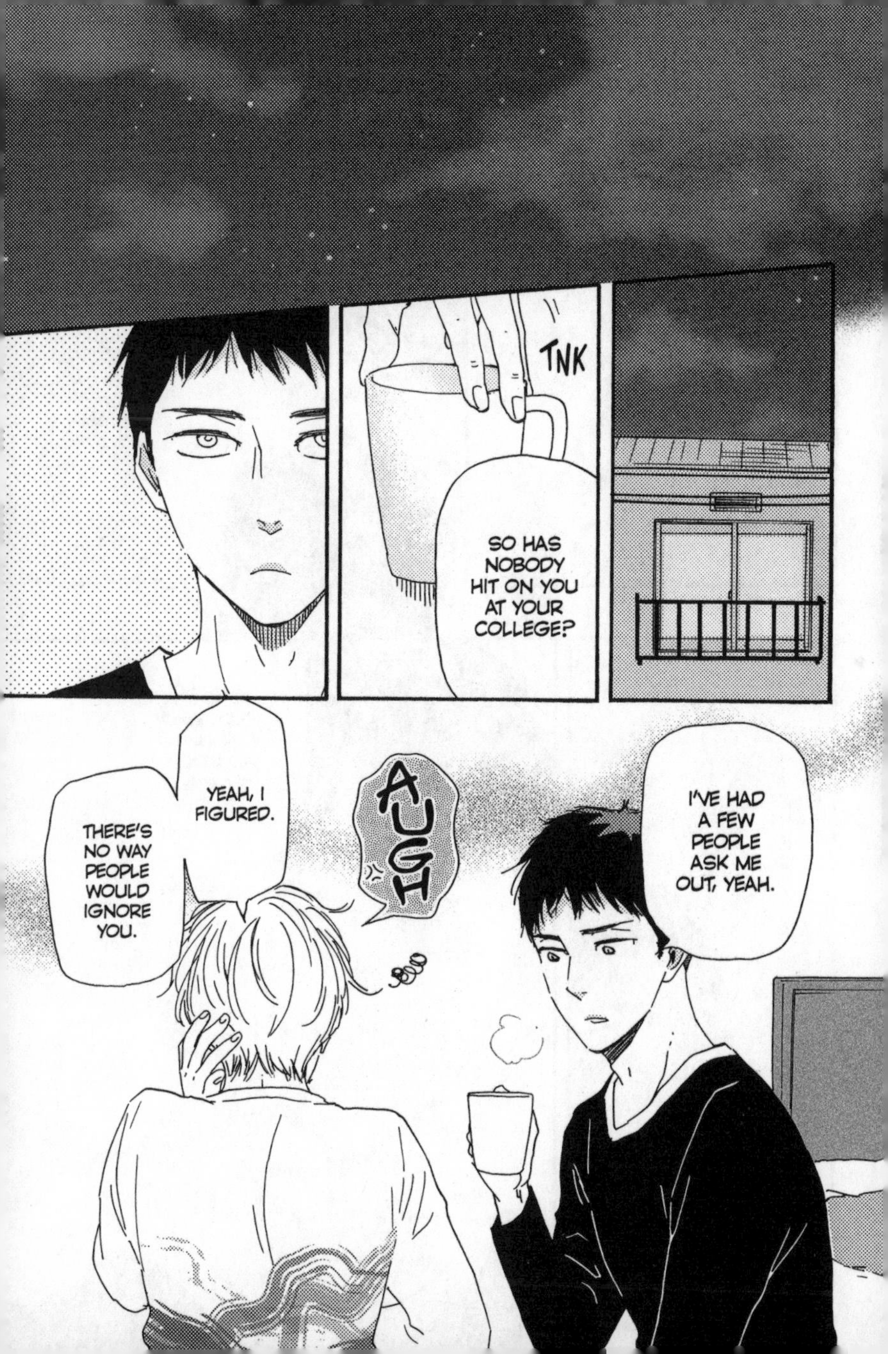
TNK
SO HAS NOBODY HIT ON YOU AT YOUR COLLEGE?
I'VE HAD A FEW PEOPLE ASK ME OUT, YEAH.
AUGH
YEAH, I FIGURED.
THERE'S NO WAY PEOPLE WOULD IGNORE YOU.

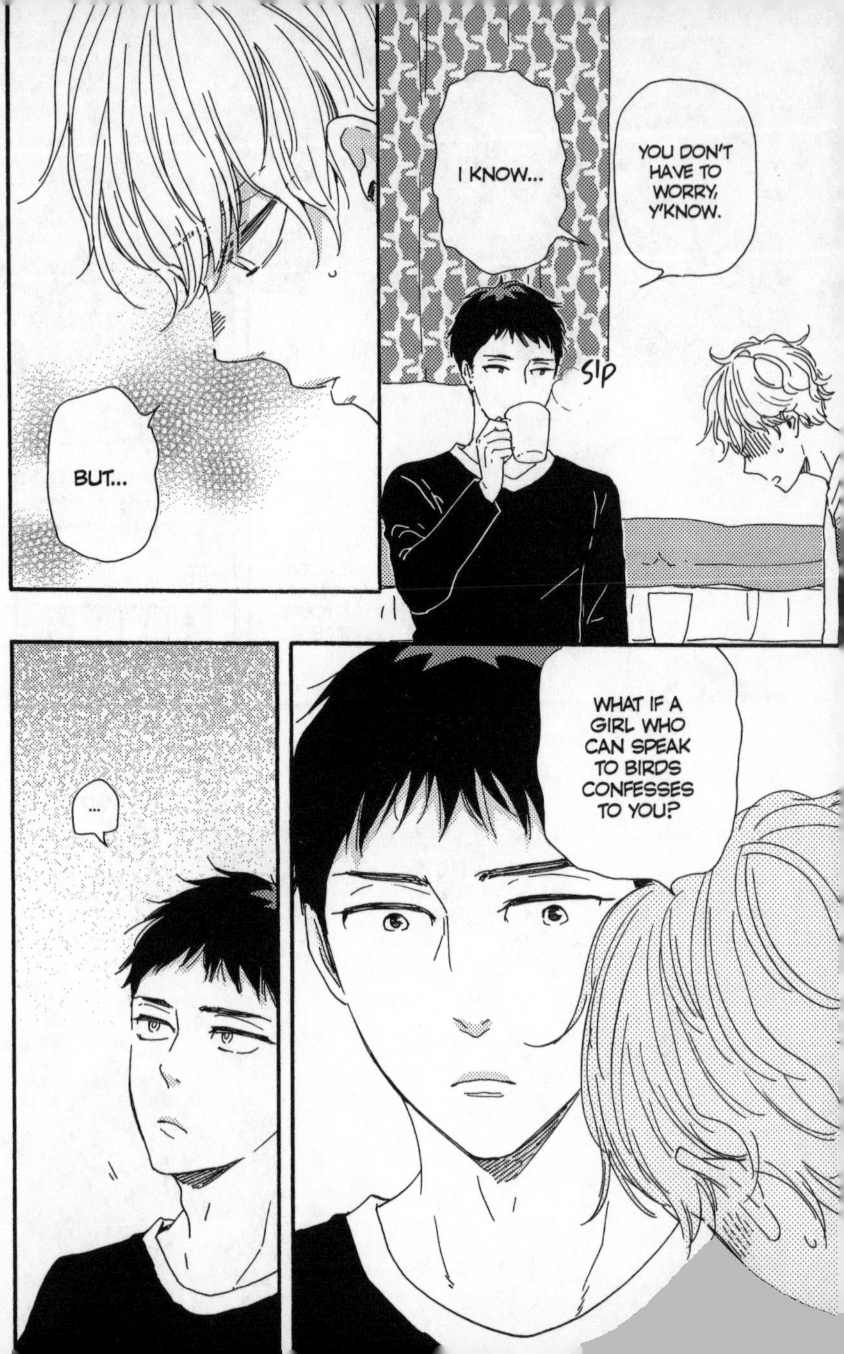
YOU DON'T HAVE TO WORRY, Y'KNOW.
I KNOW...
SIP
BUT...
WHAT IF A GIRL WHO CAN SPEAK TO BIRDS CONFESSES TO YOU?
...

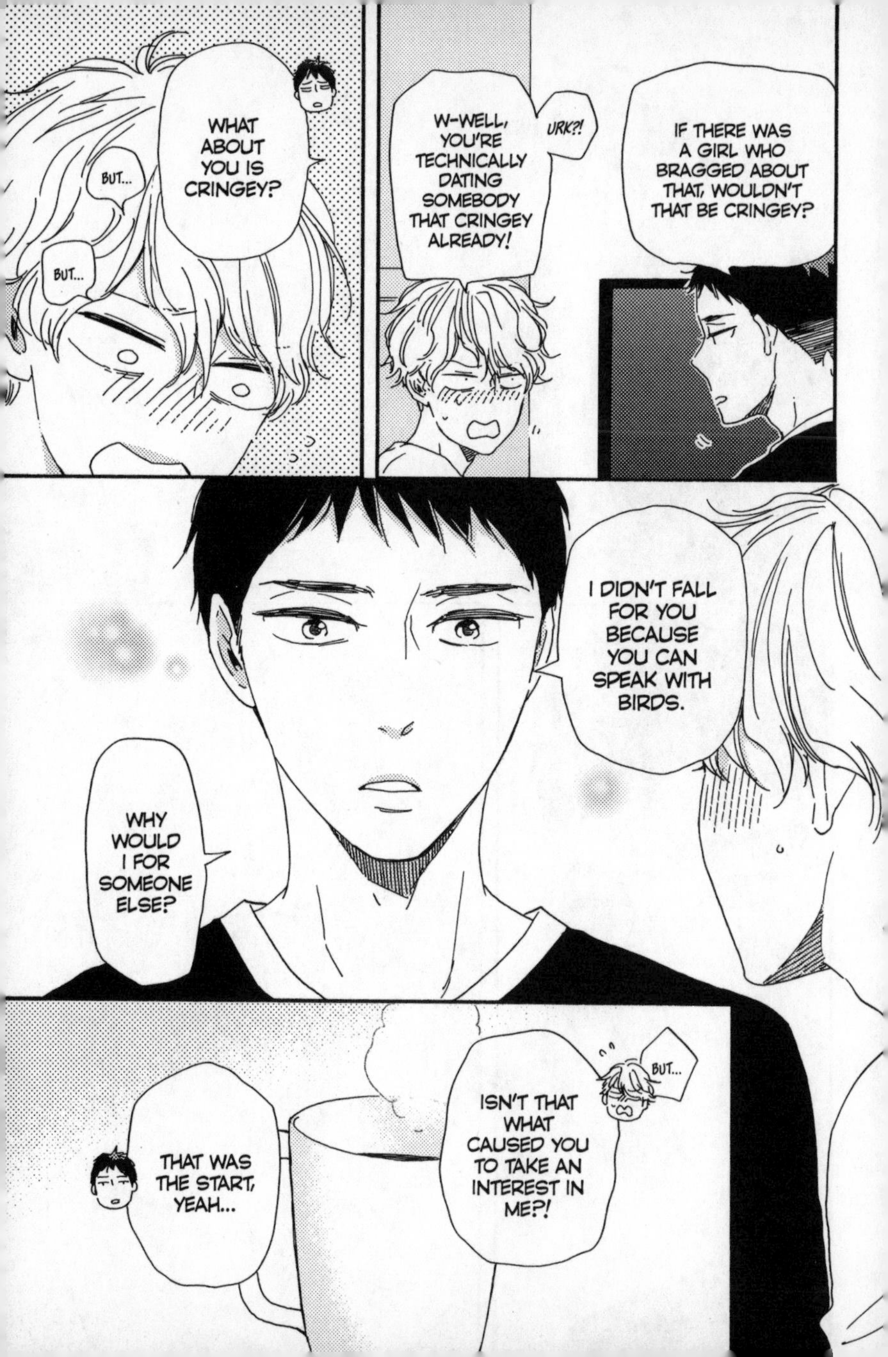
IF THERE WAS A GIRL WHO BRAGGED ABOUT THAT, WOULDN'T THAT BE CRINGEY?
URK?!
W-WELL, YOU'RE TECHNICALLY DATING SOMEBODY THAT CRINGEY ALREADY!
WHAT ABOUT YOU IS CRINGEY?
BUT...
BUT...
I DIDN'T FALL FOR YOU BECAUSE YOU CAN SPEAK WITH BIRDS.
WHY WOULD I FOR SOMEONE ELSE?
BUT...
ISN'T THAT WHAT CAUSED YOU TO TAKE AN INTEREST IN ME?!
THAT WAS THE START, YEAH...

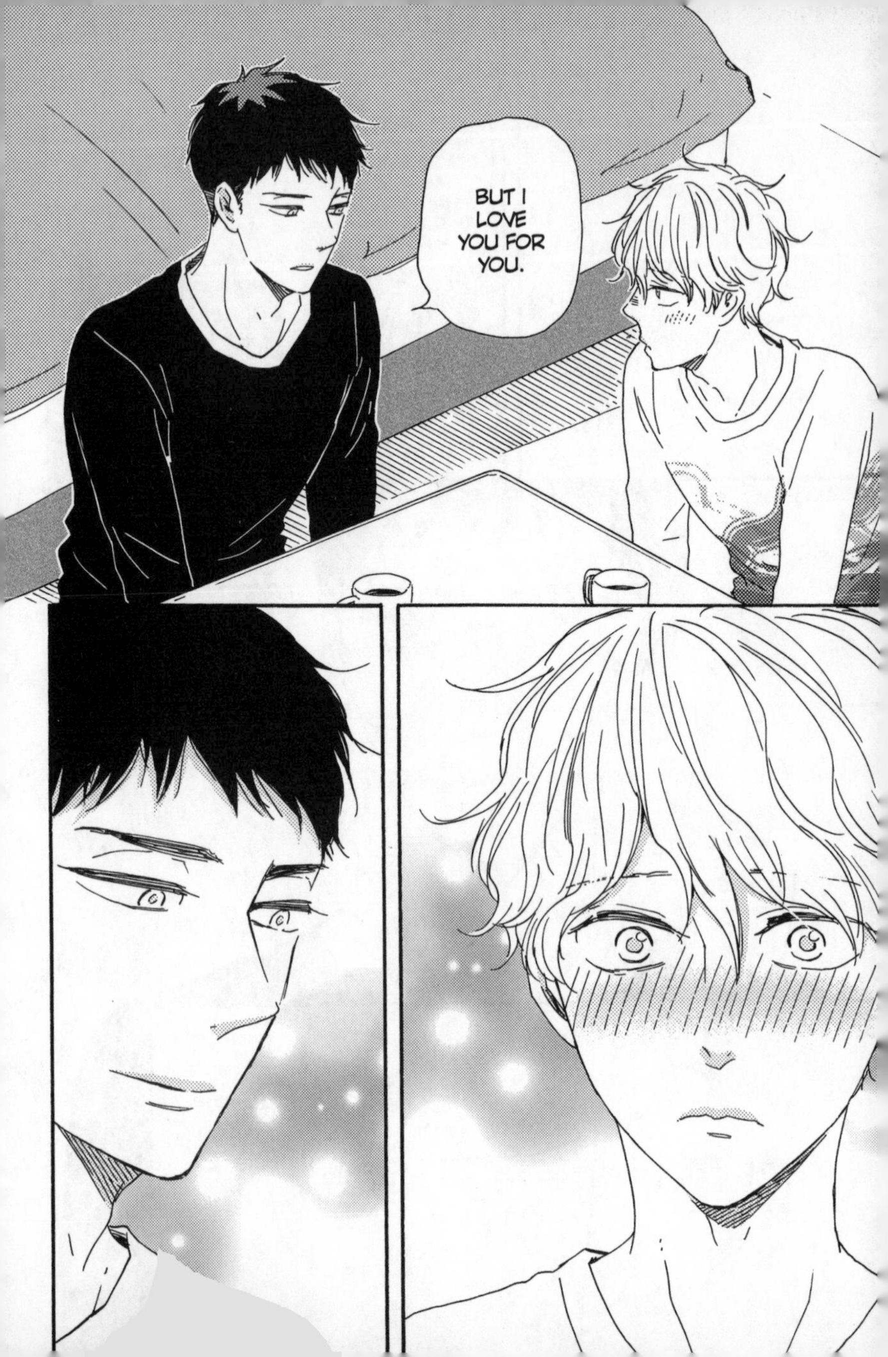
BUT I LOVE YOU FOR YOU.

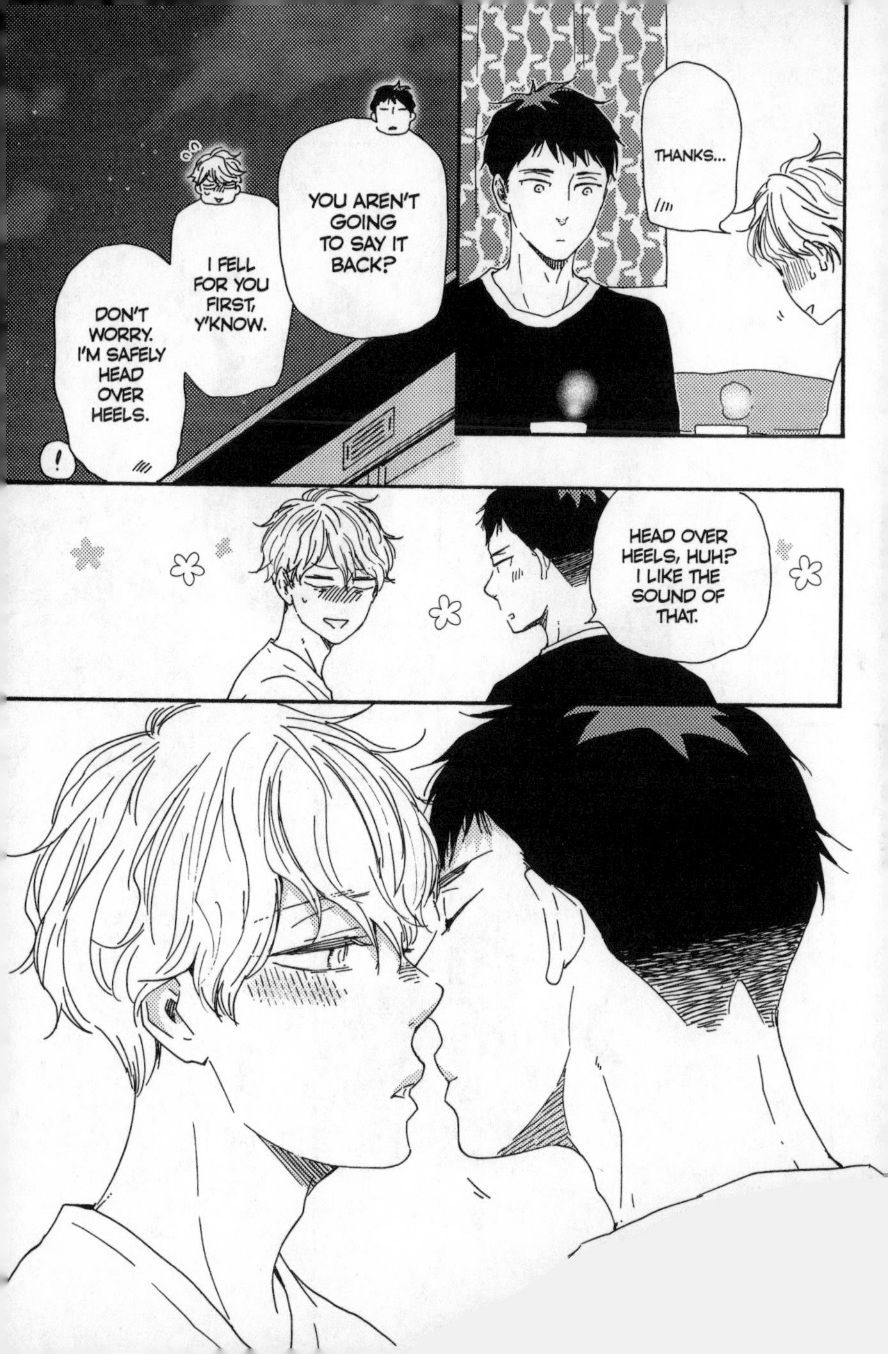
THANKS...
YOU AREN'T GOING TO SAY IT BACK?
I FELL FOR YOU FIRST, Y'KNOW.
DON'T WORRY. I'M SAFELY HEAD OVER HEELS.
!
HEAD OVER HEELS, HUH? I LIKE THE SOUND OF THAT.

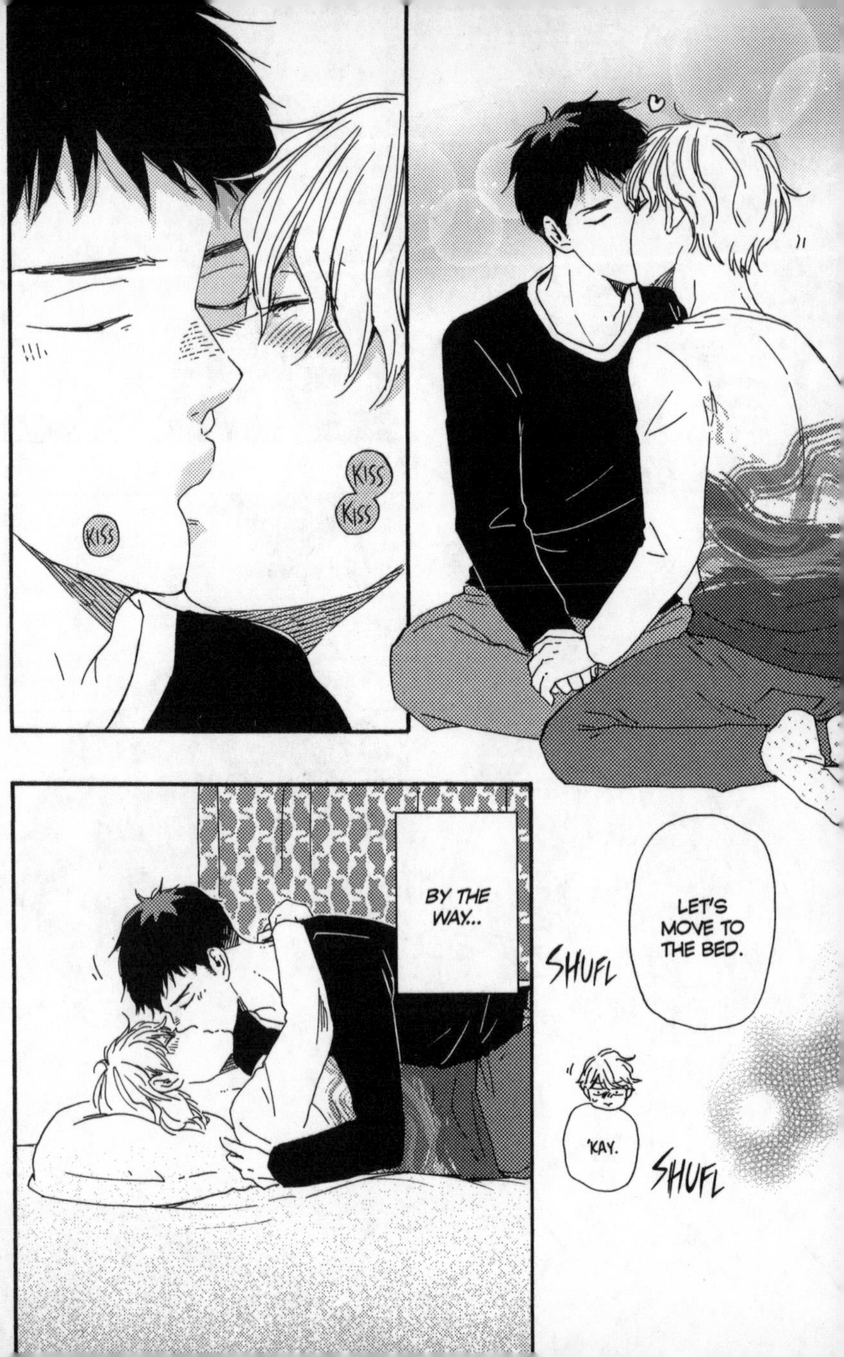
KISS
KISS
KISS
LET'S MOVE TO THE BED.
SHUFL
'KAY.
SHUFL
BY THE WAY...

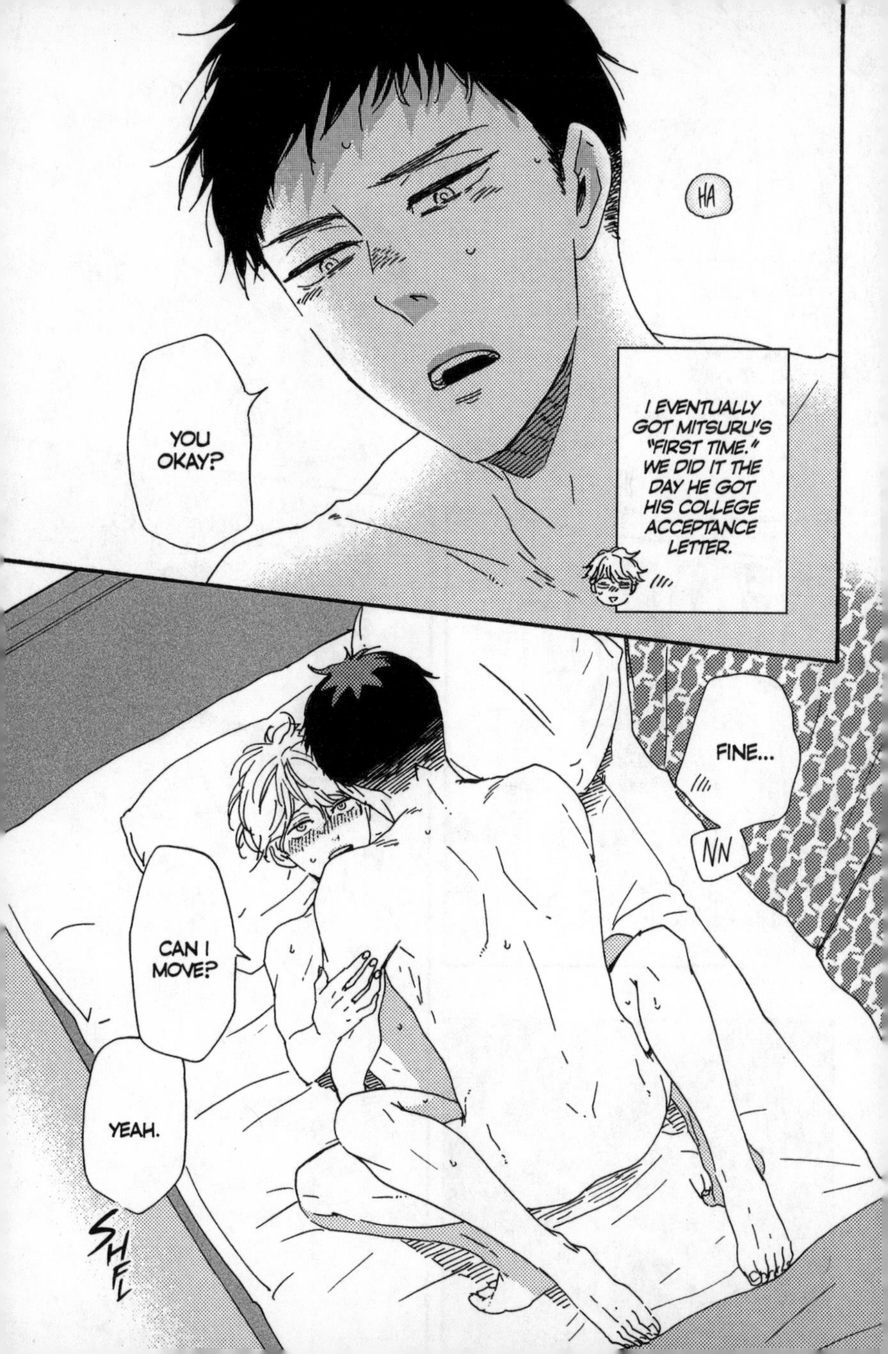
HA
I EVENTUALLY GOT MITSURU'S "FIRST TIME." WE DID IT THE DAY HE GOT HIS COLLEGE ACCEPTANCE LETTER.
YOU OKAY?
FINE...
NN
CAN I MOVE?
YEAH.
SHFL

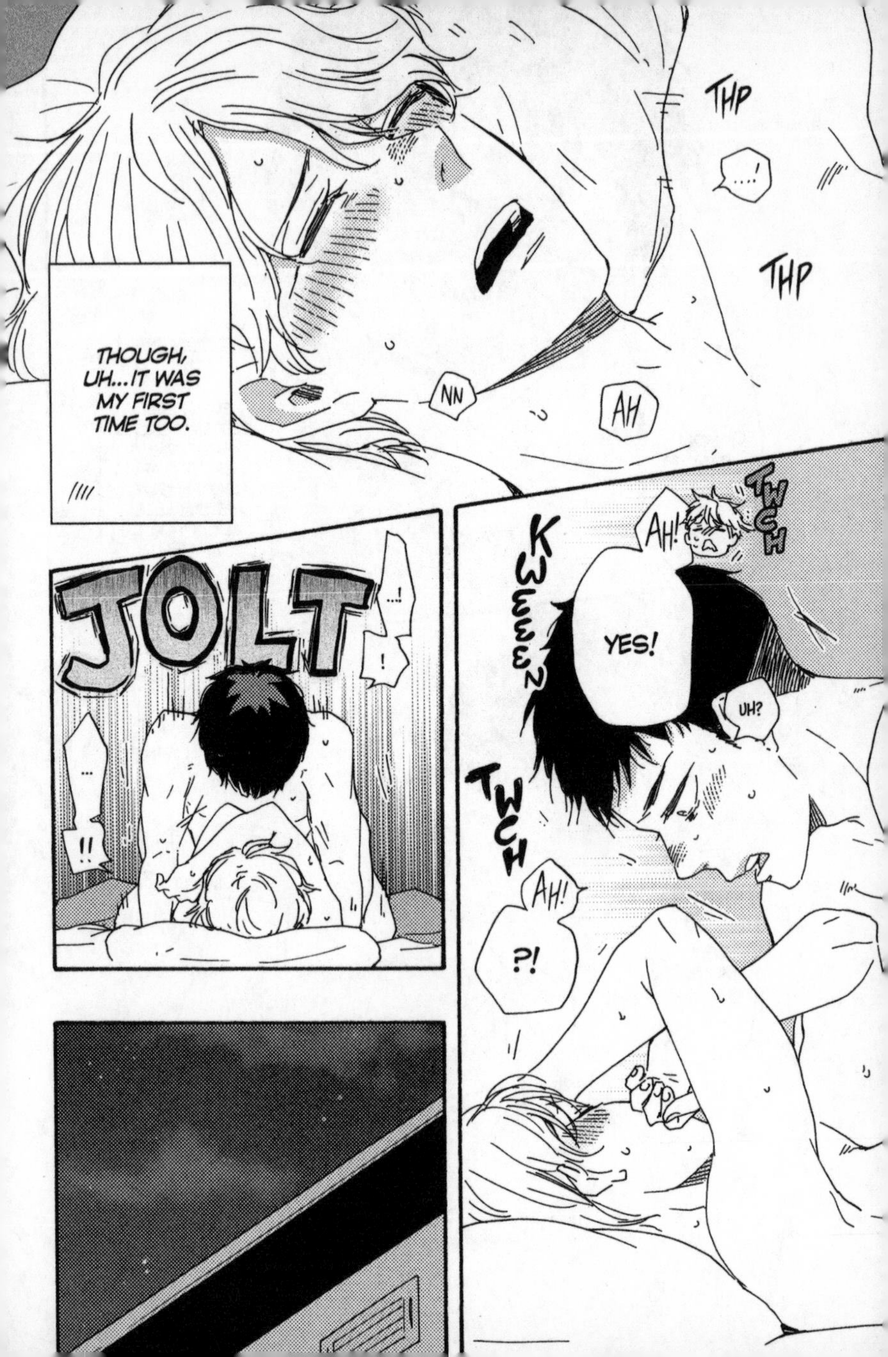
THP
....!
THP
AH
NN
THOUGH, UH...IT WAS MY FIRST TIME TOO.
TWCH
AH!
KWEEEZ
YES!
UH?
TWCH
AH!
?!
JOLT
...!
!
...
!!

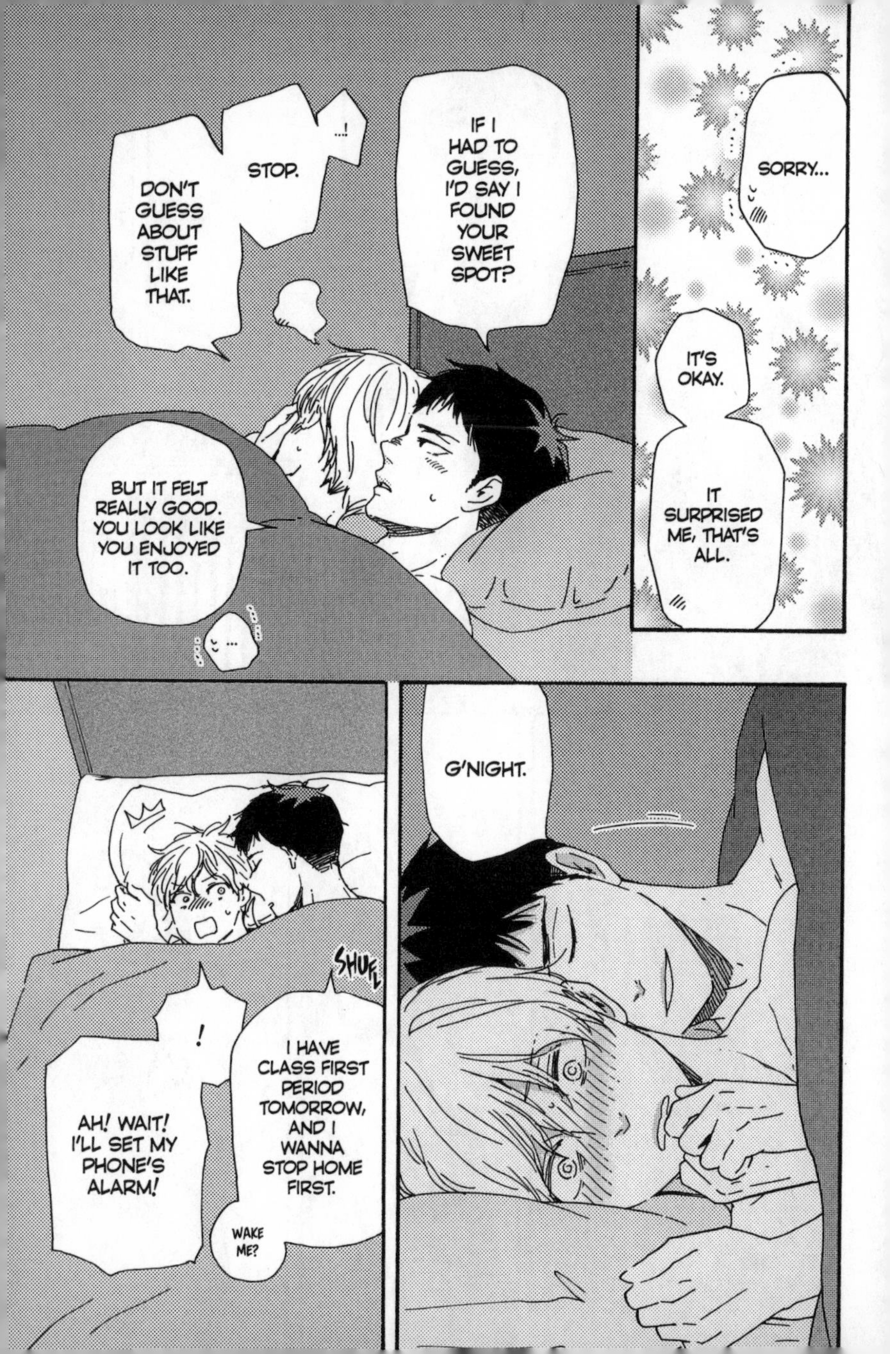
SORRY...
IT'S OKAY.
IT SURPRISED ME, THAT'S ALL.
IF I HAD TO GUESS, I'D SAY I FOUND YOUR SWEET SPOT?
...!
STOP.
DON'T GUESS ABOUT STUFF LIKE THAT.
BUT IT FELT REALLY GOOD. YOU LOOK LIKE YOU ENJOYED IT TOO.
...
G'NIGHT.
SHUFL
I HAVE CLASS FIRST PERIOD TOMORROW, AND I WANNA STOP HOME FIRST.
WAKE ME?
!
AH! WAIT! I'LL SET MY PHONE'S ALARM!

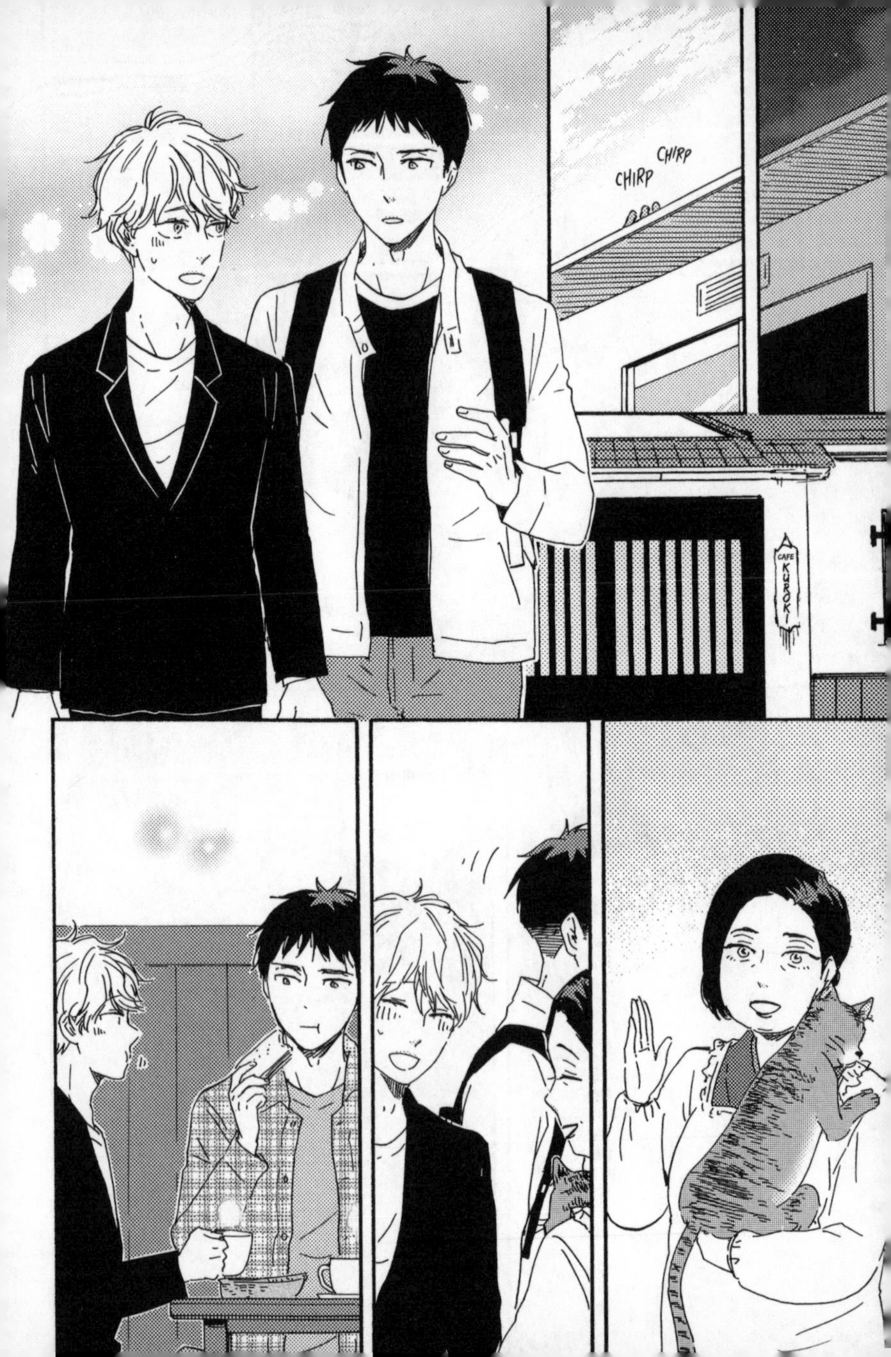
CHIRP
CHIRP
CAFE KUROKI

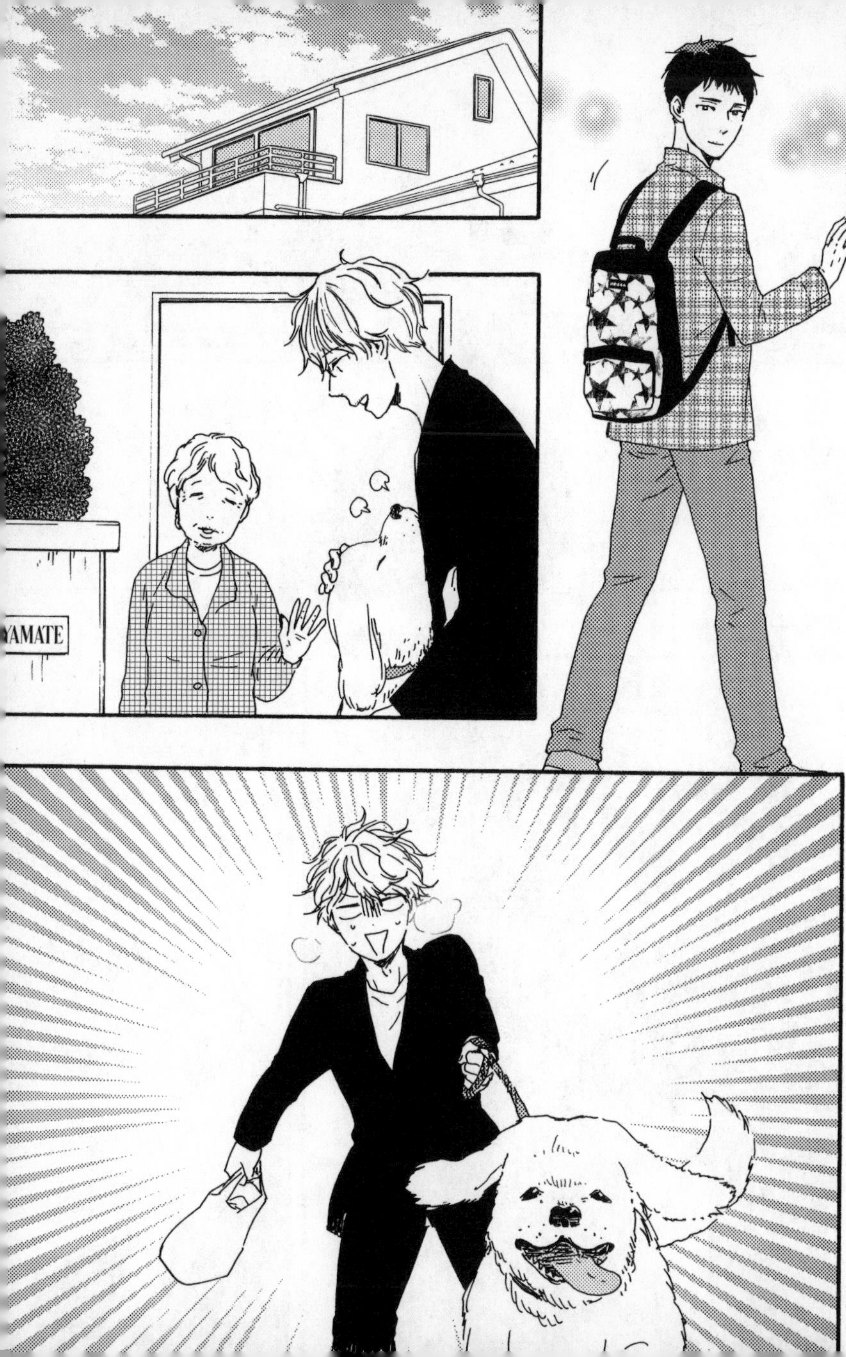
YAMATE

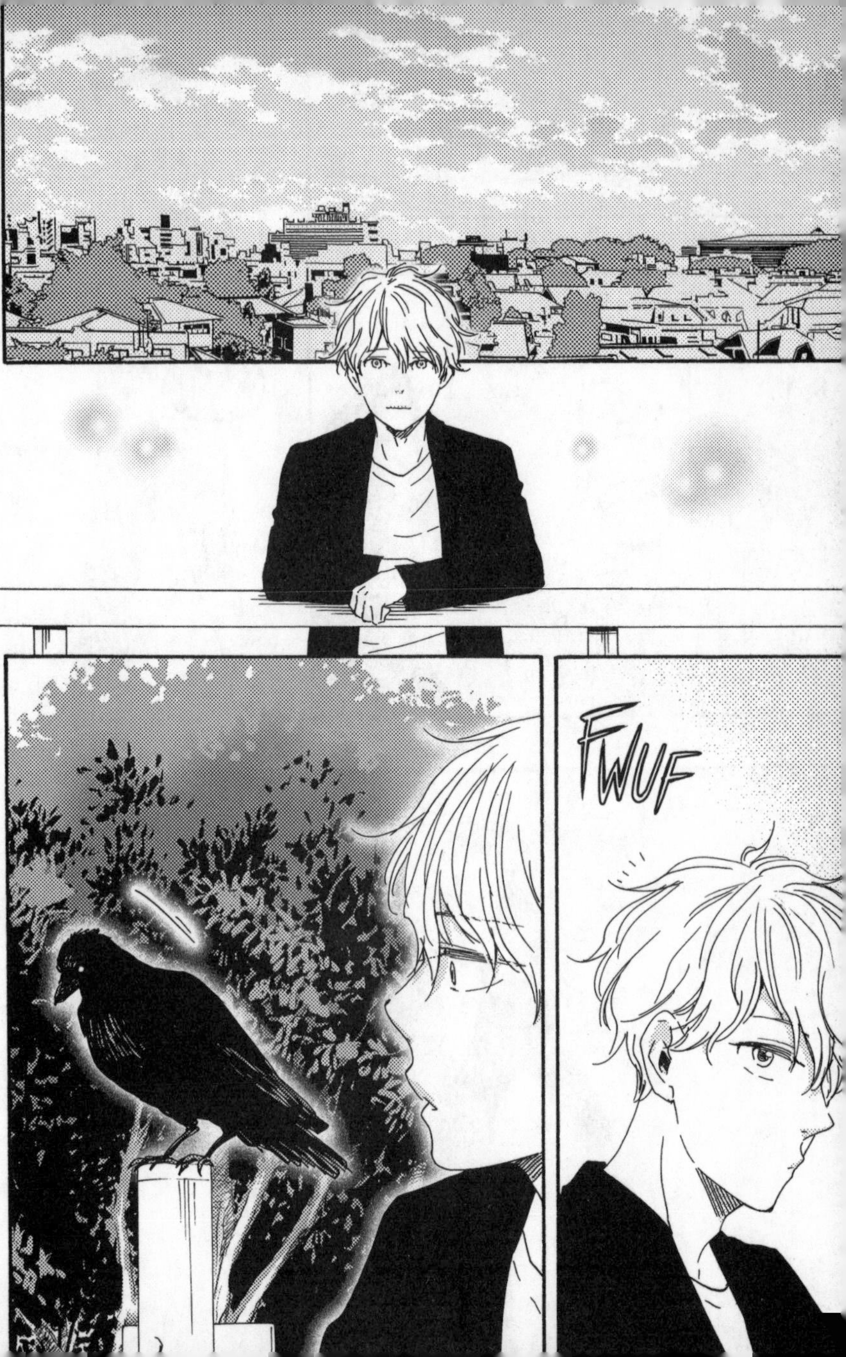
FWUF

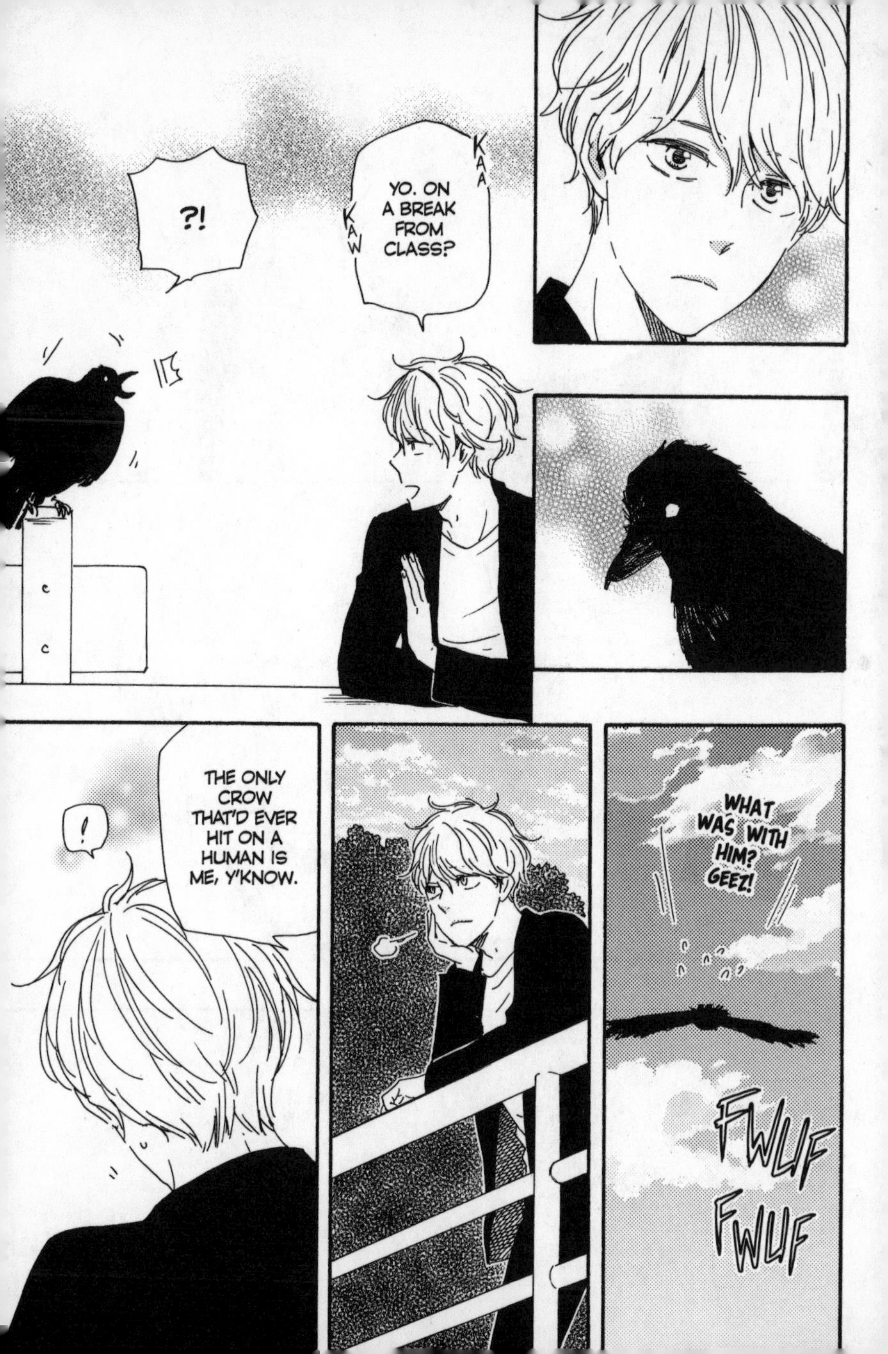
KAA
KAW
YO. ON A BREAK FROM CLASS?
?!
WHAT WAS WITH HIM? GEEZ!
FWUF FWUF
THE ONLY CROW THAT'D EVER HIT ON A HUMAN IS ME, Y'KNOW.
!

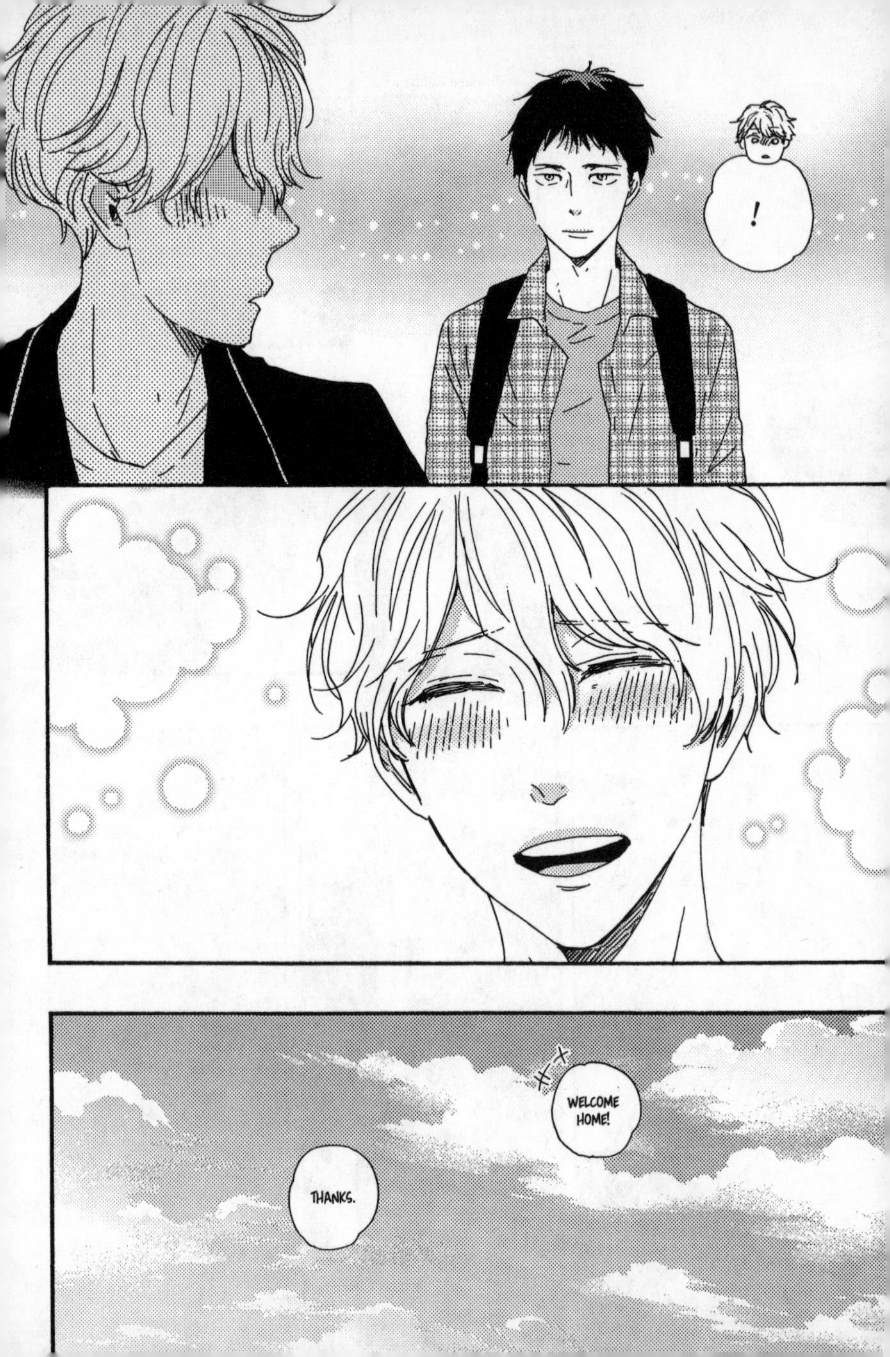
!
WELCOME HOME!
THANKS.

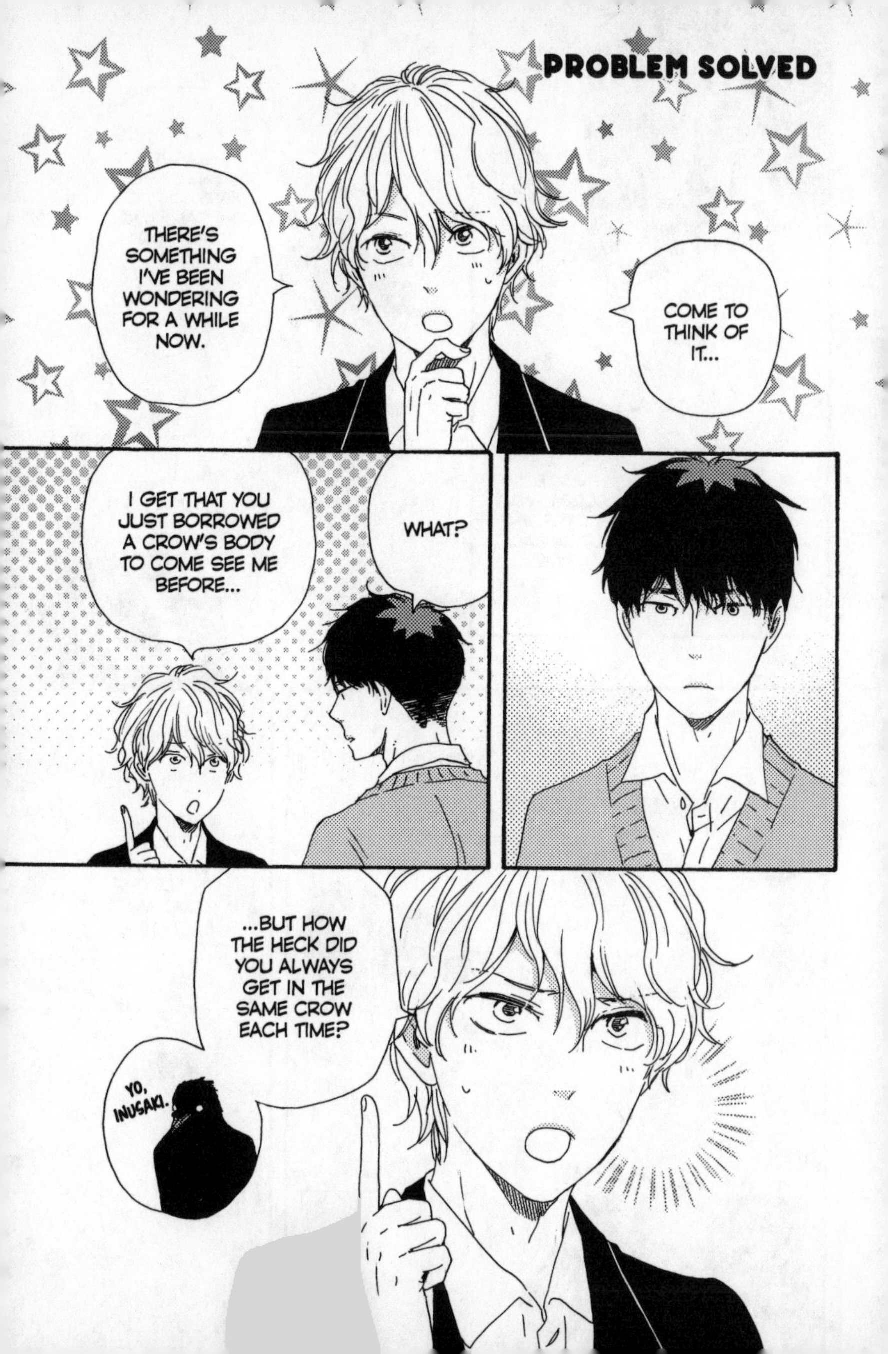
PROBLEM SOLVED
COME TO THINK OF IT...
THERE'S SOMETHING I'VE BEEN WONDERING FOR A WHILE NOW.
WHAT?
I GET THAT YOU JUST BORROWED A CROW'S BODY TO COME SEE ME BEFORE...
...BUT HOW THE HECK DID YOU ALWAYS GET IN THE SAME CROW EACH TIME?
YO, INUSAKI.

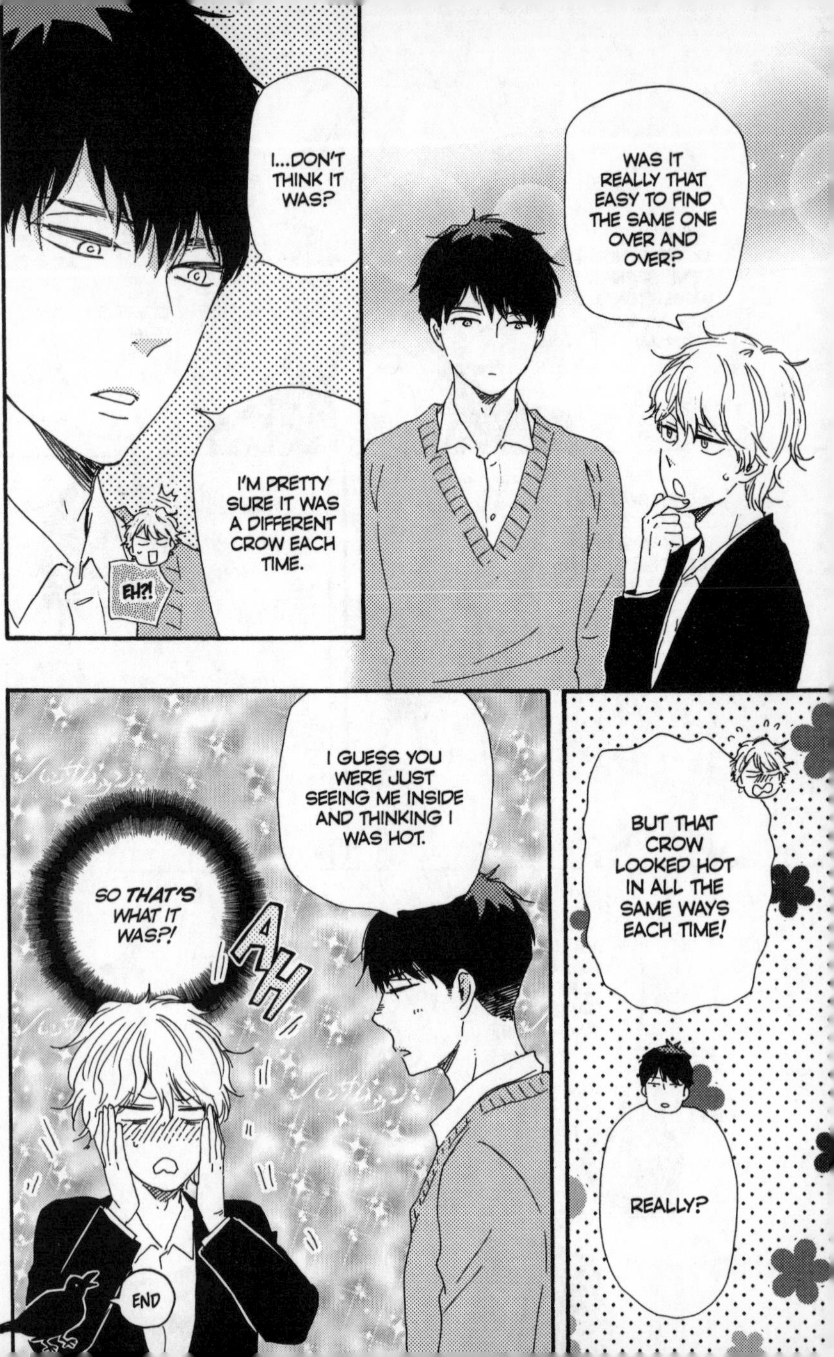
WAS IT REALLY THAT EASY TO FIND THE SAME ONE OVER AND OVER?
I...DON'T THINK IT WAS?
I'M PRETTY SURE IT WAS A DIFFERENT CROW EACH TIME.
EH?!
BUT THAT CROW LOOKED HOT IN ALL THE SAME WAYS EACH TIME!
REALLY?
I GUESS YOU WERE JUST SEEING ME INSIDE AND THINKING I WAS HOT.
AH
SO *THAT'S* WHAT IT WAS?!
END

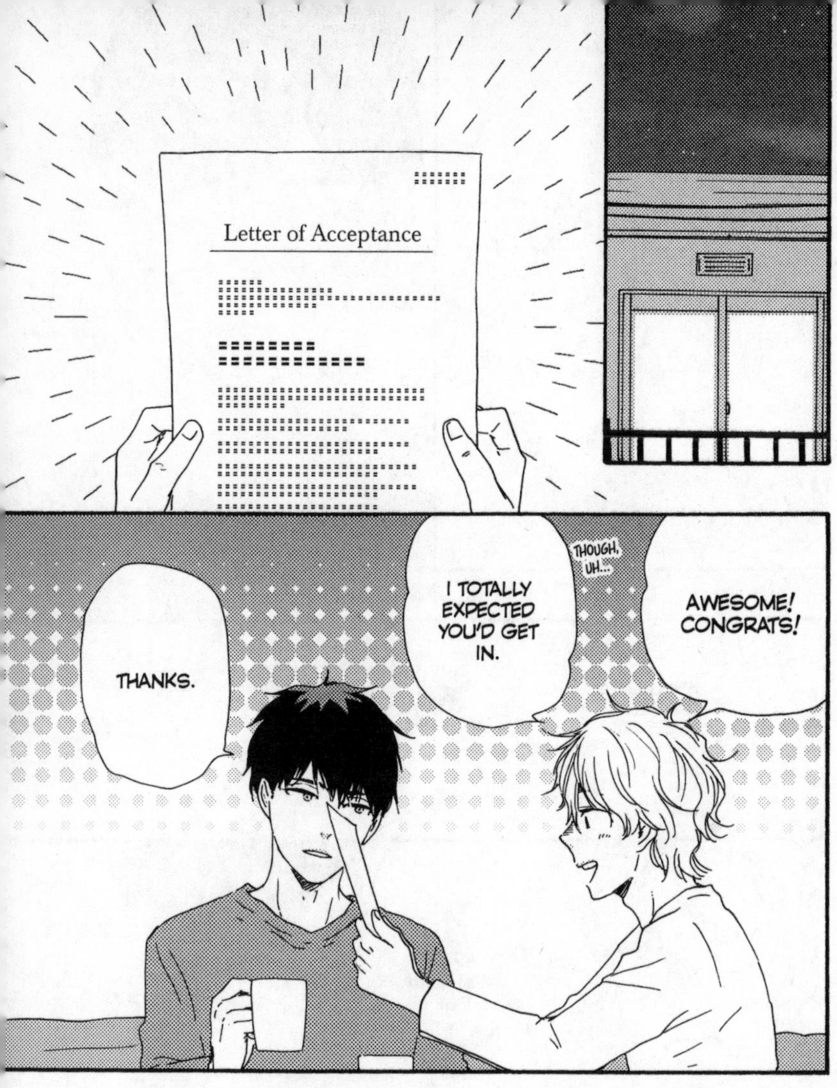
Letter of Acceptance
AWESOME! CONGRATS!
THOUGH, UH...
I TOTALLY EXPECTED YOU'D GET IN.
THANKS.

OUR FIRST...

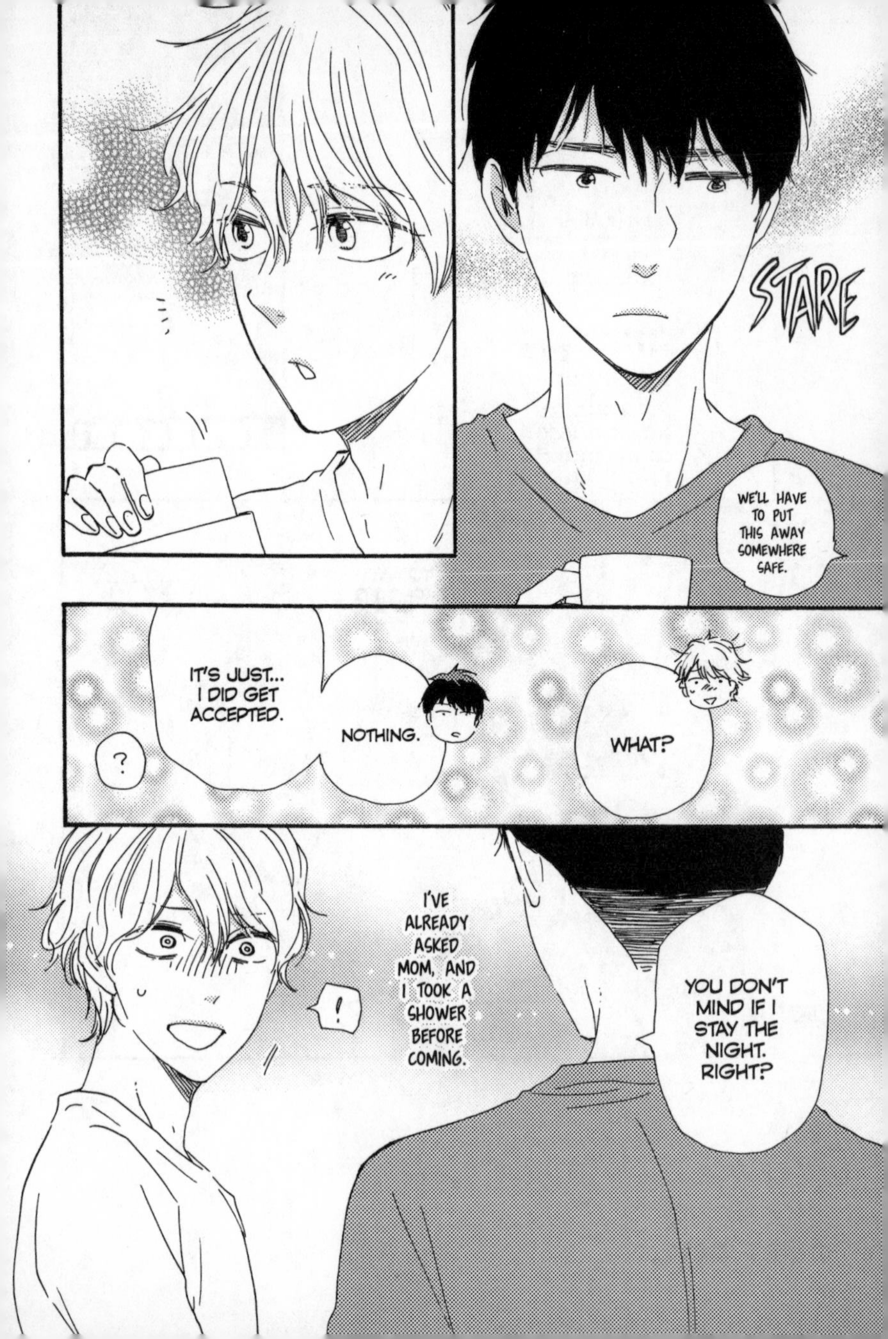
STARE
WE'LL HAVE TO PUT THIS AWAY SOMEWHERE SAFE.
WHAT?
NOTHING.
IT'S JUST... I DID GET ACCEPTED.
?
YOU DON'T MIND IF I STAY THE NIGHT. RIGHT?
I'VE ALREADY ASKED MOM, AND I TOOK A SHOWER BEFORE COMING.
!

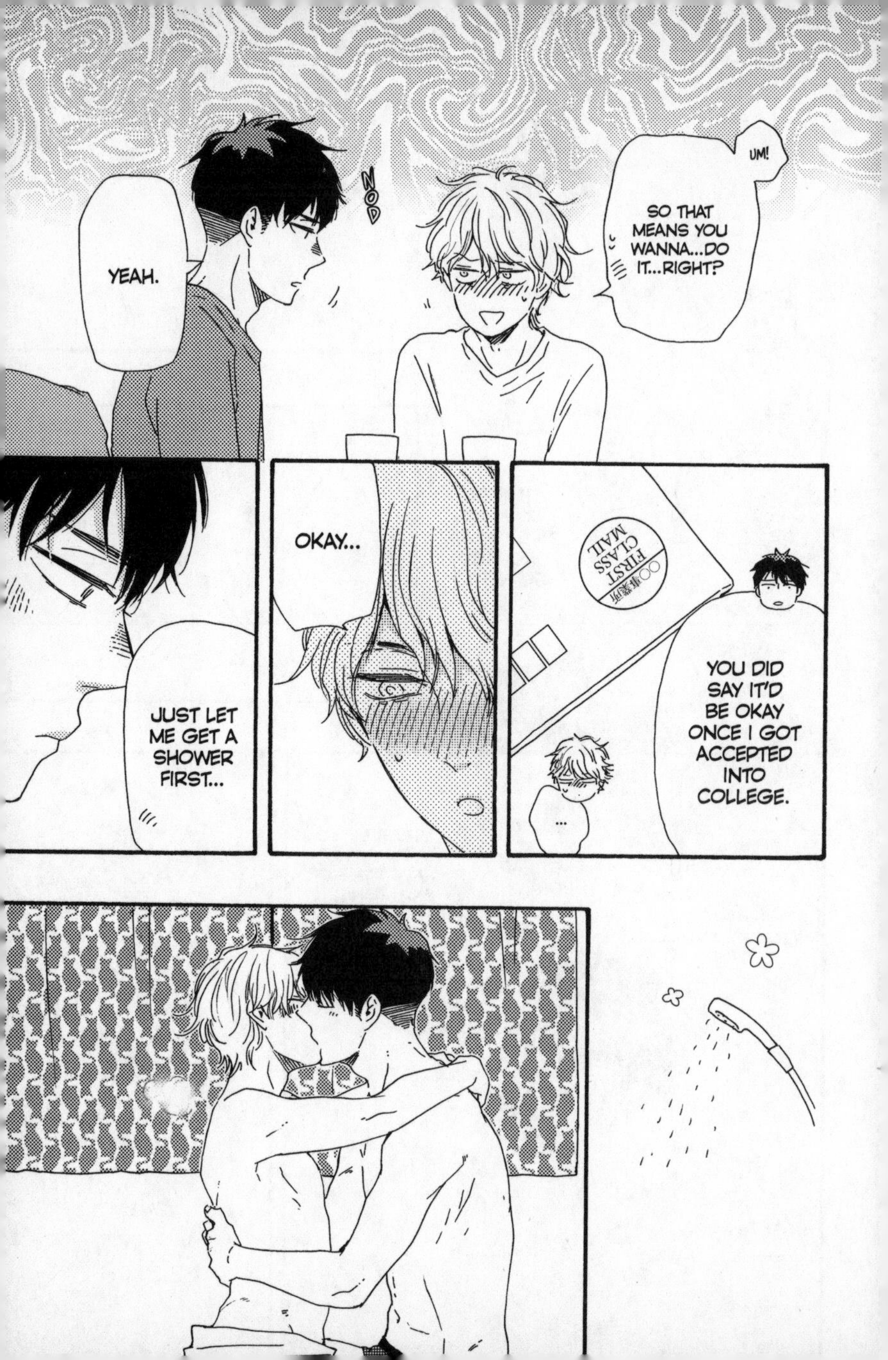
UM!
SO THAT MEANS YOU WANNA...DO IT...RIGHT?
NOD
YEAH.
○○事業所 FIRST CLASS MAIL
YOU DID SAY IT'D BE OKAY ONCE I GOT ACCEPTED INTO COLLEGE.
...
OKAY...
JUST LET ME GET A SHOWER FIRST...

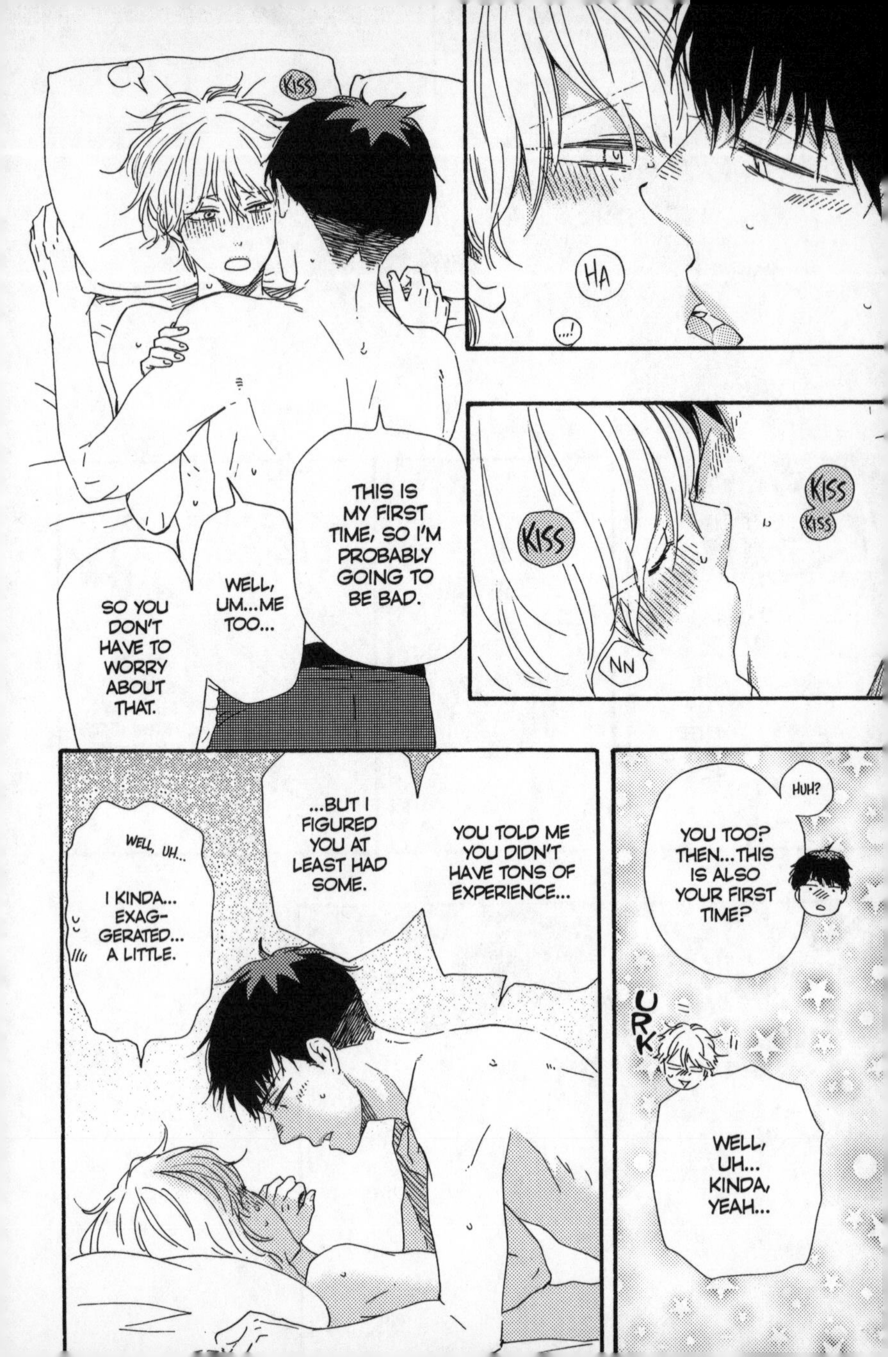
HA
...!
KISS
KISS
KISS
NN
KISS
THIS IS MY FIRST TIME, SO I'M PROBABLY GOING TO BE BAD.
WELL, UM...ME TOO...
SO YOU DON'T HAVE TO WORRY ABOUT THAT.
HUH?
YOU TOO? THEN...THIS IS ALSO YOUR FIRST TIME?
URK
WELL, UH... KINDA, YEAH...
YOU TOLD ME YOU DIDN'T HAVE TONS OF EXPERIENCE...
...BUT I FIGURED YOU AT LEAST HAD SOME.
WELL, UH...
I KINDA... EXAG-GERATED... A LITTLE.

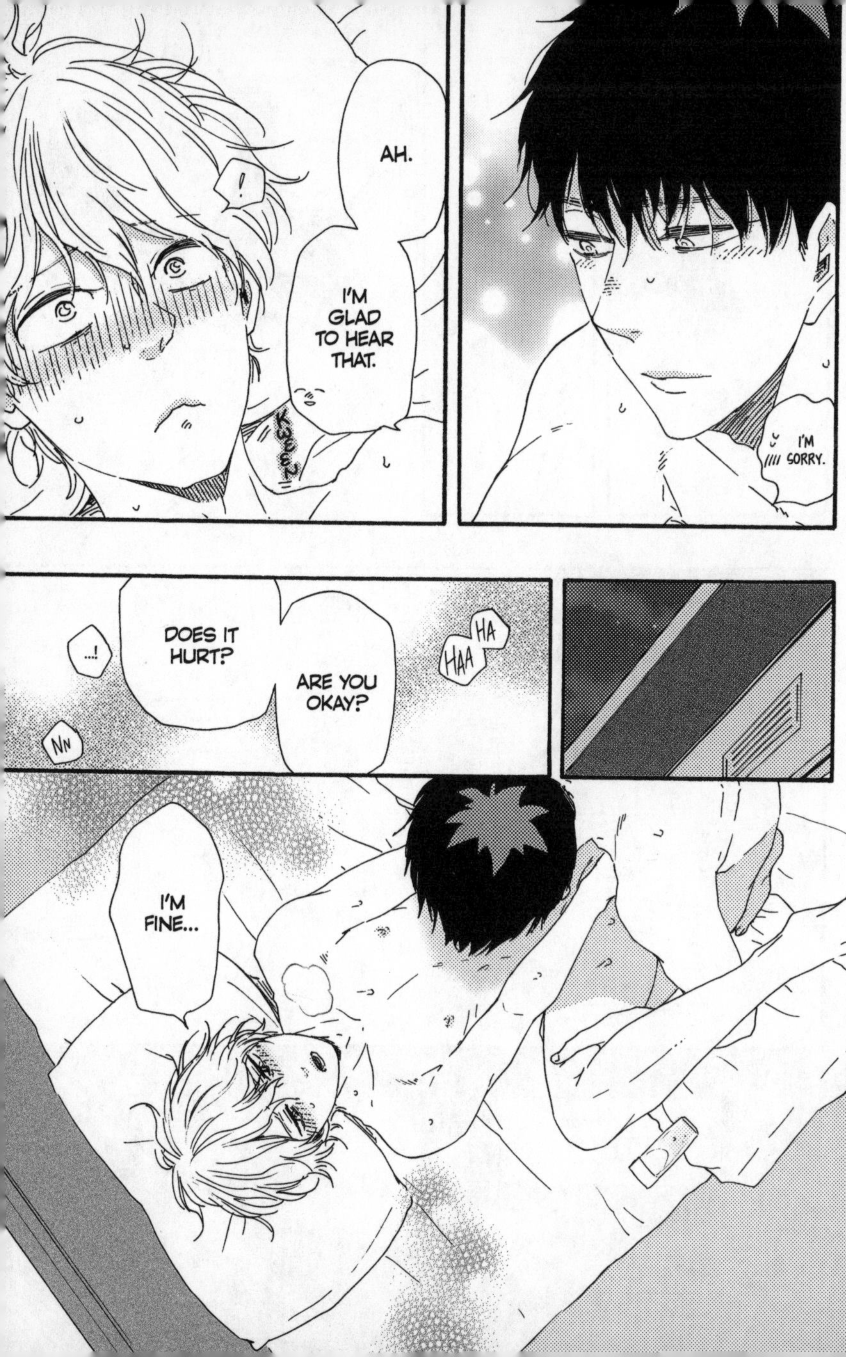
I'M SORRY.
!
AH.
I'M GLAD TO HEAR THAT.
HA
HAA
ARE YOU OKAY?
DOES IT HURT?
...!
Nn
I'M FINE...

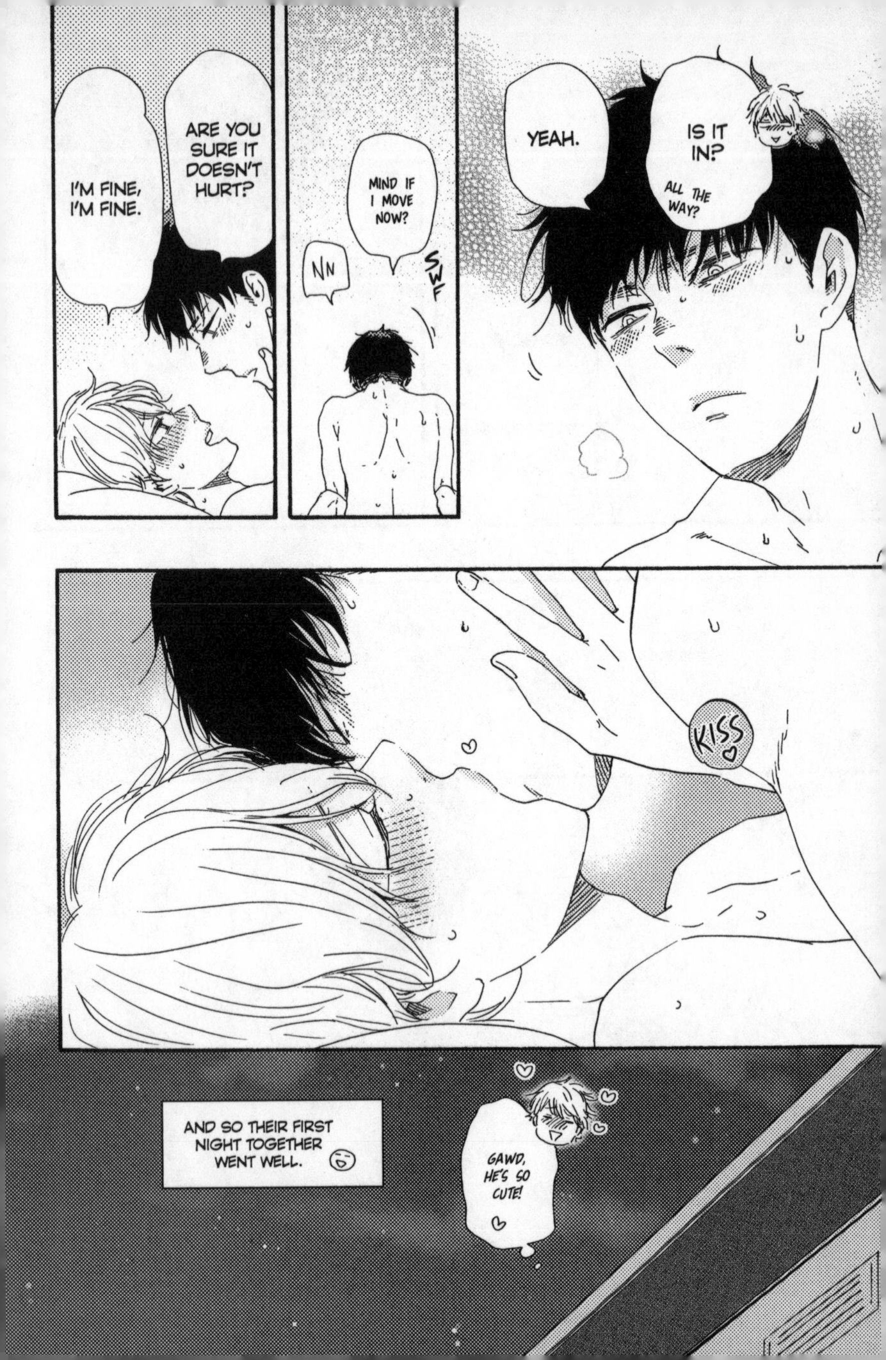
IS IT IN? ALL THE WAY?
YEAH.
MIND IF I MOVE NOW?
SWF
NN
ARE YOU SURE IT DOESN'T HURT?
I'M FINE, I'M FINE.
KISS
GAWD, HE'S SO CUTE!
AND SO THEIR FIRST NIGHT TOGETHER WENT WELL.

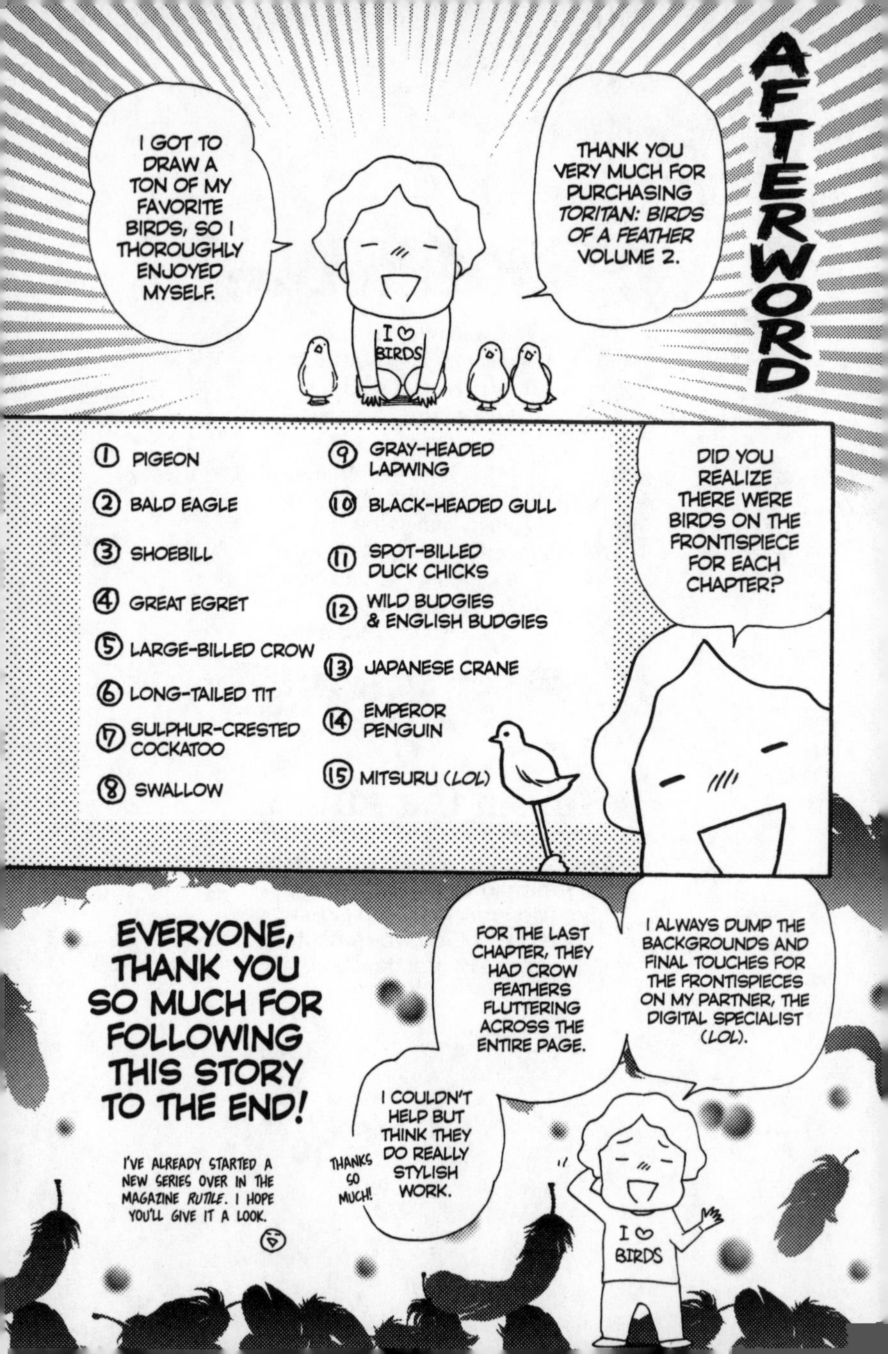
AFTERWORD
THANK YOU VERY MUCH FOR PURCHASING *TORITAN: BIRDS OF A FEATHER* VOLUME 2.
I GOT TO DRAW A TON OF MY FAVORITE BIRDS, SO I THOROUGHLY ENJOYED MYSELF.
I ♡ BIRDS
DID YOU REALIZE THERE WERE BIRDS ON THE FRONTISPIECE FOR EACH CHAPTER?
① PIGEON
② BALD EAGLE
③ SHOEBILL
④ GREAT EGRET
⑤ LARGE-BILLED CROW
⑥ LONG-TAILED TIT
⑦ SULPHUR-CRESTED COCKATOO
⑧ SWALLOW
⑨ GRAY-HEADED LAPWING
⑩ BLACK-HEADED GULL
⑪ SPOT-BILLED DUCK CHICKS
⑫ WILD BUDGIES & ENGLISH BUDGIES
⑬ JAPANESE CRANE
⑭ EMPEROR PENGUIN
⑮ MITSURU (*LOL*)
I ALWAYS DUMP THE BACKGROUNDS AND FINAL TOUCHES FOR THE FRONTISPIECES ON MY PARTNER, THE DIGITAL SPECIALIST (*LOL*).
FOR THE LAST CHAPTER, THEY HAD CROW FEATHERS FLUTTERING ACROSS THE ENTIRE PAGE.
I COULDN'T HELP BUT THINK THEY DO REALLY STYLISH WORK.
THANKS SO MUCH!
I ♡ BIRDS
EVERYONE, THANK YOU SO MUCH FOR FOLLOWING THIS STORY TO THE END!
I'VE ALREADY STARTED A NEW SERIES OVER IN THE MAGAZINE *RUTILE*. I HOPE YOU'LL GIVE IT A LOOK.

> This volume is the end of
> the detective and birds story
> *Toritan: Birds of a Feather*.
> I decided to do this story
> because I wanted to draw
> a lot of birds, but I wound
> up having to draw a bunch
> of other animals too. It was
> harder than I thought (*laughs*).
> Oh, and despite Mitsuru being
> mostly expressionless, he was
> actually fun to draw.

About the Author

Toritan: Birds of a Feather is **Kotetsuko Yamamoto**'s first SuBLime title. Born January 4, she's a Capricorn with an A blood type who loves professional baseball.

Toritan: Birds of a Feather
Volume 2
SuBLime Manga Edition

Story and Art by **Kotetsuko Yamamoto**

Translation—**Adrienne Beck**
Touch-Up Art and Lettering—**E. K. Weaver**
Cover and Graphic Design—**Yukiko Whitley**
Editor—**Jennifer LeBlanc**

TORITAN Vol.2
© YAMAMOTO KOTETSUKO 2019
All rights reserved. Reproducing this work in the form of copying, duplicating, reprinting, performing, broadcasting, distribution or sharing of data, in whole or in part, except as permitted by the copyright holder or under applicable copyright laws is strictly forbidden.
First published in Japan in 2019 by GENTOSHA COMICS INC., Tokyo
English translation rights arranged with GENTOSHA COMICS INC. through Tuttle-Mori Agency, Inc., Tokyo

GENTOSHA COMICS INC.

Printed in the U.S.A.

Published by SuBLime Manga
P.O. Box 77010
San Francisco, CA 94107

10 9 8 7 6 5 4 3 2 1
First printing, March 2021

 **PARENTAL ADVISORY**
TORITAN: BIRDS OF A FEATHER is rated M for Mature and is recommended for mature readers. This volume contains graphic imagery and mature themes.

SUBLIME
www.SuBLimeManga.com

For more information

on all our products, along with the most up-to-date news on releases, series announcements, and contests, please visit us at:

 SuBLimeManga.com

 twitter.com/**SuBLimeManga**

 facebook.com/**SuBLimeManga**

 instagram.com/**SuBLimeManga**

 SuBLimeManga.tumblr.com

SUBLIME
MANGA

The rules were clear: they could date for a week.
But someone forgot to tell love!

SEVEN DAYS

MONDAY→SUNDAY

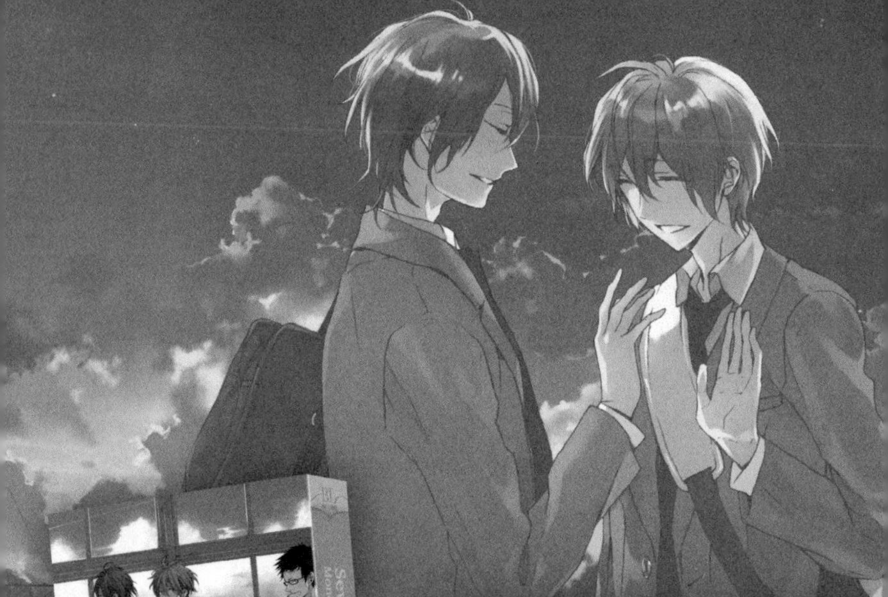

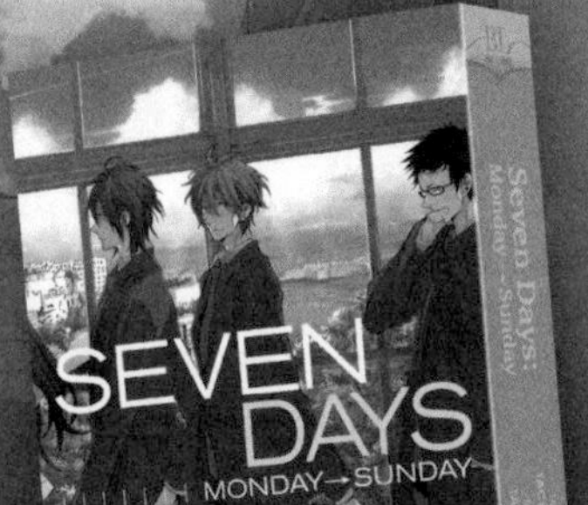
SEVEN DAYS
MONDAY→SUNDAY
Seven Days:
Monday→Sunday
STORY BY • VENIO TACHIBANA
ART BY • RIHITO TAKARAI

On a whim, high school third-year Yuzuru Shino asks out first-year Toji Seryo, who is notorious for being a weeklong lover—he'll date the first girl to ask him out Monday morning and then promptly dump her by the following Monday! The boys start dating, and by Tuesday, the first inklings of attraction hit. Can these two put words to their feelings before Monday comes, or are old habits too hard to break?

T
TEEN

SUBLIME
SuBLimeManga.com

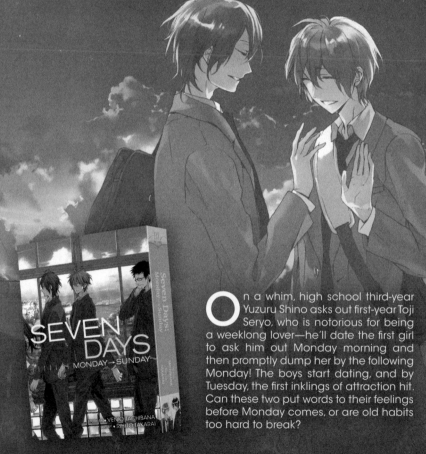

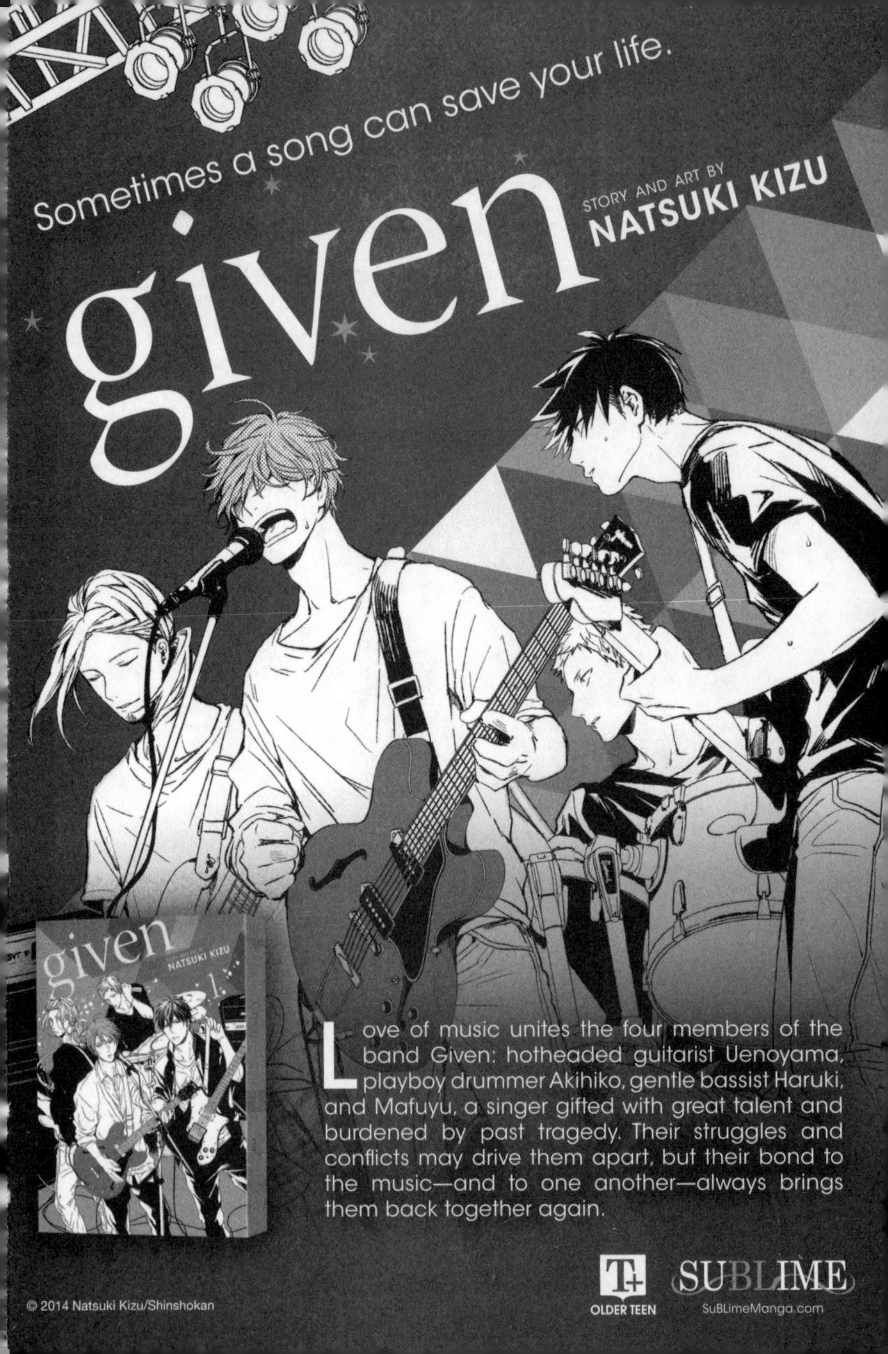

Sometimes a song can save your life.

given

STORY AND ART BY
NATSUKI KIZU

Love of music unites the four members of the band Given: hotheaded guitarist Uenoyama, playboy drummer Akihiko, gentle bassist Haruki, and Mafuyu, a singer gifted with great talent and burdened by past tragedy. Their struggles and conflicts may drive them apart, but their bond to the music—and to one another—always brings them back together again.

T+
OLDER TEEN

SuBLIME
SuBLimeManga.com